Welcome to your year of discovery

We all remember that moment we discovered something special for the first time.

I'll never forget my first trip to the National Trust's Crom Estate in Northern Ireland (below). When you come over the top of the hill, you get an extraordinary view where the land blends into the water. It gave me a feeling of such serenity.

In the months ahead, I want to make more of those exciting discoveries. In particular, I'll be looking out for our Riverlands activities, where we're bringing seven of our cherished waterways flowing back to life. I'll be visiting the Derwent in the Lake District, for example, where we're making the water cleaner to keep otters and Atlantic salmon happy.

I hope you'll also enjoy discovering some extraordinary wildlife this year. And, whether you want to get close to nature or step back in time at a historic property, I hope this *Handbook* will be your constant companion.

For now, I want to thank you again, personally, for helping to protect the places we all love, across England, Wales and Northern Ireland. So start planning those discoveries; I'll be doing the same myself.

Hilary McGrady
Director-General

Seven easy ways to get more from your membership

1. Go off-peak to beat the rush

Get a bit of space to yourself by popping in at the start or end of your day. It needn't be a big day out – you could drop by for a mid-week stroll on your way to work, or take a detour for an impromptu picnic after school.

2. Stay longer, later

We're keeping doors (and gates) open longer to help you make more brilliant memories at places you love, throughout the year. So come rain or shine you can refresh your mind, soothe your soul and boost your body. (Just remember last entry is usually 30 minutes before closing – it's best to check with the place you're planning to visit.)

3. Chart the changing seasons

Your favourite places deserve a return trip – and the wonder of the changing seasons means your visits will be different every time. From darling buds to golden hues, and from crunchy mornings to hazy evenings, you don't need to travel far for special moments.

4. Expect the unexpected

It's not just nature that changes. Many National Trust places run an ever-changing programme of experiences, indoors and outside, right through the year. From festive craft workshops to torchlight tours, there's always an opportunity to learn something new or make a surprising discovery.

5. Put special places in your pocket

Download the National Trust app to access maps, opening times, up-coming events and more while you're out and about. For more inspiration, head to **nationaltrust.org.uk**, look us up on social media or chat to staff and volunteers on your next visit.

6. Get off the beaten track

Some of the places in this *Handbook* are a bit off the beaten track, and a simple postcode won't get you all the way there. For more detailed directions and maps, download your free copy of our *Getting Here* guide at **nationaltrust.org.uk/gettinghere** or call us on **0344 800 1895** for a booklet.

7. Manage your membership, your way

- Choose how you want to hear from us
- Don't miss out on what matters to you
- Manage your list of favourite places
- Update your contact details and payment preferences

Register with My National Trust today at: **nationaltrust.org.uk/mynt**

Planning your journey

By car: rac.co.uk/route-planner

By bike: sustrans.org.uk

By train: nationalrail.co.uk or 03457 484950

By taxi (from a station): traintaxi.co.uk

By public transport (England, Wales and Scotland): traveline.info or 0871 200 2233

By public transport (Northern Ireland): translink.co.uk or 028 9066 6630

By public transport (London): tfl.gov.uk or 0343 222 1234

Where will this year take you?

Whether you want to get your heart pumping, forget your cares or just stay in touch with friends – your membership can make it all possible, come rain or shine.

Ignite your imagination, indoors

When it's grey outside, you'll find colour and drama inside our historic houses. You could take a trip back in time in a real Elizabethan kitchen, discover the hidden meaning of Chinese design, or spark your creativity with a Renaissance masterpiece.

Curious about our collections?
From furniture to fashion and from silverware to ceramics, find the places to follow your passion on page 465.

Feel the magic of spring

As nature wakes from its slumber, it's time to come out of hibernation. Why not dust off the cobwebs on a hilly bike ride or take a woodland wander beside a carpet of bluebells? And when the showers come, head inside for a hard-earned slice of freshly baked carrot cake.

Start your own chain reaction
Find out where to hire a bike on page 461 or bring your own to explore our cycle trails through beautiful countryside.

What will you do this spring?

- Fill the senses on a guided wildflower tour.
- Enjoy the fun and laughter on an Easter egg trail at Mottisfont.
- Reimagine upstairs-downstairs life in a historic house such as Ickworth.
- Treat mum to a slice of cake on Mother's Day.
- Get stuck in planting bulbs in a walled garden.

Soak up the fun of the sun

Splash into summer with some seaside sensations. Keep little hands busy with epic sandcastles and rock-pool hunts. Taste the salty spray as you paddle out for a coastal kayaking adventure. Or make your legs ache and your heart soar on a clifftop jog.

Feel some flower power
Surround yourself with scent and colour – find a garden in bloom near you on page 461.

What will you do this summer?

- Turn off the screens and read a book under a favourite tree.
- Go glamping in a Mongolian yurt and wake up to birdsong at Langdale.
- Find an enchanted forest (and imagine fairies in the waterfalls).
- Feel squelchy sand between your toes on a shoreline stroll.
- Load a scone with cream and jam.

Long days, endless delights

Live the al fresco life and feel the difference in your mind, body and soul. Keep in touch with those you cherish over a spur-of-the-moment garden picnic. Expand your horizons with one of our open-air plays under the stars. Or wear out little legs on endless swings, slides or zip wires.

Change your perspective
Experience a place you love from the water. You can hire boats at a number of the places we look after – find out where on page 461.

Become a location hunter
From *Poldark* to *Pride and Prejudice* ... and from *Harry Potter* to *Game of Thrones*, find the stunning locations of your favourite TV shows and films on page 469.

Fill your autumn with colour

As the air gets chilly and the nights draw in, it's time to look forward to those little harvest rituals. You could wrap up for fireworks and enjoy steaming jacket potatoes, carve a show-stopping pumpkin with the kids, or dig out your wellies for a long walk with good friends, surrounded by autumnal colours.

After a ghostly encounter?
Centuries of spooky happenings make Newton House at Dinefwr one of our most hair-raising haunted places. Turn to page 461 to plan your visit ... if you dare.

What will you do this autumn?

- Pop in after school and hunt for champion conkers.
- Forage for sweet blackberries for a comforting pie.
- Crunch crispy, golden leaves under your feet.
- Have a go at apple bobbing at Killerton.
- Book a half-term getaway overlooking Dorset's Chesil Beach.

Share the comfort and joy, together

Celebrate your Christmas traditions with us this year. Whether you want to blast away the overindulgence on a chilly Boxing Day walk, choose (or even make) festive gifts for your loved ones, or cosy up with a cuppa after a tour of a medieval castle, your membership will help make it happen.

What will you do this Christmas?

- Leave nuts out for your favourite winter birds.
- Feel family love by recreating grandma's Christmas cake.
- Keep kids busy in an indoor playground.
- Brighten dark nights with a winter lightshow at Anglesey Abbey.
- Warm up with mulled wine at a busy festive market.

Cornwall

Sweeping down to the Fal Estuary, the parkland at Trelissick offers panoramic views

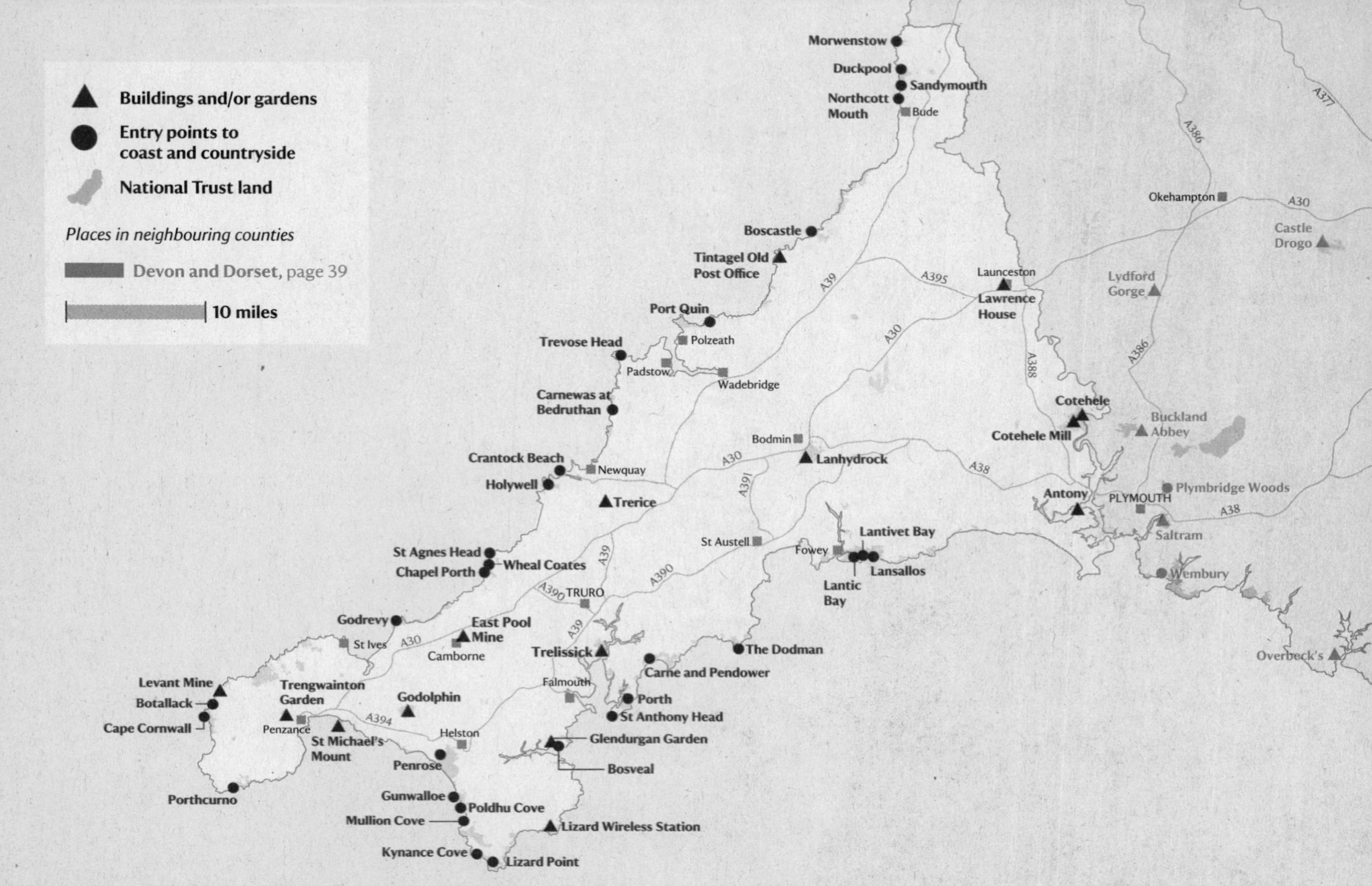

Buildings and/or gardens
Entry points to coast and countryside
National Trust land
Places in neighbouring counties
Devon and Dorset, page 39
10 miles
Morwenstow
Duckpool
Sandymouth
Northcott Mouth
Bude
Boscastle
Tintagel Old Post Office
Port Quin
Polzeath
Trevose Head
Padstow
Wadebridge
Carnewas at Bedruthan
Crantock Beach
Newquay
Holywell
Trerice
St Agnes Head
Wheal Coates
Chapel Porth
TRURO
Godrevy
St Ives
Camborne
East Pool Mine
Trelissick
Levant Mine
Botallack
Cape Cornwall
Porthcurno
Trengwainton Garden
Penzance
St Michael's Mount
Godolphin
Helston
Penrose
Gunwalloe
Poldhu Cove
Mullion Cove
Kynance Cove
Lizard Point
Lizard Wireless Station
Falmouth
Glendurgan Garden
Bosveal
Porth
St Anthony Head
Carne and Pendower
The Dodman
St Austell
Fowey
Lantic Bay
Lantivet Bay
Lansallos
Bodmin
Lanhydrock
Launceston
Lawrence House
Cotehele
Cotehele Mill
Antony
PLYMOUTH
Saltram
Wembury
Plymbridge Woods
Buckland Abbey
Lydford Gorge
Okehampton
Castle Drogo
Overbeck's
A30
A39
A395
A388
A386
A377
A38
A390
A391
A394

Antony

Torpoint, Cornwall PL11 2QA

1961

Still the family home of the Carew Poles after hundreds of years, this intimate and much-loved early 18th-century house contains personal treasures collected over generations. With sweeping views to the River Lynher and playful topiary, the garden transports you to a different world and offers a touch of Cornish charm.

Eat, shop, stay: a tea-room in the colonnade courtyard offers light lunches and afternoon tea. Indoor and outdoor seating available. Picnics welcome. Gift shop selling souvenirs and plants. Small second-hand bookshop.

Things to see and do: **Indoors** Trails. Activity room with games, books and dressing up. **Outdoors** '50 things' (self-led and delivered workshops), programme of trails and events. Games and croquet on lawn. Den-building. Garden sculpture. **Dogs**: assistance dogs only.

Access:
House **Grounds**
Parking: 250 yards.

Find out more: 01752 812191 or antony@nationaltrust.org.uk

Antony		M	T	W	T	F	S	S
2 Apr–30 May	12–5	·	T	W	T	·	·	·
2 Jun–29 Aug	12–5	·	T	W	T	·	·	S
3 Sep–31 Oct	12–5	·	T	W	T	·	·	·

House: open 12:30 to 4:30. Timed ticket entry to house allocated on arrival. Also open Good Friday and Easter Sunday, Sunday 5 May, Sunday 26 May and Bank Holiday Mondays.

Rising from the morning mist, bottom, dreamy Antony is a warm, lived-in family home

Boscastle

near Tintagel, Cornwall

1955

There has been a fishing and trading port here for centuries and you can still watch boats come and go between the high cliffs that guard the snaking harbour entrance. Much of Boscastle can be discovered on foot, with footpaths leading in all directions. You can walk in the footsteps of the young Thomas Hardy through the wildlife-rich ancient woodland in the Valency Valley, or explore the rare medieval field system known as 'the Forrabury Stitches' high above the village. Nearby is the striking lookout building on Willapark headland, and the historic churches of Minster and Forrabury. **Note**: toilet by main car park (not National Trust).

Eat, shop, stay: harbourside café with courtyard seating. Large shop and visitor centre offering a wide range of gifts, seasonal plant sales plus a wealth of guides and information about the local area. Second-hand bookshop. Five holiday cottages. Free Wi-Fi throughout.

Things to see and do: children's quiz/trail. Coasteering available nearby. Visitor centre shows short film about the 2004 flood. Why not combine with a visit to Tintagel Old Post Office, 4 miles down the coast? **Dogs**: welcome on walks and in café courtyard.

With paths leading in all directions, Boscastle, above and below, is a delight to explore on foot

Access: **Grounds**
Sat Nav: use PL35 0HD. **Parking**: 100 yards, pay and display, not National Trust (charge including members).

Find out more: 01840 250010 or boscastle@nationaltrust.org.uk

Boscastle		M	T	W	T	F	S	S
Shop, café and visitor centre								
Open all year	*	**M**	**T**	**W**	**T**	**F**	**S**	**S**

*Opening times vary throughout year, ranging from 10:30 to 4 in winter to 10 to 5:30 in high summer. Closed 25 and 26 December.

Bosveal

near Mawnan Smith, Falmouth, Cornwall 1980

Walks from here take in wooded valleys, secluded coves and soft, sheltered shores of the Helford River and Falmouth Bay. **Note**: toilets and refreshments at nearby Glendurgan Garden. Holiday cottages at Bosloe and Durgan. For Sat Nav use TR11 5JR.

Find out more: 01326 252020 or bosveal@nationaltrust.org.uk

Botallack

on the Tin Coast, near St Just, Cornwall

1995

On the wild Tin Coast, the famed Crowns engine houses (above) cling to the foot of the cliffs in a landscape transformed by its industrial past. Part of the Cornish Mining World Heritage Site, and the filming location for Wheal Leisure in BBC's *Poldark*, from here Cornish miners changed the world.
Note: industrial landscape with mine shafts and exposed cliffs – keep to paths.

Eat, shop, stay: light refreshments with views to the Isles of Scilly (opening days/times vary, check before visiting), pasties, cakes, ice cream, hot and cold drinks. Picnic blankets to borrow. Two can stay at romantic Botallack Count House Cottage, with dramatic coastal views.

Things to see and do: displays in the café celebrating the Tin Coast and mining heritage. Explore mining history on the outdoors trail and enjoy an easy clifftop walk to Levant Mine. **Dogs**: welcome everywhere on short leads. Please take care near mine shafts and cliff edges.

Access:
Sat Nav: use TR19 7QQ. Beware, some Sat Navs misdirect. Keep to the B3306 until you reach Botallack village. **Parking**: just beyond Botallack Count House.

Find out more: 01736 786934 or botallack@nationaltrust.org.uk

Botallack
Botallack Workshop café open most days (telephone for details).

Cape Cornwall

on the Tin Coast, near St Just, Cornwall

1987

The distinctive headland of Cape Cornwall juts out into the ocean where two great bodies of water meet. Once a heavily industrialised landscape, it is now part of the Cornish Mining World Heritage Site, and a wild and rugged home to the many seabirds that nest on the Brisons rocks. **Note**: narrow lanes, unsuitable for caravans. Industrial landscape – please keep to paths for your own safety.

Eat, shop, stay: light refreshments (not National Trust) available throughout the year, weather permitting – please check Tin Coast Facebook page. Toilets in car park. Many facilities in St Just (none National Trust). Holiday cottage in nearby Cot Valley.

Wild seas batter the coast at Cape Cornwall

Things to see and do: perfect beach for rock-pooling and wild swimming. Working cove for crab and lobster fishermen. Short walk to the top of the Cape for views to the Isles of Scilly. **Dogs**: welcome, but not on the beach and slipway from Easter to October.

Sat Nav: use TR19 7NN for Cape Cornwall car park. Beware some Sat Navs misdirect. Follow the signs in St Just town to Cape Cornwall. **Parking**: at Cape Cornwall, Porth Nanven (Cot Valley) and Ballowall.

Find out more: 01736 786934 or capecornwall@nationaltrust.org.uk

Carne and Pendower

near Veryan, Cornwall

1961

Carne and Pendower: view across the beaches to Nare Head

Two of the best beaches on the Roseland peninsula: fine stretches of sand and rock pools, popular with families. Walks along the coast and inland reveal the area's wildlife – great for butterflies in summer and birds in winter. Lots of history to discover nearby, from Bronze Age to Cold War. **Note**: seasonal toilets in both car parks.

Eat, shop, stay: seasonal refreshments available (concession). You can stay close to Carne Beach at the five holiday cottages at Gwendra and Caragloose.

Things to see and do: the beaches are ideal for swimming and rock-pooling. A path leads inland to Carne Beacon, one of Britain's largest Bronze Age barrows. Downloadable walking trails cover the wider area. **Dogs**: seasonal dog restrictions on beaches (please keep under control near livestock).

Sat Nav: for Carne use TR2 5PF; Pendower TR2 5PF (turn right at sign for Pendower Beach). **Parking**: car parks at both Carne and Pendower.

Find out more: 01872 580553 or carne@nationaltrust.org.uk

Carnewas at Bedruthan

near Padstow, Cornwall

1930

Since Victorian times this has been one of the most popular destinations on the Cornish coast, known for its spectacular clifftop views of giant rock stacks striding across Bedruthan Beach (not National Trust). Those with a head for heights can climb down the cliff staircase to the beach (closed during the winter) but beware of being cut off by the tide. For a longer walk, follow the coast path to Park Head and the sheltered cove of Porth Mear beyond. Carpets of spring and autumn squill bedeck these clifftops, and birds nesting from March include linnets, stonechats and skylarks. **Note**: unsafe to enter the sea here at any time.

Carnewas at Bedruthan: the striking clifftop views of these giant rock stacks have been popular since Victorian times

For information about getting to National Trust places, please see page 3

Eat, shop, stay: shop offering gifts, many locally sourced and produced, and popular tea-room (concession) with adjoining clifftop tea garden. Picnic area. Holiday cottages offering expansive sea views at Park Head.

Things to see and do: children's quiz. Carnewas awarded 'dark sky status', so ideal for stargazing. Why not combine with a visit to Trevose Head (7 miles away) or Trerice (9 miles away)? **Dogs**: welcome under control.

Access: Car park and clifftop
Sat Nav: use PL27 7UW. **Parking**: on site.

Find out more: 01637 860563 or carnewas@nationaltrust.org.uk

Carnewas at Bedruthan		M	T	W	T	F	S	S
Tea-room*								
9 Feb–31 Mar	11–4	M	T	W	T	F	S	S
1 Apr–27 Oct	10:30–5	M	T	W	T	F	S	S
27 Dec–31 Dec	11–4	M	T	·	·	F	S	S
Shop								
9 Feb–31 Mar	10:30–4	M	T	W	T	F	S	S
1 Apr–27 Oct	10–5	M	T	W	T	F	S	S
2 Nov–29 Dec	10:30–4	·	·	·	·	·	S	S

Cliff staircase closed from 28 October to mid-February.
*Telephone 01637 860701 to check opening times in winter.

Chapel Porth

near St Agnes, Cornwall

At the foot of a steep valley between high heathery cliffs, Chapel Porth Beach is a shingle strip at high tide and a huge expanse of sand at low tide. The area is steeped in mining history, with many remains to be discovered on walks. **Note**: seasonal toilets. Take care not to get cut off by incoming tide. Seasonal lifeguards.

Eat, shop, stay: Chapel Porth Beach Café (concession) open daily in summer and most winter weekends (01872 552487). Picnics welcome.

Things to see and do: great walking country – the coast path and inland paths link you with Porthtowan, St Agnes Head and the World Heritage Site mining remains at Charlotte United, Wheal Coates and Trevellas. **Dogs**: seasonal dog ban on the beach (Easter Sunday to 30 September inclusive).

Access:
Sat Nav: use TR5 0NS. **Parking**: car park (very busy in summer), accessed down single track with passing places. Additional parking at nearby Wheal Coates and St Agnes Head.

Find out more: 01872 552412 or chapelporth@nationaltrust.org.uk

Chapel Porth: a popular surfing beach

Cotehele

St Dominick, near Saltash, Cornwall PL12 6TA

1947

The Edgcumbes built their rambling granite and slate-stone home high above the River Tamar, and it remained in their family for nearly 600 years. Time has stood still here. The hall, with its ancient timber roof and displays of weaponry, and the warren of tapestry-clad rooms beyond have changed little since Tudor times. The 5-hectare (12-acre) garden features historic daffodils, terraces, ponds and orchards with 150 local apple varieties. The Valley Garden, with medieval stewpond and dovecote, leads to Cotehele Quay – thriving in Victorian times – where you'll find the 1899 Tamar sailing barge *Shamrock*, lime kilns and the Discovery Centre. **Note**: the house has no electricity, so feel free to bring a torch.

Eat, shop, stay: restaurant near house serving hot lunches and cakes. Tea-room on quay offering light lunches, cakes and cream teas. Gift shop and plant centre. Art and craft gallery featuring West Country artists. Second-hand bookshop. Picnic area. Eight holiday cottages on estate.

Things to see and do: **Indoors** 'Words and Pictures' features the work of people who were inspired by and influenced Cotehele. Renowned floral garland display at Christmas. **Outdoors** Play area. Year-round events and walks. **Dogs**: welcome on estate walks. Assistance dogs only in formal garden.

Access:
Building **Grounds**
Sat Nav: ignore from Tavistock, follow brown signs. **Parking**: at house and on quay.

Find out more: 01579 351346 or cotehele@nationaltrust.org.uk

Cotehele		M	T	W	T	F	S	S
House								
9 Mar–27 Oct	11–4	**M**	**T**	**W**	**T**	**F**	**S**	**S**
28 Oct–31 Dec*	10:30–4	**M**	**T**	**W**	**T**	**F**	**S**	**S**
Garden and estate								
Open all year	Dawn–dusk	**M**	**T**	**W**	**T**	**F**	**S**	**S**
Restaurant, tea-room, gallery, shop, plant sales								
9 Feb–8 Mar**	10–4	**M**	**T**	**W**	**T**	**F**	**S**	**S**
9 Mar–27 Oct	10–5	**M**	**T**	**W**	**T**	**F**	**S**	**S**
28 Oct–31 Dec	10–4	**M**	**T**	**W**	**T**	**F**	**S**	**S**

*Hall only. Christmas garland from 16 November. Everything closed 25 and 26 December, except garden and estate.
**Tea-room on quay open daily from 1 January.

Exploring Cotehele's Great Hall, above, and the terraced garden, below

Support the places you visit: please scan your member card for free parking ticket

Cotehele Mill

St Dominick, near Saltash, Cornwall PL12 6TA

1947

A peaceful walk alongside the Morden stream from Cotehele Quay takes you to the restored 19th-century Cotehele Mill (above). On Thursdays and Sundays you can watch corn being ground into flour. Traditional woodworker and potter on site, as well as recreated wheelwright's, saddler's and blacksmith's workshops. Look out for baking days. **Note**: nearest toilets and parking at Cotehele Quay.

Eat, shop, stay: Cotehele flour, gifts and ice cream for sale. The Edgcumbe tea-room at nearby Cotehele Quay serves light lunches and cream teas. Snacks available from the kiosk on the quay. Picnics welcome in meadow. Two holiday cottages.

Things to see and do: **Indoors** Events, including milling and bakery demonstrations, as well as dress-up days. Opportunity to mill grain at the hand quern. **Outdoors** Family trails. **Dogs**: welcome, but assistance dogs only in bakery and mill.

Access: **Building** **Grounds**
Parking: on Cotehele Quay (at the mill by arrangement only). Shuttlebus from Cotehele House.

Find out more: 01579 350606 (mill). 01579 351346 (Cotehele) or cotehele@nationaltrust.org.uk

Cotehele Mill		M	T	W	T	F	S	S
9 Mar–29 Sep	11–4:30	M	T	W	T	F	S	S
30 Sep–27 Oct	11–4	M	T	W	T	F	S	S

Crantock Beach

near Newquay, Cornwall

1956

Close to Newquay, this feels like a different Cornwall: Crantock Beach is an expanse of golden sand, great for sandcastles and surfing. Wonderful walking country – through the dunes on Rushy Green, along the banks of the Gannel Estuary, or around the headland of West Pentire, carpeted with wild flowers. **Note**: danger, unpredictable currents.

Eat, shop, stay: refreshments (not National Trust) in village and West Pentire. Fern Pit café (not National Trust), across the estuary from Crantock Beach, reached by ferryboat or footbridge during main season (tide-dependent). Seasonal refreshments on beach (one concession, not National Trust).

Things to see and do: surf school and board hire. Spot seals from the coast path. There are vibrant displays of summer wild flowers to discover in the fields above nearby Polly Joke Beach. **Dogs**: welcome under control everywhere, including the beach.

An expanse of golden sand on Crantock Beach

Access:
Sat Nav: use TR8 5RN for Crantock Beach and TR8 5QS for Treago Mill. **Parking**: on site (height restriction barrier when unmanned) and at Treago Mill for Polly Joke Beach (also known as Porth Joke).

Find out more: 01208 863046 or crantockbeach@nationaltrust.org.uk

The Dodman

Penare, near Gorran Haven, Cornwall 1919

The highest headland on Cornwall's south coast, with massive Iron Age ramparts. Great walking, wildlife and beaches on either side. **Note**: park at Penare: footpaths to Hemmick Beach and Dodman Point. For Sat Nav use PL26 6NY – don't go to Treveague Farm but continue down hill.

Find out more: 01872 580553 or thedodman@nationaltrust.org.uk

Duckpool

near Bude, Cornwall 1960

Remote beach with rock pools at the mouth of the wooded Coombe Valley, overlooked by cliffs carpeted with wild flowers. **Note**: toilets open seasonally. For Sat Nav use EX23 9JN.

Find out more: 01208 863046 or duckpool@nationaltrust.org.uk

East Pool Mine

Pool, near Redruth, Cornwall TR15 3NP

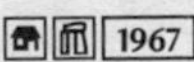 1967

East Pool celebrates the extraordinary lives of people who worked at the very heart of what is now the Cornish Mining World Heritage Site. With two giant beam engines, preserved in towering engine houses, this is a place for all the family to discover the dramatic story of Cornish mining.

Eat, shop, stay: small shop selling gifts, food and souvenirs, also a good selection of minerals and Cornish history books. Hot and cold drinks, snacks and ice cream available to enjoy outside on picnic benches in the sun, or inside the Discovery Centre.

At East Pool Mine, visitors can get hands-on as they discover the story of Cornish mining

Things to see and do: working beam engine and hands-on exhibits. Family activities, trails and free guided tours. Trevithick Cottage, home of the celebrated Cornish engineer Richard Trevithick, is nearby at Penponds. **Dogs**: welcome in outdoor areas.

Access: Grounds
Taylor's Engine House **Michell's Engine House**
Sat Nav: for main site, use TR15 3NH; for Trevithick Cottage use TR14 0QG. **Parking**: for main site, use Morrisons' car park (far end). Additional parking at Michell's Engine House nearby.

Find out more: 01209 315027 or eastpool@nationaltrust.org.uk
Trevithick Road, Pool, Cornwall TR15 3NP

East Pool Mine		M	T	W	T	F	S	S
Mine and Taylor's Engine House								
19 Mar–26 Oct*	10:30–5	·	**T**	**W**	**T**	**F**	**S**	·
Michell's Engine House								
19 Mar–26 Oct*	12–4	·	**T**	**W**	**T**	**F**	**S**	·
Trevithick Cottage								
3 Apr–23 Oct	2–5	·	·	**W**	·	·	·	·

*Open Easter Monday and Bank Holiday weekends in May and August (times as above). Winter opening available for arranged visits.

Glendurgan Garden

Mawnan Smith, near Falmouth, Cornwall TR11 5JZ

1962

Glendurgan Garden was described by its creators, the Quakers Alfred and Sarah Fox, as a 'small peace [sic] of heaven on earth'. Visitors can find out why it proved to be just this for the Foxes and their 12 children by exploring Glendurgan's three valleys, running down to the sheltered beach at Durgan on the Helford River. There's a puzzling maze, created by Alfred and Sarah to entertain the family. You can enjoy camellias, magnolias and primroses in early spring, then rhododendrons and bluebells in May, followed by the exotic greens of summer and dramatic autumn colour in the trees. **Note**: steep paths, steps, uneven terrain.

Eat, shop, stay: tea-house (concession) serving homemade cakes, soups, sandwiches, light lunches and daily changing specials. Small shop and plant centre. Holiday lets close by – from waterside cottages for two, to large country houses for eight or more.

Things to see and do: you can find out about local history from the friendly volunteer team in Durgan Fish Cellar. Durgan Beach on the Helford River. Children's activities. Introductory talks (call to check availability). **Dogs**: assistance dogs only in garden. Walks in surrounding countryside (details available at Glendurgan).

Access: Garden entrance Garden
Parking: on site.

Find out more: 01326 252020 or glendurgan@nationaltrust.org.uk

Glendurgan Garden		M	T	W	T	F	S	S
16 Feb–31 Jul	10:30–5:30	·	T	W	T	F	S	S
1 Aug–31 Aug	10:30–5:30	M	T	W	T	F	S	S
1 Sep–3 Nov	10:30–5:30	·	T	W	T	F	S	S

Last entry one hour before closing. Closes dusk if earlier. Open Bank Holiday Mondays.

Glendurgan Garden, clockwise from top right: view down the valley, Durgan Beach and the maze

Godolphin

Godolphin Cross, Helston, Cornwall TR13 9RE

2000

Hidden in shaded woodland, Godolphin escaped modernisation and contemporary fashions. The granite-faced terraces and sunken lawns of the Side Garden have seen little change since the 16th century, and Victorian farm buildings tell the story of Godolphin as a tenant farm. The estate, once busy with prosperous tin mines, is now part of the Cornish Mining World Heritage Site and is wonderful walking country, rich in archaeology, rare plants and wildlife. There are panoramic views from the top of Godolphin Hill. The historic house is a holiday home, where you can stay and experience the splendour that mining riches bought. **Note**: house is open to visitors on limited dates between holiday bookings (please check before visiting).

Eat, shop, stay: small tea-room in the Piggery serving drinks, sandwiches, cakes, ice cream. Local gifts and souvenirs. Picnic benches in the orchard or borrow a blanket to relax in the garden. You can soak up the atmosphere by staying in Godolphin House.

Things to see and do: gardener's potting shed has information on flora and fauna. Free guided tours and waymarked walks. Discover the active conservation programme of the farm buildings. Barefoot trail from Easter to October. **Dogs**: welcome outdoors and in tea-room on short leads. Water bowl and dog biscuits available.

Access: **House** **Cider House** **Garden**
Parking: 300 yards.

Find out more: 01736 763194 or godolphin@nationaltrust.org.uk

Godolphin		M	T	W	T	F	S	S
Garden, outbuildings and tea-room								
1 Jan–27 Oct	10–5	M	T	W	T	F	S	S
28 Oct–31 Dec*	10–4	M	T	W	T	F	S	S
Estate								
Open all year	Dawn–dusk	M	T	W	T	F	S	S
House								
Limited opening**		·	·	·	·	·	·	·

Tea-room last orders 30 minutes before closing.
*Closed 24 and 25 December. **House open first Saturday to Thursday of every month, February to October (except August), plus weekends 30 November to 15 December (please check house opening before visiting).

Modernisation and fashion fads have passed Godolphin by, leaving the garden and buildings remarkably unchanged since their creation

Godrevy

near Hayle, Cornwall 1939

Long sandy beaches on St Ives Bay with wildlife-rich cliffs and walks. Godrevy café in dunes (concession) open most days. **Note**: unstable cliffs and incoming tides. Toilets open in top field. For Sat Nav use TR27 5ED. Car-parking fields on headland open summer, subject to weather and ground conditions.

Find out more: 01872 552412 or godrevy@nationaltrust.org.uk

Gunwalloe

near Helston, Cornwall 1974

Two family-friendly sandy beaches and reedbeds rich in wildlife. Between the two coves, a medieval church shelters behind Castle Mound. **Note**: lifeguards patrol Church Cove in summer holidays. Dogs welcome all year at Dollar Cove, council-enforced ban at Church Cove (Easter to 1 October).

Find out more: 01326 222170 or gunwalloe@nationaltrust.org.uk

Holywell

near Newquay, Cornwall

1951

A classic north Cornish beach with a sweep of golden sand and a towering dune system. There's lots of history to explore, including the remains of an Iron Age castle on Kelsey Head, a Bronze Age barrow on Cubert Common and the holy well in a cave on the beach.

Eat, shop, stay: seasonal refreshments, traditional seaside shopping and pubs at Holywell and a convenience store and café year round at Cubert, 2 miles (none National Trust).

Holywell, with Carter's Rocks just offshore

Things to see and do: surf schools. Beach has a stream running down one side and is great for building sandcastles. Wildlife-rich grasslands and coastline. **Dogs**: welcome everywhere, including the beach, but under close control (especially around livestock).

Access:
Sat Nav: use TR8 5PF. **Parking**: on site.

Find out more: 01208 863046 or holywell@nationaltrust.org.uk

Kynance Cove

on the Lizard peninsula, Cornwall 1935

It's a ⅓-mile walk down through Lizard heathland to this famous beach, with its serpentine stacks, islands and caves. **Note**: for Sat Nav use TR12 7PJ. Car park very busy in summer – arrive early to avoid disappointment. Council-enforced seasonal dog ban on beach. Level access route to viewpoint only; path to beach steep and uneven. No vehicle access to café track. Café open Easter to November.

Find out more: 01326 222170 or kynancecove@nationaltrust.org.uk

Lanhydrock

Bodmin, Cornwall PL30 5AD

1953

A tragic fire in 1881 meant that the Agar-Robartes family had to rebuild most of their 17th-century home. Out of the ashes came the country house you see today, presented as if time has stood still with the family having just popped out to tea. There are more than 50 rooms to discover – from the extensive kitchens, which reveal the servants' daily lives, to the elegant Victorian luxury of the family rooms. Outside is a garden, full of colour all year round and famed for its magnolias, and ancient woodlands with miles of footpaths to explore. The off-road cycle trails have different routes to suit all levels of experience, and you can even hire a bike when you get here.

A family-friendly cycling trail at Lanhydrock

Eat, shop, stay: the Park Café offers homemade dishes all year. At the house, there's the Stables tea-room, plus waitress service in the Victorian restaurant. Shop sells local food and gifts. Second-hand bookshop. A holiday cottage on the estate sleeps six.

Things to see and do: **Indoors** There's a remarkable early 17th-century ceiling in the gallery which survived the fire and is the oldest room in the house. As you explore you will experience everyday life in both the upstairs and downstairs worlds. Free children's trail daily. At Christmas, there's a traditional Victorian atmosphere. **Outdoors** Guided tours (telephone for availability) help you discover one of the great Cornish gardens, as well as the more remote corners of the parkland and riverside woods. There are waymarked routes for exploring alone, as well as family-friendly cycle trails and a popular adventure playground. **Dogs**: dog-friendly walks throughout the estate (assistance dogs only in house and garden).

Levant Mine and Beam Engine

on the Tin Coast, near Pendeen, St Just, Cornwall TR19 7SX

Levant Mine and Beam Engine on the cliffs

High up on the exposed cliffs of the Tin Coast is Levant, part of the Cornish Mining World Heritage Site, and at its heart the restored 1840s beam engine running on steam. Here you can discover how Cornish miners, engineers and inventors risked everything to help shape the modern world. **Note**: exposed clifftop location, uneven ground/mine ruins, please take care. Engine steaming (timed tickets when busy).

Eat, shop, stay: light refreshments, hot and cold drinks, pasties and ice cream with outdoor picnic benches. Small shop selling books, minerals, souvenirs and postcards. You can stay nearby in the heart of the Tin Coast at Botallack Count House Cottage (sleeps two).

Things to see and do: **Indoors** Restored beam engine steams daily. **Outdoors** Waymarked walks to Botallack and Geevor. Free guided tours of mining landscape, archaeology and tunnel to the man-engine shaft. Mineral panning activity. **Dogs**: welcome on short leads, but not in man-engine tunnel.

Access: **Reception** **Engine house** **Grounds**
Parking: 328 yards. Narrow road, please drive slowly and be considerate of our neighbours. Motorhomes and caravans should park at Geevor Tin Mine (½ mile via coastal path).

Find out more: 01736 786156 or levant@nationaltrust.org.uk

Levant Beam Engine		M	T	W	T	F	S	S
18 Mar–27 Oct	10:30–5	M	T	W	T	F	S	S

Access to man-engine tunnel by guided tour only.
Winter opening available for arranged visits.

Lizard Point

on the Lizard peninsula, near Helston, Cornwall

This is mainland Britain's most southerly point, infamous as a site of shipwrecks in the past and overlooking what is still one of the busiest shipping lanes in the world. The cliffs and farmland are incredibly rich in wildlife and in early summer the wild flowers are at their best. From the Wildlife Watchpoint you can spot seals and occasionally dolphins, as well as the iconic Cornish choughs that breed close by. At Bass Point, a short walk along the coast path, you'll find the tiny Lizard Wireless Station.

Watching wildlife at Lizard Point

The coast path leading to Lizard Point, above, and remains of the old lifeboat station at Polpeor Cove, top

Eat, shop, stay: highly rated Polpeor Café at Lizard Point (concession) open all year – weather-dependent – with outside seating and great views. Gifts on sale at information point (Easter to end October). One holiday cottage at Wireless Station, and more elsewhere on Lizard peninsula.

Things to see and do: take a walk along the coast path for superb coastal views, or try one of the inland routes to search for rare and unique plants. **Dogs**: welcome on leads (please note that livestock graze in some areas).

Access: [access symbols]
Sat Nav: use TR12 7NT.
Parking: at Lizard Point.

Find out more: 01326 222170 or lizard@nationaltrust.org.uk

Lizard Point		M	T	W	T	F	S	S
Wildlife Watchpoint*								
1 Apr–15 Sep	10–4	**M**	**T**	**W**	**T**	**F**	**S**	**S**

*Weather permitting.

Lizard Wireless Station

Bass Point, Lizard, near Helston, Cornwall 1996

The oldest surviving wireless station in the world – a tiny hut on the cliffs where Marconi conducted his world-changing experiments. **Note**: best access is by foot from Lizard Point, 1 mile via coast path. Accessible parking by arrangement. Nearest parking at Lizard Point, use TR12 7NT. Opening hours vary throughout year (please check before setting out).

Find out more: 01326 222170 or lizardwirelessstation@nationaltrust.org.uk

Morwenstow

near Bude, Cornwall 1956

Coastal realm of a great Victorian character – Parson Hawker. Hawker's Hut, driftwood-built, is on the cliff edge near his church. **Note**: sorry no toilets. For Sat Nav use EX23 9SR. Rectory Tea-rooms (tenant-run) open seasonally for cream teas and more.

Find out more: 01208 863046 or morwenstow@nationaltrust.org.uk

Mullion Cove

on the Lizard peninsula, near Helston, Cornwall 1945

Originally built in the 1890s, the picturesque harbour at Mullion Cove shelters a small fishing fleet from powerful westerly storms. **Note**: toilets open seasonally. Dogs on leads welcome all year. Kayaking and boat trips available. National Trust campsite nearby at Teneriffe Farm. Parking 200 yards approximately, not National Trust (charge including members).

Find out more: 01326 222170 or mullioncove@nationaltrust.org.uk

Northcott Mouth

near Bude, Cornwall 1981

Quiet and ruggedly beautiful, this small rocky beach opens up to expansive sand and rock pools as the tide drops. **Note**: sorry no toilets. Dogs welcome, under control. Lifeguards in high season. For Sat Nav use EX23 9ED.

Find out more: 01208 863046 or northcottmouth@nationaltrust.org.uk

Loe Bar at Penrose, right, separates Cornwall's largest natural lake from the sea

Penrose

near Helston and Porthleven, Cornwall TR13 0RD

1974

Home to Loe Pool, Cornwall's largest natural lake, Penrose is a mix of woods, farmland, parkland, cliffs and beaches: a great place to explore. There are 16 miles of bridleways and footpaths, including a trail around the pool and many coast path links. **Note**: to maintain the sense of peace, we don't allow watercraft on the pool. No fishing.

Eat, shop, stay: Stables Café (concession) with parkland views. Picnics welcome in the neighbouring walled garden. There are several holiday cottages around Penrose, some hidden away and others with sea or lake views.

Things to see and do: you can hire a bike at Helston, try the easy-access route from Helston to the café, or choose a downloadable trail to follow. **Dogs**: welcome under control, please note livestock graze in the fields.

Access: **Stables Cafe** **Helston Drive**
Sat Nav: use TR13 0RA for Fairground car park and TR13 0RD for Penrose Hill car park.
Parking: several small car parks around Loe Pool, plus Fairground car park in Helston (not National Trust).

Find out more: 01326 222170 or penroseestate@nationaltrust.org.uk

Penrose		M	T	W	T	F	S	S
Stables Café								
5 Jan–7 Apr	10–4	·	·	·	·	·	S	S
8 Apr–27 Oct	10–4	M	T	W	T	F	S	S
2 Nov–29 Dec	10–4	·	·	·	·	·	S	S

Poldhu Cove

Poldhu, near Mullion, Helston,
Cornwall TR12 7JB

1984

Poldhu is an unspoilt beach popular with locals and visitors. The beach, dunes and reedbeds are designated as a Site of Special Scientific Interest for their rich wildlife. South of the cove the Marconi Monument and visitor centre celebrate Poldhu's role as the site of the first transatlantic wireless signal. **Note**: lifeguards on duty throughout summer. Car park and toilets not National Trust. Charge for parking (including members).

Eat, shop, stay: the café at Poldhu Beach is open all year (not National Trust). A Trust campsite is close by at Teneriffe Farm, near Mullion, and there are holiday cottages further away at Bass Point, Penrose and Cadgwith.

Things to see and do: popular surf school offers lessons for all the family with ex-professional Dan Joel. **Dogs**: welcome on coast path. Council-enforced beach ban from Easter to 1 October.

Poldhu Cove: popular with locals and visitors

Access: **Marconi Centre**
Sat Nav: use TR12 7BU. **Parking**: on site, not National Trust (charge including members).

Find out more: 01326 222170 or poldhucove@nationaltrust.org.uk

Port Quin

near Wadebridge, Cornwall

1936

Walking the coast path on the Rumps, near Port Quin

Once a busy fishing port, Port Quin is now a peaceful sheltered inlet on an outstanding stretch of unspoilt coast. Nearby are the headlands of Pentire and the Rumps, with spectacular views and wild flowers; Lundy Bay at the foot of a wildlife-filled valley; and Pentireglaze Haven with great rock-pooling. **Note**: nearest toilets in Polzeath, 3 miles (not National Trust).

Eat, shop, stay: nearest pubs, cafés and shops in Polzeath and Port Isaac (none National Trust). Holiday cottages on this stretch of coast include the quirky Doyden Castle and a number of coastal apartments and characterful cottages.

Things to see and do: seals, rare bats, corn buntings and puffins to spot. Well-preserved Iron Age ramparts on the Rumps. Sea kayaking and coasteering available nearby. **Dogs**: welcome under control. Seasonal dog ban on Polzeath Beach (including Pentireglaze Haven).

Sat Nav: use PL29 3SU for Port Quin; PL27 6QY Pentireglaze and Pentire Farm; PL27 6QZ Lundy Bay. **Parking**: at Port Quin, Lead Mines (Pentireglaze) and Lundy Bay. Also at Polzeath (not National Trust).

Find out more: 01208 863046 or portquin@nationaltrust.org.uk

Porth

on the Roseland peninsula, near Portscatho, Cornwall 1958

Creekside and coastal footpaths make for great walking and wildlife spotting, or spend the day on the beach at Towan. **Note**: for Sat Nav use TR2 5EX. The Thirstea Company (concession) serves drinks, cakes, sandwiches and ice cream. Toilets. Holiday cottages here and nearby Bohortha.

Find out more: 01872 580553 or porth@nationaltrust.org.uk

Porthcurno

near Penzance, Cornwall 1994

Soft, white shell beach with freshwater stream, surrounded by turquoise seas. Great for watching birds, basking sharks and dolphins. **Note**: for Sat Nav use TR19 6JU. Parking and toilets not National Trust (charge including members).

Find out more: 01736 761853 or porthcurno@nationaltrust.org.uk

St Agnes Head

near St Agnes, Cornwall 1967

A patchwork of gorse and heather carpets these clifftops high above the Atlantic Ocean, overlooked by lofty St Agnes Beacon. **Note**: car park height restriction 1.83 metres. For Sat Nav use TR5 0NU. Coast path walk to Wheal Coates and café and toilets at Chapel Porth.

Find out more: 01872 552412 or stagneshead@nationaltrust.org.uk

St Anthony Head

on the Roseland peninsula, near Portscatho, Cornwall

1959

Standing guard on the eastern entrance to Falmouth harbour, this headland has been strategically important for centuries. It commands magnificent views up the Fal Estuary and across Falmouth Bay towards the Lizard, and you'll find plenty of historic fortifications from various eras to explore.

Eat, shop, stay: you can stay here in the old officers' quarters on the headland itself (two adapted for disabled visitors), or nearby at Bohortha and Porth holiday cottages. There are many wonderful spots for picnicking. At Porth there's a seasonal café (concession).

Things to see and do: St Anthony Battery tours on certain summer dates. Bird hide for spotting peregrine falcons. You can walk the coast path to Porth or Place, or scramble down to Molunan Beach. **Dogs**: welcome.

Access:
Sat Nav: use TR2 5HA. **Parking**: on site.

Find out more: 01872 580553 or stanthonyhead@nationaltrust.org.uk

Looking towards St Anthony Head and its lighthouse from Molunan Beach

St Michael's Mount

Marazion, Cornwall TR17 0HS

1954

This iconic rocky island, crowned by a medieval church and castle, is home to the St Aubyn family and a 30-strong community of islanders. Visiting the Mount, you are immersed in history, islanders' tales and legends, such as the famous 'Jack the Giant Killer'. There's a subtropical terraced garden to explore, and spectacular views of Mount's Bay and the Lizard from the castle battlements. If the tide is high, you can take an evocative boat trip to the island harbour; at low tide you walk across the ancient cobbled causeway from Marazion on the mainland, as pilgrims have done for centuries. **Note**: steep climb to the castle over uneven, cobbled, historic pathway. St Aubyn Estates/National Trust partnership. Members have to pay for car parking and boat trips to the Mount at high tide.

Eat, shop, stay: Island Café for pasties, sandwiches, ice cream. Sail Loft for Newlyn fish specials, homemade bread, cakes. Both serve local ales, cider, cream teas. Island and Courtyard shops sell emerging contemporary artists' ranges, local produce, jewellery, homewares. None National Trust.

St Michael's Mount, clockwise from above: the medieval castle, the Blue Drawing Rooms and the iconic island seen from Marazion

Things to see and do: Indoors Children's castle quest. Find out more about the castle's history by asking our knowledgeable room guides. Sunday church services (Whitsun to September). **Outdoors** Storytelling and family activities during school holidays. **Dogs**: assistance dogs only in castle and garden.

Access: **Castle** **Village**
Parking: numerous spaces in Marazion, opposite St Michael's Mount, not National Trust (charge including members).

Find out more: 01736 710265 (information, tides and boats) or stmichaelsmount@nationaltrust.org.uk
stmichaelsmount.co.uk
Estate Office, King's Road, Marazion TR17 0EL

St Michael's Mount		M	T	W	T	F	S	S
Castle								
24 Mar–28 Jun	10:30–5	**M**	**T**	**W**	**T**	**F**	·	**S**
30 Jun–30 Aug	10–5:30	**M**	**T**	**W**	**T**	**F**	·	**S**
1 Sep–1 Nov	10:30–5	**M**	**T**	**W**	**T**	**F**	·	**S**
Garden								
15 Apr–28 Jun	10:30–5	**M**	**T**	**W**	**T**	**F**	·	·
4 Jul–30 Aug	10–5:30	·	·	·	**T**	**F**	·	·
5 Sep–27 Sep	10:30–5	·	·	·	**T**	**F**	·	·

Last admission one hour before castle closes (remember to allow enough time for travel from mainland). Telephone for details of November and December opening arrangements.

Sandymouth

near Bude, Cornwall

1978

A popular destination, yet Sandymouth remains unspoilt and breathtakingly beautiful. You'll find an extreme difference between the beach at low tide – when it is a huge sweep of sand and rocky outcrops – and at high tide, when it shrinks back to a pebbly cove, backed by twisted cliffs.

Eat, shop, stay: Sandymouth Café (concession) has outdoor and indoor seating and also sells beach goods. Pubs, shops and cafés in Kilkhampton and Bude (none National Trust).

Walking the coast path above Sandymouth

Things to see and do: surf school. Fantastic rock-pooling and coastal walks. Look out for the waterfall and amazing geological formations backing the beach. You may also catch sight of skylarks, song thrushes and stonechats. **Dogs**: welcome everywhere, including the beach, but under close control (especially around livestock).

Access:
Sat Nav: use EX23 9HW. **Parking**: on site.

Find out more: 01208 863046 or sandymouth@nationaltrust.org.uk

Sandymouth
Café at Sandymouth open daily April to October and Thursday to Sunday during the winter, telephone 01288 354286 for opening times.

Tintagel Old Post Office

Fore Street, Tintagel, Cornwall PL34 0DB

1903

A medieval manor house in miniature, at more than 600 years old this is one of Cornwall's oldest domestic buildings. Used by a number of businesses throughout the Victorian period, its final function was as the village's letter-receiving office. The cottage garden hidden at the back (above) offers a welcome retreat. **Note**: nearest toilet 54 yards in Trevena Square (not National Trust).

Eat, shop, stay: small souvenir shop in the Post Room selling craft items, gifts and books inspired by the Old Post Office's history and events. Picnics are welcome in the relaxing cottage garden at the back of the house.

Things to see and do: **Indoors** Events all year, including traditional craft workshops, baking demonstrations and activities to provide entertainment during school holidays. **Outdoors** Family trail, games and dressing up. **Dogs**: assistance dogs only.

Access: **Building**
Grounds
Parking: pay and display village car parks, not National Trust (charges including members). Nearest Trust parking at Glebe Cliff, ½ mile.

Find out more: 01840 770024 or tintageloldpo@nationaltrust.org.uk

Tintagel Old Post Office		M	T	W	T	F	S	S
16 Feb–24 Feb	11–4	M	T	W	T	F	S	S
9 Mar–31 Mar	11–4	M	T	W	T	F	S	S
1 Apr–29 Sep	10:30–5:30	M	T	W	T	F	S	S
30 Sep–3 Nov	11–4	M	T	W	T	F	S	S

 For information about getting to National Trust places, please see page 3

Trelissick

Feock, near Truro, Cornwall TR3 6QL

1955

Trelissick is set on its own peninsula, with panoramic views over the Fal Estuary. The house provides the perfect setting to enjoy the ever-changing seascape and countryside. Visitors can explore meandering paths through the garden, leading to exotic planting and formal lawns with herbaceous borders bursting with colour. There are also longer walks to discover through the historic park and woodland, which sweep down towards the estuary, and along Lamouth Creek to the Iron Age promontory fort and 18th-century quay at Roundwood.

An adventure among the ferns at Trelissick

Access: **Reception** **House** **Garden**
Parking: 80 yards.

Eat, shop, stay: Crofters Café open daily. Barn Restaurant and Courtyard Room both available for functions and private hire. Large shop with plant and garden centre. Second-hand bookshop. Cornish art and craft gallery. Six holiday cottages on the estate.

Things to see and do: **Indoors** Friendly family house. You're welcome to play the piano and sit in the East Library. House and garden Christmas events. **Outdoors** You can walk and run throughout the estate. **Dogs**: welcome in the park and woodland walks. Assistance dogs only in garden.

Find out more: 01872 862090 or trelissick@nationaltrust.org.uk

Trelissick		M	T	W	T	F	S	S
Garden, café, shop, gallery and bookshop								
Open all year	10:30–5:30*	M	T	W	T	F	S	S
House								
19 Jan–17 Nov	11–5**	M	T	W	T	F	S	S
Parkland and walks								
Open all year		M	T	W	T	F	S	S

*1 January to 15 February and 28 October to 31 December: closes 4:30. Garden closes dusk if earlier. **19 January to 15 February and 28 October to 17 November: closes 4. Late-night openings and Christmas events in December. Closed 25 and 26 December.

Trelissick: sitting on its very own peninsula, the house commands sweeping views over the Fal Estuary

Trengwainton Garden

Madron, near Penzance, Cornwall TR20 8RZ

1961

Here in this warm sheltered garden, you can follow in the footsteps of the great 1920s plant hunters to see colourful species that flowered in Britain for the first time. Award-winning magnolias and rhododendrons are still nurtured by those with a passion for plants, and subtropical varieties from around the world thrive in the shelter of the walled gardens, including a kitchen garden built to the dimensions of Noah's Ark. Winding wooded paths follow a ½-mile incline to sea views across Mount's Bay, and the descent via the drive is bordered by a stream garden and open meadows.

Bursting with produce, this sloping bed at Trengwainton Garden is angled to catch the the best of the sun for as long as possible

Eat, shop, stay: award-winning tea-room (concession) with indoor and outdoor seating. Shop sells local gifts, food, souvenirs and Trengwainton-inspired plants. Second-hand bookshop and gallery in the former head gardener's cottage. Nearby, you can stay in an 18th-century former laundry house (sleeps nine).

Things to see and do: seasonal family holiday activities including trails, Easter egg hunts, summer play, pumpkin fun and Christmas lantern walk. 1940s garden plot with replica Anderson shelter and medicinal plant border. **Dogs**: welcome on leads. Water, free biscuits and poo-bags available.

Access: **Reception** **Tea-room** **Garden**
Sat Nav: TR20 8RZ. **Parking**: 150 yards.

Find out more: 01736 363148 or trengwainton@nationaltrust.org.uk

Trengwainton Garden		M	T	W	T	F	S	S
17 Feb–27 Oct	10:30–5	**M**	**T**	**W**	**T**	·	·	**S**

Open Good Friday. Tea-room opens at 10.

Trerice

Kestle Mill, near Newquay, Cornwall TR8 4PG

1953

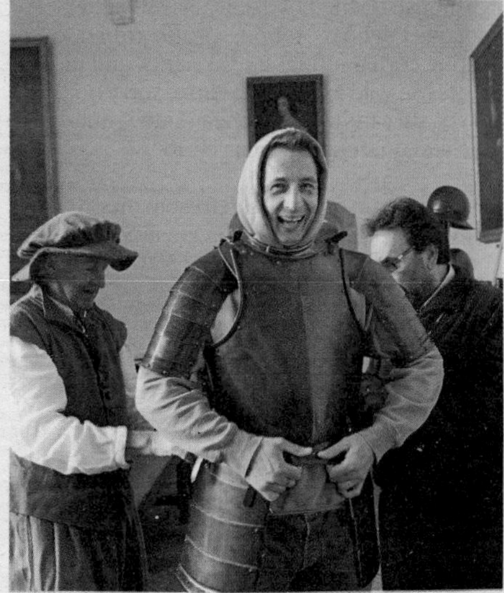

Clockwise from left: 'kayles' on the lawn at Trerice, the house in its peaceful setting and trying on the armour

Once the Cornish seat of the Arundell family, Trerice remains little changed since it was built in 1573, thanks to long periods under absentee owners. With golden stone, ornate gables and a magnificent hall window, Trerice is a grand Elizabethan house on a small scale. From the highest point of the garden, views stretch out over a landscape rich in history. Shouts of excitement ring out from the kayling lawn as the Cornish game of 'kayles' is played, bringing back some of the bustle and noise that must have typified its time as a working manor farm. **Note**: we occasionally need to close parts or all of Trerice for private functions.

Eat, shop, stay: the barn restaurant serves light meals, snacks, Cornish cream teas and our famous lemon meringue pie. The shop sells local products, souvenirs and plants. The west wing of the house contains a holiday flat that sleeps two.

Things to see and do: **Indoors** Costume days, introductory talks and conservation events. Replica armour to try on. **Outdoors** Family activities, Cornish 'kayles' and other traditional games. **Dogs**: welcome in car park only.

Access: **House** **Barn** **Garden**
Sat Nav: enter Kestle Mill A3058. **Parking**: 300 yards. Electric vehicle charging point available.

Find out more: 01637 875404 or trerice@nationaltrust.org.uk

Trerice		M	T	W	T	F	S	S
2 Mar–3 Nov	10:30–5*	**M**	**T**	**W**	**T**	**F**	**S**	**S**
9 Nov–22 Dec**	11–4	·	·	·	·	·	**S**	**S**

*House opens 11. **Selected rooms, garden, shop and restaurant open.

Trevose Head

near Padstow, Cornwall

2016

Jutting into the Atlantic, Trevose Head commands views for miles along the coast. Exposed western cliffs contrast starkly with a gentler eastern coastline. Home of Trevose lighthouse (owned by Trinity House) and Padstow Lifeboat Station, it's also famed for nesting corn buntings and skylarks, and rare plants like wild asparagus. **Note**: sorry no toilets. Be careful of the sheer-sided round hole and quarry near Dinas Head.

Eat, shop, stay: seasonal refreshments. Convenience store and pub/café in St Merryn and Harlyn (1 to 2 miles). None National Trust. Picnics welcome.

Commanding unrivalled views, Trevose Head, below, is home to corn buntings, above

Things to see and do: wonderful coastal walks with views and chances to watch wildlife. Access to Booby's Bay Beach. Carnewas at Bedruthan, just a few miles along the coast, is another spectacular coastal destination. **Dogs**: welcome under control. Please be aware of ground-nesting birds and keep to signed footpaths.

Sat Nav: use PL28 8SL. **Parking**: on site. Open all year at scenic car park; summer car park for beaches open May to September.

Find out more: 01208 863046 (North Cornwall office) or trevosehead@nationaltrust.org.uk

Wheal Coates

near St Agnes, Cornwall 1956

Dramatic mining ruins – an iconic Cornish sight – hugging the heather and gorse-carpeted clifftops. **Note**: for Sat Nav use TR5 0NT. Follow the coast path for a steep, but lovely, walk down to Chapel Porth for beach, café and toilets.

Find out more: 01872 552412 or whealcoates@nationaltrust.org.uk

Additional coastal and countryside car parks in Cornwall

Strangles Beach	EX23 0LQ	St Agnes Beacon	TR5 0NU	Chyvarloe	TR12 7PY
Glebe Cliff, Tintagel	PL34 0DL	Reskajeage Downs	TR14 0JG	Predannack	TR12 7EZ
Lundy Bay	PL27 6QZ	Derrick Cove	TR14 0JG	Poltesco	TR12 7LR
Pentireglaze	PL27 6QY	Fishing Cove	TR27 5EE	Nare Head	TR2 5PQ
Trevose Head	PL28 8SL	Trencrom	TR27 6NP	Lamledra (Vault Beach)	PL26 6JS
Park Head	PL27 7UU	Carn Galver	TR20 8YX	Coombe Farm	PL23 1HW
Treago Mill (Polly Joke)	TR8 5QS	Cot Valley	TR19 7NS	Hendersick	PL13 2HZ

Devon and Dorset

Blacksmith working at historic Finch Foundry, Devon

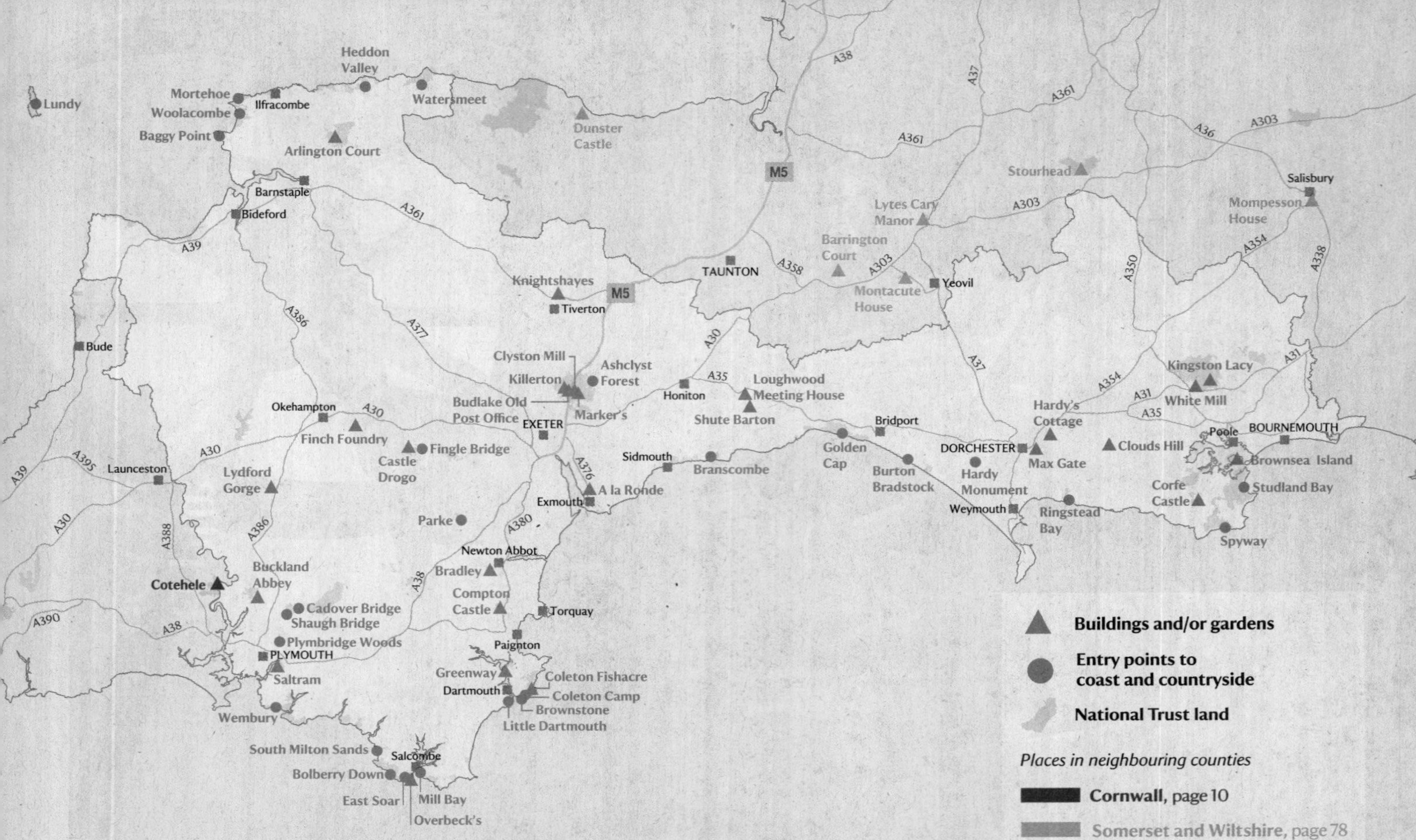

Lundy
Mortehoe
Woolacombe
Baggy Point
Ilfracombe
Heddon Valley
Watersmeet
Arlington Court
Dunster Castle
Barnstaple
Bideford
A39
A361
A38
A37
A36
A303
A338
A350
A354
A358
A377
A386
A395
A388
A390
A30
A35
A31
A376
A380
M5
Stourhead
Salisbury
Mompesson House
Lytes Cary Manor
Barrington Court
TAUNTON
Montacute House
Yeovil
Knightshayes
Tiverton
Bude
Clyston Mill
Killerton
Ashclyst Forest
Budlake Old Post Office
Marker's
EXETER
Honiton
Loughwood Meeting House
Shute Barton
Bridport
Kingston Lacy
White Mill
Hardy's Cottage
Okehampton
Finch Foundry
Castle Drogo
Fingle Bridge
Launceston
Lydford Gorge
Sidmouth
Branscombe
Golden Cap
Burton Bradstock
DORCHESTER
Hardy Monument
Max Gate
Clouds Hill
Poole
BOURNEMOUTH
Brownsea Island
Studland Bay
Corfe Castle
Spyway
A la Ronde
Exmouth
Weymouth
Ringstead Bay
Parke
Newton Abbot
Bradley
Buckland Abbey
Cotehele
Cadover Bridge
Shaugh Bridge
Compton Castle
Torquay
Plymbridge Woods
PLYMOUTH
Saltram
Paignton
Greenway
Coleton Fishacre
Dartmouth
Coleton Camp
Brownstone
Little Dartmouth
Wembury
South Milton Sands
Salcombe
Bolberry Down
East Soar
Mill Bay
Overbeck's
Buildings and/or gardens
Entry points to coast and countryside
National Trust land
Places in neighbouring counties
Cornwall, page 10
Somerset and Wiltshire, page 78
10 miles

A la Ronde

Summer Lane, Exmouth, Devon EX8 5BD

1991

Full of creativity and treasures from around the world, this amazing 16-sided house was the work of cousins Jane and Mary Parminter in the 1790s. Step inside and enter another world, one where their imaginations ran wild in design and ornamentation. They decorated walls with feathers, shells and pictures made of seaweed and sand, and every space contains mementoes from their travels. With the 360° touchscreen virtual tour, you can view the fragile shell gallery made with 25,000 shells. Outside, there's a sense of harmony around the orchard, hay meadow and colourful borders, and views over the Exe Estuary. **Note**: small and delicate rooms. Photography welcome without flash.

Endearingly eccentric 16-sided A la Ronde, Devon, contains wonderfully wild ornamentation

Eat, shop, stay: licensed café serving morning coffee, light lunches and afternoon tea. Indoor and outdoor seating with views of the Exe Estuary. Picnic areas available. A range of high-quality and local products in the stables shop. Pre-loved book sales.

Things to see and do: **Indoors** Eclectic, artistic collection. Play the piano. **Outdoors** Family trail and activities. Short walk around hay meadow and orchard, with seating and views. Estate tours. Garden games, croquet and trails. **Dogs**: dogs on leads welcome everywhere (excluding house).

Access:
House **Grounds**
Sat Nav: postcode unreliable, enter Summer Lane. **Parking**: on site.

Find out more: 01395 265514 or alaronde@nationaltrust.org.uk

A la Ronde		M	T	W	T	F	S	S
2 Feb–27 Oct	10:30–5:30*	**M**	**T**	**W**	**T**	**F**	**S**	**S**

*House: opens 11 and closes 5 (last entry 4). Open by guided tour only 4 to 8 and 11 to 15 February, 25 February to 1 March and 4 to 8 March; freeflow all other dates. Café last orders at 5.

Arlington Court and the National Trust Carriage Museum

Arlington, near Barnstaple, Devon EX31 4LP

1949

Hidden in the lichen-draped landscape of North Devon, Arlington is a surprise and a delight. The starkly classical exterior of the house gives no clue to what lies inside – recently redisplayed to share the passions of the Chichester family who lived here. The stable block houses a nationally important display of more than 40 carriages, from grand state coaches to humble governess cars. The garden is restored to its colourful Victorian glory, and the conservatory's exotic plantings reveal the Chichesters' world travels.

Eat, shop, stay: seasonal pop-up dog-friendly café. Reduced menu in winter. Two holiday cottages on edges of estate, sleeping two or three (dogs welcome).

Things to see and do: **Indoors** Bat-cam for watching rare bats. Rooms in the cellar tell the servants' stories. Children's activities.

Outdoors Two woodland play areas. Bring your walking boots for exploring the large estate. **Dogs**: welcome on leads in garden, Carriage Museum and wider estate.

Access:
House **Museum** **Grounds**
Sat Nav: from South Molton, don't turn left into unmarked lane. **Parking**: 150 yards.

Find out more: 01271 850296 or arlingtoncourt@nationaltrust.org.uk

Arlington Court		M	T	W	T	F	S	S
16 Feb–15 Mar	11–4*	**M**	**T**	**W**	**T**	**F**	**S**	**S**
16 Mar–27 Oct	11–5*	**M**	**T**	**W**	**T**	**F**	**S**	**S**
2 Nov–22 Dec	11–4	·	·	·	·	·	**S**	**S**

*Garden, shop and tea-room open 10:30. Grounds open all year, dawn to dusk.

Classical Arlington Court and the National Trust Carriage Museum in Devon, inside and out

Baggy Point

near Croyde, Devon

1939

Baggy Point is the impressive headland at Croyde, once owned by the Hyde family and overlooking one of the best surfing beaches in the South West. Huge coastal views out to Lundy Island, great walking and opportunities to climb, surf and coasteer make it a must-do destination for anyone visiting North Devon. Baggy Point also appeals to wildlife and nature lovers – keep a look out for seals and porpoises, as well as many bird species, including peregrine falcons, linnets and Dartford warblers. **Note**: toilets and outdoor shower in courtyard next to car park.

The impressive headland of Baggy Point, Devon

Eat, shop, stay: Sandleigh tea-room, garden and shop (tenant-run) serves drinks and food grown in the walled garden. Open-air covered seating area overlooking garden. Tea-room is next to car park, close to beach slipway. Car-park kiosk serves cold drinks and snacks.

Things to see and do: free family activity pack to borrow (or download). Walks leaflets available from car-park kiosk. Easy-access route to the Point. Arlington Court and the National Trust Carriage Museum nearby. **Dogs**: welcome on leads (except for seasonal ban on Croyde Beach, May to September).

Access:
Sat Nav: use EX33 1PA. **Parking**: car park in Moor Lane, Croyde.

Find out more: 01271 870555 or baggypoint@nationaltrust.org.uk

Bolberry Down

between Salcombe and Hope Cove, near Malborough, Devon

1938

The starting point for a spectacular stretch of coast between Salcombe and Hope Cove, including the headlands of Bolt Head and Bolt Tail and the sandy beach at Soar Mill Cove. The majestic ragged cliffs have claimed countless ships over the centuries. There's an easy-access clifftop route.

Eat, shop, stay: refreshments and meals at Oceans Restaurant (not National Trust). At East Soar Outdoor Experience (tenant-run), there's the Walkers' Hut café for hot drinks and homemade cakes, catered camping and a holiday cottage. Nearest National Trust holiday cottage at Wembury.

Things to see and do: level circular trail (just under a mile), accessible for most wheelchair users and pushchairs. **Dogs**: welcome (on leads where animals grazing).

Access:
Sat Nav: use TQ7 3DY. **Parking**: at Bolberry Down and Hope Cove (not National Trust).

Find out more: 01752 346585. 01548 561904 (East Soar Outdoor Experience) or bolberrydown@nationaltrust.org.uk

Bolberry Down in Devon: Soar Mill Cove

Bradley

Totnes Road, Newton Abbot, Devon TQ12 6BN

1938

Surrounded by riverside meadows and woodland, this unspoilt medieval manor house is still a relaxed family home. There are original features to look out for, such as the medieval cat hole and drip stones, as well as the peaceful chapel that was licensed for services in 1428. **Note**: sorry no toilet. Parking from 10:30 on open days.

Eat, shop, stay: table-top shop selling honey, souvenirs, gifts and postcards. Picnics welcome in the meadows surrounding the house and garden.

Things to see and do: free children's trail. Open-air theatre performances in the garden. Walks in Bradley meadow and woodland. **Dogs**: welcome in meadows and woodland. Assistance dogs only in garden and house.

Access:
Building **Grounds**
Sat Nav: TQ12 1LX directs to gate lodge (follow driveway for parking). **Parking**: in meadow (for designated parking call 07745 236836).

Find out more: 01803 661907 or bradley@nationaltrust.org.uk

Bradley		M	T	W	T	F	S	S
2 Apr–31 Oct	11–5	·	T	W	T	·	·	·

Bradley, Devon: unspoilt medieval manor house

Branscombe

on the Jurassic Coast, near Seaton, Devon

1965

Nestling in a valley that reaches down to the sea on East Devon's dramatic Jurassic Coast (below), the village of Branscombe is surrounded by picturesque countryside with miles of tranquil walking through woodland, farmland and beach. Charming thatched houses, forge and restored watermill add to its timeless magic. **Note**: nearest toilets at information point, village hall and beach car park.

Eat, shop, stay: Old Bakery tea-room (tenant-run) serving sandwiches, cakes and cream teas. Quality ironwork on sale from the Old Forge. Forge Cottage, just across the road, is a holiday cottage in an ideal location for exploring.

Things to see and do: trail (graded as easy) winding up from the beach to the village, passing Manor Mill, Old Bakery and Old Forge. The beach is great for swimming and picnics. **Dogs**: welcome on leads in the Old Bakery garden, orchard, beach and wider countryside.

Access: **Tea-room** **Mill** **Grounds**
Sat Nav: use EX12 3DB. **Parking**: next to Old Forge, limited spaces. Also village hall and beach car parks (neither National Trust).

Find out more: 01752 346585 or branscombe@nationaltrust.org.uk

Branscombe		M	T	W	T	F	S	S
Manor Mill								
14 Apr–29 Sep*	2–4	·	·	·	·	·	·	S
Old Forge								
Open all year	10–5**	M	T	W	T	F	S	S

*31 July to 28 August: also open Wednesdays, 2 to 4.
**Telephone 01297 680481 to check forge opening times.
For Old Bakery tea-room openings, telephone 01297 680764.

 For information about getting to National Trust places, please see page 3

Brownsea Island

Poole Harbour, Poole, Dorset

1962

The perfect day's adventure, this island wildlife sanctuary is easy to get to but feels like another world from the moment you step ashore. The island sits in the middle of Poole Harbour, with dramatic views to the Purbeck Hills. Thriving natural habitats, including woodland, heathland and a lagoon, have created havens for wildlife, such as the red squirrel and a huge variety of birds. The island is rich in history too. It is the birthplace of the Scouting and Guiding movements, and there are the remains of daffodil farming, pottery works and Maryland village to explore. **Note**: half-hourly ferry service from Poole and Sandbanks (not National Trust). Seahorse wheelchair ferry service available. Voluntary donation to enter the Dorset Wildlife Trust area (including members). No visitor or member access to castle.

Eat, shop, stay: Villano Café; coffee bar; self-service hot drinks at the Outdoor Centre. Engine Gift Shop selling National Trust gifts and local products. Scout and Guide Trading Post sells memorabilia. Two quayside holiday cottages as well as a large campsite and bunkhouse.

Things to see and do: visitor centre offers free family trails and island stories display. Seasonal event programme plus activities and camping at the Outdoor Centre. Relaxing picnic spots and fun natural play area. **Dogs**: assistance dogs only.

Access: **Reception** **Visitor centre** **Grounds**
Sat Nav: for Sandbanks Jetty use BH13 7QJ; for Poole Quay BH15 1HP. **Parking**: near Sandbanks and Poole Quay, not National Trust (charge including members).

Find out more: 01202 707744 or brownseaisland@nationaltrust.org.uk

Brownsea Island		M	T	W	T	F	S	S
2 Feb–10 Mar*	10–4	·	·	·	·	·	**S**	**S**
16 Mar–3 Nov**	10–5	**M**	**T**	**W**	**T**	**F**	**S**	**S**

*Hourly ferry service from Poole Quay and Sandbanks Jetty from 10. **Half-hourly ferry service from Poole Quay and Sandbanks Jetty from 10. Winter Bird Boats (landing at Brownsea) run from Poole on 6, 10, 20 January and 3 February. Last ferry leaves island at 5.

Brownsea Island, Dorset: this wildlife sanctuary, below, is easily reached by ferries, above

Brownstone

Brownstone Road, Kingswear, Devon TQ6 0EH 1981

Spectacular views on a coastal walk that leads to a rare Second World War gun battery at Froward Point. **Note**: naturally uneven coastal paths, steep in places – be aware of cliff edges and keep children and dogs supervised.

Find out more: 01803 752776 (rangers) or brownstone@nationaltrust.org.uk

Buckland Abbey

Yelverton, Devon PL20 6EY

1948

Hundreds of years ago, Cistercian monks chose this tranquil valley as the perfect spot in which to worship, farm their estate and trade. The Abbey, later converted into a house, today combines furnished rooms with museum galleries, bringing to life the story of how seafaring adventurers Sir Richard Grenville and Sir Francis Drake changed the shape of Buckland Abbey and the fate of England. Outdoors you'll find the walled kitchen garden, Cider House garden and wild garden; the impressive medieval Great Barn; community growing areas; orchards and woodland walks with far-reaching views and late spring bluebells.

Eat, shop, stay: Ox Yard Restaurant serves freshly cooked local produce, often using ingredients grown in the kitchen garden. Picnics welcome in garden and grounds. Shop selling gifts and plants. Galleries and second-hand bookshop. Holiday cottage.

Exploring the garden and grounds at Buckland Abbey, Devon, below and right. Kitchen, top right

Support the places you visit: please scan your member card for free parking ticket

Things to see and do: **Indoors** Look for traces of the medieval abbey and its Elizabethan conversion. **Outdoors** Higher Paddock natural play area and zip wire for younger visitors. Year-round events, estate walks and trails. **Dogs**: welcome on leads in farmland and on woodland walks. Assistance dogs only in garden.

Access: [access symbols]
Abbey [access symbols] **Visitor Welcome** [access symbols]
Grounds [access symbols]
Sat Nav: do not use. **Parking**: 150 yards.

Find out more: 01822 853607 or
bucklandabbey@nationaltrust.org.uk

Buckland Abbey		M	T	W	T	F	S	S
5 Jan–10 Feb*	10–4	·	·	·	·	·	S	S
16 Feb–31 Dec	10–5**	M	T	W	T	F	S	S

*Garden, estate, restaurant and shop open; Abbey closed.
**Abbey opens 11. From 28 October, everything closes at 4. Everything closed 25 and 26 December. 1 and 2 January: everything open. 3 and 4 January: everything except Abbey open.

Burton Bradstock

on the Jurassic Coast, near Bridport, Dorset

[symbols] 1973

Spectacular cliffs at Burton Bradstock in Dorset

One of the main gateways to Dorset's Jurassic Coast. Here are spectacular sandstone cliffs – Burton Cliff glows bright gold in sunlight – and miles of unspoilt beaches. Hive Beach is a popular family destination, nearby Cogden is quieter; both are part of Chesil Bank – the largest shingle ridge in the world.

Eat, shop, stay: tenant-run Hive Beach Café on Chesil Bank serving local seafood.

Things to see and do: paddling, swimming and outdoor activities. Circular and clifftop walks. **Dogs**: welcome. Dog-free zone on Hive Beach, 1 June to 30 September.

Access: [access symbol]
Sat Nav: use DT6 4RF for Burton Bradstock; DT6 4RL for Cogden. **Parking**: on site.

Find out more: 01297 489481 or
burtonbradstock@nationaltrust.org.uk

Cadover Bridge

on Dartmoor, near Shaugh Prior, Devon 1960

Tranquil moorland by River Plym, with pools. Starting point for walks through ancient woodland or across open moors and tors. **Note**: for Sat Nav use PL7 5EH.

Find out more: 01626 834748 or
cadoverbridge@nationaltrust.org.uk

Castle Drogo

Drewsteignton, near Exeter, Devon EX6 6PB

1974

High above the ancient woodlands of the Teign Gorge stands Castle Drogo. Inspired by the rugged Dartmoor tors surrounding it, the castle was designed and built by renowned 20th-century architect Sir Edwin Lutyens for the self-made millionaire Julius Drewe. Times are changing at Drogo, as the project to restore the castle and grounds to a state worthy of the Drewe family nears completion after six years of major conservation work. Inside the castle a programme of conservation and redisplay reveals what it takes to care for the building and collection, telling the stories of Drogo and celebrating its architecture. **Note**: access may be restricted or changed due to reinstatement works. Access guide available.

Eat, shop, stay: popular licensed café in the visitor centre, with outside seating, serving light meals, homemade cakes and scones. Picnics welcome in orchard. Shop stocking gifts, local beers, jams and a good-sized plant centre. Holiday cottage nearby at Chagford.

Castle Drogo, Devon, clockwise from right: Lutyens's vaulted staircase, walking on the estate, the Bunty House

Things to see and do: **Indoors** Programme of specialised guided tours, family trails and events. **Outdoors** Lutyens-designed terraced garden, games on the lawn. Walks into the Teign Gorge, views across Dartmoor, riverside paths. **Dogs**: welcome on leads in grounds and wider estate. Assistance dogs only in formal garden.

Access:
Castle **Grounds**
Parking: 400 yards from visitor centre.

Find out more: 01647 433306 or castledrogo@nationaltrust.org.uk

Castle Drogo		M	T	W	T	F	S	S
Castle								
9 Mar–27 Oct	11–5	**M**	**T**	**W**	**T**	**F**	**S**	**S**
Garden, visitor centre, café and shop								
1 Jan–8 Mar*	10–4	**M**	**T**	**W**	**T**	**F**	**S**	**S**
9 Mar–27 Oct	9:30–5**	**M**	**T**	**W**	**T**	**F**	**S**	**S**
28 Oct–31 Dec†	10–4	**M**	**T**	**W**	**T**	**F**	**S**	**S**
Estate								
Open all year	Dawn–dusk	**M**	**T**	**W**	**T**	**F**	**S**	**S**

*Closed 14 to 27 January. **Garden opens at 10; visitor centre and garden close 5:30; café and shop close 5:30 in July and August. †Closed 23 to 26 December.

Clouds Hill

Bovington, Dorset BH20 7NQ

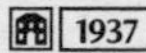

In this tiny woodsman's cottage you can discover the essentials and the luxuries chosen by T. E. Lawrence after he had abandoned the 'Lawrence of Arabia' persona and remodelled himself as a private in the army at Bovington Camp. Much of the furniture and fittings was designed by Lawrence himself.

Eat, shop, stay: self-service tea and coffee available. Small shop selling gifts, books and Lawrence memorabilia.

Things to see and do: you can visit the nearby homes of Thomas Hardy – Max Gate and Hardy's Cottage – along the very roads on which Lawrence himself rode.
Dogs: welcome on leads in grounds only.

Access: **Building** **Grounds**
Parking: on site.

Find out more: 01929 405616 or cloudshill@nationaltrust.org.uk

Clouds Hill		M	T	W	T	F	S	S
1 Mar–31 Oct	11–5	**M**	**T**	**W**	**T**	**F**	**S**	**S**

Timed tickets may apply on busy days. No electric light, so last admission at dusk.

T. E. Lawrence's book room in Clouds Hill, Dorset

Coleton Camp

between Dart Estuary and Brixham, Devon 1981

Great walks along the coast path to Scabbacombe and Man Sands beaches on this rugged stretch of coast. **Note**: naturally uneven coastal paths, steep in places – be aware of cliff edges and keep children and dogs supervised. For Sat Nav use TQ6 0EQ.

Find out more: 01803 753010 or coletoncamp@nationaltrust.org.uk

Coleton Fishacre

Brownstone Road, Kingswear, Devon TQ6 0EQ

1982

This evocative 1920s Arts and Crafts-style house, with its elegant art deco interiors, perfectly encapsulates the spirit of the Jazz Age. The former country home of the D'Oyly Carte family, it has a light, joyful atmosphere and inspiring sea views. You can glimpse life 'downstairs' in the servants' rooms. In the RHS-accredited garden, paths weave through glades and past tranquil ponds and rare tender plants from New Zealand and South Africa; many exotic plants thrive beneath the tree canopy. You can walk down to a coastal viewpoint through the valley garden.

Playing the piano in Coleton Fishacre's Saloon

Step back to the 1920s at Coleton Fishacre, Devon, above. Right, the glorious garden

Eat, shop, stay: Café Coleton serving light bites, hearty lunches, cakes and bakes. Shop selling souvenir guides, gifts, food, music and plants. Why not stay in Chauffeur's Flat, Coleton Barton Cottages or nearby Higher Brownstone to enjoy after-hours access to the garden?

Things to see and do: family trails in the house and garden. Daily guided garden walks from Easter to October, led by a member of the garden team. Events, including open-air theatre. Wild play area. **Dogs**: welcome on short leads in garden and Café Coleton. Tethering rings by house.

Access:
Building **Grounds**
Parking: 20 yards from reception; overflow parking 150 yards.

Find out more: 01803 842382 or
coletonfishacre@nationaltrust.org.uk

Coleton Fishacre		M	T	W	T	F	S	S
16 Feb–27 Oct	10:30–5	M	T	W	T	F	S	S
2 Nov–22 Dec	11–4	·	·	·	·	·	S	S
23 Dec–31 Dec	11–4	M	T	·	·	F	S	S

Compton Castle

Marldon, Paignton, Devon TQ3 1TA

1951

A rare survivor, this medieval fortified manor house (above) has high curtain walls and portcullises. It was once the home of Sir Humphrey Gilbert, part-founder of the New World, and his descendants still live here today. Outside, you can discover roses climbing pergolas, knot and herb gardens and a picnic orchard. **Note**: hall, sub-solar, solar, study, kitchen, scullery, guard room, chapel open. Sorry, credit cards not accepted.

Eat, shop, stay: table-top shop selling souvenirs, guidebooks, gifts and postcards. Pop-up outdoors shop during summer holidays. Picnics welcome in the lower orchard. Why not stay a little longer and have a holiday in the Watchtower? Castle Barton restaurant (not National Trust) opposite.

Things to see and do: family activities, including indoor and outdoor trails for children, medieval dressing up and garden games. You can join a 1½-mile circular walk opposite the castle. **Dogs**: welcome in the lower orchard on leads. Assistance dogs only in castle and garden.

Access: **Building** **Grounds**
Parking: in Castle Barton's car park for cars and campervans, opposite entrance, 100 yards. Overflow parking on grass verges at castle entrance.

Find out more: 01803 661906 or
comptoncastle@nationaltrust.org.uk

Compton Castle		M	T	W	T	F	S	S
2 Apr–31 Oct	10:30–4:30	·	T	W	T	·	·	·

Open Bank Holiday Mondays.

Corfe Castle

Corfe, Wareham, Dorset BH20 5EZ

1982

This fairytale fortress is an evocative survivor of the English Civil War, partially demolished by the Parliamentarians in 1646. It's a favourite haunt for adults and children alike – all ages are captivated by these romantic ruins with their breathtaking views. There are 1,000 years of the castle's history as a royal palace and fortress to be discovered here. Fallen walls and secret places tell tales of treachery and treason around every corner. Corfe Castle's brooding presence is a backdrop to some of Britain's most beautiful coast and countryside. Corfe Common and Hartland Moor are close by – you can explore them by walking or cycling, discovering rare wild flowers and masses of wildlife along the way. **Note**: steep, uneven slopes; steps; sudden drops throughout castle. All/parts of castle close in high winds.

Eat, shop, stay: 18th-century tea-room and garden in village serving cream teas with a view of the castle. Locally made gifts available in the shop in the village square. Three National Trust holiday cottages in the village, and more in the wider Purbeck landscape.

Things to see and do: an action-packed programme of fun family history events runs from April until September, with something most weekends and school holidays. Highlights include Saxon and Viking and Civil War re-enactments, wildlife events, open-air theatre and winter lights. Throughout the year, discover more about the castle's trebuchet and rich history. There's a children's activity trail and activities which run throughout the year. Beyond the castle walls, you can explore a wildlife-rich landscape of hills and heathland on walks through Purbeck. **Dogs**: welcome on short leads.

Access: Grounds
Sat Nav: use BH20 5DR. **Parking**: 800 yards uphill walk. Norden car park (½ mile) and West Street in village, neither National Trust (charge including members).

Why not share your pictures with us? #nationaltrust

A survivor of the Civil War, Corfe Castle in Dorset, left and below, is steeped in history, which is brought to life by re-enactments, above

Find out more: 01929 481294 (ticket office). 01929 480921 (shop). 01929 481332 (tea-room) or corfecastle@nationaltrust.org.uk

Corfe Castle		M	T	W	T	F	S	S
1 Jan–15 Feb	10–4	**M**	**T**	**W**	**T**	**F**	**S**	**S**
16 Feb–29 Sep	10–6*	**M**	**T**	**W**	**T**	**F**	**S**	**S**
30 Sep–27 Oct	10–5	**M**	**T**	**W**	**T**	**F**	**S**	**S**
28 Oct–31 Dec	10–4	**M**	**T**	**W**	**T**	**F**	**S**	**S**

Castle, shop and tea-room: closed 7 March and 25 to 26 December. *Shop and tea-room close 5:30.

East Soar

between Salcombe and Hope Cove, near Malborough, Devon

1950

East Soar in Devon: the coast path near Bolt Head

This is a great starting point for exploring the isolated and rugged coast between Bolt Head and Bolt Tail. There's lots of history to discover, including the remains of Bronze Age settlements, shipwrecks and a top-secret Second World War installation. There is a waymarked 1-mile route to Overbeck's, overlooking Salcombe. **Note**: sorry no toilet.

Eat, shop, stay: the quirky Walkers' Hut café (tenant-run) at East Soar Outdoor Experience serves hot drinks and homemade cakes. There are also catered camping options and a pretty holiday cottage. Nearby Overbeck's offers crab sandwiches and cream teas with sea views.

Things to see and do: this is a good stretch of coast for wildlife-spotting – look out for cirl buntings, silver-studded blue butterflies and large flocks of swallows and house martins gathering for their autumn migration.

Access:
Sat Nav: use TQ7 3DR.
Parking: at East Soar car park.

Find out more: 01752 346585.
01548 561904 (Walkers' Hut) or
eastsoar@nationaltrust.org.uk

Finch Foundry

Sticklepath, Okehampton, Devon EX20 2NW

1994

The foundry was a 19th-century family-run business producing a range of tools for West Country industries, including farming and mining. The huge waterwheels and tilt hammer spring into action during regular demonstrations. Products of the business are displayed in the carpenters' workshop. Outside is a delightful cottage garden. **Note**: narrow entrance to car park, plus height restrictions.

Eat, shop, stay: cosy tea-room, with tables in the garden, offering snacks, cakes, ice cream, hot and cold drinks. Gift shop, plant sales.

Things to see and do: **Indoors** Demonstrations and talks on machinery, blacksmithing and edge tools. St Clement's Day (patron saint of blacksmithing) in November. **Outdoors** Starting point for moorland walks. Tom Pearse's summerhouse in garden. **Dogs**: welcome in all areas (excluding tea-room).

Sparks fly during a demonstration at Finch Foundry in Devon

Access: [icons] **Foundry** [icons] **Grounds** [icon]
Parking: on site (height/width restrictions).

Find out more: 01837 840046 or finchfoundry@nationaltrust.org.uk

Finch Foundry		M	T	W	T	F	S	S
16 Feb–24 Feb	11–3	M	T	W	T	F	S	S
2 Mar–27 Oct	11–5	M	T	W	T	F	S	S
2 Nov–22 Dec	11–3	·	·	·	·	·	S	S

Demonstrations of the working machinery throughout day. One day a month conservation maintenance days when the machinery may not be fully operational.

Fingle Bridge

Teign Gorge, near Drewsteignton, Exeter, Devon 1990

Popular spot in Dartmoor's Teign Gorge. Walkers can explore the footpaths in nearby Fingle Woods, or climb towards Castle Drogo. **Note**: uneven terrain. Fingle Woods are being restored and managed in partnership with the Woodland Trust.

Find out more: 01647 433356 or finglebridge@nationaltrust.org.uk

Golden Cap

on the Jurassic Coast, near Bridport, Dorset

[icons] 1961

Spectacular countryside estate on the Jurassic Coast – one of England's only natural World Heritage Sites. The great rocky shoulder of Golden Cap is the south coast's highest point, with breathtaking views in all directions. Stonebarrow Hill is a good starting point for discovering the 25 miles of footpaths around the estate.

Eat, shop, stay: small volunteer-run shop and information centre (open Easter to October), with toilets and bunkhouse, in the old radar station at Stonebarrow car park, Charmouth. Six holiday cottages, mostly thatched, make ideal bases for getting to know the wider estate.

Things to see and do: play trail on Langdon Hill. Smugglers' trail on Stonebarrow Hill. Family activities and events all year. Charmouth Beach for fossils and traces of 185 million years of Earth's history. **Dogs**: welcome.

Sat Nav: for Stonebarrow use DT6 6RA; Langdon Hill DT6 6EP. **Parking**: at Stonebarrow Hill and Langdon Hill.

Find out more: 01297 489481 (Golden Cap) or goldencap@nationaltrust.org.uk

Golden Cap
Stonebarrow shop and information centre open seasonally, Easter to October.

The view east from the high point of Golden Cap, Dorset, on a glorious golden evening

Greenway

Greenway Road, Galmpton, near Brixham, Devon TQ5 0ES

2000

Here you are given a glimpse into the lives of the famous author Agatha Christie and her family. Their holiday home is set in the 1950s, when Greenway overflowed with friends and family gathered together for holidays and Christmas. The family were great collectors: the house is brimming with their books, archaeology, Tunbridgeware, silver and porcelain. The informal woodland garden drifts down the hillside towards the Dart Estuary and the Boathouse, scene of the crime in *Dead Man's Folly*. Please consider 'green ways' to travel here: ferry (courtesy vehicle available from quay), steam train (½-mile woodland walk), cycling or walking. **Note**: booking essential for parking (01803 842382).

Eat, shop, stay: Barn Café serving lunches and sweet treats. Tack-room open at peak times offering drinks, ice cream and snacks. Shop selling souvenir guides, Agatha Christie books and plants. Second-hand bookshop. Four holiday cottages, with after-hours access to the garden.

Things to see and do: why not start your visit with an introductory film in the Stables? Guided garden tours daily until October. Events such as open-air theatre. Family activities, including croquet, tennis and trails. **Dogs**: welcome on garden paths on short leads (tethering rings available in courtyard).

Access:
Buildings **Garden**
Parking: spaces must be booked – same-day booking possible by telephone. No parking on Greenway Road or Galmpton.

Find out more: 01803 842382 (Greenway car-park booking and infoline). 01803 882811 (Greenway Ferry Company). 01803 555872 (Dartmouth Steam Railway and River Boat Company) or greenway@nationaltrust.org.uk

Greenway		M	T	W	T	F	S	S
16 Feb–27 Oct	10:30–5	**M**	**T**	**W**	**T**	**F**	**S**	**S**
2 Nov–22 Dec	11–4	·	·	·	·	·	**S**	**S**
23 Dec–31 Dec	11–4	**M**	**T**	·	·	**F**	**S**	**S**

Greenway in Devon, above and below: Agatha Christie's much-loved family holiday home

Hardy Monument

Black Down, near Portesham, Dorset 1938

Memorial to Vice-Admiral Hardy, Flag-Captain of HMS *Victory* at Trafalgar, designed to look like a spyglass. Views over the Channel. **Note**: nearest postcode for Sat Nav is DT2 9HY. Open Wednesday to Sunday, 17 April to 29 September, 11 to 4 (subject to weather).

Find out more: 01297 489481 or hardymonument@nationaltrust.org.uk

Hardy's Cottage

Higher Bockhampton, near Dorchester, Dorset DT2 8QJ

1948

You can find yourself 'far from the madding crowd', as you explore Hardy's rural childhood home and the birthplace of his literary land of 'Wessex'. Visitors are invited to make themselves at home, whether sitting next to the fire or wandering through the quintessential cottage garden.
Note: nearest toilet at visitor centre.

Parents' bedroom at Hardy's Cottage, Dorset

The exuberant garden at Hardy's Cottage

Eat, shop, stay: postcards, gifts and Thomas Hardy's books are on sale at the cottage, and at Hardy's Birthplace Visitor Centre near the car park. Café (not National Trust) at the visitor centre.

Things to see and do: why not combine your visit with a trip to Max Gate, Hardy's later home in Dorchester, and Clouds Hill, the retreat of Hardy's friend T. E. Lawrence, both nearby? **Dogs**: welcome on leads in the garden and woods only.

Access: **Building** **Grounds**
Parking: 700 yards (not National Trust, however free to members displaying valid National Trust car sticker). Telephone for accessible parking arrangements. Path to cottage very uneven.

Find out more: 01305 262366 or hardyscottage@nationaltrust.org.uk

Hardy's Cottage		M	T	W	T	F	S	S
3 Jan–28 Feb	11–4	·	·	·	T	F	S	S
1 Mar–31 Oct	11–5	M	T	W	T	F	S	S
1 Nov–29 Dec*	11–4	·	·	·	T	F	S	S

Last admission 45 minutes before closing (dusk if earlier). Admission by timed tickets, only available from visitor centre (590 yards from cottage). Visitor centre: open daily 10 to 4. Café: closing times vary with season (call 01305 251228 for details). *Closed 26 December.

Heddon Valley

on Exmoor, near Combe Martin, Devon

1963

The dramatic West Exmoor coast, favourite landscape of the Romantic poets, offers not only the beautiful Heddon Valley to explore, but also Woody Bay and the Hangman Hills nearby. At the heart of the valley sits the historic Hunter's Inn, a good place to relax after discovering the spectacular coastal, moorland and woodland walks in the area. Nature highlights include one of the UK's last surviving colonies of high brown fritillary butterflies, which can be seen in July and August on the bracken-clad hillsides of Heddon Valley. Look out for the rich diversity of fungi in autumn.

Eat, shop, stay: shop selling walking equipment, clothing, maps, postcards, local history books, Exmoor products, gifts and ice cream. Hunter's Inn has all you would expect from a classic Exmoor pub and hotel. Heddon Orchard Bothy offers basic accommodation – camping without a tent.

Things to see and do: all-terrain children's buggies and all-terrain mobility scooter available to borrow (call 01598 763556 to book mobility scooter). **Dogs**: welcome.

Access: **Countryside**
Sat Nav: use EX31 4PY. **Parking**: opposite Trust shop.

Find out more: 01598 763402 or heddonvalley@nationaltrust.org.uk

Heddon Valley		M	T	W	T	F	S	S
Shop								
1 Apr–1 Nov	10:30–5*	M	T	W	T	F	S	S

Shop also open daily 16 to 24 February and every weekend in March, 11 to 3:30. *Closes at 4 from 1 October.

Dramatic Heddon Valley, Devon, above and below, offers many spectacular paths

Killerton

Broadclyst, Exeter, Devon EX5 3LE

1944

Would you give away your family home for your political beliefs? Sir Richard Acland did just that with his Killerton Estate in the heart of Devon, when he gave it to the Trust in 1944. Today you'll find a welcoming Georgian house set in 2,600 hectares (6,400 acres) of working farmland, woods, parkland, cottages and orchards. There's plenty of calm space in the glorious garden, beautiful year-round with rhododendrons, magnolias, champion trees and formal lawns. You can explore winding paths, climb an extinct volcano, discover an Iron Age hill fort and take in distant views towards Dartmoor. More family home than grand mansion, the relaxed house holds the National Trust's largest fashion collection, with selected items exhibited annually.

Eat, shop, stay: table service in the highly rated Killerton Kitchen. Snacks and cake in the Stables Coffeeshop or Dairy Café. Picnics welcome. Plant centre, bookshop and shop selling gifts and award-winning estate produce. Five holiday cottages on the estate.

Things to see and do: **Indoors** Interactive, family-friendly house. You're welcome to play the piano, read library books and sit on chairs. Daily family trail.

Welcoming and relaxed Killerton, Devon: the Library, below, and glorious blooms in the garden, bottom

Even heavy rain can't dampen spirits at Killerton

Outdoors You can walk, run and cycle throughout the estate, which is made up of parkland, woods, orchards and rolling Devon countryside. Winding garden paths to the Bear's Hut, ice house and chapel. There are giant redwoods, rhododendrons and far-reaching views to discover. Many seasonal events and trails, including Easter trails, apple festival and Christmas at Killerton. **Dogs**: welcome in the parkland and estate. Assistance dogs only in garden and chapel grounds.

Access:
House **Grounds**
Sat Nav: postcode leads to house, so follow brown signs to main car park. **Parking**: main car park 280 yards. Additional smaller car parks, including Ashclyst Forest Gate, Ellerhayes Bridge, Danes Wood.

Find out more: 01392 881345 or killerton@nationaltrust.org.uk

Killerton		M	T	W	T	F	S	S
House and Killerton Kitchen restaurant								
16 Feb–29 Mar	11–4	**M**	**T**	**W**	**T**	**F**	**S**	**S**
30 Mar–3 Nov	11–5	**M**	**T**	**W**	**T**	**F**	**S**	**S**
23 Nov–31 Dec*	11–4	**M**	**T**	**W**	**T**	**F**	**S**	**S**
Garden, Stables Coffeeshop, chapel, shop, plant centre**								
1 Jan–15 Feb	11–4	**M**	**T**	**W**	**T**	**F**	**S**	**S**
16 Feb–31 Dec*	10–5:30	**M**	**T**	**W**	**T**	**F**	**S**	**S**
Parkland								
Open all year	8–7	**M**	**T**	**W**	**T**	**F**	**S**	**S**

House: entry by timed tickets at peak times. Fashion collection exhibition open with house, 16 February to 3 November. *Special Christmas opening until 5 January 2020: closes at 3 on 24 December, everything except park closed 25 December, house closed 26 December. **Open 9 on Saturdays. Garden and park: open daily to 7, or dusk if earlier. Dairy Café: open at peak times.

Killerton Estate: Budlake Old Post Office

Broadclyst, Exeter, Devon EX5 3LW 1944

Visiting this old post office with its cottage garden and outbuildings is like stepping back into the 1950s. **Note**: nearest parking/toilets at Killerton. Open Monday, Tuesday, Wednesday, weekends, 1 April to 30 October, 1 to 5.

Find out more: 01392 881345 or budlakepostoffice@nationaltrust.org.uk

Killerton Estate: Clyston Mill

Broadclyst, Exeter, Devon EX5 3EW 1944

A historic working water-powered corn mill in a picturesque setting by the River Clyst. **Note**: nearest parking and toilets in Broadclyst village. Open Monday, Tuesday, Wednesday and weekends, 1 April to 30 October, 1 to 5.

Find out more: 01392 462425 or clystonmill@nationaltrust.org.uk

Killerton Estate: Ashclyst Forest

near Broadclyst, Exeter, Devon 1944

One of the largest woods in East Devon, with waymarked trails for exploring. A haven for butterflies, bluebells and birds. **Note**: for Sat Nav use EX5 3DT, follow signs to Ashclyst. Nearest toilets, café and shop at main Killerton car park.

Find out more: 01392 881345 or ashclystforest@nationaltrust.org.uk

Killerton Estate: Marker's

Broadclyst, Exeter, Devon EX5 3HS 1944

A medieval hall-house with a thatched roof, smoke-blackened timbers, a rare painted screen, garden and cob summerhouse. **Note**: nearest parking and toilets in Broadclyst village. Open Monday, Tuesday, Wednesday and weekends, 1 April to 30 October, 1 to 5.

Find out more: 01392 461546 or markers@nationaltrust.org.uk

Kingston Lacy

Wimborne Minster, Dorset BH21 4EA

1982

Home to the Bankes family for over 300 years, Kingston Lacy is a monument to the family's exceptional taste and desire to surround themselves with beauty. After the family lost their Corfe Castle stronghold to the Parliamentarians in the Civil War, they moved here and gradually created an astonishing Italian palace in the heart of rural Dorset. Today you can discover an internationally acclaimed art collection, including paintings by Rubens, Velázquez and Titian, exquisite carvings and lavish interiors. There's even more to explore outside, with sweeping lawns, a Japanese Garden, kitchen garden, woodland and parkland walks – look out for the award-winning herd of Red Ruby Devon cattle – and a huge 3,500-hectare (8,500-acre) countryside estate to enjoy. **Note**: timed tickets only. Some rooms may close at short notice. Low light levels.

Eat, shop, stay: hot meals at lunchtime, light bites, cream teas and cakes in the Stables Café. Drinks, cakes and ice cream in kitchen garden (March to October). The old kitchen shop stocks local food, plants, gifts and souvenirs. Second-hand bookshop. Holiday cottage.

Things to see and do: **Indoors** Lavish interiors, world-class art collection, sculptures and wood carvings (levels of light are kept low to protect these treasures). **Outdoors** The garden changes with the seasons from snowdrops, blossom and bluebells to summer flowers and autumn colour. There are deckchairs for relaxing on the lawn, or why not explore the kitchen garden or join a garden tour? Activities all year include guided walks, family trails and evening events. Longer walks across the estate include a riverside route past Eye Bridge or the Iron Age hill fort of Badbury Rings, home to 14 varieties of orchid. **Dogs**: welcome on leads in café courtyard and 'horseshoe' seats, park, woodlands and wider estate.

Access:
Building **Grounds**
Sat Nav: unreliable, follow B3082 to main entrance. Use BH21 4EL for Eye Bridge; BH21 4EE for Pamphill Green; DT11 9JL for Badbury Rings. **Parking**: on site or at Eye Bridge, Pamphill Green and Badbury Rings, where there is a charge on point-to-point race days (including members).

 For information about getting to National Trust places, please see page 3

Kingston Lacy, Dorset, this page and opposite: a great day out for all ages, indoors and out

Find out more: 01202 883402 or kingstonlacy@nationaltrust.org.uk

Kingston Lacy		M	T	W	T	F	S	S
House								
1 Mar–27 Oct	11–5	**M**	**T**	**W**	**T**	**F**	**S**	**S**
Part of house: for exhibition or seasonal experience only								
1 Jan–28 Feb	11–4	**M**	**T**	**W**	**T**	**F**	**S**	**S**
28 Oct–24 Nov	11–4	**M**	**T**	**W**	**T**	**F**	**S**	**S**
29 Nov–31 Dec	11–4*	**M**	**T**	**W**	**T**	**F**	**S**	**S**
Garden, park, shop and café								
Open all year	10–4**	**M**	**T**	**W**	**T**	**F**	**S**	**S**

House: last admission one hour before closing; open by timed-entry tickets only, bookable online up to 24 hours in advance (limited places available on day); some rooms and areas may close at short notice (please check before visiting). *Christmas experience: Wednesday through to Sunday, house open until 6 and garden (with light displays) to 7. Everything closed 16 January and 25 December. **1 March to 28 October: close at 6.

Knightshayes

Bolham, Tiverton, Devon EX16 7RQ

1972

One of the finest in the South West and the only existing 'garden in a wood', Knightshayes garden is a masterpiece of architectural planting. As well as one of the largest plant collections in the National Trust, there are hidden glades and pathways to discover and far-reaching views. The Gothic Revival house is a rare example of the genius of William Burges, whose opulent designs are guaranteed to inspire extremes of opinion. Alongside this, the restored walled garden merges full productivity with aesthetic appeal, and it's one of the best examples of a Victorian kitchen garden in the country. **Note**: access to the house and garden is restricted during spring and winter.

Eat, shop, stay: Stables Café serves hot meals, made using ingredients from the kitchen garden, also soup, sandwiches, cakes and drinks. Conservatory tea-room (seasonal) selling cakes, ice cream and drinks. Well-stocked shop and plant centre, with plants from the Knightshayes collection.

Things to see and do: **Indoors** Family trails around the house. Traditional Victorian Christmas. **Outdoors** Two play areas. Animal topiary. Kitchen garden restoration project. Events, including summer maze festival, Christmas fairs and winter garden illuminations. **Dogs**: welcome on leads in parkland and woods; in formal garden, November to February only.

Access:
House
Stables
Gardens
Sat Nav: do not use, follow brown signs on nearing Tiverton/Bolham. **Parking**: on site.

Find out more: 01884 254665 or knightshayes@nationaltrust.org.uk

Knightshayes		M	T	W	T	F	S	S
1 Jan–28 Feb	10–4	**M**	**T**	**W**	**T**	**F**	**S**	**S**
1 Mar–31 Oct	10–5	**M**	**T**	**W**	**T**	**F**	**S**	**S**
1 Nov–30 Nov	10–4	**M**	**T**	**W**	**T**	**F**	**S**	**S**
1 Dec–31 Dec	10–5	**M**	**T**	**W**	**T**	**F**	**S**	**S**

House: opens 11; upstairs open 11 to 3:30 only (closed November and December). Selected rooms open January and February. Parkland and woodland: open 7:30 to 5:30. Garden, café and shop: open to 5:30, July and August. Everything closed 24, 25 and 26 December.

The garden of Gothic Revival Knightshayes in Devon is a masterpiece of architectural planting. The Pool Garden is a place of perfect peace

Little Dartmouth

near Dartmouth, Devon 1970

A gentle coastal landscape west of Dartmouth, with wonderful views, wild flowers and the remains of a Civil War encampment. **Note**: toilets at Dartmouth Castle (not National Trust). For Sat Nav use TQ6 0JP.

Find out more: 01752 346585 or littledartmouth@nationaltrust.org.uk

Loughwood Meeting House

Dalwood, Axminster, Devon EX13 7DU 1969

Atmospheric 17th-century thatched Baptist meeting house dug into the hillside. **Note**: sorry no toilet. Open daily, 10 to 5. Services held twice yearly (details at Meeting House).

Find out more: 01752 346585 or loughwood@nationaltrust.org.uk

Lundy

Bristol Channel, Devon

1969

Rugged Lundy off the Devon coast, above and left: a place of stark beauty and abundant wildlife

Lundy is a remarkable island in the Bristol Channel, a place of solitude, stark beauty and abundant wildlife, much loved by its regular visitors and residents. A day trip on the MS *Oldenburg* allows time to explore the rugged cliff tops, discover seabirds and visit the church, castle and welcoming tavern. **Note**: 2019 marks the 50th anniversary of the National Trust and Landmark Trust protecting Lundy together. The Landmark Trust administers and manages Lundy. The *Oldenburg* runs from Bideford or Ilfracombe, and National Trust members pay fares (discounts available).

Eat, shop, stay: the Marisco Tavern serves hot and cold food and drinks. General store sells groceries, souvenirs, Lundy stamps, snacks and ice cream. To really get to know Lundy, you can stay in one of the Landmark Trust's 23 holiday cottages.

Things to see and do: coastal walking, letterboxing, photography, bird- and wildlife-watching. **Dogs**: assistance dogs only.

Access: **Building**
Sat Nav: use EX34 9EQ for Ilfracombe; EX39 2EY for Bideford.
Parking: at Bideford and Ilfracombe, not National Trust (charge including members).

Find out more: 01271 863636 or lundy@nationaltrust.org.uk lundyisland.co.uk The Lundy Shore Office, The Quay, Bideford, Devon EX39 2LY

Lundy

MS *Oldenburg* sails from Bideford or Ilfracombe up to four times a week from the end of March until the end of October carrying both day and staying passengers. A helicopter service operates from Hartland Point from November to mid-March, Mondays and Fridays only, for staying visitors.

Lydford Gorge

Lydford, near Tavistock, Devon EX20 4BH

This magical legend-rich river gorge (the deepest in the South West) offers a variety of adventurous walks. The gorge provides a truly breathtaking experience: around every corner the River Lyd plunges, tumbles, swirls and gently meanders as it travels through the steep-sided, oak-wooded valley. There are amazing features carved out by the water over thousands of years, from the 30-metre Whitelady Waterfall to the turbulent pothole called the Devil's Cauldron. Throughout the seasons there is an abundance of wildlife and plants to see, from woodland birds to wild garlic in the spring and fungi in the autumn. **Note**: rugged terrain, vertical drops. Booking required for Tramper.

Eat, shop, stay: shop selling gifts, books, plants, local food and drink, outdoor clothing, footwear and accessories. Two tea-rooms either end of the gorge, with outside seating, serving cream teas, cakes, light lunches and ice cream. Takeaway available.

Things to see and do: waterfall suspension bridge, wildlife-themed and bushcraft activities, spotter sheets, Halloween trail in October half term, children's play area and bird hide along the old railway line. **Dogs**: welcome on leads (excluding tea-rooms).

Legend-rich Lydford Gorge in Devon, above and below, is the deepest in the South West

Access: **Buildings**
Sat Nav: EX20 4BH (Devil's Cauldron entrance); EX20 4BL (waterfall entrance).
Parking: on site.

Find out more: 01822 820320 or lydfordgorge@nationaltrust.org.uk

Lydford Gorge		M	T	W	T	F	S	S
Gorge, shop and tea-rooms								
2 Mar–27 Oct	10–5*	**M**	**T**	**W**	**T**	**F**	**S**	**S**
Gorge (part of), shop and tea-room								
16 Feb–24 Feb	10–3:30	**M**	**T**	**W**	**T**	**F**	**S**	**S**
1 Nov–22 Dec	10–3:30	·	·	·	·	**F**	**S**	**S**

*Waterfall tea-room: opens 10:30, closing dependent on weather. October: last admission to gorge 3:30; shop and tea-room close at 4.

Max Gate

Alington Avenue, Dorchester, Dorset DT1 2FN

1940

Max Gate, home to Dorset's most famous author and poet, Thomas Hardy, was designed by the writer himself in 1885. This atmospheric Victorian house is where Hardy wrote some of his most famous novels, including *Tess of the d'Urbervilles* and *Jude the Obscure*, as well as most of his poetry.

Eat, shop, stay: Thomas Hardy's books, souvenirs and small gifts on sale. Tea, coffee, cakes and ice cream available.

Thomas Hardy designed his home, Max Gate in Dorset, above and right

Things to see and do: visit nearby Hardy's Cottage, the thatched cottage in which the writer was born and grew up, and Clouds Hill, the retreat of Hardy's friend T. E. Lawrence ('Lawrence of Arabia'). **Dogs**: welcome on leads in garden only.

Access: **Building** **Garden**
Sat Nav: enter Max Gate not postcode.
Parking: on roadside in front of the house (50 yards, limited spaces, not National Trust).

Find out more: 01305 262538 or maxgate@nationaltrust.org.uk

Max Gate		M	T	W	T	F	S	S
3 Jan–28 Feb	11-4	·	·	·	T	F	S	S
1 Mar–31 Oct	11-5	M	T	W	T	F	S	S
1 Nov–29 Dec*	11-4	·	·	·	T	F	S	S

Closes dusk if earlier. *Closed 26 December.

Mill Bay

East Portlemouth, near Salcombe, Devon 1991

There are sandy beaches at Mill Bay, Sunny Cove and Seacombe Sands, with rugged walking past coastguard lookouts towards Prawle. **Note**: for Sat Nav use TQ8 8PU. Toilets and Mill Bay Beach not National Trust.

Find out more: 01752 346585 or millbay@nationaltrust.org.uk

Mortehoe

near Ilfracombe, Devon 1909

Gateway to a wild, remote coast with a rich history of wrecking and smuggling. Amazing walking, wildlife and sunbathing seals.
Note: use EX34 7DT for village car park and toilets, not National Trust (charge including members). Town Farmhouse (tenant-run) offers cream teas in summer.

Find out more: 01271 870555 or mortehoe@nationaltrust.org.uk

Overbeck's

Sharpitor, Salcombe, Devon TQ8 8LW

Tucked away on the cliffs above Salcombe is this hidden paradise: a subtropical garden, bursting with colour, filled with exotic and rare plants and surprises round every corner. The views over the estuary and coast are truly breathtaking. The garden surrounds the seaside home of scientist and inventor Otto Overbeck. Inside, among Otto's eclectic collections – glimpses of a bygone age – are his 'Rejuvenator', once believed to cure all ills, and the melodious giant music box called a polyphon. The house has another evocative story to tell as well, from when it was a convalescent hospital during the First World War. **Note**: entrance path and grounds are very steep in places.

The garden at Overbeck's, Devon, is a hidden paradise, full of colourful subtropical plants

Eat, shop, stay: licensed tea-room serving light lunches (crab sandwiches a speciality), cream teas and afternoon tea. Terrace seating with sea views. Shop selling the unique 'First Flight' statuette inspired by the bronze sculpture in the garden. Local prints, plants and coast-inspired gifts.

Things to see and do: **Indoors** Generations of children return to hunt for Fred the ghost. Choose a polyphon disc to play. Children's museum trail. **Outdoors** Children's garden trail. Wednesday garden tour with question time. **Dogs**: assistance dogs only.

Access:
Building **Grounds**
Sat Nav: follow brown signs through Salcombe. **Parking**: small car park at top of drive and on approach lane. Additional parking at East Soar (1½ miles along coast path).

Find out more: 01548 842893 or overbecks@nationaltrust.org.uk

Overbeck's		M	T	W	T	F	S	S
*9 Feb–3 Nov	11–5	**M**	**T**	**W**	**T**	**F**	**S**	**S**

Tea-room closes at 4:45.

 Places may occasionally close for events or bad weather

Parke

near Bovey Tracey, Devon TQ13 9JQ

1974

Parke in Devon: tranquil, historic parkland

On the south-eastern edge of Dartmoor sits this tranquil historic parkland. Riverside paths follow the course of the River Bovey as it meanders through woodlands and meadows rich in plants and wildlife. Look out for the medieval weir, walled garden and historic orchard.

Eat, shop, stay: Home Farm Café (not National Trust) – freshly cooked food from the seasonal menu board, coffee, teas and homemade cakes. Parke Lodge holiday cottage at the entrance to Parke.

Things to see and do: orienteering trails to follow. Apple Day in autumn. Self-guided woodland trails leaflet available in courtyard. Dartmoor Pony Heritage Trust (not National Trust). **Dogs**: welcome under close control.

Access: Countryside
Sat Nav: use TQ13 9JQ.
Parking: on site (limited).

Find out more: 01626 834748 or parke@nationaltrust.org.uk

Parke	
Open every day all year	Dawn–dusk

Home Farm Café open 10 to 5 daily (10 to 4 November to March), plus Thursday, Friday and Saturday evenings (booking essential).

Plymbridge Woods

near Plymouth, Devon

1968

The wooded valley of the River Plym creates a link from the edge of Plymouth to the heights of Dartmoor. Footpaths lead through woodlands and alongside industrial ruins. There's also a family-friendly cycle path (NCN27) along an old railway line, a wooded mountain-bike trail and a variety of running routes.

Eat, shop, stay: mobile refreshment van in Plymbridge car park. Riverside picnic spots. A short cycle ride away is Saltram, with its popular Park Café and Chapel Tea-room in the garden.

Things to see and do: plenty of options for walkers, runners, cyclists and birdwatchers. Peregrine falcons can be watched from the viewpoint on Cann Viaduct in spring. Downloadable walking, cycling and orienteering trails. **Dogs**: welcome under close control.

Access:
Sat Nav: use PL7 4SR for Plymbridge.
Parking: at Plymbridge.

Find out more: 01752 341377 or plymbridgewoods@nationaltrust.org.uk

The River Plym at Plymbridge Woods in Devon

Ringstead Bay

on the Jurassic Coast, near Weymouth, Dorset

1949

This quiet, unspoilt stretch of the Jurassic Coast in West Dorset is like the seaside of childhood memories: a perfect sweep of shingle beach with rock pools inviting you to explore, backed by farmland and cliffs covered with flowers and butterflies. The seawater is incredibly clear and safe for bathing.

Eat, shop, stay: picnics welcome at the Trust car park at the top of the hill, with its views of the Jurassic Coast World Heritage Site. Shop and café at the beach car park (not National Trust).

Things to see and do: spectacular views of the bay and across to the Isle of Portland to enjoy. Why not walk out to the chalk headland of White Nothe? **Dogs**: welcome, including on the South West Coast Path.

Sat Nav: use DT2 8NQ for Southdown. **Parking**: on the clifftop farmland at Southdown Farm and beach car park (not National Trust).

Find out more: 01297 489481 or ringsteadbay@nationaltrust.org.uk

Ringstead Bay, Dorset: perfect sweep of shingle

Saltram

Plympton, Plymouth, Devon PL7 1UH

1957

High above the River Plym, with magnificent views across the estuary, Saltram's rolling landscape parkland now provides wooded walks and open space for rest and play on Plymouth's outskirts. Saltram was home to the Parker family from 1743 and the house reflects their increasingly prominent lifestyle during the Georgian period. The magnificent decoration and original contents include Robert Adam's Neo-classical Saloon, original Chinese wallpapers, 18th-century oriental, European and English ceramics and a superb country-house library. Outside, the garden's planting offers something

of interest all year, and there are also an 18th-century orangery and follies to explore. After wandering along scented pathways and the magnificent lime avenue, why not treat yourself to afternoon tea in the Chapel Tea-room?

Eat, shop, stay: Park Café serving meals, drinks, snacks and ice cream. The Chapel Tea-room in the garden offers light lunches and afternoon tea with waitress service. Shop selling seasonal gifts, local food, books and plants.

Things to see and do: **Indoors** Dressing up, guided tours, themed family trails, conservation in action. Visit at Christmas to see the house decorated. **Outdoors** Seasonal

The opulent Neo-classical Saloon at Saltram in Devon, below, was designed by Robert Adam. Right, enjoying a game of croquet

spectacles of winter snowdrops, spring daffodils, summer blooms and autumn colour in the garden. The park is ideal for anyone wanting a stroll with the dog, a run, cycle ride or simply to feed the ducks, whatever the weather. Garden illuminated at Christmas. Activities, '50 things', guided walks and tours throughout the year. Why not book the outdoor classroom for a Forest School session or a child's birthday? **Dogs**: very welcome in the park (identified on- and off-lead areas).

Access:
House **Grounds**

Saltram's magnificent façade, below. A young visitor takes a closer look, bottom

Sat Nav: enter Romilly Gardens, not postcode (look for Saltram sign). **Parking**: 50 yards.

Find out more: 01752 333500 or saltram@nationaltrust.org.uk

Saltram		M	T	W	T	F	S	S
House								
21 Jan–28 Feb†	11–3:30	**M**	**T**	**W**	**T**	**F**	**S**	**S**
1 Mar–31 Oct	12–4:30*	**M**	**T**	**W**	**T**	**F**	**S**	**S**
Garden, Park Café, Chapel Tea-room and shop								
Open all year	10–5**	**M**	**T**	**W**	**T**	**F**	**S**	**S**
Park								
Open all year	Dawn–dusk	**M**	**T**	**W**	**T**	**F**	**S**	**S**
Christmas at Saltram††								
21 Nov–30 Dec	12–8	**M**	**T**	**W**	**T**	**F**	**S**	**S**

†Winter route. *11 to 12: house entry by guided tour only (places limited). Last house admission 45 minutes before closing.**Closes at 4, November to February; Chapel Tea-room last orders one hour before closing.††Christmas: house closes at 4 on 24 December; everything (except park) closed 25 and 26 December.

Shaugh Bridge

on Dartmoor, near Shaugh Prior, Devon 1960

Ancient oakwoods and mossy boulders cloak the Plym Valley; riverside walks pass the atmospheric Dewerstone Rocks and industrial ruins. **Note**: for Sat Nav use PL7 5HD. Watch out for climbers on the Dewerstone Rocks.

Find out more: 01626 834748 (Dartmoor countryside office) or shaughbridge@nationaltrust.org.uk

Shute Barton

Shute, near Axminster, Devon EX13 7PT 1959

Medieval manor house, with later Tudor gatehouse and battlemented turrets – now a holiday cottage. **Note**: for Sat Nav use EX13 7PT. Very limited parking. Open weekends, 18/19 May, 15/16 June, 19/20 October and 16/17 November, 10:30 to 3:45 by guided tour only (no need to book).

Find out more: 01752 346585 or shute@nationaltrust.org.uk

 For information about getting to National Trust places, please see page 3

South Milton Sands

Thurlestone, near Kingsbridge, Devon

1980

This popular beach – a long sweep of golden sand and rock pools – edges a sheltered bay of crystal-clear water and looks out to the iconic Thurlestone Rock offshore. The nearby wetland is home to many bird species and is an ideal place to spot rare migratory visitors.

Eat, shop, stay: the beach café (tenant-run) serves freshly prepared food, for eat-in and takeaway, inspired by its seaside location.

Things to see and do: great for swimming and watersports. Wetsuits, as well as windsurf and paddle boards, for hire (seasonal). The South West Coast Path offers great walks.
Dogs: welcome on coast path and beach.

Sheltered South Milton Sands in Devon, left and above, is perfect for wildlife-spotting, watersports or just simply splashing in the sea

Access: **Café and toilets** **Beach**
Sat Nav: use TQ7 3JY. **Parking**: behind beach.

Find out more: 01752 346585 or southmiltonsands@nationaltrust.org.uk

South Milton Sands

Beachhouse café seasonal opening, telephone 01548 561144.

Spyway

on the Purbeck coast, Langton Matravers, near Swanage, Dorset 1982

Gateway to a dramatic coast of grassy clifftops teeming with wildlife, and Dancing Ledge. Fabulous walking – some steep slopes.
Note: sorry no toilet. For Sat Nav use BH19 3HG.

Find out more: 01929 450002 or spyway@nationaltrust.org.uk

Studland Bay

Studland, near Swanage, Dorset

 1982

This glorious slice of Purbeck coastline is famed for its 4-mile stretch of golden sand, gently shelving bathing waters and views of Old Harry Rocks and the Isle of Wight. With four beaches to choose from, Studland is loved by young families and watersports fans of all ages, and it includes the most popular naturist beach in Britain. The vast swathe of heathland behind the beach is a haven for native wildlife and features all six British reptiles. Footpaths and bridleways through sand dunes, woods and wild open landscape encourage you to explore. Wildlife to spot includes deer, insects and birds, as well as numerous wild flowers. Studland was the inspiration for Toytown in Enid Blyton's *Noddy*. **Note**: toilets at Shell Bay, Knoll Beach and Middle Beach; also South Beach (not National Trust).

Studland Bay, Dorset, clockwise from right: the 4-mile beach, heathland and windy table tennis

Eat, shop, stay: Knoll Beach Café on the beach with spectacular views of Old Harry Rocks; indoor and open-air seating. Log burner in winter. Wood-fired pizza oven in summer. Beach goods and seaside gifts for sale. Thirteen holiday cottages in the area.

Things to see and do: year-round events programme, family trails and multitude of watersports and beach sports – geocaching, slacklining, orienteering, beach volleyball, snorkelling, swimming, beach table tennis, paddle-boarding, sea kayaking and sailing. And don't forget sandcastles and rock-pooling. You can hire bikes or go horse-riding to explore inland. You can also hire a beach hut for the day or longer. Signposted trails, including one of the most popular coastal walks to Old Harry Rocks. Second World War remains tell of Studland's role in the build-up to D-Day.

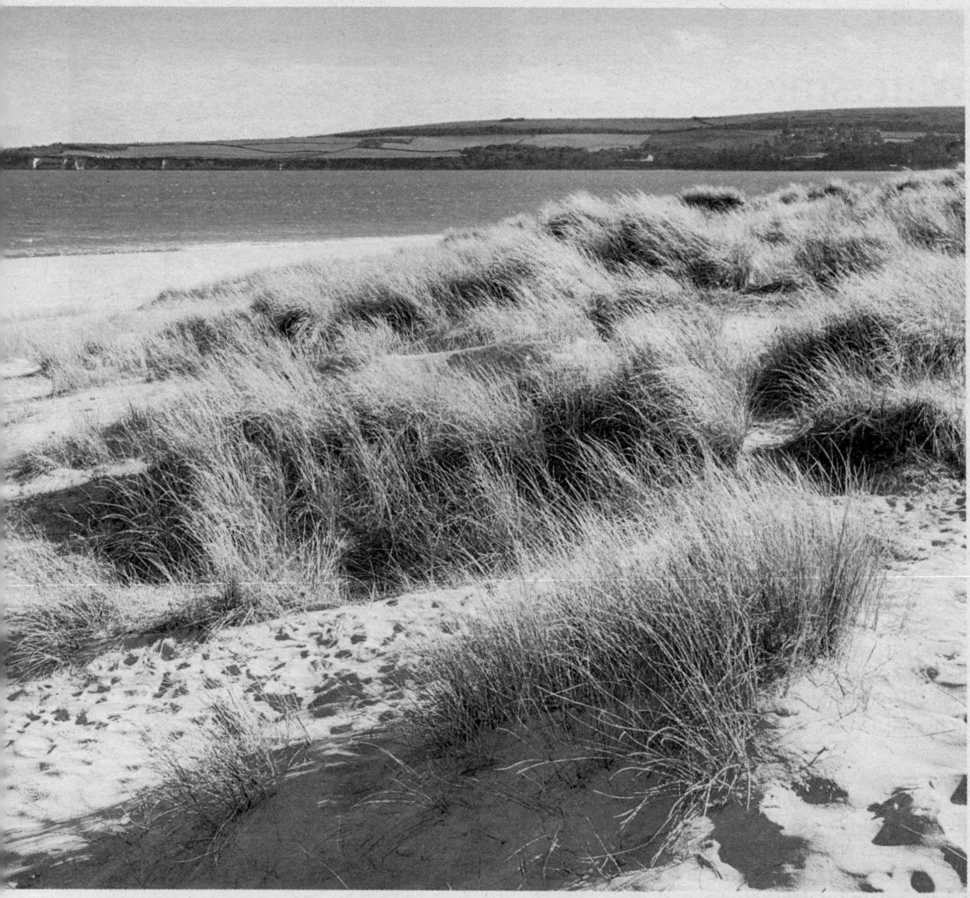

Five bird hides overlook Poole Harbour and Little Sea. Discovery Centre for private hire. **Dogs**: welcome 1 May to 30 September on short leads. Under control in winter.

Access: **Grounds**
Sat Nav: use BH19 3AQ for Knoll Beach.
Parking: at Shell Bay (7 to 9); South Beach (9 to 11); Knoll Beach and Middle Beach (9 to 8, or dusk if earlier).

Find out more: 01929 450500 or studlandbay@nationaltrust.org.uk

Studland Bay	
Shop and café	
Open every day all year	9:30–5*

*31 March to 26 October: open to 6 at weekends. July and August: open daily, 9 to 6. Reduced hours in winter, 10 to 4. Shop and café: closed 6 and 7 March and 25 December.

Watersmeet

on Exmoor, near Lynmouth, Devon

1955

This area, where the lush valleys of the East Lyn and Hoar Oak Water tumble together, is a haven for wildlife and offers excellent walking. At the heart sits Watersmeet House, a 19th-century fishing lodge, which is now a tea garden, shop and information point. **Note**: deep gorge with steep walk down to house.

Eat, shop, stay: tea garden serving hot and cold food and drinks in a magnificent wooded setting. Shop selling Exmoor produce and gifts, walking gear and maps. Nearby holiday cottages offer the chance of a longer stay to explore the area.

Things to see and do: Exmoor Spotter chart for families and 'Exmoor Coast of Devon' walks leaflet available. **Dogs**: allowed on leads in tea garden.

Access: Building Grounds
Sat Nav: use EX35 6NT. **Parking**: pay and display (not National Trust) on Watersmeet Road; steep walk down to house. Trust car parks nearby at Combe Park and Countisbury. Please call to book accessible parking.

Watersmeet, Devon: a glimpse of the house, right, and one of the footpaths, below

Find out more: 01598 752648 or watersmeet@nationaltrust.org.uk

Watersmeet		M	T	W	T	F	S	S
Tea-room and tea garden								
1 Apr–1 Nov	10:30–5*	**M**	**T**	**W**	**T**	**F**	**S**	**S**

Also open daily 16 to 24 February, weekends in March, November and December, and daily 26 December to 1 January, 11 to 3:30. *Opens 8:30 at weekends, 6 July to 1 September; closes at 4 in October.

Wembury

near Wembury village, Plymouth, Devon

1939

A great beach, and more: some of the best rock pools in the country, good surfing, masses of wildlife and views of a distinctive island – the Great Mewstone. Starting point for lovely coastal walks to Wembury Point and the Yealm Estuary. **Note**: toilet (not National Trust).

Eat, shop, stay: Old Mill Café serves coffees, homemade cakes, soups, pasties and ice cream, as well as beach shop (tenant-run). Part of the old mill house adjoining the café, Mill Cottage is an idyllic holiday let right on the shore.

Things to see and do: Marine Centre full of information. Rock-pooling, surfing and snorkelling. **Dogs**: welcome on coast path all year, and on beach 1 October to 30 April.

Access: [icons] Café [icon] **Marine Centre** [icon]
Sat Nav: use PL9 0HP.
Parking: just above beach.

Find out more: 01752 346585.
01752 862538 (Marine Centre) or
wembury@nationaltrust.org.uk

Wembury
For details of the Old Mill Café seasonal opening, telephone 01752 863280.

As well as kite-flying, Wembury in Devon offers wonderful surfing, some of the best rock pools in the country and wildlife galore

White Mill

Sturminster Marshall, near Wimborne Minster, Dorset BH21 4BX 1982

An 18th-century corn mill with original wooden machinery, built on a Domesday Book site in a peaceful riverside setting. **Note**: open weekends, 30 March to 27 October, 12 to 5 and Bank Holiday Mondays. Guided tours available, last tour at 4.

Find out more: 01258 858051 or
whitemill@nationaltrust.org.uk

Woolacombe

near Ilfracombe, Devon 1935

A golden beach and huge dunes, amazing surfing, perfect coves for rock-pooling and numerous headland walks with views of Lundy. **Note**: for Sat Nav use EX34 7BG (car park). Nearest toilets are by the beach (neither toilets nor car park are National Trust). Members have to pay for parking.

Find out more: 01271 870555 or
woolacombe@nationaltrust.org.uk

Additional coastal and countryside car parks in Devon and Dorset

Devon	
Countisbury	EX35 6NE
Combe Park	EX35 6LF
Woody Bay	EX31 4QU
Trentishoe Down	EX34 0PF
Torrs Walk, Ilfracombe	EX34 8BA
Hartland: Brownsham	EX39 6AN
Exmansworthy	EX39 6AR
East Titchberry	EX39 6AU
Stoke	PL8 1JG
Ringmore	TQ7 4HR
Snapes Point	TQ8 8NQ
Prawle Point	TQ7 2BX
Scabbacombe	TQ6 0EF
Man Sands	TQ6 0EF
Salcombe Hill	EX10 0NY
Dunsland	EX22 7AA
Steps Bridge	EX6 7EQ
Hembury Woods	TQ11 0HW
Holne Woods	TQ13 7ST
Danes Wood	EX5 3LH
Ellerhayes	EX5 4PY
Dorset	
Cogden	DT6 4RJ
Lambert's Castle	DT6 5QJ
Acton	BH19 3JN
Dean Hill Viewpoint	BH19 3AA

Bursting with colour, the exuberant garden borders at Montacute House in Somerset are accessible to all

Somerset and Wiltshire

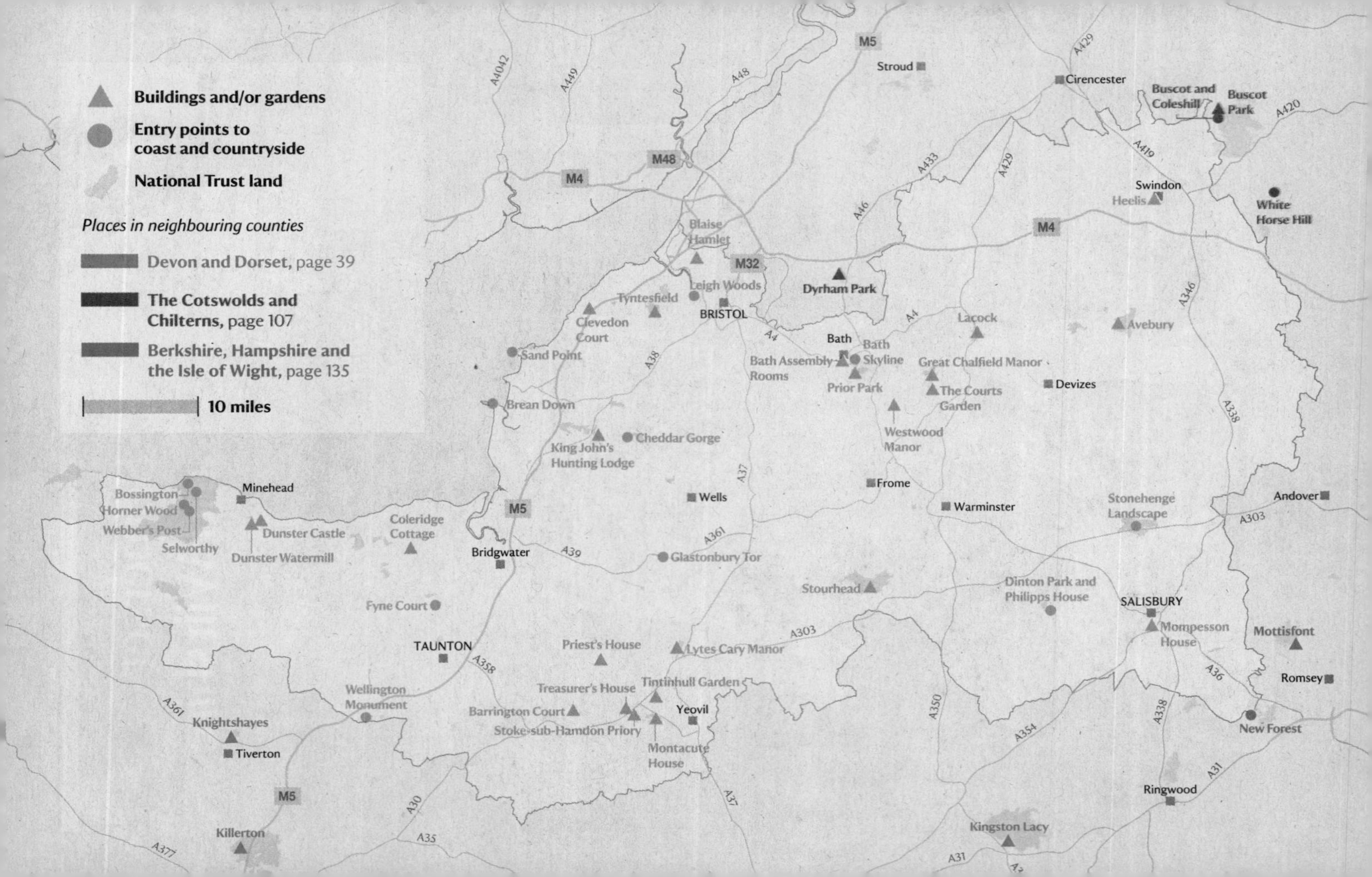

Buildings and/or gardens
Entry points to coast and countryside
National Trust land
Places in neighbouring counties
Devon and Dorset, page 39
The Cotswolds and Chilterns, page 107
Berkshire, Hampshire and the Isle of Wight, page 135
10 miles
Stroud
Cirencester
Buscot and Coleshill
Buscot Park
Swindon
Heelis
White Horse Hill
Blaise Hamlet
Leigh Woods
Tyntesfield
BRISTOL
Dyrham Park
Clevedon Court
Sand Point
Bath
Bath Assembly Rooms
Bath Skyline
Prior Park
Lacock
Avebury
Great Chalfield Manor
The Courts Garden
Devizes
Brean Down
King John's Hunting Lodge
Cheddar Gorge
Westwood Manor
Bossington
Horner Wood
Webber's Post
Selworthy
Minehead
Dunster Castle
Dunster Watermill
Coleridge Cottage
Bridgwater
Wells
Frome
Warminster
Stonehenge Landscape
Andover
Glastonbury Tor
Stourhead
Fyne Court
Dinton Park and Philipps House
SALISBURY
Mompesson House
Mottisfont
Romsey
TAUNTON
Priest's House
Lytes Cary Manor
Treasurer's House
Tintinhull Garden
Wellington Monument
Barrington Court
Stoke-sub-Hamdon Priory
Yeovil
Montacute House
Knightshayes
Tiverton
New Forest
Ringwood
Kingston Lacy
Killerton
M4
M48
M32
M5
A4042
A449
A48
A429
A433
A46
A4
A419
A420
A346
A338
A38
A37
A39
A361
A303
A358
A350
A354
A36
A31
A30
A35
A377

Avebury

near Marlborough, Wiltshire

1943

At Avebury, the world's largest prehistoric stone circle partially encompasses a pretty village. Avebury forms part of the Stonehenge and Avebury World Heritage Site. The millionaire archaeologist Alexander Keiller excavated here in the 1930s, and Avebury's museum is named after him. Arranged in two parts, the Alexander Keiller Museum is divided into the Stables, displaying archaeological treasures from across the local area, and the Barn, a 17th-century threshing barn housing interactive displays and children's activities that reveal the story of this ancient landscape. Avebury Manor, on the edge of the village, was transformed in a partnership between the National Trust and the BBC, creating a hands-on experience that celebrates and reflects the lives of the people who once lived here. **Note**: English Heritage holds guardianship of Avebury Stone Circle (owned and managed by the National Trust). Toilets open during business hours.

Eat, shop, stay: Circles Café; Avebury Manor Tea-room serving cream teas and light lunches (seasonal); Coach House Café (weekends/school holidays). Shop selling local gifts. Cobblestones second-hand bookshop. Holiday cottage within the stone circle available all year.

Things to see and do: **Indoors** Specialist talks and guided tours of Avebury Manor. Family activities in the Alexander Keiller Museum and children's events during holidays.

Avebury Manor, on the edge of the Wiltshire village, has an abundant garden

Walking the gigantic bank and ditch that enclose Avebury's prehistoric stone circles, above, and getting hands-on in the kitchen of Avebury Manor, left

Find out more: 01672 539250 or
avebury@nationaltrust.org.uk
National Trust Estate Office, High Street,
Avebury, Wiltshire SN8 1RF

Avebury		M	T	W	T	F	S	S
Stone circle								
Open all year	Dawn–dusk	**M**	**T**	**W**	**T**	**F**	**S**	**S**
Manor and garden								
5 Jan–10 Feb	Tour	·	·	·	·	·	**S**	**S**
16 Feb–30 Mar	11-4	**M**	**T**	**W**	**T**	**F**	**S**	**S**
31 Mar–26 Oct*	11-5	**M**	**T**	**W**	**T**	**F**	**S**	**S**
27 Oct–31 Dec	11-4	**M**	**T**	**W**	**T**	**F**	**S**	**S**
Museum								
1 Jan–30 Mar	10-4	**M**	**T**	**W**	**T**	**F**	**S**	**S**
31 Mar–26 Oct	10-6	**M**	**T**	**W**	**T**	**F**	**S**	**S**
27 Oct–31 Dec	10-4	**M**	**T**	**W**	**T**	**F**	**S**	**S**

Shop and café open daily. Entry to manor by timed tickets, last entry one hour before closing. In winter, parts of garden, manor and museum may be closed. Everything except stone circle closed 24 to 26 December. *Manor closed 20 to 22 June.

Outdoors Guided tours of the stone circle all year. Talks and guided tours of the landscape. Family trails and activities during the school holidays. **Dogs**: on leads welcome. Assistance dogs only in the manor, garden and café.

Access:
Museum **Manor** **Grounds**
Sat Nav: use SN8 1RD. **Parking**: 300 yards. Please do not park on village streets.

Barrington Court

Barrington, near Ilminster, Somerset TA19 0NQ

1907

Colonel Lyle, whose family firm became part of Tate & Lyle, rescued the partially derelict 16th-century Court House in the 1920s, surrounding it with a productive estate. A keen collector of architectural salvage, Colonel Lyle filled the house with his collection of panelling, fireplaces and staircases. Now without furniture, the light, empty spaces provide atmospheric opportunities to explore their stories freely. The walled White Garden, Rose and Iris Garden and Lily Garden were influenced by Gertrude Jekyll, with playing fountains, vibrant colours and intoxicating scents. The original kitchen garden supplies the restaurant and continues the Lyle family's vision of self-sufficiency. **Note**: independently run artisan workshops (opening times vary).

Rescued from dereliction, Barrington Court in Somerset is now full of light, empty spaces

Eat, shop, stay: Strode dining and tea-rooms offering tea, homemade cakes and meals with ingredients often grown in the kitchen garden. Children's menu available. Shop selling gifts, plants and award-winning cider and apple juice. Second-hand bookshop. Artisan workshops. Holiday cottage in Strode House.

Things to see and do: **Indoors** House tours and children's trail, seasonal events. Activities in artisan workshops. **Outdoors** Trails and tours. Seasonal events, including Easter and Christmas activities. **Dogs**: assistance dogs only in formal garden.

Access:
Building **Grounds**
Sat Nav: misdirects visitors to rear entrance – follow brown signs from Barrington village.
Parking: 200 yards.

Find out more: 01460 241938 or barringtoncourt@nationaltrust.org.uk

Barrington Court		M	T	W	T	F	S	S
4 Jan–17 Feb	10:30–3	M	·	·	·	F	S	S
18 Feb–3 Nov	10:30–5	M	T	W	T	F	S	S
4 Nov–30 Dec	10:30–3	M	·	·	·	F	S	S

Bath Assembly Rooms

Bennett Street, Bath, Somerset BA1 2QH 1931

The Assembly Rooms were at the heart of fashionable Georgian society. The Fashion Museum is on the lower ground floor. **Note**: limited access during functions. Bath Assembly Rooms is run by Bath and North East Somerset Council. Entry charge for the Fashion Museum (including members). Open daily 10:30 to 6 (closes at 5 in January, February, November and December; closed 25 and 26 December). Last admission one hour before closing.

Find out more: 01225 477789 or bathassemblyrooms@nationaltrust.org.uk

Bath Skyline

Bath, Somerset

1959

One of Bath's unique features, leading to its World Heritage Site designation, is its 'green setting' – encircling meadows and wooded hillsides where you can walk and relax with grandstand views over the historic cityscape. There's a 6-mile Bath Skyline waymarked walk, plus shorter routes to follow from the city centre. **Note**: sorry no toilet or parking.

Bath Skyline, Somerset: breathtaking views, above, and plenty of play opportunities, left

Eat, shop, stay: there are many places to picnic around the Skyline. Food and snacks are available nearby at Prior Park Landscape Garden. Also from Widcombe cafés, the American Museum in Britain and the Holburne Museum (none National Trust, some entry fees).

Things to see and do: 'Walk to the view' is a 3-mile self-led circular route starting from the Abbey. Geocaching trail and other family activities. Bath parkrun every Saturday. Regular guided walks. **Dogs**: welcome under control (on leads in some areas). Cattle grazing April to November.

Access:
Parking: none on site, nearest city centre, not National Trust (charge including members).

Find out more: 01225 833977 or bathskyline@nationaltrust.org.uk

Blaise Hamlet

Henbury, Bristol BS10 7QY 1943

Delightful hamlet of nine picturesque cottages, designed by John Nash in 1809 for Blaise Estate pensioners. **Note**: access to green only; cottages not open. Sorry no toilet.

Find out more: 01275 461900 or blaisehamlet@nationaltrust.org.uk

 For information about getting to National Trust places, please see page 3

Bossington

on Exmoor, near Minehead, Somerset

1944

Part of the Holnicote Estate, Bossington is a peaceful coastal hamlet with distinctive thatched cottages. You can play Pooh sticks from the footbridge in the woods, or wander down to the pebble beach. There's plenty of wildlife to spot and far-reaching views to Wales and along the Exmoor coastline. **Note**: nearest toilets in car park.

Eat, shop, stay: barbecue pits provided in the picnic field next to the car park. Kitnors tea-room is open all year for cream teas and light lunches (not National Trust). Why not stay a little longer? Picturesque Lower House holiday cottage sleeps 10.

Things to see and do: there are limekilns to discover on the beach, or take the South West Coast Path to Hurlstone Point's ruined coastguard lookout, which is a top spot for porpoise sightings. **Dogs**: welcome on leads.

Access:
Sat Nav: use TA24 8HF. **Parking**: on site.

Find out more: 01643 862452 or bossington@nationaltrust.org.uk

Bossington, Somerset: looking down on Porlock Bay on the Holnicote Estate from Bossington Hill

Brean Down

near Weston-super-Mare, North Somerset

1954

One of Somerset's most striking coastal landmarks: a dramatic limestone peninsula (above) jutting out into the Bristol Channel. You can relax on the beach at the foot of the down or take a walk along this spectacular 'natural pier' to the fort, which provides a unique insight into Brean's military past. **Note**: steep climbs and cliffs; please stay on main paths. Tide comes in quickly.

Eat, shop, stay: Cove Café – with winter woodburner or summer courtyard and picnic benches – serving cooked breakfasts, lunches or tea and cakes. Shop with popular ice-cream bar, buckets, spades, beach games and souvenirs. Holiday apartment (sleeps four).

Things to see and do: you can walk to the end of the down and discover the historic fort, spotting birds, feral goats and flowers on the way. Downloadable circular walk available. Events throughout year.
Dogs: welcome on leads, please note stock may be grazing on the down.

Access: **Building**
Sat Nav: use TA8 2RS.
Parking: at Cove Café and shop.

Find out more: 01278 751874 or breandown@nationaltrust.org.uk

Brean Down		M	T	W	T	F	S	S
Café and shop								
1 Jan–28 Feb	10–4	**M**	**T**	**W**	**T**	**F**	**S**	**S**
1 Mar–31 Oct	9–5	**M**	**T**	**W**	**T**	**F**	**S**	**S**
1 Nov–31 Dec*	10–4	**M**	**T**	**W**	**T**	**F**	**S**	**S**

*Closed 25 December.

Cheddar Gorge

in the Mendips, near Wells, Somerset

1910

Cheddar Gorge, Somerset: a haven for wildlife

At almost 400 feet deep and 3 miles long, Cheddar is Britain's largest gorge. It was formed during successive ice ages, when glacial meltwater carved into the limestone creating steep cliffs. The gorge is a haven for wildlife and contains many rare plants and flowers, including the Cheddar pink. **Note**: terrain is steep away from the road. Caves and car parks privately owned (charge including members).

Eat, shop, stay: seasonal shop and information centre providing leaflets, information on National Trust membership, local information and walks, gifts and souvenirs. Free Wi-Fi and computer tablets available for use to help plan days out in the area.

Things to see and do: 4-mile circular gorge walk (details from shop and information centre) and Strawberry Line (NCN26) cycle route to Cheddar. Top of the Gorge festival takes place in June. **Dogs**: welcome on leads in shop and gorge.

Sat Nav: use BS27 3QE. **Parking**: car parks on both sides of gorge, not National Trust (charge including members).

Find out more: 01934 744689 or cheddargorge@nationaltrust.org.uk

Cheddar Gorge		M	T	W	T	F	S	S
Shop and information centre								
5 Jan–17 Feb	10–5	·	·	·	·	·	**S**	**S**
18 Feb–1 Nov	10–5	**M**	**T**	**W**	**T**	**F**	**S**	**S**
2 Nov–29 Dec	10–5	·	·	·	·	·	**S**	**S**

Clevedon Court

Tickenham Road, Clevedon, North Somerset BS21 6QU

1961

Home to Clevedon's lords of the manor for centuries, Clevedon Court features rare domestic architecture from the medieval period and a beautiful terraced garden. The house was bought by Abraham Elton in 1709 and is still the well-loved family home of the Eltons today. **Note**: no debit or credit card facilities.

Eat, shop, stay: kiosk serving cakes, cream teas and hot and cold drinks.

Things to see and do: an extensive collection of Elton Ware pottery, Nailsea glass and prints of industrial archaeology. Family guide and children's trail. **Dogs**: assistance dogs only.

Access:
House **Garden**
Parking: 50 yards (unsuitable for trailer or motor caravans). Alternative parking 100 yards east of entrance in cul-de-sac.

Find out more: 01275 872257 or clevedoncourt@nationaltrust.org.uk

Clevedon Court		M	T	W	T	F	S	S
3 Apr–29 Sep	2–5	·	·	**W**	**T**	·	·	**S**

Tea kiosk and car park open 1:15. House entry by timed ticket, not bookable. Open Bank Holiday Mondays.

Medieval Clevedon Court in North Somerset

Support the places you visit: please scan your member card for free parking ticket

Coleridge Cottage

35 Lime Street, Nether Stowey, Bridgwater, Somerset TA5 1NQ

1909

Home to Samuel Taylor Coleridge for three years, this simple house – the birthplace of literary Romanticism – was where he wrote his best-known poems. Now an award-winning experience offers the chance to immerse yourself in 18th-century sights and sounds. Coleridge's poetry is brought to life in the cottage and wildflower garden.

Eat, shop, stay: tea-room serving light refreshments. Shop selling gifts reflecting Coleridge's life and work.

Things to see and do: **Indoors** Writing with a quill, dressing up in Georgian costumes or following a family trail. **Outdoors** You can listen to poetry in the garden, or draw water from the well.

Access: **Building** **Garden**
Parking: in pub car park (not National Trust).

Find out more: 01278 732662 or coleridgecottage@nationaltrust.org.uk

Coleridge Cottage		M	T	W	T	F	S	S
2 Mar–3 Nov	11–5	M	T	W	T	F	S	S
7 Dec–22 Dec	11–4	·	·	·	·	·	S	S

Private tours/educational visits by arrangement.

Award-winning Coleridge Cottage in Somerset

The Courts Garden

Holt, near Bradford on Avon, Wiltshire BA14 6RR

1943

This curious English country garden (above) is a hidden gem. Garden rooms of different styles, shaped by the vision of past owners and gardeners, reveal themselves at every turn. You'll find herbaceous borders, topiary, a peaceful water garden, statuary, an arboretum, kitchen garden, naturally planted spring bulbs and a sunken garden.

Eat, shop, stay: seasonal produce from the kitchen garden for sale, as well as a small selection of gifts and guidebooks. Sales from the second-hand bookshop support conservation work. Rose Garden tea-room (concession) serving lunch and afternoon tea. Picnics welcome in the arboretum.

Things to see and do: new views to and from a recently installed bridge, garden history in the Orchard Room. Trails and wildlife garden for young explorers. Pick up gardening tips from the friendly team. **Dogs**: assistance dogs only.

Access: **Garden**
Parking: 80 yards in village hall car park (not National Trust). Follow signs for overflow parking. Please avoid parking on village streets.

Find out more: 01225 782875 or courtsgarden@nationaltrust.org.uk

The Courts Garden		M	T	W	T	F	S	S
2 Feb–24 Feb	11–5:30	·	·	·	·	·	S	S
25 Feb–3 Nov	11–5:30	M	T	·	T	F	S	S

Tea-room: last orders 45 minutes before closing.

Dinton Park and Philipps House

Dinton, Salisbury, Wiltshire SP3 5HH 1943

Tranquil rolling parkland, perfect for walks and picnics, surrounds a neo-Grecian house designed by Jeffry Wyatville in 1820. **Note**: the house is closed this year. The park is open daily all year. Sorry no toilet.

Find out more: 01672 538014 or sw.customerenquiries@nationaltrust.org.uk

Dunster Castle

Dunster, near Minehead, Somerset TA24 6SL

1976

Dramatically sited on top of a tor, a castle has existed here since Norman times. Its impressive medieval gatehouse and ruined tower are a reminder of its turbulent history. The castle that you see today, owned by the Luttrell family for more than 600 years, became an elegant country home during the 19th century. The terraced garden displays varieties of Mediterranean and subtropical plants, while the tranquil riverside wooded garden below, with its natural play area, leads to the historic working watermill. There are panoramic views over the Bristol Channel and surrounding countryside from the castle and grounds.

Now an elegant country home, dramatic Dunster Castle, Somerset, sits atop a high tor

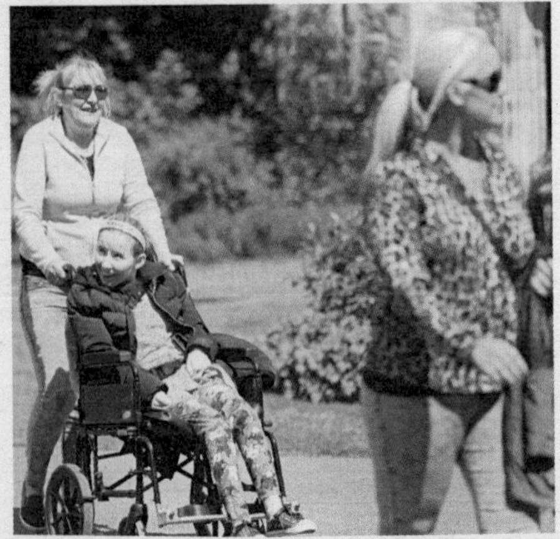

Eat, shop, stay: 17th-century stables and watermill shops selling local gifts, guidebooks, plants and mill produce. Light refreshments available at the Camellia House. Riverside tea-room and tea garden serving breakfast, light lunches and afternoon tea. Picnic area in grounds.

Things to see and do: **Indoors** Interactive exhibitions and 'Chapters' bring stories to life. Tours of kitchens and behind the scenes. Explore the vaulted Victorian reservoir beneath the Keep Garden. **Outdoors** Events, including living history. **Dogs**: welcome in parkland and garden on short leads.

Access:
Castle Stables Grounds
Parking: 300 yards (enter from A39).

Find out more: 01643 823004 (Infoline). 01643 821314 or dunstercastle@nationaltrust.org.uk

Dunster Castle		M	T	W	T	F	S	S
Castle								
1 Jan–15 Feb	Tour*	M	T	W	T	F	S	S
16 Feb–3 Nov	11–5	M	T	W	T	F	S	S
4 Nov–13 Dec	Tour*	M	T	W	T	F	S	S
14 Dec–15 Dec	11–4	·	·	·	·	·	S	S
16 Dec–19 Dec	Tour*	M	T	W	T	·	·	·
20 Dec–31 Dec	11–4	M	T	·	T	F	S	S
Garden, park, shop and tea-room								
Open all year	10–5**	M	T	W	T	F	S	S

*Entry by tour only (places limited). 'Dunster by Candlelight': Friday 6 and Saturday 7 December, castle open 4 to 9.
**Close dusk if earlier. Everything closed 24 and 25 December.

Dunster Working Watermill

Mill Lane, Dunster, near Minehead, Somerset TA24 6SL

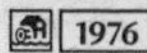

Close to Dunster Castle on the peaceful River Avill (below) is this fully operating 18th-century watermill, built on the site of a mill mentioned in the Domesday survey of 1086. This is a rare surviving example of a double-overshot mill and continues to produce flour today. **Note**: the mill is within the grounds of Dunster Castle, access via the normal entry points.

Eat, shop, stay: mill produces stoneground wholemeal flour from organic wheat, and the milling team packs porridge oats, jumbo oats and the mill's own muesli mix – all for sale in the shop. Riverside tea-room and tea garden serving light lunches and afternoon tea.

Things to see and do: milling takes place on the first Wednesday of every month throughout the year. A 1-mile circular walk suitable for families takes in the mill and Dunster Castle. **Dogs**: welcome in the Watermill tea-room garden.

Access: Building
Parking: at Dunster Castle car park, 800 yards (enter from A39).

Find out more: 01643 821759 (mill). 01643 821314 (Dunster Castle) or dunstercastle@nationaltrust.org.uk

Dunster Working Watermill	
Open every day all year	10–5*

*Closes at dusk if earlier. 'Dunster by Candlelight' on 6 and 7 December, Watermill open until 9. Closed 24 and 25 December.

Fyne Court

near Bridgwater, Somerset

1967

This is a hidden gem in the Quantock Hills. While the house (former home of amateur scientist Andrew Crosse) no longer stands, the site remains simply beautiful within its woods and meadows. A great place for gentle walks, splashing in streams, building dens and discovering ruins (above). Information available in courtyard.

Eat, shop, stay: Courtyard tea-room serving light lunches, cream teas and cakes. Fyne Court Cottage (once a shooting lodge, then the family's retreat when the main house burnt down in a fire in 1894) is now a holiday cottage (sleeps six).

Things to see and do: three walking trails, including accessible trail. Natural play and den-building areas. You can observe the skies at the Skyglade and enjoy a picnic in the walled garden. Events year round. **Dogs**: welcome on leads.

Access: Grounds
Sat Nav: use TA5 2EQ. **Parking**: on site.

Find out more: 01823 451587 or fynecourt@nationaltrust.org.uk

Fyne Court		M	T	W	T	F	S	S
Estate								
Open all year		M	T	W	T	F	S	S
Tea-room								
3 Jan–17 Feb	10:30–3:30	·	·	·	T	F	S	S
18 Feb–3 Nov	10:30–4	M	T	W	T	F	S	S
7 Nov–29 Dec	10:30–3:30	·	·	·	T	F	S	S

Opening days and times can vary due to weather conditions.

Glastonbury Tor

near Glastonbury, Somerset 1933

Iconic tor topped by a 15th-century tower, with spectacular views over the Somerset Levels, Dorset and Wiltshire. **Note**: sorry no toilet. Nearest free parking at Somerset Rural Life Museum (not National Trust), BA6 8DB.

Find out more: 01278 751874 or glastonburytor@nationaltrust.org.uk

Great Chalfield Manor and Garden

near Melksham, Wiltshire SN12 8NH

1943

A monkey, soldiers and griffins adorn the rooftops of this moated medieval manor, looking over the terraces of the romantic garden with topiary houses, rose garden and spring-fed fishpond. All is lovingly looked after by the Floyd family. The manor has featured in several television dramas, including *Wolf Hall*. **Note**: home to the donor family tenants, who manage it for the National Trust. Charge for events outside normal opening times (including members).

Great Chalfield Manor and Garden, Wiltshire: moated medieval manor with a romantic garden

Eat, shop, stay: guidebooks, postcards and plants for sale. Tea and coffee, homemade cakes and soup served in the Motor House (not National Trust).

Things to see and do: visits to house are by guided tour (limited). Garden and parish church may be enjoyed at any time (during opening hours). Map for cross-country walk to The Courts Garden available.
Dogs: assistance dogs only.

Access: [access symbols]
Manor [access symbols] **Garden** [access symbols]
Parking: 100 yards, on grass verge outside manor gates.

Find out more: 01225 782239 or greatchalfieldmanor@nationaltrust.org.uk

Great Chalfield		M	T	W	T	F	S	S
Manor								
2 Apr–31 Oct	Tour*	·	T	W	T	·	·	S
Garden								
2 Apr–31 Oct	11–5	·	T	W	T	·	·	S
7 Apr–27 Oct	1–5	·	·	·	·	·	·	S

*Manor: admission by 45-minute guided tour (places limited, not bookable) Tuesday, Wednesday and Thursday at 11, 12, 2, 3 and 4; Sunday at 2, 3 and 4. Group visits welcome Friday and Monday (not Bank Holidays); please contact the tenant, Mrs Robert Floyd, on 01225 782239 (charge including members).

Heelis

Kemble Drive, Swindon, Wiltshire SN2 2NA
2005

The Trust's award-winning central office is a remarkable example of an innovative and sustainable building. **Note**: shop and café open all year except 1 January, 21 April, 25 to 26 December. Admission to offices by booked guided tour only.

Find out more: 01793 817575 or heelis@nationaltrust.org.uk

Horner Wood

on Exmoor, near Minehead, Somerset

[symbols] 1944

Playing in the river at Horner Wood, Somerset

One of the largest and most beautiful ancient oak woods in Britain, Horner Wood is part of the Holnicote Estate. 324 hectares (800 acres) of woodland clothe the lower slopes of surrounding moorland, following river and stream valleys. This National Nature Reserve is home to a rich variety of wildlife. **Note**: toilets in car park.

Horner Wood: ancient oak adorned with ferns

Eat, shop, stay: you can picnic by the river or enjoy a light lunch or cream tea at Horner Tea Garden or Horner Vale tea-room (neither National Trust). There are four holiday cottages on the Holnicote Estate for staying a bit longer.

Things to see and do: there's a 17th-century packhorse bridge and a Tudor iron-smelting site in the woods, plus some of Britain's rarest lichens, mosses and bats, and the General, a 500-year-old oak tree. **Dogs**: welcome under close control so as not to disturb wildlife and grazing animals.

Sat Nav: use TA24 8HY. **Parking**: on site.

Find out more: 01643 862452 or hornerwood@nationaltrust.org.uk

King John's Hunting Lodge

The Square, Axbridge, Somerset BS26 2AP
1968

This early Tudor timber-framed wool merchant's house (dating from around 1500) provides a fascinating insight into local history. **Note**: run as a local history museum by Axbridge and District Museum Trust. Open daily, 1 April to 31 October, 1 to 4.

Find out more: 01934 732012 or kingjohns@nationaltrust.org.uk

Lacock Abbey, Fox Talbot Museum and Village

Lacock, near Chippenham, Wiltshire SN15 2LG

1944

You can see why Ela of Salisbury chose this spot for her abbey in 1232: nestled alongside the River Avon in a rolling Wiltshire landscape, Lacock invites you to stay. The Abbey reveals evidence of a legacy of almost 800 years of past owners with sophisticated taste, who sensitively turned it from a nunnery into an unusual family home, furnished with well-loved mementoes and furniture. Seasonal colour can be discovered in the wooded grounds, botanic garden, greenhouse and orchard. The museum celebrates William Henry Fox Talbot, who created the first photographic negative and established this as a birthplace of photography. Lacock has a homely feel, and the village, with its timber-framed cottages, is to this day a bustling community. **Note**: please check opening arrangements for the Abbey in winter as access is limited.

Lacock Abbey, Fox Talbot Museum and Village in Wiltshire: exploring the garden

The golden stone of Lacock Abbey's west front glows in the light of the summer's setting sun

Eat, shop, stay: many places to eat and drink in Lacock village, including the Stables café and recently opened courtyard tea-room at the Abbey. Two National Trust shops, independent village businesses and a beautiful holiday cottage make Lacock a great place to visit.

Things to see and do: **Indoors** The Abbey offers two distinct experiences: a peaceful ground-floor monastic cloister and first-floor furnished rooms. The museum gives an insight into the history of photography and includes changing exhibitions. **Outdoors** The level grounds are great for picnics and walks. Range of events and exhibitions, seasonally changing family trails in the Abbey grounds, open-air theatre and a play area in the village. Lacock is a famous filming location, and its appearances include *Harry Potter*, *Wolf Hall* and *Pride and Prejudice*. **Dogs**: 1 November to 31 March welcome on short leads in Abbey grounds.

Access:
Abbey **Museum**
Grounds
Sat Nav: may direct down closed road. Set to Hither Way, Lacock, for car park. **Parking**: 220 yards. No visitor parking on village streets.

Find out more: 01249 730459 or lacockabbey@nationaltrust.org.uk

Lacock		M	T	W	T	F	S	S
2 Jan–15 Feb*	11–4	**M**	**T**	**W**	**T**	**F**	**S**	**S**
16 Feb–3 Nov	10:30–5	**M**	**T**	**W**	**T**	**F**	**S**	**S**
4 Nov–31 Dec*	11–4	**M**	**T**	**W**	**T**	**F**	**S**	**S**

Abbey: first-floor rooms open 30 minutes later.
Last admission to the Abbey rooms and last orders at tea-room 45 minutes before closing. Closed 25, 26 December and 1 January 2020. *Abbey cloister only, plus Great Hall at weekends (to 3:30). Village businesses operate independently.

Leigh Woods

Bristol

1909

Leigh Woods, Bristol: views of Clifton Suspension Bridge

A tranquil wilderness on Bristol's doorstep, with woodland, wildlife, Iron Age fort and wonderful views of the Avon Gorge and suspension bridge. Excellent network of paths, including 1¾-mile easy-access trail, links to the National Cycle Network and popular 'Yer Tiz' off-road cycle trail. Unique whitebeam trees grow in these woods. **Note**: toilet open during office hours.

Eat, shop, stay: picnics welcome.

Things to see and do: welcome hub. Natural play features. Events programme. Permanent orienteering course (map available to download). Iron Age hill fort – Stokeleigh Camp. Great views. Listen out for the calls of peregrine falcons. **Dogs**: welcome (but be aware of cattle in summer).

Access:
Sat Nav: use BS8 3QB for Leigh Woods car park (not National Trust). **Parking**: limited, on site (not National Trust).

Find out more: 0117 973 1645 or leighwoods@nationaltrust.org.uk

Lytes Cary Manor

near Somerton, Somerset TA11 7HU

1949

This intimate medieval manor house, with its beautiful Arts and Crafts-inspired garden (below), was originally home to the Lyte family, who lived here for several generations until the 18th century. After years of neglect, Lytes Cary was lovingly restored in the 20th century by Sir Walter Jenner, and is arranged as it was in his time. A stroll around the garden rooms, divided by high yew hedges, reveals collections of topiary (including the Twelve Apostles), sensuous herbaceous borders, orchards and manicured lawns. **Note**: parts of the garden may be closed to preserve the grass.

Eat, shop, stay: small tea-room offering cakes and drinks. Picnic tables in the courtyard. Shop selling gifts, garden accessories and plants. Second-hand books. The west wing of the house is available as a holiday let, as is a Victorian cottage on the estate.

Things to see and do: tranquil walks on the wider estate and children's outdoor natural play area. Allotments are bursting with creative and colourful designs. **Dogs**: welcome on leads in the courtyard and on estate walks.

Access: **Building** **Tea-room** **Grounds**
Parking: 40 yards.

Find out more: 01458 224471 or lytescarymanor@nationaltrust.org.uk

Lytes Cary Manor		M	T	W	T	F	S	S
2 Mar–3 Nov	10:30–5*	M	T	W	T	F	S	S
9 Nov–29 Dec**	10–2	·	·	·	·	·	S	S

*House: open 11 to 4:30 (tea-room closes 4:45). Timed tickets at peak times. **Garden (limited viewing), tea-room and shop only. Estate walks open dawn to dusk.

Mompesson House

The Close, Salisbury, Wiltshire SP1 2EL

1952

Visiting Salisbury's Cathedral Close, you step back into a past world. As you enter Mompesson House, featured in the film *Sense and Sensibility*, the feeling of leaving the modern world behind deepens. The tranquil atmosphere is enhanced by the magnificent plasterwork, graceful oak staircase and fine period furniture, which are the main features of this perfectly proportioned Queen Anne town house. Mompesson House has one of the finest displays of English 18th-century drinking glasses and a collection of stumpwork, a fascinating example of raised embroidery. The garden, with traditional herbaceous borders and pergola, is an oasis of calm in Salisbury.

Eat, shop, stay: the garden tea-room has indoor and outdoor seating and serves tea, coffee, light bites and cakes. The Studio shop in the courtyard offers a range of gifts for you and your home.

Things to see and do: exhibition 'Standing by My Darling's Side: a Victorian experience of life, love and loss'. Family trails and croquet on the lawn. Events including music in the garden.
Dogs: assistance dogs only.

Access:
Building **Grounds**
Parking: 260 yards in city centre, not National Trust (charge including members).

Find out more: 01722 335659 or mompessonhouse@nationaltrust.org.uk

Mompesson House		M	T	W	T	F	S	S
9 Mar–3 Nov	11–5	**M**	**T**	**W**	**T**	**F**	**S**	**S**
23 Nov–22 Dec*	11–3:30	·	·	·	**T**	**F**	**S**	**S**

*Ground-floor rooms decorated for Christmas.

Graceful Mompesson House, Wiltshire, stands within the city's picturesque Cathedral Close

Montacute House

Montacute, Somerset TA15 6XP

1931

This architecturally daring Elizabethan mansion was built to flaunt both wealth and power. Today its glittering façade shelters nationally important collections of furniture and textiles: 500-year-old tapestries exquisitely worked with heroes, saints, fishes and flowers; samplers touchingly stitched by little fingers; and more than 50 portraits on loan from the National Portrait Gallery. Outside, you can walk in Elizabethan footsteps through a formal garden, broken by cloud-pruned hedges and Victorian floral profusion. Wide lawns create open spaces, while avenues of trees lead you out into parkland, bluebell woods and a former motte-and-bailey castle now topped by an 18th-century folly. **Note**: this year there may be conservation work happening to the staircases – please check before visiting.

Eat, shop, stay: café serving freshly made seasonal lunches and tempting cakes; dogs welcome in outside courtyard. Gift shop, plant sales and second-hand bookshop. Farmers' markets. Two historic holiday cottages on the estate.

Elizabethan Montacute House, Somerset, above and left: built to flaunt power and wealth

Things to see and do: **Indoors** National Portrait Gallery exhibition 'Elizabeth of Bohemia: the Winter Queen'. **Outdoors** Regular 'Welcome' tours, seasonal events, family trails and open-air theatre. **Dogs**: welcome in garden and café courtyard (on short leads). Elsewhere, assistance dogs only.

Access:
Building **Grounds**
Parking: on site.

Find out more: 01935 823289 or montacute@nationaltrust.org.uk

Montacute House		M	T	W	T	F	S	S
House								
1 Jan–3 Mar	11–3*	M	T	W	T	F	S	S
4 Mar–3 Nov	11–4:30	M	T	W	T	F	S	S
4 Nov–31 Dec	11–3	M	T	W	T	F	S	S
Garden, parkland, café and shop								
1 Jan–3 Mar	10–4*	M	T	W	T	F	S	S
4 Mar–3 Nov	10–5	M	T	W	T	F	S	S
4 Nov–31 Dec	10–4	M	T	W	T	F	S	S

House: visitor routes will vary depending on essential conservation work. *1 to 6 January: house open 3 to 6:30; everything else 11 to 7. Everything closed 24 and 25 December.

Priest's House, Muchelney

Muchelney, Langport, Somerset TA10 0DQ

1911

Medieval hall-house, built in 1308.
Note: private home. Sorry no toilet or parking. Open Monday and Sunday, 14 April to 30 September, 2 to 5.

Find out more: 01935 823289 or priestshouse@nationaltrust.org.uk

Prior Park Landscape Garden

Ralph Allen Drive, Bath, Somerset BA2 5AH

1993

Perched on a hillside overlooking Bath, this elevated spot was chosen by Ralph Allen to show off his estate to the city. The magical landscape garden that he created captures a moment in time: 1764, the year of Allen's death. There is a lot to discover, including winding paths leading to hidden retreats, dramatic views over Bath and a rare Palladian Bridge. This year we're embarking on a major restoration project to repair the 18th-century dams. Access to the lakes may be restricted, but you'll have a once-in-a-lifetime opportunity to see the work in progress. **Note**: no parking on site. Steep slopes, steps, uneven paths. House not accessible (not National Trust).

Eat, shop, stay: Tea Shed by the lakes serves light snacks, cakes and refreshments (outdoor seating only). Refreshments will be relocated during the dam's restoration project. Small shop next to visitor reception with a selection of National Trust products.

Things to see and do: events and activities all year. Free guided tours and seasonal trails. The Bath Skyline 6-mile circular walk is just minutes from the garden. **Dogs**: welcome on short leads.

Prior Park Landscape Garden overlooking Bath, Somerset, below, and a young gardener, above

The Palladian Bridge at magical Prior Park

Access:

Parking: on site for disabled visitors only. Car parks in city centre, 1 mile (steep, uphill walk), not National Trust (charge including members). Frequent bus services from bus station or City Sightseeing bus (Skyline route) from city centre.

Find out more: 01225 833977 or priorpark@nationaltrust.org.uk

Prior Park Landscape Garden		M	T	W	T	F	S	S
5 Jan–27 Jan*	10–4	·	·	·	·	·	S	S
1 Feb–1 Nov	10–5:30	M	T	W	T	F	S	S
2 Nov–29 Dec*	10–4	·	·	·	·	·	S	S

Last admission one hour before closing. Closes dusk if earlier than 5:30. Tea Shed opening times vary. *Also open 1 January and 26 December.

Sand Point

near Kewstoke, Weston-super-Mare, North Somerset 1964

A natural pier into the Bristol Channel, north of Weston-super-Mare and Brean Down. Perfect for picnics; views across Sand Bay. **Note**: steep climbs and cliffs – please stay on main paths. Tide comes in quickly. Sorry, no toilets. For Sat Nav use BS22 9UD.

Find out more: 01278 751874 or sandpoint@nationaltrust.org.uk

Selworthy

on Exmoor, near Minehead, Somerset

1944

Selworthy is a good place to start discovering the wonderfully varied Exmoor landscapes within the 4,856-hectare (more than 12,000-acre) Holnicote Estate. This is a timeless rural landscape of thatched cottages, a medieval church, woodland walks and sweeping views across the vale to Dunkery Beacon, Exmoor's highest point.

Eat, shop, stay: Periwinkle Cottage tea-room and Clematis Cottage shop (tenant/National Trust partnership) are top spots for treats and trinkets. Or stay a little longer in the romantic, thatched Ivy's Cottage (sleeps two).

Things to see and do: a walk through the woods leads to Bury Castle, an Iron Age hill fort. The whitewashed church of All Saints looks out over the vale.
Dogs: welcome on leads.

Sat Nav: use TA24 8TP. **Parking**: on site.

Find out more: 01643 862452 or selworthy@nationaltrust.org.uk

Cycling near Selworthy, on Exmoor, Somerset

Stoke-sub-Hamdon Priory

North Street, Stoke-sub-Hamdon, Somerset TA14 6QP 1946

Fascinating small complex of buildings, formerly the home of priests serving the Chapel of St Nicholas (now destroyed). **Note**: sorry no toilet or parking. Please respect the privacy of tenants in the main house. Open Monday and Sunday, 14 April to 30 September, 2 to 5.

Find out more: 01935 823289 or stokehamdonpriory@nationaltrust.org.uk

Stonehenge Landscape

near Amesbury, Wiltshire

1927

You can wander freely through thousands of acres of downland within the Stonehenge and Avebury World Heritage Site. The landscape around the famous stones is studded with ancient monuments, such as the Avenue and Cursus, and abounds with wildlife. The visitor centre shuttle stops at Fargo woodland on request. **Note**: English Heritage manages stone circle, visitor centre/car park. Bookings via english-heritage.org.uk. Pay and display car park free to Trust members (booking essential).

Stonehenge Landscape, Wiltshire, above and left: the downland around the famous stones is full of ancient monuments easily accessible to walkers

Trust members enter free (excluding International National Trust or affiliate membership organisation members).

Eat, shop, stay: café and shop at visitor centre (not National Trust).

Things to see and do: guided walks and family activities throughout the year. **Dogs**: assistance dogs only.

Access:
Sat Nav: use SP3 4DX. **Parking**: at visitor centre (English Heritage), free to Trust members displaying Trust sticker. Booking is recommended to guarantee a space. Limited parking at Woodhenge.

Find out more: 0870 333 1181 (English Heritage). 01980 664780 (National Trust) or stonehenge@nationaltrust.org.uk

Stourhead

near Mere, Wiltshire BA12 6QF

1946

'A living work of art' is how Stourhead was described when it first opened over 250 years ago. The world-famous landscape garden surrounds a glistening lake. There are towering trees, exotic rhododendrons, classical temples and a magical grotto to explore. Stourhead House was one of the first in the country to showcase Palladian architecture. With a unique Regency library, Chippendale furniture and inspirational paintings, this was a grand family home, shaped by generations of the Hoare family. Outside, views stretch across the Wiltshire countryside, and the lawns are perfect for picnics. Great for walking and wildlife spotting, with 1,072 hectares (2,650 acres) of chalk downs, ancient woods, Iron Age hill forts and farmland to explore.

Eat, shop, stay: restaurant and shop with garden and plant selection. Second-hand bookshop. Spread Eagle Inn, ice-cream parlour, Red Lion pub, farm shop and art gallery (all concessions). Picnics welcome. Holiday cottage by garden entrance, CL site for Caravan Club members.

Stourhead in Wiltshire, clockwise from above: the unique Regency library, vivid autumn colour and walking around the glistening lake

Things to see and do: **Indoors** The house is the perfect start to your 'Genius of the Place' experience. This year's programme focuses on the creative professionals who designed or built the vision we see today, including Henry Flitcroft, Frances Faugoin, Colen Campbell and Thomas Chippendale the Younger. Explore behind the scenes on a guided tour (January and February). **Outdoors** Your 'Genius of the Place' journey continues in the world-famous landscape revealing the origins of the design, temples and trees. The garden changes in harmony with the seasons: from spring blooms and fresh greens of summer, to spectacular autumn colours and exposed winter views. **Dogs**: garden – on leads after 4 (March to October); 3 (November); daytime (December to February).

Access: [icons]
House [icons] **Landscape garden** [icons]
Parking: 400 yards. King Alfred's Tower, 100 yards.

Find out more: 01747 841152 or stourhead@nationaltrust.org.uk

Stourhead		M	T	W	T	F	S	S
Garden								
Open all year	9–5*	M	T	W	T	F	S	S
House								
9 Mar–10 Nov	11–4:30**	M	T	W	T	F	S	S
23 Nov–22 Dec†	11–3:30	M	T	W	T	F	S	S
King Alfred's Tower								
9 Mar–3 Nov	12–4**	·	·	·	·	·	S	S

*Closes at 6 in main season (30 March to 27 October) or dusk if earlier. **Closes at 3:30 after 27 October.†Selected show rooms only, decorated for Christmas. Everything closed 25 December. King Alfred's Tower is open more often at popular times, including Bank Holidays (check before setting out).

Tintinhull Garden

Farm Street, Tintinhull, Yeovil, Somerset BA22 8PZ

[icons] 1953

The vision of Phyllis Reiss, amateur gardener, lives on in this small yet perfectly formed garden, with 'living rooms' of colour and scent. Created in the last century around a 17th-century manor house, it's one of the most harmonious small gardens in Britain, featuring secluded lawns, pools and imaginative borders.

Harmonious Tintinhull Garden in Somerset, above and left: small but perfectly formed

Eat, shop, stay: tea-room serving cakes and cream teas. Small shop and plant sales. You can soak up the atmosphere for longer by staying in the holiday cottage that forms part of Tintinhull House.

Things to see and do: arboretum and orchard producing apple juice sold on site. Why not combine with a visit to Montacute House or Lytes Cary Manor? **Dogs**: welcome in courtyard only.

Access: [icons] **Gardens** [icons]
Parking: 150 yards.

Find out more: 01458 224471 or tintinhull@nationaltrust.org.uk

Tintinhull Garden		M	T	W	T	F	S	S
30 Mar–29 Sep	11–5	M	T	W	T	F	S	S

Tea-room closes at 4:45.

Treasurer's House, Martock

Martock, Somerset TA12 6JL 1971

Completed in 1293, this medieval house includes a Great Hall, 15th-century kitchen and an unusual wall-painting. **Note**: private home. Sorry no toilets or parking. Open Monday and Sunday, 14 April to 30 September, 2 to 5.

Find out more: 01935 823289 or treasurersmartock@nationaltrust.org.uk

 For information about getting to National Trust places, please see page 3

Tyntesfield

Wraxall, Bristol, North Somerset BS48 1NX

2002

Cocooned in the Somerset countryside, Tyntesfield is a rare survivor – a near-complete Victorian Gothic country house and estate. This extraordinary home and working landscape was created for the Gibbs family as a place where they could celebrate their achievements, raise their children and share their passions for family and faith. The richly decorated and furnished house is home to more than 60,000 of the family's possessions – a remarkable collection. Every part of the estate, every possession, tells a story about the Gibbs family, their estate workers and the world they lived in. Today you are welcomed into this cherished place to discover an ornate private chapel, flower-filled terraces, towering trees, abundant kitchen garden and views across the Somerset hills. **Note**: entry to the house is by timed ticket only (booking online in advance is advised).

Eat, shop, stay: the Cow Barn restaurant, Pavilion café and roaming trailers serving a range of dishes inspired by Tyntesfield's history, made using ingredients from the estate. Shop offering plant sales and local artisan products. Second-hand bookshop. Three holiday cottages across the estate.

Extraordinary Tyntesfield in North Somerset

High Victorian Gothic in the Hall at Tyntesfield, left. The house, top, sits cocooned in the countryside. A detail of a fireplace, above

Things to see and do: **Indoors:** Guided storytelling tours on weekdays in January, February and November as Tyntesfield house is carefully cleaned and conserved during the winter months. A 'Very Victorian' Christmas in December. **Outdoors:** Free daily guided walks on the history of the Tyntesfield Estate (check times on arrival). Three play areas, including a woodland adventure trail and den-building village. Events all year, including open-air theatre, family trails and living history. **Dogs**: welcome on short leads in specified areas (map available from ticket office).

Access: [icons]
House [icons] **Grounds** [icons]
Parking: 550 yards.

Find out more: 0344 800 4966 (Infoline). 01275 461900 or tyntesfield@nationaltrust.org.uk

Tyntesfield		M	T	W	T	F	S	S
House								
1 Jan–28 Feb†	Tour	**M**	**T**	**W**	**T**	**F**	**S**	**S**
1 Mar–3 Nov	11–3*	**M**	**T**	**W**	**T**	**F**	**S**	**S**
4 Nov–22 Nov†	Tour	**M**	**T**	**W**	**T**	**F**	**S**	**S**
23 Nov–31 Dec	11–3	**M**	**T**	**W**	**T**	**F**	**S**	**S**
Estate and garden								
Open all year	10–5**	**M**	**T**	**W**	**T**	**F**	**S**	**S**

†Tours only on weekdays, freeflow visits on 1 to 2 January and weekends. Timed tickets to house (limited), booking via website advised. Last entry one hour before closing.
*House: 16 March to 28 October (main season), closes at 5.
**Estate and garden: close at 6 in main season. Shop and restaurant: close 30 minutes before estate and garden. Christmas: 24 and 31 December house closes at 2, estate closes at 3. Everything closed 25 December.

Webber's Post

on Exmoor, near Minehead, Somerset 1944

Great spot for views over Horner Wood, short strolls, cycling, picnics and walking up to Dunkery Beacon, Exmoor's highest point. **Note**: sorry no toilets. For Sat Nav use TA24 8TB and follow signs to Webber's Post.

Find out more: 01643 862452 or webberspost@nationaltrust.org.uk

Wellington Monument

near Wellington, Somerset

 1934

Standing in an informal rural setting on the edge of the Blackdown Hills, Wellington Monument is in urgent need of repairs. The Trust is currently raising vital funds towards these, and welcomes donations and involvement in the campaign. **Note**: essential repairs due to start early summer. Sorry no toilet.

Sat Nav: use TA21 9PB.
Parking: small car park, ⅓ mile.

Find out more: 01823 451587 or wellingtonmonument@nationaltrust.org.uk

Wellington Monument, Somerset: a favourite place

Westwood Manor

Westwood, near Bradford on Avon, Wiltshire BA15 2AF

1960

Over the centuries, the residents of this small late medieval, Tudor and Jacobean house have modified the building to their own tastes, each leaving a permanent mark. The interiors are rich with decorative plasterwork, fine furniture and beautiful tapestries. Highlights are two rare keyboard instruments: a spinet and a virginal. **Note**: Westwood Manor is a family home, administered by the tenants.

Westwood Manor, Wiltshire: still a family home

Eat, shop, stay: guidebook telling the fascinating history of Westwood, postcards and CD of Elizabethan music recorded on the virginal and spinet. Tea and cake (and toilets) available in the parish room next door (not National Trust).

Things to see and do: children's quizzes (house suitable for over fives). Close to Lacock Abbey, The Courts Garden at Holt and Great Chalfield Manor and Garden.

Access: **Manor** **Garden**
Parking: 90 yards.

Find out more: 01225 863374 or westwoodmanor@nationaltrust.org.uk

Westwood Manor		M	T	W	T	F	S	S
2 Apr–29 Sep	2–5	·	**T**	**W**	·	·	·	**S**

Groups (eight people plus): please contact tenant on 01225 863374 to arrange private tour.

Additional coastal and countryside car parks in Somerset and Wiltshire

Somerset	
Sand Point	BS22 9UD
Staple Plain, Quantock Hills	TA4 4DQ
Holford	TA5 1SE
Quarts Moor	EX15 3UZ
King's Wood, Mendip Hills	BS25 1DH
Ivy Thorn, Polden Hills	BA16 0TZ
Walton Hill, Polden Hills	BA16 9RD
Wiltshire	
Whitesheet Hill	BA12 6RP
Win Green Hill	SP5 5AW
Overton Hill	SN8 1QG
Pepperbox Hill	SP5 3QL
Cley Hill	BA12 7QU

The Cotswolds and Chilterns

The garden at Hidcote in Gloucestershire is full of surprises

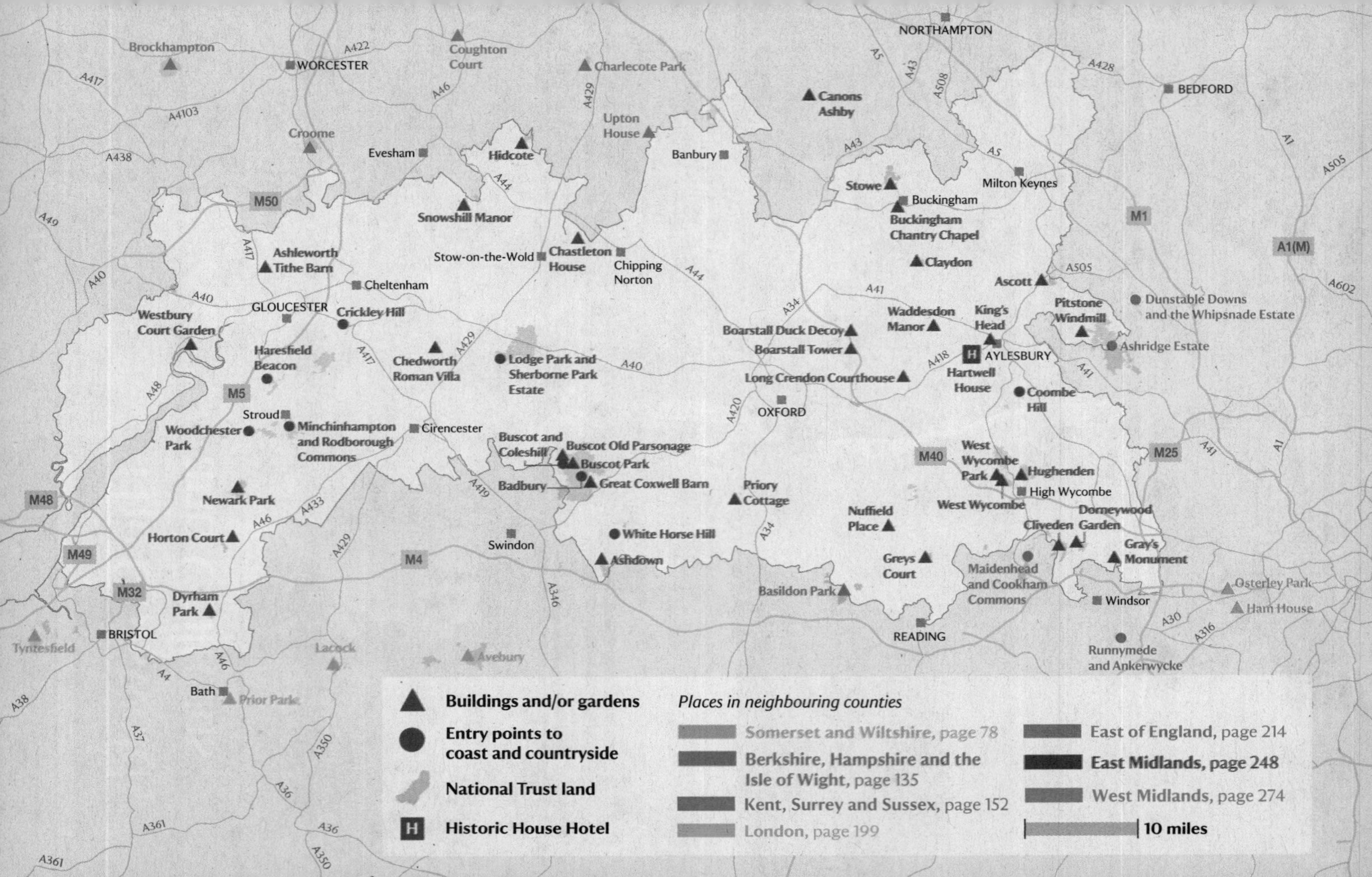

Brockhampton
WORCESTER
Coughton Court
Charlecote Park
NORTHAMPTON
BEDFORD
Croome
Evesham
Hidcote
Upton House
Banbury
Canons Ashby
Stowe
Buckingham
Buckingham Chantry Chapel
Milton Keynes
Snowshill Manor
Ashleworth Tithe Barn
Stow-on-the-Wold
Chastleton House
Chipping Norton
Claydon
Ascott
Cheltenham
GLOUCESTER
Crickley Hill
Westbury Court Garden
Haresfield Beacon
Chedworth Roman Villa
Lodge Park and Sherborne Park Estate
Boarstall Duck Decoy
Boarstall Tower
Waddesdon Manor
King's Head
AYLESBURY
Hartwell House
Pitstone Windmill
Dunstable Downs and the Whipsnade Estate
Ashridge Estate
Long Crendon Courthouse
OXFORD
Coombe Hill
Stroud
Woodchester Park
Minchinhampton and Rodborough Commons
Cirencester
Buscot and Coleshill
Buscot Old Parsonage
Buscot Park
Badbury
Great Coxwell Barn
Priory Cottage
West Wycombe Park
Hughenden
High Wycombe
West Wycombe
Newark Park
Nuffield Place
Dorneywood Garden
Cliveden
Horton Court
Swindon
White Horse Hill
Ashdown
Greys Court
Gray's Monument
Maidenhead and Cookham Commons
Basildon Park
Osterley Park
Ham House
Windsor
Dyrham Park
BRISTOL
Tyntesfield
Lacock
Avebury
READING
Runnymede and Ankerwycke
Bath
Prior Park
Buildings and/or gardens
Entry points to coast and countryside
National Trust land
Historic House Hotel
Places in neighbouring counties
Somerset and Wiltshire, page 78
Berkshire, Hampshire and the Isle of Wight, page 135
Kent, Surrey and Sussex, page 152
London, page 199
East of England, page 214
East Midlands, page 248
West Midlands, page 274
10 miles

Ascott

Wing, near Leighton Buzzard, Buckinghamshire LU7 0PR

1949

Ascott House, an 'Old English' half-timbered manor, dates back to the 16th century. It was transformed by the Rothschilds towards the end of the 19th century and houses several exceptional collections. The extensive gardens are an attractive mix of formal and natural, with specimen trees, shrubs and beautiful herbaceous borders. **Note**: Ascott is a family home, administered by the de Rothschild family.

Eat, shop, stay: tea-room offering light lunches, afternoon tea, ice cream and hot and cold drinks. Shop and takeaway outlet selling food and drinks, souvenirs, guidebooks, calendars, postcards, plants, flowers and kitchen garden produce in season.

Things to see and do: Dutch Masters and paintings by Stubbs (above), Gainsborough and Reynolds. Fine furniture and amazing collection of oriental porcelain. Discover the Rothschilds' passion for innovative gardening. Relaxing cricket matches most summer weekends. **Dogs**: assistance dogs only.

Access:
Building **Grounds**
Sat Nav: nearest LU7 0PP.
Parking: on site (218 yards).

Find out more: 01296 688242 or ascott@nationaltrust.org.uk

Ascott		M	T	W	T	F	S	S
19 Mar–15 Sep	1–6*	·	**T**	**W**	**T**	**F**	**S**	**S**

Open Bank Holiday Mondays. *House: open 2 to 5 (entrance by timed ticket only); tea-room open 12 to 5:30. National Gardens Scheme: 6 May and 26 August (£6, including members); house closed. Grounds: last entry at 5.

Ashdown

Lambourn, Newbury, Oxfordshire RG17 8RE

1956

Unique 17th-century chalk-block hunting lodge, with doll's-house appearance, built for the Queen of Bohemia by the Earl of Craven, set in a historic woodland. The guided tour, which reveals an intriguing family history, leads up the staircase hung with fine 17th-century paintings. Outstanding rooftop views across three counties. **Note**: access to roof via 100-step staircase.

Things to see and do: guided staircase tour. White Horse Hill nearby. **Dogs**: on leads in woodland only.

Access: **Building** **Grounds**
Sat Nav: follow local brown signs from B4000.
Parking: in main estate car park, 437 yards.

Find out more: 01793 762209 or ashdown@nationaltrust.org.uk

Ashdown		M	T	W	T	F	S	S
House								
3 Apr–30 Oct	Tour*	·	·	**W**	·	·	**S**	·
Woodland								
Open all year	Dawn–dusk	**M**	**T**	**W**	**T**	**F**	**S**	**S**

*House: admission by guided tour only, 2:15, 3:15 and 4:15 (advance booking not necessary).

Ashdown, Oxfordshire: the pretty 17th-century hunting lodge is set in historic woodland

Ashleworth Tithe Barn

Ashleworth, Gloucestershire GL19 4JA 1956

Barn, with immense stone-tiled roof, picturesquely situated close to the River Severn. **Note**: sorry no toilet.

Find out more: 01452 814213 or ashleworth@nationaltrust.org.uk

Badbury

Coleshill, near Swindon

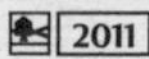 2011

This former plantation woodland is criss-crossed with easy circular walks, offering stunning views over the Upper Thames Valley. A spread of snowdrops heralds spring, followed by a carpet of bluebells. A copse of military-straight beech trees defines the Iron Age hill fort. **Note**: sorry no toilets.

Eat, shop, stay: three holiday cottages on the Buscot and Coleshill Estates.

The woodland at Badbury near Swindon, above, offers endless opportunities for adventure, below

Things to see and do: perfect woodland for family adventures and den-building. Natural woodland wild play area. Great Coxwell Barn nearby. **Dogs**: under close control.

Sat Nav: use SN7 7NJ.
Parking: at countryside car park.

Find out more: 01793 762209 or badbury@nationaltrust.org.uk

Boarstall Duck Decoy

Boarstall, near Bicester, Buckinghamshire HP18 9UX 1980

One of the last remaining decoys in the country, a fascinating insight into rural life. Natural play area for children. **Note**: open Mondays and weekends, 9 March to 3 November, 11 to 5. Also open Good Friday.

Find out more: 01280 817156 or boarstalldecoy@nationaltrust.org.uk

Boarstall Tower

Boarstall, near Bicester, Buckinghamshire HP18 9UX 1943

Charming 14th-century moated gatehouse set in beautiful gardens, retaining original fortified appearance. Grade I listed. **Note**: access to upper levels is via a spiral staircase. Restricted opening due to building and restoration work, telephone for opening details.

Find out more: 01280 817156 or boarstalltower@nationaltrust.org.uk

Buckingham Chantry Chapel

Market Hill, Buckingham, Buckinghamshire MK18 1JX 1912

Atmospheric 15th-century chapel, restored by Sir Gilbert Scott in 1875. Today it is a thriving coffee shop and second-hand bookshop. **Note**: open Tuesday, Wednesday, Friday and Saturday, 4 January to 21 December, 10 to 3 (to 4 on Saturday). Volunteer-run, opening subject to availability (call before visiting).

Find out more: 01280 817156 or buckinghamchantry@nationaltrust.org.uk

The Buscot and Coleshill Estates

Coleshill, near Swindon

1956

The Buscot and Coleshill Estates near Swindon, above and right: breathtaking countryside

These countryside estates on the western border of Oxfordshire include the attractive, unspoilt villages of Buscot and Coleshill, each with a thriving tea-room. There are circular walks of differing lengths and a series of footpaths criss-crossing the estates, with breathtaking countryside and wildlife at Buscot Lock and Badbury Hill. **Note**: toilets in Coleshill Estate office yard and next to village shop and tea-room in Buscot.

Eat, shop, stay: Buscot tea-room offering lunches and afternoon tea. Locally sourced produce served at Coleshill shop and tea-room and The Radnor Arms (none National Trust). Three holiday cottages.

Things to see and do: guided walks throughout the year, including tours of the Second World War bunker. See the restored watermill in action and visit the replica operational bunker on special open afternoons. **Dogs**: on leads near livestock and under close control at all times.

Sat Nav: use SN6 7PT. **Parking**: at Buscot village and by Coleshill Estate office.

Find out more: 01793 762209 or buscotandcoleshill@nationaltrust.org.uk

The Buscot and Coleshill Estates
Coleshill watermill and replica operational bunker open second Sunday of the month: April to October, 2 to 5. Countryside and footpaths open dawn to dusk.

Buscot Old Parsonage

Buscot, Faringdon, Oxfordshire SN7 8DQ 1949

Beautiful early 18th-century house with small walled garden, on the banks of the Thames. **Note**: sorry no toilets. Open Wednesdays, 3 April to 30 October, 2 to 6. Admission by written appointment with tenant (please mark envelope 'National Trust booking').

Find out more: 01793 762209 or buscot@nationaltrust.org.uk

Buscot Park

Faringdon, Oxfordshire SN7 8BU

1949

Lord Faringdon's family live in the house, maintain the interior, manage the grounds, gardens (above) and tea-room, and are responsible for the public display of the contents owned by The Faringdon Collection Trust. This unusual arrangement with the National Trust breathes life into the property and gives it an individualistic air.

Eat, shop, stay: tea-room (not National Trust), serving cream teas, cakes, ice cream and a selection of hot and cold drinks. Local honey and cider, peppermints, plants and kitchen garden produce (when available). Ice cream also available in ticket office. Picnic area.

Things to see and do: occasional events in grounds and theatre (available for hire). **Dogs**: in Paddock (overflow car park) only.

Access:
House **Grounds**
Parking: on site.

Find out more: 01367 240932 (Infoline). 01367 240786 or buscotpark@nationaltrust.org.uk buscotpark.com

Buscot Park		M	T	W	T	F	S	S
House, grounds and tea-room								
3 Apr–27 Sep*	2–6	·	·	**W**	**T**	**F**	·	·
Grounds only								
1 Apr–30 Sep	2–6	**M**	**T**	·	·	·	·	·

*Weekend openings: 13/14, 20/21 April; 4/5, 11/12, 25/26 May; 8/9, 22/23, 29/30 June; 13/14, 27/28 July; 10/11, 24/25 August; 14/15, 28/29 September (tea-room open 2 to 5:30). Last admission to house one hour before closing. Open Bank Holiday Mondays.

Chastleton House

Chastleton, near Moreton-in-Marsh, Oxfordshire GL56 0SU

1991

Within the warm, weathered Cotswold stone walls of this ancient country house (below), lie faded elegant interiors full of myths and memories – a compelling time capsule of 400 years of family life. Discover the secrets they hide, then explore the garden, a sleeping beauty preserved in graceful decline.

Eat, shop, stay: plants, local ice cream, home-grown produce and honey from Chastleton's hives for sale. Second-hand books in the stables. Light refreshments available most days in the local church (not National Trust). Picnics welcome in the garden.

Things to see and do: **Indoors** You can experience the romantic decline of a country manor, watch our introductory film and enjoy our family explorer packs. **Outdoors** Croquet on the lawn. **Dogs**: on leads in car park and Dovecote Field. Assistance dogs only in garden.

Access: **Building** **Garden**
Sat Nav: use GL56 0SP to the Greedy Goose pub, then follow brown signs. **Parking**: footpath to house, steep in places, 273 yards.

Find out more: 01494 755560 (Infoline). 01608 674355 or chastleton@nationaltrust.org.uk

Chastleton House		M	T	W	T	F	S	S
6 Mar–3 Nov	1–5*	·	·	**W**	**T**	**F**	**S**	**S**

*Last entry one hour before closing.

 For information about getting to National Trust places, please see page 3

Chedworth Roman Villa

Yanworth, near Cheltenham, Gloucestershire GL54 3LJ

1924

Cradled in a beautiful wooded valley and fed by a natural spring, this high-status Roman villa saw imperial fashions and local spirits living side by side. Nature took over and hid the magnificent mosaics, intricate hypocaust systems, bathhouses and ancient water-shrine for more than 1,500 years until Victorian gamekeepers rediscovered the site. The National Trust has, in turn, looked after Chedworth's Roman treasures and Victorian legacy for nearly a century, providing its modern villa guests with new facilities, as well as astonishing archaeology to enjoy. It remains a hidden place of natural beauty and continual discovery.

Eat, shop, stay: café serving sandwiches, soup, jacket potatoes, cakes, snacks, hot and cold drinks and ice cream. You can find books, games, Roman-themed souvenirs, seasonal plants and National Trust gifts in the shop.

Things to see and do: **Indoors** Guidebooks, audio guides, free guided tours. Activities, including Roman dressing up for children. Costumed interpreters and living history events. **Outdoors** Family activities and trails (Bank Holiday weekends and school holidays). **Dogs**: assistance dogs only.

Access: **Reception** **West Range** **Grounds**
Parking: on lane at entrance, plus woodland overflow (March to October).

Find out more: 01242 890256 or chedworth@nationaltrust.org.uk

Chedworth Roman Villa		M	T	W	T	F	S	S
9 Feb–22 Mar	10–4	**M**	**T**	**W**	**T**	**F**	**S**	**S**
23 Mar–27 Oct	10–5	**M**	**T**	**W**	**T**	**F**	**S**	**S**
28 Oct–24 Nov	10–4	**M**	**T**	**W**	**T**	**F**	**S**	**S**

Chedworth Roman Villa, Gloucestershire: fabulous mosaics and treasures lay hidden for centuries

Claydon

Middle Claydon, near Buckingham,
Buckinghamshire MK18 2EY

1956

Nestled in peaceful parkland, the Georgian exterior (above) hides a lavish interior filled with oddities. The collection encompasses the unique and wonderful, alongside intricate Rococo carvings and portraits of interesting characters from 300 years of Verney family history. An inspirational place, where Florence Nightingale, Lady Verney's sister, spent her summers. **Note**: garden entry charges apply (including members).

Eat, shop, stay: shop, second-hand bookshop, courtyard shops, galleries and tea-room (not National Trust). Picnics welcome.

Things to see and do: **Indoors** Relax in the Great Red Room and enjoy a game of checkers. Children's activities, trails and dressing-up costumes. **Outdoors** The classic English garden opened by the Verney family. **Dogs**: welcome on leads in the park.

Access:
House **Grounds**
Parking: on site, limited hard-standing parking.

Find out more: 01296 730349 or claydon@nationaltrust.org.uk

Claydon		M	T	W	T	F	S	S
9 Mar–3 Apr	11–4	M	T	W	·	·	S	S
6 Apr–21 Jul	11–5	M	T	W	·	·	S	S
22 Jul–8 Sep	11–5	M	T	W	·	F	S	S
9 Sep–3 Nov	11–4	M	T	W	·	·	S	S

Open Good Friday. Phoenix Kitchens (not National Trust): open same dates as house, 10 to 4.

Cliveden

Cliveden Road, Taplow, Maidenhead,
Buckinghamshire SL1 8NS

1942

High above the River Thames with panoramic views over the Buckinghamshire and Berkshire countryside, these gardens capture the grandeur of a bygone age. Over the course of 350 years, each family added their own extravagant touch, creating a series of distinct gardens. You can discover vibrant floral displays on the elaborate Parterre, award-winning herbaceous borders, an intimate Rose Garden and rich autumn colour filling the oriental Water Garden. Each area is designed purely for enjoyment, and all echo Cliveden's rich history of passion, pleasure and

 Support the places you visit: please scan your member card for free parking ticket

politics. Miles of walks meander through majestic woodlands and along riverbank paths, while a yew-tree maze, storybook-themed play area and acres of space to run around in, make this a great place to play. **Note**: overnight mooring available on Cliveden Reach, £10 per 24 hours (£5 for members), not including entry.

Eat, shop, stay: Conservatory Café (refurbishment this spring/summer) serving lunch (11:30 to 3:30) and snacks. Outdoor kiosk (dog-friendly) serving light refreshments. Doll's House seasonal 'grab-and-go' beside play area, designed for families. Shop and plant centre. Second-hand bookshop. Picnic areas.

Things to see and do: **Indoors** Guided tours of the house (now a hotel) on certain days. **Outdoors** More than 70,000 bedding plants create striking displays in spring, summer and early autumn. The Rose Garden blooms from June. Miles of picturesque pathways through seasonal colour. Highlights for families include

Cliveden, Buckinghamshire, above and below: the gardens capture the grandeur of a bygone age

The colourful Parterre at Cliveden

a play area, maze, woodland play trail and den-building area. Events include open-air theatre, seasonal trails, guided walks and workshops. Boat trips on the Thames, April to October (additional charge including members). Throughout the year enjoy events celebrating 100 years since Nancy Astor became the first female MP to take her seat in Parliament. **Dogs**: welcome under close control in woodlands and other locations on a short lead.

Access:
House (hotel) **Garden**
Sat Nav: for gardens use Cliveden Road and SL1 8NS. For woodlands use SL6 0HJ.
Parking: on site.

Find out more: 01628 605069 or cliveden@nationaltrust.org.uk

Cliveden	
Garden, shop, café and woodland	
Open every day all year	10–5*

House and chapel: limited opening April to October (call for details). House: admission by timed ticket only from Information Centre. *1 January to 15 February and 3 November to 31 December: estate closes 4. Everything closed 24 and 25 December.

Coombe Hill

Butler's Cross, near Wendover, Buckinghamshire 1918

Nationally important chalk grassland site and the highest viewpoint in the Chilterns with stunning views over the Aylesbury Vale.
Note: picnic area and play trail. Sorry no toilet. For Sat Nav use HP17 0UR.

Find out more: 01494 755573 (Hughenden Estate Office) or coombehill@nationaltrust.org.uk

Crickley Hill

Birdlip, Gloucestershire 1935

Sitting high on the Cotswold escarpment with views towards the Welsh hills, Crickley Hill overlooks Gloucester and Cheltenham.
Note: car park, café, toilets and visitor centre not National Trust. For Sat Nav use GL4 8JY. Parking charges (including members).

Find out more: 01452 814213 or crickleyhill@nationaltrust.org.uk

Dorneywood Garden

Dorneywood, Dorney Wood Road, Burnham, Buckinghamshire SL1 8PY 1942

Ministerial residence since 1954 with country garden. Afternoon teas. Open selected afternoons (dates may change at short notice).
Note: no photography. Visitor details recorded for security reasons. House and garden open daily, 7 to 17 July, 2 to 4:30. Garden open Wednesday and Thursday, 15 May to 4 July and 14 August and 19 September, 2 to 4. Booking essential. May be closed at short notice, please check before travelling.

Find out more: dorneywood@nationaltrust.org.uk

Dyrham Park

Dyrham, near Bath,
South Gloucestershire SN14 8HY

1961

Dyrham is a place of exploration. Parkland adventurers can savour far-reaching views towards the Welsh hills or encounter the resident herd of majestic fallow deer, while in the garden we are creating a haven of tranquillity and inspiration. Sumptuous planting in the pool garden contrasts with the Dutch formality of the avenue, as well as with the wilder wooded terraces. The house is an intimate encounter with the late 17th century. There are treasures gathered from across the world, reflecting an age of exploration and empire, revealing the personal passions of William Blathwayt – Secretary at War to William of Orange. The house interior is evolving as we develop new ways of revealing Dyrham's stories.

Eat, shop, stay: tea-room (indoor seating) and tea garden (outdoor seating) serving lunch, cakes and refreshments. Courtyard kiosk offering drinks, ice cream and snacks on busy days. Picnics are welcome in the parkland. Shop selling plants, books, local products and gifts. Second-hand bookshop.

Things to see and do: **Indoors** You can get a taste of 17th-century luxury with a collection of Delftware and fine Dutch art dating from William Blathwayt's time in Holland. Though the house collection is being reconfigured, there is always plenty to see but please check for the latest tours and up-to-date information. **Outdoors** Year-round events and activities, guided tours of the park and garden, self-led trails and walks. For families there are two natural play areas: younger children will enjoy the ride-on trucks, tractor, allotment and wooden climbing area at Old Lodge; older ones can find carved creatures and get active at Hollow Ways. **Dogs**: assistance dogs only.

The garden and mirror-like lake at Dyrham Park in South Gloucestershire

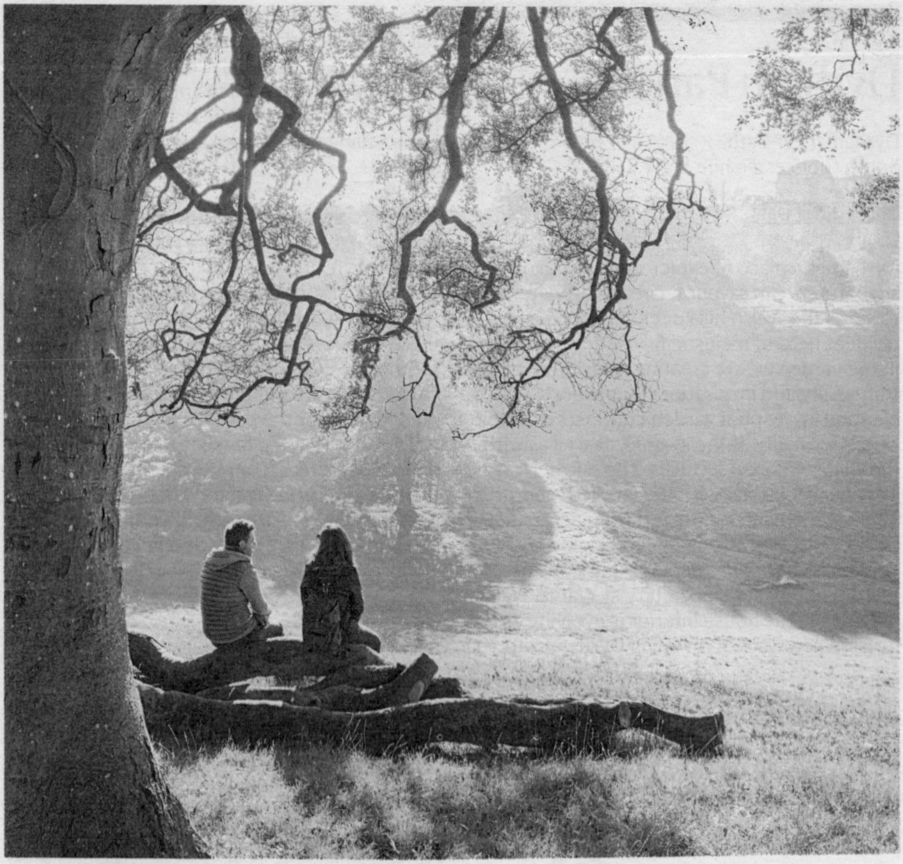

Dyrham Park: the parkland, top, and visitors exploring the house, above

Access:
House **Grounds**
Sat Nav: use SN14 8HY and enter via A46.
Parking: on site (just over ½ mile from house).

Find out more: 0117 937 2501 or dyrhampark@nationaltrust.org.uk

Dyrham Park		M	T	W	T	F	S	S
House								
1 Jan–15 Feb	Tour*	**M**	**T**	**W**	**T**	**F**	**S**	**S**
16 Feb–26 Oct	11–5	**M**	**T**	**W**	**T**	**F**	**S**	**S**
27 Oct–31 Dec**	Tour*	**M**	**T**	**W**	**T**	**F**	**S**	**S**
Park, garden, shop, tea-room and basement								
1 Jan–15 Feb	10–4	**M**	**T**	**W**	**T**	**F**	**S**	**S**
16 Feb–26 Oct	10–5	**M**	**T**	**W**	**T**	**F**	**S**	**S**
27 Oct–31 Dec**	10–4	**M**	**T**	**W**	**T**	**F**	**S**	**S**

Last admission one hour before closing. Everything closed until 1 on 4, 11, 18, 25 September; 6, 13, 20, 27 November; 4, 11 December. *During busy periods, the house may open as freeflow instead of tours. **Everything closed 24 and 25 December.

Gray's Monument

Stoke Poges, Buckinghamshire SL2 4NZ 1925

This 5-metre-high monument, surrounded by expansive parkland views, captures the poet Thomas Gray's long association with the village. **Note**: sorry no toilet or tea-room. Limited parking at St Giles's Church (not National Trust).

Find out more: graysmonument@nationaltrust.org.uk

Great Coxwell Barn

Great Coxwell, Faringdon, Oxfordshire SN7 7LZ 1956

Former 13th-century monastic barn, a favourite of William Morris, who would regularly bring his guests to wonder at its structure. **Note**: sorry no toilet; narrow access lanes leading to property. Open daily, dawn to dusk.

Find out more: 01793 762209 or greatcoxwellbarn@nationaltrust.org.uk

Greys Court

Rotherfield Greys, Henley-on-Thames, Oxfordshire RG9 4PG

1969

Picturesque Greys Court in Oxfordshire, left, is set in the rolling hills of the Chilterns. The kitchen, above

Set in the rolling hills of the Chilterns, Greys Court is a picturesque Tudor manor house surrounded by layers of history, intimate walled gardens and glorious wooded parkland. The house is warm and welcoming, unfurling the memories of the Brunner family through the rooms of their comfortable home. Across the perfect lawn, a medieval tower and patchwork of mellow brick buildings conceal an English country garden. Through an ancient arch, seasonal blooms are revealed, from bright bulbs through clematis and wisteria to glorious peonies and roses in the summer. Winter walks in the woodland are a must.

Eat, shop, stay: tea-room serving morning coffee, afternoon tea, lunches and snacks. Shop selling books, gifts, souvenirs and plants. Seasonal organic produce and plants from the gardens (when available).

Things to see and do: **Indoors** Enjoy the Brunner home's comfortable family rooms. Learn about the wider history in the Cromwellian Building. **Outdoors** Discover 'rooms' in the walled gardens and explore rambling woodland walks. **Dogs**: welcome on leads (excluding house and walled gardens).

Access: House Tea-room Grounds
Parking: 220 yards.

Find out more: 01491 628529 or greyscourt@nationaltrust.org.uk

Greys Court		M	T	W	T	F	S	S
Garden, tea-room and shop								
Open all year	10-5*	M	T	W	T	F	S	S
House								
1 Jan-28 Feb	11-3	M	T	W	T	F	S	S
1 Mar-31 Oct	1-5**	M	T	W	T	F	S	S
1 Nov-31 Dec	11-3	M	T	W	T	F	S	S

*1 January to 4 February and 29 October to 31 December: closes 4. **House tours at 11 and 12, tickets available from Visitor Reception (places limited). Everything opens at 12 on 1 September for annual village fête. Closed 24 and 25 December.

Haresfield Beacon

near Stroud, Gloucestershire

1931

Prominently positioned on three spurs of the Cotswold escarpment. Views across the Severn Estuary towards the Forest of Dean and Brecon Beacons. The wildlife is some of the best in the Cotswolds and there's a wealth of archaeological features, including long and round barrows, a hill fort and cross dyke. **Note**: Cotswold Way National Trail runs through estate.

Eat, shop, stay: pubs in Randwick and Haresfield (not National Trust). Ice-cream vendor (not Trust) in Shortwood car park on sunny days. Picnics welcome.

Things to see and do: bluebells and butterflies to spot and woods to explore – there are superb veteran beech trees on Shortwood's slopes. Great place to fly a kite and watch buzzards and kestrels. **Dogs**: welcome

Haresfield Beacon in the Cotswolds, Gloucestershire

(on leads near livestock). Dog bins available in Shortwood car park.

Sat Nav: use GL6 6PP for Shortwood car park.
Parking: at Shortwood.

Find out more: 01452 814213 or haresfieldbeacon@nationaltrust.org.uk

Hartwell House Hotel, Restaurant and Spa

Oxford Road, near Aylesbury, Buckinghamshire HP17 8NR

2008

Elegant Grade I listed stately home, having both Jacobean and Georgian façades, contains magnificent Great Hall with exceptional ceiling and elegant drawing rooms serving morning coffee or afternoon tea. Set in beautifully landscaped grounds, including ruined Gothick church, lake, bridge and 36 hectares (90 acres) of parkland. Only one hour from central London. **Note**: access is for paying guests of the hotel, including for luncheon, afternoon tea and dinner. Children over the age of six welcome. Held on a long lease from the Ernest Cook Trust.

Find out more: 01296 747444. 01296 747450 (fax) or info@hartwell-house.com hartwell-house.com

Hidcote

Hidcote Bartrim, near Chipping Campden, Gloucestershire GL55 6LR

1948

This world-famous Arts and Crafts-inspired garden nestles in a north Cotswolds hamlet. Created by the talented American horticulturist Major Lawrence Johnston, Hidcote's colourful and intricately designed outdoor spaces are full of surprises, which change in harmony with the seasons. Many of the unusual plants found growing in the garden were collected from Johnston's plant-hunting trips around the world. Wandering along the narrow paved pathways, you come across secret gardens, unexpected views and plants that burst with colour.

Eat, shop, stay: Winthrop's Café serving hot food until 2:30. 'Grab and go' Barn Café serving lighter snacks. The National Trust's largest plant centre. Shop selling exclusive Hidcote-inspired gifts. Picnics welcome in the picnic area, close to the car park.

Things to see and do: **Indoors** Exhibitions in the chapel and manor house. **Outdoors** Croquet on the Great Lawn, or tennis using period wooden racquets (activities are weather dependent). Seasonal spectaculars throughout the garden. **Dogs**: assistance dogs only.

Hidcote in Gloucestershire, above and below: a world-famous Arts and Crafts-inspired garden

Access:
Visitor reception **Grounds**
Sat Nav: follow signs to Mickleton.
Parking: 100 yards.

Find out more: 01386 438333 or hidcote@nationaltrust.org.uk

Hidcote		M	T	W	T	F	S	S
Garden, shop and Winthrop's Café								
9 Feb-3 Mar	11-4	·	·	·	·	·	**S**	**S**
4 Mar-27 Oct	10-6*	**M**	**T**	**W**	**T**	**F**	**S**	**S**
2 Nov-15 Dec	11-4	·	·	·	·	·	**S**	**S**

Garden: last admission one hour before closing.
*4 to 31 March and 30 September to 27 October: closes at 5 (Barn Café, plant centre and shop close one hour earlier). Barn Café open only at weekends in March and October.

Horton Court

Horton, near Chipping Sodbury, South Gloucestershire BS37 6QR [1949]

Atmospheric Norman hall and Tudor loggia, in the beautiful secluded setting of Horton Court's historic grounds. **Note**: main manor house is tenanted and not open to public. Sorry no toilets. Advance booking may be required. Limited spring-summer opening (call for opening details/booking).

Find out more: 01453 842644 (Newark Park) or hortoncourt@nationaltrust.org.uk

Hughenden

High Wycombe, Buckinghamshire HP14 4LA

[1947]

It's hardly surprising that the unconventional Victorian Prime Minister Benjamin Disraeli so loved Hughenden. His handsome home, set in an unspoiled Chiltern valley with views of ancient woods and rolling hills, is full of fascinating personal memorabilia of this charismatic colourful statesman. Disraeli's country retreat later became the headquarters for a top-secret, Second World War operation codenamed 'Hillside' and put Hughenden high on Hitler's target list. The Hillside exhibition and ice-house bunker bring wartime Britain to life. The estate also offers a variety of walks in the parkland and wider countryside, rewarding visitors with views of the Chiltern Hills.

Eat, shop, stay: Stableyard café serving hot meals, sandwiches, cakes and drinks. Dizzy's tea-room open weekends and holidays serving sandwiches, cakes and drinks. The shop stocks local produce, as well as Disraeli and 'Hillside' memorabilia. Second-hand bookshop, plants and estate produce available.

Things to see and do: **Indoors** Historical introductory talks throughout the day. **Outdoors** Woodland walks. Children's trails in

Handsome Hughenden, Buckinghamshire, below and top right, sits in an unspoilt Chiltern valley

Walled Garden and woodland play at the top of the picnic orchard. **Dogs**: welcome on short leads in orchard and gardens. Assistance dogs only in manor.

Access:
Manor **Grounds**
Parking: on site.

Find out more: 01494 755565 (Infoline). 01494 755573 or hughenden@nationaltrust.org.uk

Hughenden		M	T	W	T	F	S	S
House*								
1 Jan–6 Jan	11–3	·	**T**	**W**	**T**	**F**	**S**	**S**
26 Jan–15 Feb	12–3	**M**	**T**	**W**	**T**	**F**	**S**	**S**
16 Feb–27 Oct	11–5	**M**	**T**	**W**	**T**	**F**	**S**	**S**
28 Oct–31 Dec	11–3	**M**	**T**	**W**	**T**	**F**	**S**	**S**
Gardens, shop, café and kiosk								
Open all year	10–5**	**M**	**T**	**W**	**T**	**F**	**S**	**S**

*House: admission by timed ticket at certain peak times; closed 7 January to 25 January for conservation work.
**1 January to 15 February and 27 October to 31 December close at 4. Whole property closed 24 and 25 December.

King's Head

King's Head Passage, Market Square, Aylesbury, Buckinghamshire HP20 2RW 1925

Historic public house dating back to 1455, with a pleasant family atmosphere. This is one of England's best-preserved coaching inns. **Note**: Farmers' Bar leased by Chiltern Brewery. Closed 25 December. Open Bank Holiday Mondays and other public holidays (please check before visiting).

Find out more: 01296 718812 (Farmers' Bar). 01280 817156 (National Trust) or kingshead@nationaltrust.org.uk

Lodge Park and Sherborne Park Estate

Aldsworth, near Cheltenham, Gloucestershire GL54 3PP

1983

Within the tranquil Sherborne Park Estate sits England's only surviving 17th-century deer-coursing grandstand (below). Lodge Park was built in 1634 to satisfy John 'Crump' Dutton's love of gambling and entertaining. There are dramatic views from the roof. The Sherborne Park Estate has a variety of peaceful walks through the Cotswold countryside. **Note**: toilets at Lodge Park only.

Eat, shop, stay: tea, cake, ice cream and plants for sale at Lodge Park, when open. Tea-room and shop in Sherborne village (not National Trust). Nearby holiday cottages: Deer Park Lodge at Lodge Park, West Lodge in Sherborne and 9 Arlington Row, Bibury.

Things to see and do: living history, family events, lawn games, talk and tea events, historic shepherd's hut and beautiful walk in Bridgeman landscape at Lodge Park. Walks through the wider estate, including guided walks. **Dogs**: on leads in Lodge Park grounds and near livestock. Under control at all times.

Access: **Lodge**
Sat Nav: for Lodge Park use GL54 3PP; for Sherborne Estate use GL54 3DT (Ewe Pen Barn) or GL54 3DL (Water Meadows).

Parking: on site for Lodge Park. For Sherborne Estate use either Ewe Pen Barn or Water Meadows car parks.

Find out more: 01451 844130 (Lodge Park) or lodgepark@nationaltrust.org.uk

Lodge Park and Sherborne Park		M	T	W	T	F	S	S
Lodge Park								
1 Mar–27 Oct*	11–4	**M**	·	·	·	**F**	**S**	**S**
Sherborne Park Estate								
Open all year	Dawn–dusk	**M**	**T**	**W**	**T**	**F**	**S**	**S**

*Also open Tuesdays, Wednesdays and Thursdays from 6 to 29 August. Lodge Park occasionally closes for private functions (call to check).

Long Crendon Courthouse

Long Crendon, Aylesbury, Buckinghamshire HP18 9AN 1900

Superb example of a 14th-century courthouse with a wealth of local history – the second building acquired by the National Trust. **Note**: extremely steep stairs. Sorry no toilet. Parking limited. Open Wednesday and weekends, 9 March to 3 November, 11 to 5. Volunteer-run, so opening subject to availability, please call to check before visiting. Open all public and Bank Holidays.

Find out more: 01280 817156 or longcrendon@nationaltrust.org.uk

Minchinhampton and Rodborough Commons

near Stroud, Gloucestershire

1913

These historic Cotswold commons, traditionally grazed, are famed for rare flowers and butterflies, prehistoric remains and far-reaching views. Minchinhampton Common

contains a nationally important complex of Neolithic and Bronze Age burial mounds, while Rodborough Common's limestone grasslands have abundant wild flowers, including rare pasqueflowers and many varieties of orchid.

Eat, shop, stay: many great picnic spots (no tables). The historic Winstones ice-cream factory is on Rodborough Common; ice-cream vans usually found in Reservoir car park in summer. Several pubs around the edge of both commons (none National Trust). Two holiday cottages nearby.

Things to see and do: the commons are great places to walk, picnic or spot rare butterflies and moths, such as the wood tiger moth (above). Downloadable Rodborough Common butterfly walk available. **Dogs**: welcome everywhere (under close control near livestock). Dog bins in car parks.

Sat Nav: use GL5 5BJ for Minchinhampton; GL5 5BP Rodborough (postcodes may be approximate). **Parking**: at Reservoir car park on Minchinhampton Common; Rodborough Fort car park on Rodborough Common.

Find out more: 01452 814213 or minchinhampton@nationaltrust.org.uk

Newark Park

Ozleworth, Wotton-under-Edge, Gloucestershire GL12 7PZ

1949

With splendid views from the Cotswold escarpment, Newark Park is a secluded estate with a historic country home at its heart. From Tudor beginnings to dramatic rescue by a 20th-century Texan, the house has many stories to tell. The informal garden and estate provide space to play, explore and contemplate. **Note**: toilets in car park (additional toilets in Newark House).

Eat, shop, stay: gift shop on the first floor of Newark House and plant sales next to visitor reception. Tea pavilion in the garden serving light lunches, cakes, drinks and ice cream. Outdoor seating, with indoor seating available in house. Holiday cottage.

Splendid view from Newark Park, Gloucestershire

Things to see and do: **Indoors** Exhibitions in house. **Outdoors** Waymarked walks, geocaching and play garden. Open-air theatre, croquet on the lawn with peacocks for company. Seasonal garden specials include snowdrops, cyclamen and wild garlic.
Dogs: welcome on leads in garden and estate (please mind peacocks and grazing livestock).

Access:
Building **Grounds**
Sat Nav: only works when approaching from north; if approaching from south follow brown signs from Wotton-under-Edge and A46.
Parking: 100 yards from house.

Find out more: 01453 842644 or newarkpark@nationaltrust.org.uk

Newark Park		M	T	W	T	F	S	S
2 Feb–3 Nov	11–5*	**M**	**T**	**W**	**T**	**F**	**S**	**S**
8 Nov–15 Dec	11–4	·	·	·	·	**F**	**S**	**S**

*2 February to 3 March: closes 4. Estate walks open daily dawn to dusk (weather permitting). Car park: reduced opening in winter.

Nuffield Place

Huntercombe, near Henley-on-Thames, Oxfordshire RG9 5RY

2011

Nuffield Place was the home of William Morris, who rose from modest circumstances as a backyard bicycle repairer to become one of the richest men in the world. As founder of Morris

The tool cupboard at Nuffield Place, Oxfordshire

Motors, Lord Nuffield was an innovator in mass production. He was also a great philanthropist, donating millions to charitable causes. Despite their great wealth, Lord and Lady Nuffield lived modestly in their Oxfordshire country home. The Arts and Crafts-style house is full of personal curiosities, such as the tool cupboard in Lord Nuffield's wardrobe, and gives an intriguing glimpse into the home life of this private couple.

Eat, shop, stay: tea-room serving light lunches and afternoon tea. Shop selling unique Nuffield Place mementoes, gifts, books and postcards.

A Morris Minor sits outside Nuffield Place: the home of William Morris, an innovator in mass production and founder of Morris Motors

Things to see and do: **Indoors** Immerse yourself in the wonderful stories of Lord and Lady Nuffield. **Outdoors** Charming Arts and Crafts-style garden with colourful herbaceous borders, kitchen garden and croquet lawn. Greys Court nearby. **Dogs**: welcome on leads in the gardens and woodlands.

Access: **House** **Shop** **Grounds**
Parking: on site.

Find out more: 01491 641224 or nuffieldplace@nationaltrust.org.uk

Nuffield Place		M	T	W	T	F	S	S
25 Feb–3 Nov*	10–5**	**M**	**T**	**W**	**T**	**F**	**S**	**S**

*Closed 28 April, 30 June, 9 July. **House: access from 11; timed tickets may be used on busy days (available from visitor reception, places limited).

Pitstone Windmill

Ivinghoe, Buckinghamshire LU7 9EJ 1937

Believed to be the oldest postmill in England. Stunning views of the Chilterns. **Note**: access to windmill 262 yards via a grassy field track. Sorry no facilities. Limited parking. Open Sundays, 5 May to 25 August, 10 to 4 (also open Mondays, 6 and 27 May and 26 August).

Find out more: 01442 851227 or pitstonemill@nationaltrust.org.uk

Priory Cottage

1 Mill Street, Steventon, Abingdon, Oxfordshire OX13 6SP 1939

Now converted into two houses, these former monastic buildings were gifted to the National Trust by the famous Ferguson's Gang.
Note: administered by tenant. Sorry no toilet. Open Tuesdays, 2 April to 24 September, 2 to 6 (Great Hall only open). Admission by written appointment with the tenant.

Find out more: 01793 762209 or priorycottages@nationaltrust.org.uk

Snowshill Manor and Garden

Snowshill, near Broadway,
Gloucestershire WR12 7JU

1951

Charles Wade was an artist and architect who took delight in creating a home for his unlikely treasures. He collected beautiful and interesting objects, which for him were a celebration of colour, craftsmanship and design. With a sense of fun and theatre, he took great pleasure in turning his home into a stage for these varied and curious finds. Next to the manor house is the small cottage where Charles Wade lived. Both manor house and cottage are surrounded by an intimate terraced garden, where he created 'different courts for different moods'. **Note**: entry by timed ticket (including members); places limited.

Eat, shop, stay: café serving hot meals, sandwiches, cakes and drinks using home-grown produce where possible. Shop selling gifts, plants and local produce. Second-hand bookshop. Picnics welcome. Why not stay a while longer at one of four picturesque holiday cottages in the village?

Things to see and do: **Indoors** Family trail, handling collection and, through regular demonstrations, a chance to see how we care for the collection. **Outdoors** Family trail, natural play area and introductory talks.
Dogs: assistance dogs only.

Access:
Manor **Garden**
Sat Nav: follow signs from centre of village.
Parking: 500 yards.

Find out more: 01386 852410 or
snowshillmanor@nationaltrust.org.uk

Snowshill Manor and Garden		M	T	W	T	F	S	S
Manor								
18 Mar–3 Nov	12–5	M	T	W	T	F	S	S
9 Nov–1 Dec	11–2:30	·	·	·	·	·	S	S
Garden, shop and café								
18 Mar–3 Nov	11–5:30	M	T	W	T	F	S	S
9 Nov–1 Dec	10:30–3:30	·	·	·	·	·	S	S

Manor: admission by non-bookable timed tickets (may run out on busy days). Last admission one hour before closing. Charles Wade's cottage opens at 11.

Snowshill Manor and Garden, Gloucestershire: filled with unlikely treasures collected by Charles Wade

Stowe

Buckingham, Buckinghamshire MK18 5EQ

1989

The beauty of Stowe has attracted visitors since 1717. Picture-perfect views, lakeside walks and temples create a monumental landscape that changes with the seasons. Full of hidden meaning and classical references, the garden remains an earthly paradise. Follow in the footsteps of 18th-century tourists by beginning your visit at the New Inn visitor centre. From here it is a short walk or buggy-ride to the garden, where another world awaits. Our restoration programme continues to return Stowe to its former glory. The sheer size and scale is perfect for a steady stroll or vigorous ramble but will leave you overwhelmed by its awe-inspiring splendour. We're celebrating 30 years looking after Stowe; join us for a year of celebrations.

Eat, shop, stay: New Inn café serving light lunches, cakes, soups and scones. Café in courtyard and covered porch welcomes dogs. Shop selling local products inspired by Stowe, as well as gifts and plants. A second-hand bookshop is a must for bookworms. Picnics welcome.

Things to see and do: **Indoors** 18th-century parlour rooms in the New Inn. Visitor centre at New Inn provides details about visiting Stowe House state rooms (not National Trust). House visitor centre open, includes exhibition and family-friendly activities. St Mary's Church open for visits. **Outdoors** Crisp winter walks, blooming spring displays, lazy summer days and vivid autumn colour – Stowe is forever changing. Fun family activities and outdoor event programme. We're restoring paths, returning replica statues and opening new garden areas all year, so there will be more to explore however many times you visit. **Dogs**: welcome on leads (downloadable dog trail available). Tie-up points and water provided. Monthly walk.

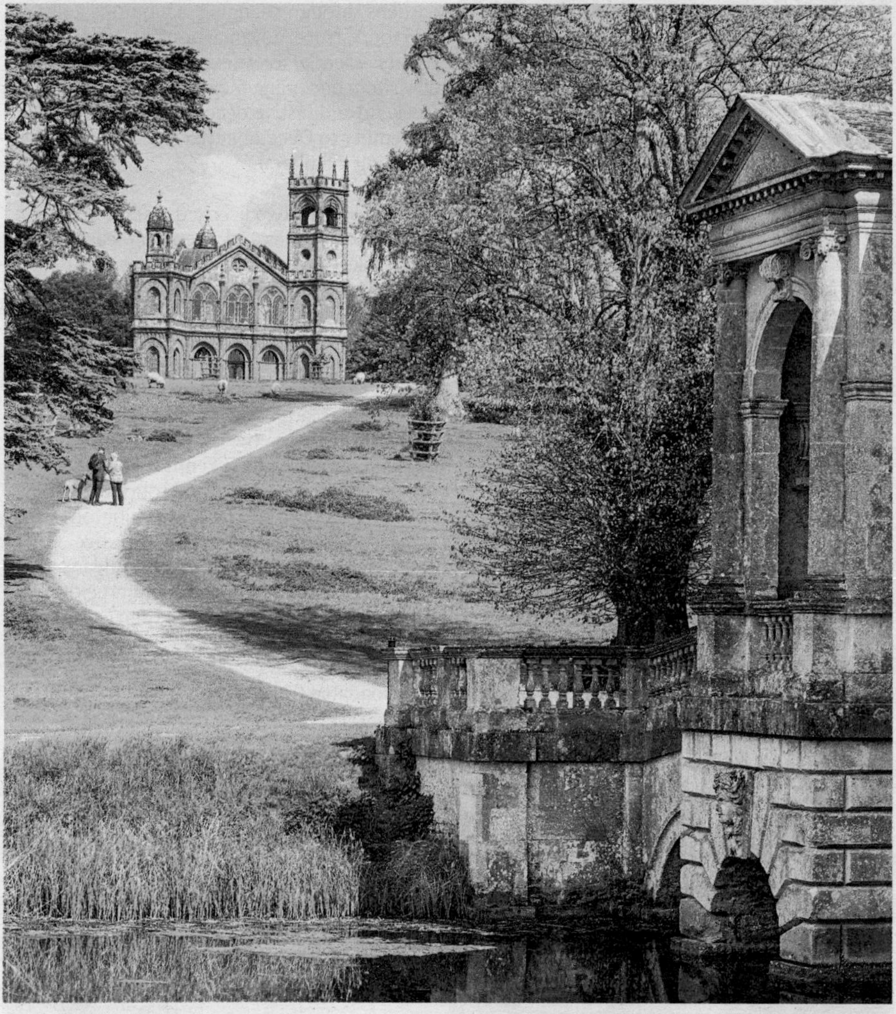

Access:
Visitor centre **Grounds**
Parking: 545 yards.

Find out more: 01280 817156 or stowe@nationaltrust.org.uk

Stowe	
Open every day all year*	10–5**

*Gardens: closed 25 May (New Inn, parkland, café and shop open); recommended last entry 90 minutes before closing.
**1 January to 3 February and 4 November to 31 December: closes 4. Closed 24 and 25 December.

Stowe in Buckinghamshire, clockwise from right: visitors with resident sheep, the Temple of Ancient Virtue, and Gothic Temple and Palladian Bridge

Waddesdon Manor

Waddesdon, near Aylesbury,
Buckinghamshire HP18 0JH

1957

Baron Ferdinand de Rothschild started building the manor – managed by the Rothschild Foundation – in 1874 to display his outstanding collection of art treasures and entertain fashionable society. His choice of a French-style château, typical of the Loire Valley, surprises many visitors. The highest quality 18th-century French decorative arts are displayed alongside magnificent English portraits and Dutch Old Master paintings in 40 elegant interiors. Outside is one of the finest Victorian gardens in Britain, famous for its parterre and ornate working aviary, and enhanced with classical and contemporary sculpture. Today, the manor continues its tradition of entertainment and hospitality, with events celebrating food and wine. Visitors can explore Waddesdon's history, collections and gardens through changing exhibitions, talks and tours. **Note**: advance booking for house tickets essential for weekends and holidays for all visitors (including members). July Festival weekend and festive decorated interiors, November to December (£5 charge, including members).

Eat, shop, stay: two licensed restaurants for breakfasts, lunches and afternoon teas. Snacks and drinks at the Treaterie, Summer House and Coffee Bar. Gift and wine shop; regular wine tastings. Five Arrows Hotel in Waddesdon village. None National Trust.

Things to see and do: **Indoors** House timed ticket entry March to October, with furnished interiors displaying the collections (advance booking advised for weekends and holidays). Annual exhibitions. Talks and tours about the house, collection, archive and exhibitions with experts. November to December festive decorations, only east wing open (advance booking essential). Rolling programme of films. **Outdoors** Daily free guided garden walks and tours of the aviary and cellars, online tree and sculpture trails, dog walks and other maps downloadable from waddesdon.org.uk.

Waddesdon Manor in Buckinghamshire: the magnificent French-style château

For information about getting to National Trust places, please see page 3

Opulent dining room at Waddesdon Manor laid for a banquet, top, and ornate parterre, above

Children's woodland playground and den-building. Weekend and school holiday family events. Open-air film and theatre. Food festivals, Winter Light and Christmas fair.
Dogs: welcome outdoors on short leads (except parterre and aviary gardens, woodland playground and buses).

Access:
House **Coach House Gallery**
Grounds
Parking: ¾ mile (frequent free shuttle service). Electric vehicle charging points in main car park.

Find out more: 01296 820414 or waddesdonmanor@nationaltrust.org.uk

Waddesdon Manor		M	T	W	T	F	S	S
Gardens, aviary, playground, wine cellars, shop, restaurant								
1 Jan–2 Jan	11–6	·	**T**	**W**	·	·	·	·
5 Jan–24 Mar	10–4	·	·	·	·	·	**S**	**S**
16 Feb–24 Feb	10–4	**M**	**T**	**W**	**T**	**F**	**S**	**S**
27 Mar–3 Nov	10–5	·	·	**W**	**T**	**F**	**S**	**S**
25 May–2 Jun	10–5	**M**	**T**	**W**	**T**	**F**	**S**	**S**
26 Oct–3 Nov	10–5	**M**	**T**	**W**	**T**	**F**	**S**	**S**
16 Nov–29 Dec	11–6	·	·	**W**	**T**	**F**	**S**	**S**
30 Dec–31 Dec**	11–6	**M**	**T**	·	·	·	·	·
House*								
27 Mar–25 Oct	12–4	·	·	**W**	**T**	**F**	·	·
30 Mar–27 Oct	11–4	·	·	·	·	·	**S**	**S**
27 May–31 May	12–4	**M**	**T**	**W**	**T**	**F**	·	·
Christmas House (partial opening)*								
16 Nov–29 Dec	11:30–6	·	·	**W**	**T**	**F**	**S**	**S**
30 Dec–31 Dec**	11:30–6	**M**	**T**	·	·	·	·	·
Coach House Gallery								
25 May–2 Jun	11–5	**M**	**T**	**W**	**T**	**F**	**S**	**S**
5 Jun–20 Oct	11–5	·	·	**W**	**T**	**F**	**S**	**S**

Open Bank Holiday Mondays (plus 19 April, 28 May and 27 August): grounds 10 to 5, house 12 to 4.
*House: admission by timed ticket, available at waddesdon.org.uk or by calling 01296 820414 (booking fee). Members must book house tickets in advance to guarantee admission. Recommended entry to house before 2:30; last house entry 3:10. Special ticketed event 6 and 7 July.
**Closed 23, 24, 25 and 26 December.

West Wycombe Park

West Wycombe, Buckinghamshire

Lavish West Wycombe Park, Buckinghamshire, lies within a serene landscape garden

Alongside this historic village lies an exquisite Palladian mansion. This lavish home and serene landscape garden reflect the wealth and personality of its creator, the infamous Sir Francis Dashwood, founder of the Hellfire Club. Still home to the Dashwood family and their fine collection, it remains a busy, private estate. **Note**: opened in partnership with the Dashwood family. The Hellfire Caves and café are privately owned and National Trust members receive a discount on the admission charge.

Eat, shop, stay: refreshments available at the Hellfire Caves and café (not National Trust), where members receive a discount. A variety of shops and pubs in the National Trust village, offering refreshments and local produce (none National Trust).

Things to see and do: **Indoors** Mansion guided tours, Monday to Thursday (freeflow access Sundays). **Outdoors** Centuries-old village with historic cottages and coaching inns. West Wycombe Hill, iconic Dashwood mausoleum and church with golden ball. **Dogs**: welcome on West Wycombe Hill. Assistance dogs only in park.

Access:

Parking: 250 yards.

Find out more: 01494 755571 (Infoline). 01494 513569 or westwycombe@nationaltrust.org.uk

West Wycombe Park		M	T	W	T	F	S	S
Grounds								
1 Apr–29 Aug	2–6	M	T	W	T	·	·	S
House*								
2 Jun–29 Aug	2–6	M	T	W	T	·	·	S

*House: entry Monday to Thursday by guided tour (timed tickets). Freeflow on Sundays and Bank Holidays. Last admission 45 minutes before closing.

West Wycombe Village and Hill

West Wycombe, Buckinghamshire HP14 3AJ

1934

This historic village, with its many buildings of architectural interest, was an important coaching stop between London and Oxford. West Wycombe Hill offers commanding views over West Wycombe Park and the surrounding countryside. On top of the hill is St Lawrence Church with its famous golden ball. **Note**: church and mausoleum not National Trust.

Eat, shop, stay: refreshments available at the Hellfire Caves and café (not National Trust), where members receive a discount. Variety of shops and pubs in the National Trust village, offering refreshments and local produce (none National Trust).

Things to see and do: centuries-old historic cottages and coaching inns. West Wycombe Hill, iconic Dashwood mausoleum and church with golden ball. **Dogs**: welcome on West Wycombe Hill and in the village.

Parking: roadside parking in village and on West Wycombe Hill.

Find out more: 01494 755571 (Infoline). 01494 513569 or westwycombe@nationaltrust.org.uk

Westbury Court Garden

Westbury-on-Severn, Gloucestershire GL14 1PD

1967

Originally laid out between 1696 and 1705, this is the only restored Dutch water garden in the country. There are canals, clipped hedges, working 17th-century vegetable plots and many old varieties of fruit trees. **Note**: credit cards not accepted.

Eat, shop, stay: hot drinks machine on site. Bottled water and juice for sale. Light refreshments available in the local church (not National Trust) on some Sunday afternoons.

Things to see and do: evening garden tours, Easter egg trails and Apple Day.
Dogs: welcome on short leads at all times.

Access: Pavilion
Summerhouse **Garden**
Parking: car park 300 yards from main road.

Find out more: 01452 760461 or westburycourt@nationaltrust.org.uk

Westbury Court Garden		M	T	W	T	F	S	S
6 Mar–31 May	10–5	·	·	W	T	F	S	S
1 Jun–30 Sep	10–5	M	T	W	T	F	S	S
2 Oct–27 Oct	10–5	·	·	W	T	F	S	S

Open Bank Holiday Mondays, and other times by appointment.

Westbury Court Garden in Gloucestershire

White Horse Hill

Uffington, Oxfordshire

1979

The White Horse at Uffington is part of an ancient landscape, steeped in history and mythology. It's the oldest chalk figure in the country, dated to the late Bronze Age about 3,000 years ago. Its linear form dominates the landscape, yet no one knows how it was made. The walls of an Iron Age hill fort are visible on the hilltop, the highest point in Oxfordshire. You can also look down on a valley known as The Manger and a natural outcrop known as Dragon Hill, where St George was said to have fought and slain the dragon.
Note: archaeological monuments under English Heritage guardianship. Sorry no toilet.

White Horse Hill, Oxfordshire: rechalking the figure

Admiring the view at White Horse Hill

Things to see and do: guided walks and events to rechalk the White Horse. Stunning views can be enjoyed from the top of the hill. Ashdown House woodland walks nearby. **Dogs**: under close control on leads at all times (stock grazing and nesting birds).

Access:
Sat Nav: use SN7 7QJ. **Parking**: on site.

Find out more: 01793 762209 or whitehorsehill@nationaltrust.org.uk

Woodchester Park

Nympsfield, near Stroud, Gloucestershire

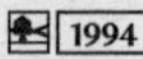 1994

This tranquil wooded valley contains a 'lost landscape': remains of an 18th- and 19th-century landscape park with a chain of five lakes. The restoration of this landscape is an ongoing project. Waymarked trails (steep in places) lead through picturesque scenery, passing an unfinished Victorian mansion. **Note**: toilet not always available. Mansion managed by Woodchester Mansion Trust (not National Trust). Admission to mansion: charges apply (including members).

Eat, shop, stay: seasonal café, shop and toilets at Woodchester Mansion (not National Trust).

Things to see and do: waymarked trails through valley and popular woodland play trail for children built along shortest route, which includes rope swings, see-saw and balance beams. Events throughout the year. **Dogs**: under close control, on leads where requested.

Sat Nav: nearest GL10 3TS, then follow signs. **Parking**: accessible from Nympsfield road, 300 yards from junction with B4066.

Find out more: 01452 814213 or woodchesterpark@nationaltrust.org.uk

Woodchester Park, Gloucestershire: a lost landscape

Additional countryside car parks in The Cotswolds and Chilterns

Buckinghamshire	
Ivinghoe Beacon	HP4 1NF
Pulpit Wood, Whiteleaf Fields	HP27 0NB
Gloucestershire	
Mayhill	GL18 1JS
Dover's Hill	GL55 6PN
Oxfordshire	
Buscot Village	SN7 8DA

Berkshire, Hampshire and the Isle of Wight

One of the characterful Belted Galloways at New Forest Commons and Foxbury in Hampshire

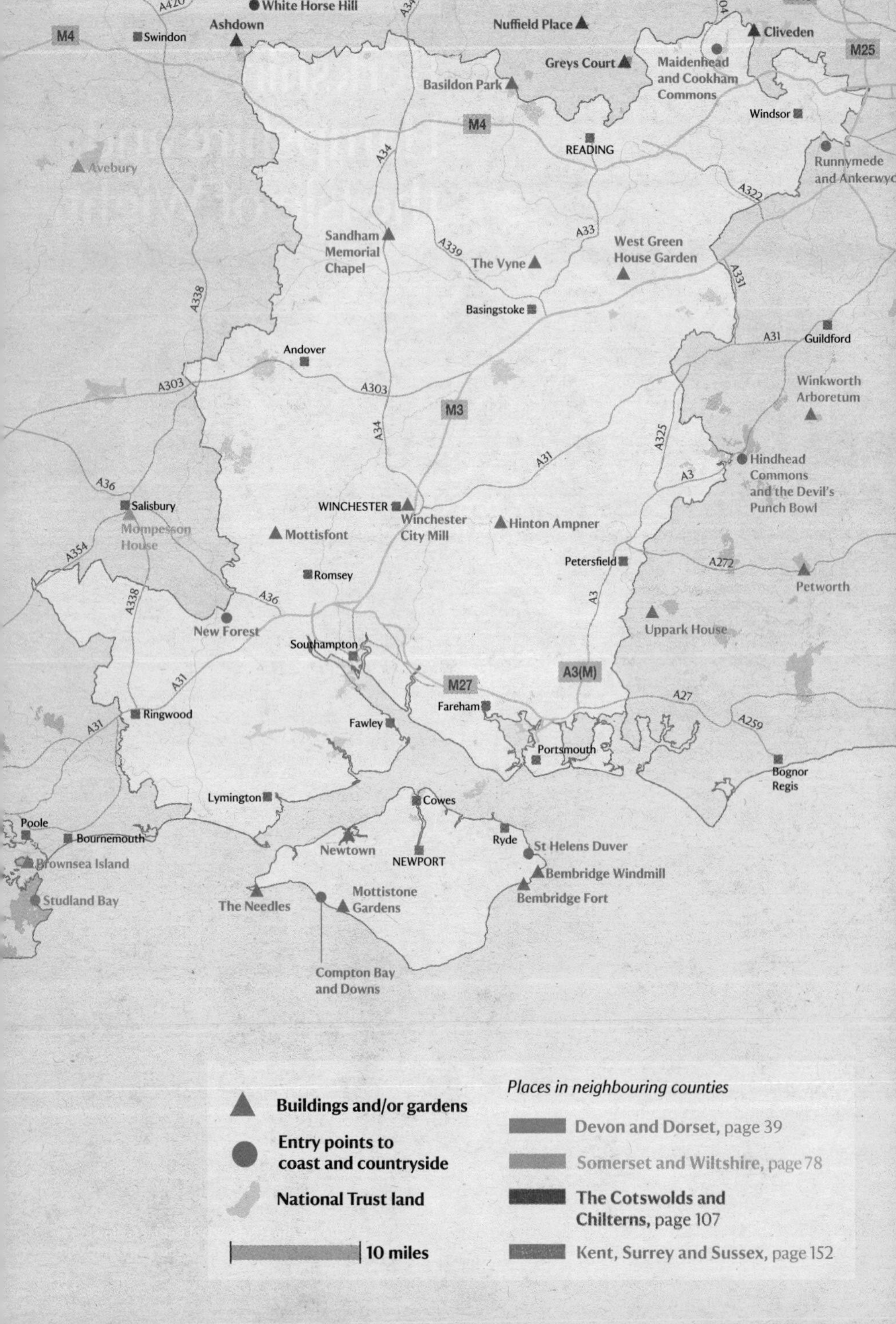

White Horse Hill
Ashdown
Swindon
M4
Nuffield Place
Cliveden
Greys Court
Maidenhead and Cookham Commons
M25
Basildon Park
Windsor
READING
Avebury
Runnymede and Ankerwycke
Sandham Memorial Chapel
West Green House Garden
The Vyne
Basingstoke
Guildford
Andover
Winkworth Arboretum
M3
Hindhead Commons and the Devil's Punch Bowl
Salisbury
WINCHESTER
Mompesson House
Winchester City Mill
Hinton Ampner
Mottisfont
Petersfield
Romsey
Petworth
New Forest
Uppark House
Southampton
A3(M)
M27
Fareham
Ringwood
Fawley
Portsmouth
Bognor Regis
Lymington
Cowes
Poole
Bournemouth
Ryde
St Helens Duver
Newtown
NEWPORT
Brownsea Island
Bembridge Windmill
Bembridge Fort
Studland Bay
The Needles
Mottistone Gardens
Compton Bay and Downs
Buildings and/or gardens
Entry points to coast and countryside
National Trust land
10 miles
Places in neighbouring counties
Devon and Dorset, page 39
Somerset and Wiltshire, page 78
The Cotswolds and Chilterns, page 107
Kent, Surrey and Sussex, page 152

Glorious Basildon Park in Berkshire

Basildon Park

Lower Basildon, Reading, Berkshire RG8 9NR

1978

Sitting elegantly in 162 hectares (400 acres) of historic parkland and gardens, this 18th-century mansion was saved from destruction by Lord and Lady Iliffe in the 1950s, when it was derequisitioned after the Second World War. In a true labour of love, the Iliffes spent nearly 50 years renovating and returning the house to its former glory, acquiring a collection of fine furnishings and carefully selected Old Masters. The wooded parkland showcases glorious seasonal colour all year round, while the landscape has been restored to offer wonderful views, peaceful trails and picnic places. **Note**: entrance to main show rooms of mansion on first floor – 21 steps from ground level.

Eat, shop, stay: mansion tea-room serving coffee, lunch, afternoon tea and snacks. Shop selling books, plants, local food, ice cream and much more.

Things to see and do: **Indoors** Exhibition space in the South Pavilion. **Outdoors** Woodland and parkland walks. Wild Play and family activities. **Dogs**: welcome on leads in grounds. Assistance dogs only in house.

Access:
Mansion **Grounds**
Sat Nav: not reliable, please follow brown tourist signs. **Parking**: 400 yards.

Find out more: 01491 672382 or basildonpark@nationaltrust.org.uk

Basildon Park	
Open every day all year	10–5*

*House: freeflow from 11. 1 January to 4 February and 29 October to 31 December: closes 4. Closed 24 and 25 December.

Bembridge Fort

Bembridge Down, near Bembridge, Isle of Wight PO36 8QY 1967

In a commanding position on top of Bembridge Down, this unrestored Victorian fort is open for volunteer-run guided tours. **Note**: sorry no toilets. Not suitable for children under 10. Open Tuesdays, 2 April to 29 October, 2 to 3:30 (access by guided tour only, booking essential).

Find out more: 01983 741020 or bembridgefort@nationaltrust.org.uk c/o Longstone Farmhouse, Strawberry Lane, Mottistone, Isle of Wight PO30 4EA

Bembridge Windmill

High Street/Mill Road, Bembridge, Isle of Wight PO35 5SQ

1961

The Isle of Wight's only surviving windmill (below), and one of the island's most iconic buildings, built more than 300 years ago. The sails last turned in 1913, but inside most of its original machinery is still intact. Climb to the top and follow the milling process down four floors. **Note**: steep steps inside the windmill.

Eat, shop, stay: reception kiosk offering hot and cold drinks, including tea and a selection of coffees. Ice cream, postcards, sweets, gifts, souvenirs and flour also available. Picnic tables in grounds. Four holiday cottages nearby – Chert, Little Chert, Wydcombe and Knowles Farm cottages.

Things to see and do: **Indoors** Hunt for the hidden millers inside the windmill. **Outdoors** Walks, including the start of Culver Trail. Nature ID trails and children's activities during school holidays. Bembridge Fort nearby. **Dogs**: welcome in grounds on leads. Assistance dogs only in windmill.

Access: **Building**
Sat Nav: do not use, look for brown signs.
Parking: free (not National Trust), 100 yards in lay-by.

Find out more: 01983 873945 or bembridgemill@nationaltrust.org.uk

Bembridge Windmill		M	T	W	T	F	S	S
9 Mar–3 Nov	10:30–5	**M**	**T**	**W**	**T**	**F**	**S**	**S**

Closes dusk if earlier. Conducted school groups and special visits March to end October (telephone or email to book).

Compton Bay and Downs

Compton, Isle of Wight

1961

The sandy beach with colourful cliffs behind at Compton Bay and Downs, Isle of Wight

With sandy beaches and colourful cliffs, Compton Bay is considered one of the best beaches on the island. It's also a prime site for fossil-hunting – look out for dinosaur foot casts. The clifftops and downs are rich in wildlife and easy-to-access walks, with views as far as Dorset. **Note**: steep steps down to the beach.

Eat, shop, stay: licensed van selling hot and cold snacks, drinks and ice cream. Two holiday cottages, Compton Farm Cottages, within walking distance – both ideally placed for exploring the coast and Downs.

Things to see and do: one of the best spots on the Isle of Wight for swimming, surfing and fossil-hunting. Scenic views from three walking trails available to download from the website. **Dogs**: welcome on beach between Hanover Point and Brook Chine all year.

Sat Nav: use PO30 4HB. **Parking**: on site.

Find out more: 01983 741020 or comptonbay@nationaltrust.org.uk

Hinton Ampner

Hinton Ampner, near Alresford, Hampshire SO24 0LA

1986

Hinton Ampner is the fulfilment of one man's vision. After a catastrophic fire in 1960, Ralph Dutton rebuilt his home in the light and airy Georgian style he loved. A passionate collector, he filled the sunny rooms with ceramics and art. Outside, Dutton designed a series of tranquil garden rooms, each with their own distinctive planting still apparent today. Geometric topiary, exotic-coloured dahlias and borders of repeat-flowering roses lead onto terraces with panoramic views across the South Downs. Extensive lawns, a park with ancient oaks and beech woodland provide plenty of space to stroll, play, relax and picnic.

Eat, shop, stay: café serving seasonal dishes made using produce grown in our walled garden, homemade cakes and cream teas. Shop selling a range of locally sourced products and estate-grown plants. Second-hand bookshop. Picnics welcome.

Things to see and do: **Indoors** Conservation demonstrations throughout the year. **Outdoors** Estate walking trails and free seasonal garden walks. Events, including open-air theatre and music in the summer. Children's trails all year. **Dogs**: welcome on short leads in the grounds (assistance dogs only in the walled garden).

Access:
Building **Grounds**
Sat Nav: use SO24 0NH – takes you to Hinton Arms pub, 21 yards west of main entrance.
Parking: on site.

Find out more: 01962 771305 or hintonampner@nationaltrust.org.uk

Hinton Ampner		M	T	W	T	F	S	S
House*								
4 Feb–31 Dec	11–3:30	**M**	**T**	**W**	**T**	**F**	**S**	**S**
Estate, garden, shop and tea-room								
Open all year**	10–5†	**M**	**T**	**W**	**T**	**F**	**S**	**S**

*House: closed 25 to 30 November for Christmas set up.
**Walled Garden and South Terrace: open all year.
†1 January to 3 February and 4 November to 31 December: open 10 to 4. Everything closed 25 and 26 December.

Light and airy Hinton Ampner in Hampshire is the fulfilment of one man's vision

Maidenhead and Cookham Commons

near Maidenhead, Berkshire

1934

Maidenhead and Cookham Commons, Berkshire

This chain of ancient commons offers footpaths through broadleaf woodlands, chalk downland, marshes dotted with orchids and hay meadows buzzing with insects in summer. These rich habitats are great for spotting wildlife throughout the year – you might see emperor dragonflies, marbled white butterflies, redwings, skylarks and fieldfares.

Eat, shop, stay: numerous shops, restaurants, pubs and cafés in nearby Cookham, Cookham Dean, Pinkneys Green and Maidenhead (none National Trust). Picnic on wildflower meadows.

Things to see and do: enjoy walking and horse-riding along bridleways and tree-lined avenues. Let your imagination run wild on family-friendly routes, with great places to try den-building and bug-hunting.
Dogs: welcome (please be mindful of ground-nesting birds and cattle grazing).

Sat Nav: use SL6 6QD for Pinkneys Green.
Parking: numerous on site.

Find out more: 01628 605069 or maidenheadandcookham@nationaltrust.org.uk

Mottisfont

near Romsey, Hampshire SO51 0LP

1957

Ancient trees, babbling brooks and rolling lawns frame this 18th-century house with a medieval priory at its heart. Maud Russell made Mottisfont her home in the 1930s, bringing artists here to relax and create works inspired by Mottisfont's past, including an extraordinary drawing room painted by Rex Whistler. We continue those artistic traditions today, with a permanent 20th-century art collection and major exhibitions in our top-floor gallery. Outside, carpets of spring bulbs, a walled rose garden, rich autumn leaves and a colourful winter garden create a feast for the senses all year round. Our world-famous collection of old-fashioned roses flowers once a year in June. There's space to run, jump and play, and always something for families to do.

Eat, shop, stay: Old Kitchen in house serving hot meals on china. Coach House Café in Stables offering lighter lunches on eco-friendly disposable tableware. Ice-cream parlour, additional kiosk in good weather. Shop and plant centre at Welcome Centre, second-hand bookshop in Stables.

Mottisfont, Hampshire: the rose garden in June, right, and the 18th-century house, below

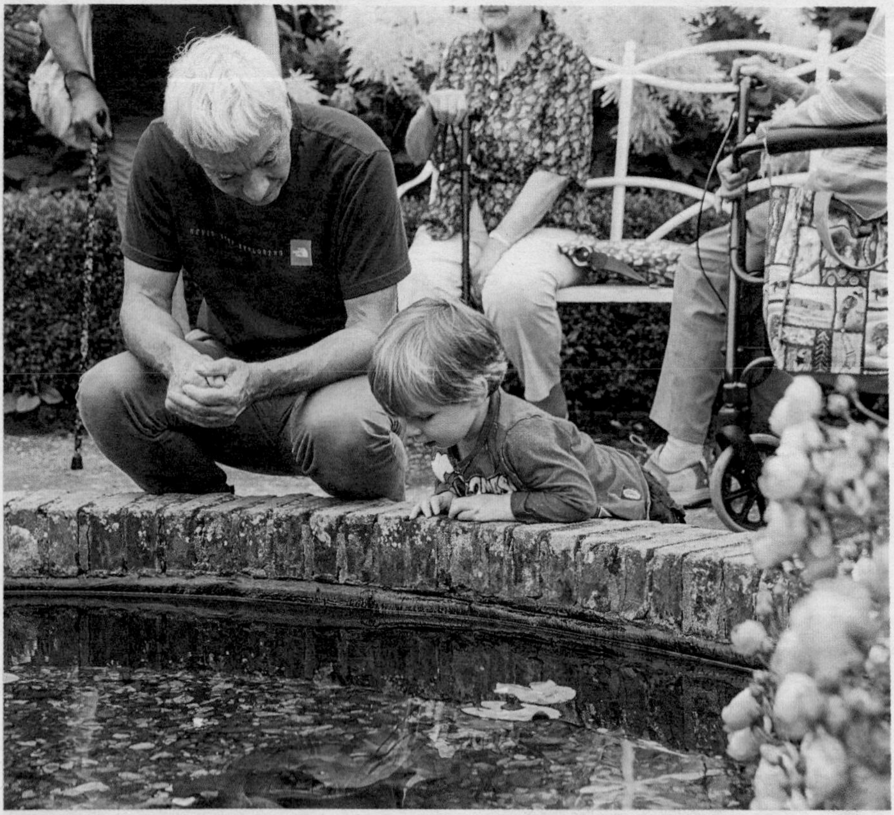

Nature-watching at Mottisfont, above, and examining the blooms in the rose garden, below

Things to see and do: **Indoors** Four major exhibitions in the art gallery every year – this year includes the artwork of Norman Thelwell and a summer family show with a creative quest trail. Changing layers of interpretation around the house, telling stories of the Russell family. **Outdoors** Free daily guided walks and talks. Family activities, including seasonal activity trails in school holidays and wild play areas. Open-air theatre events in summer. Other seasonal events throughout the year. Seasonal variety in the gardens. Wider woodland estate to explore on foot or by bike. **Dogs**: welcome on short leads at all times, with some restrictions inside the walled garden.

Access:
House **Gallery** **Grounds**
Sat Nav: use SO51 0LN. **Parking**: on site.

Find out more: 01794 340757 or mottisfont@nationaltrust.org.uk

Mottisfont	
Open every day all year	10–5*

*1 January to 3 February and 4 November to 31 December: closes 4. House and gallery open at 11. House closed 7 to 11 January and 11 to 22 November. Gallery closed in between exhibitions. Gardens open until 8 (last entry 7) Thursday to Saturday, 6 to 22 June. Everything closed 24 and 25 December.

Mottistone Gardens and Estate

Mottistone, near Brighstone,
Isle of Wight PO30 4ED

1965

Set in a sheltered valley, these 20th-century gardens are filled with shrub-lined banks, hidden pathways and colourful borders. They surround an ancient manor house (not open), and have a Mediterranean-style planting scheme, taking advantage of the southerly location, including drought-tolerant plants and an olive grove. Other features include a monocot border, an organic kitchen garden and a tea garden alongside The Shack, a cabin retreat designed as their summer drawing office by architects John Seely (2nd Lord Mottistone) and Paul Paget. A network of footpaths crosses the adjoining Mottistone Estate, taking walkers high onto the downs via the historic Longstone. **Note**: manor house open two days a year.

Eat, shop, stay: shop selling gifts, books, cards, local products and ice cream. Plant sales. Second-hand books. Tea garden serving drinks, seasonal soups, sandwiches, cake, cream teas and light refreshments. Three holiday cottages nearby – Mottistone Manor Farmhouse, Longstone Cottage and Rose Cottage.

Things to see and do: family events and garden tours. Flowerpot trail and estate walks. '50 things to do before you're 11¾' activities around the garden. The Needles Batteries and Headland are close by. **Dogs**: welcome on leads in the gardens, under close control around livestock on the estate.

Access:
The Shack **Garden**
Parking: 50 yards.

Find out more: 01983 741302 or mottistonegardens@nationaltrust.org.uk

Mottistone Gardens		M	T	W	T	F	S	S
Gardens								
10 Mar–31 Oct	10:30–5*	**M**	**T**	**W**	**T**	·	·	**S**
Shop								
7 Nov–21 Dec	11–3	·	·	·	**T**	**F**	**S**	·

Estate: open every day all year. *Gardens: close dusk if earlier. House: open two days only, 26 May by guided tour, 9:30 to 12 (timed ticket, available on day); freeflow 1 to 5, and 27 May, 10:30 to 5 by freeflow (additional charges apply).

Gardening, above, and herbaceous borders, below, at Mottistone Gardens and Estate on the Isle of Wight

The Needles Batteries and Headland

West High Down, Alum Bay, Isle of Wight PO39 0JH

1975

Walking from Freshwater Bay to The Needles Headland along Tennyson Down, there are views as far as Dorset. At the end, high above The Needles, amid acres of countryside, is the Needles Old Battery. This Victorian fortification built in 1862 was used throughout both world wars. The Parade Ground has two original guns, and the military history is brought to life with displays, models, and a series of vivid cartoons. An underground tunnel leads to a searchlight emplacement with dramatic views over the Needles Rocks at the tip of the island. The New Battery, further up the headland, was once a secret rocket-testing site and has an exhibition on the rocket tests carried out there during the Cold War. **Note**: steep paths and uneven surfaces. Spiral staircase to tunnel. Toilet at Old Battery only.

Eat, shop, stay: clifftop 1940s-style tea-room with stunning views serving soup, sandwiches, cakes, cream teas and light refreshments. Picnic tables. Shop selling ice cream, confectionery and gifts. Drinks, snacks and ice cream available at New Battery. Stay on at Coastguard clifftop holiday cottages.

The Needles Batteries and Headland: Old Battery, left, and New Battery, below

The Needles Batteries and Headland, Isle of Wight: visitors exploring the searchlight emplacement

Things to see and do: **Indoors** Soldier and photo trails. **Outdoors** Clifftop walks to Tennyson Monument and beyond.
Dogs: welcome on leads, assistance dogs only in upstairs tea-room, all dogs welcome downstairs.

Access:
Old Battery **New Battery**
Parking: no parking on site (limited disabled parking by arrangement). Nearest at Alum Bay, ¾ mile, not National Trust (minimum charge £5, with 20% reduction for National Trust members). Freshwater Bay, 3½ miles (not National Trust), or Highdown (196:SZ325856), 2 miles.

Find out more: 01983 754772 or needles@nationaltrust.org.uk

The Needles		M	T	W	T	F	S	S
Old Battery and tea-room								
9 Mar–3 Nov	10:30–5	M	T	W	T	F	S	S
Old Battery tea-room								
1 Jan–6 Jan	11–3	·	T	W	T	F	S	S
10 Jan–17 Feb	11–3	·	·	·	T	F	S	S
18 Feb–3 Mar	11–3	M	T	W	T	F	S	S
7 Nov–22 Dec	11–3	·	·	·	T	F	S	S
26 Dec–31 Dec	11–3	M	T	·	T	F	S	S
Needles Headland								
Open all year		M	T	W	T	F	S	S
New Battery								
9 Mar–3 Nov	11–4	M	T	W	T	F	S	S

Needles Batteries: close dusk if earlier and in high winds.
12 May: no disabled vehicular access due to Walk the Wight.
29 June: Old Battery early opening for Round the Island yacht race.

New Forest Commons and Foxbury

near East Wellow, Hampshire

1928

Woodland, grassland, heathland, bogs and mires make up the unique landscape of the New Forest Commons, a wilderness that's teeming with wildlife. The National Trust looks after commons at the following places: Bramshaw, Foxbury, Hale Purlieu, Hightown, as well as Rockford and Ibsley. Foxbury, a gateway to the New Forest, is a 150-hectare (370-acre) area of heathland restoration. Wide open spaces, gentle hillsides and hidden ponds are there to be discovered in this recovering landscape. This is a fragile conservation site for wildlife and we only allow access for special seasonal events. **Note**: all chargeable entrance and event fees in Foxbury apply to members.

Things to see and do: programme of events throughout the year at Foxbury focusing on the site's rich wildlife, including seasonal bird walks, volunteer tree-planting and Forest School for young children. **Dogs**: on leads or under close control March to July (due to nesting birds).

Sat Nav: follow the Omega signs; for Foxbury use SO51 6AQ, Bramshaw Commons SO51 6AQ; Hale Purlieu SP6 2QZ; Hightown Common BH24 3HH; Rockford and Ibsley Commons BH24 3NA. **Parking**: for Foxbury at Half Moon car park on Blackhill Road.

Find out more: 01425 650035 or newforest@nationaltrust.org.uk

New Forest Commons and Foxbury

For your safety we would not advise access to the New Forest between dusk and dawn. Foxbury is accessible for special seasonal events only.

New Forest Commons and Foxbury, Hampshire: heathland, above, and ponies, below

Newtown National Nature Reserve and Old Town Hall

Newtown, near Shalfleet,
Isle of Wight PO30 4PA

1933

On the water's edge, Newtown is home to a tranquil harbour, wildflower meadows and ancient woodland with rare butterflies and red squirrels. The only National Nature Reserve on the island, Newtown has been cared for by the National Trust since 1963. Tucked away in a tiny hamlet adjoining the National Nature Reserve is the small and quirky 17th-century Old Town Hall, the only remaining evidence of Newtown's former importance. This historic building was the second to be bought and donated to the National Trust by Ferguson's Gang who were battling against the sprawling development of England in the 1930s. **Note**: nearest toilet in the car park by the visitor point.

Eat, shop, stay: postcards, guidebooks, maps and souvenirs available at the Old Town Hall. Cold drinks, information and walks leaflets available at the visitor point.

The salt marsh at Newtown National Nature Reserve and Old Town Hall, Isle of Wight

Things to see and do: **Indoors** Children's quiz sheet. Exhibitions by local artists. **Outdoors** National Nature Reserve walks. Bird hides. Family activities. Seasonal events. **Dogs**: on a lead on National Nature Reserve (please observe local signs).

Access: **Building**
Parking: 15 yards.

Find out more: 01983 531785 (Old Town Hall). 01983 531622 (visitor point) or newtown@nationaltrust.org.uk

Newtown		M	T	W	T	F	S	S
Old Town Hall								
9 Mar–24 Oct	10:30–5*	·	**T**	**W**	**T**	·	**S**	**S**
Nature Reserve								
Open all year		**M**	**T**	**W**	**T**	**F**	**S**	**S**
Bird hide								
9 Mar–24 Oct	10–4	**M**	**T**	**W**	**T**	**F**	**S**	**S**

*Old Town Hall, last admission 15 minutes before closing. Closes dusk if earlier.

An oyster-catcher at Newtown National Nature Reserve

St Helens Duver

near St Helens, Isle of Wight

1928

Once a Victorian golf course with royal patronage, St Helens Duver has sandy beaches, hidden rock pools, undulating sand dunes and coastal woods to explore. It's also a fascinating place to look for wildlife, from burrowing digger wasps to wasp spiders and waterbirds over the harbour. **Note**: sorry no toilets.

Eat, shop, stay: why not stay for longer at one of two charming holiday cottages close to the Duver? Old Church Lodge, a single-storey Victorian stone cottage, sleeps four, while the Old Club House, an attractive wooden chalet overlooking the Duver, sleeps five.

Things to see and do: great spot for relaxing on the beach, exploring rock pools, admiring spring flowers or birdwatching across the harbour. You can take a coastal walk, or walk to Bembridge Windmill. **Dogs**: welcome under close control.

Sat Nav: use PO33 1XY. **Parking**: on site.

Find out more: 01983 741020 or sthelensduver@nationaltrust.org.uk

St Helens Duver, Isle of Wight: the salt marsh

Sandham Memorial Chapel

Harts Lane, Burghclere, near Newbury, Hampshire RG20 9JT

1947

Lose yourself in Stanley Spencer's extraordinarily powerful paintings, recollecting his First World War service as a medical orderly and soldier, housed within this tranquil space (above). An exhibition area gives historical context before you enter the Chapel, while the garden is somewhere to pause and reflect afterwards or perhaps to picnic.

Eat, shop, stay: small shop selling books, postcards, plants and local products. Picnics welcome.

Things to see and do: exhibition about the Chapel, paintings and the people who were instrumental in its creation. Orchard, beautiful wildflower meadow and new garden of reflection to explore. Events throughout the year. **Dogs**: in grounds on leads only.

Access: **Chapel** **Visitor reception/exhibition** **Grounds** **Parking**: opposite entrance to Chapel.

Find out more: 01635 278394 or sandham@nationaltrust.org.uk

Sandham Memorial Chapel		M	T	W	T	F	S	S
27 Feb–31 Oct*	11–4	·	·	W	T	F	S	S
1 Nov–22 Dec	11–3	·	·	·	·	F	S	S

*1 June to 25 August open to 5, weekends only. Open Bank Holiday Mondays, 11 to 4. Car park opposite Chapel available during normal opening hours, locked 15 minutes after closing. Chapel may be closed on certain days due to rehearsals for special events (please check before visiting).

The Vyne

Vyne Road, Sherborne St John, Basingstoke, Hampshire RG24 9HL

1956

Following major roof repairs last year the house is now fully open, including rooms never before open to the public. Visitors can discover the story of a brother and sister who became intertwined with The Vyne's survival; one the unexpected heir to the grand Tudor mansion, the other adopted as a companion. Outside, acres of wildlife-rich gardens, meadows and woods create a wonderful space for relaxation and exploration, while the play space gives children freedom to let their imagination take them on an adventure. Sweeping lawns offer lakeside picnicking, and a short stroll reveals a bird hide overlooking water meadows.

Eat, shop, stay: tea-room serving light lunches, soup, sandwiches, cakes and scones. Gift shop and plant sales. Second-hand bookshops in house and garden. Picnics welcome.

The wildlife-rich gardens at The Vyne, Hampshire, are perfect for explorers

The Vyne: the grand Tudor mansion, above, and visitors playing the piano, right

Things to see and do: **Indoors** Events and activities all year. Free guided tours. **Outdoors** Open-air theatre. Garden tours, trails and woodland walks. **Dogs**: welcome on short leads in woodland and gardens.

Access:
House **Grounds**
Sat Nav: not reliable, follow brown tourist signs. **Parking**: on site, limited in winter (October to April) due to ground conditions.

Find out more: 01256 883858 or thevyne@nationaltrust.org.uk

The Vyne	
Open every day all year	10–5*

*1 January to 3 February and 4 November to 31 December: closes 4. House: opens 11 for visit by tour or timed ticket (telephone for details). Shop: opens 11. Last entry one hour before closing. Closed 24 and 25 December.

West Green House Garden

West Green, Hartley Wintney, Hampshire RG27 8JB 1957

Four seasons of beauty, contrast and inspiration. Created by acclaimed garden designer and writer Marylyn Abbott. **Note**: maintained on behalf of the National Trust by Marylyn Abbott. Facilities not National Trust. Open Wednesday to Sunday, 6 March to 27 October and 7 to 30 November, 11 to 4:30, as well as 1 to 23 December, 11 to 7. Also open Bank Holiday Mondays.

Find out more: 01252 844611 or westgreenhouse@nationaltrust.org.uk

Winchester City Mill

Bridge Street, Winchester, Hampshire SO23 9BH

1929

This restored working watermill has stood at the heart of the city of Winchester for a millennium and is probably the oldest working watermill in the UK. As the official Gateway to the South Downs National Park, City Mill provides information for visitors wishing to explore local walks and attractions. **Note**: nearest toilet 220 yards (not National Trust).

Eat, shop, stay: shop selling local produce, gifts and books, as well as our freshly milled wholemeal flour.

Things to see and do: tours, workshops and exhibitions. School holiday quizzes and trails and seasonal events for the whole family, including Easter egg hunts. Flour-milling demonstrations every weekend and regular baking demonstrations. **Dogs**: assistance dogs only.

Access: Building
Sat Nav: do not use. **Parking**: at Chesil car park or park and ride, neither National Trust (charge including members).

Find out more: 01962 870057 or winchestercitymill@nationaltrust.org.uk

Winchester City Mill		M	T	W	T	F	S	S
1 Jan–24 Dec	10–5*	M	T	W	T	F	S	S

*1 January to 24 February and 4 November to 24 December: closes 4.

Learning about Winchester City Mill, Hampshire, right

Additional coastal and countryside car parks in Berkshire, Hampshire and the Isle of Wight

Berkshire

Simon's Wood	RG45 6AE

Isle of Wight

Bembridge and Culver Downs	PO36 8QY
Borthwood Copse	PO36 0LD
Knowles Farm	PO38 2NP
St Catherine's Hill and Down	PO38 2JB
Tennyson Down	PO39 0HY
Ventnor Downs	PO38 1AH

Kent, Surrey and Sussex

Having fun discovering beach beasties at Birling Gap and the Seven Sisters, East Sussex

Cliveden
Maidenhead and Cookham Commons
M25
M4
M3
M23
M26
M2
M20
Osterley Park
Ham House
Eastbury Manor House
Rainham Hall
Red House
Runnymede and Ankerwycke
Claremont Garden
Morden Hall Park
The Homewood
St John's Jerusalem
Owletts
Cobham Wood
Rochester
Margate
Hatchlands Park
Bookham Commons
Headley Heath
Clandon Park
Polesden Lacey
Box Hill
Reigate Hill and Gatton Park
Quebec House
Knole
Old Soar Manor
MAIDSTONE
Stoneacre
Faversham
Canterbury
Deal
Shalford Mill
Guildford
Denbies Hillside
Chartwell
Emmetts Garden
Ightham Mote
River Wey and Godalming Navigations and Dapdune Wharf
Abinger Roughs and Netley Park
Leith Hill Tower and Countryside
Leith Hill Place
Frensham Little Pond
Oakhurst Cottage
Winkworth Arboretum
Tunbridge Wells
Ashford
South Foreland Lighthouse
Dover
The White Cliffs
Hindhead Commons and the Devil's Punch Bowl
Standen House
Sissinghurst Castle Garden
Scotney Castle
Folkestone
Nymans
Wakehurst
Smallhythe Place
Harting Down
Haywards Heath
Sheffield Park
Bateman's
Bodiam Castle
Woolbeding Gardens
Petworth
Lamb House
Uppark House
Ditchling Beacon
Devil's Dyke
LEWES
Hailsham
Hastings
Slindon Estate
Brighton
Monk's House
Littlehampton
Worthing
Alfriston Clergy House
Bognor Regis
East Head
Eastbourne
Birling Gap and the Seven Sisters
A3
A31
A322
A331
A30
A40
A406
A41
A13
A2
A205
A20
A24
A232
A21
A22
A249
A299
A256
A28
A229
A26
A2070
A259
A264
A272
A23
A27
Buildings and/or gardens
Entry points to coast and countryside
National Trust land
Places in neighbouring counties
The Cotswolds and Chilterns, page 107
Berkshire, Hampshire and the Isle of Wight, page 135
London, page 199
10 miles

Abinger Roughs and Netley Park

White Downs Lane, Abinger Hammer, Surrey RH5 6QS 1940

Hidden woods with 300-year-old oak trees and flower-sprinkled grasslands make this the perfect spot for young nature explorers. **Note**: sorry no toilets.

Find out more: 01306 887485 (rangers) or abingerroughs@nationaltrust.org.uk

Alfriston Clergy House

The Tye, Alfriston, Polegate, East Sussex BN26 5TL

 1896

This rare 14th-century Wealden 'hall-house' was the first building to be acquired by the National Trust, in 1896. The thatched, timber-framed house is in an idyllic setting, with views across the River Cuckmere, and is surrounded by a tranquil cottage garden full of wildlife. **Note**: nearest toilet in village car park.

Alfriston Clergy House, East Sussex, above and below: the first house acquired by the National Trust

Eat, shop, stay: shop selling souvenirs, plants and gifts.

Things to see and do: **Indoors** Children's quizzes and trails. Varied events all year. **Outdoors** Short circular walks and longer hikes over the South Downs.
Dogs: assistance dogs only.

Access:
Building **Grounds**
Parking: 500 yards in village car parks (not National Trust).

Find out more: 01323 871961 or alfriston@nationaltrust.org.uk

Alfriston Clergy House		M	T	W	T	F	S	S
2 Mar–3 Jul	10:30–5	M	T	W	·	·	S	S
5 Jul–30 Aug	10:30–5	M	T	W	·	F	S	S
31 Aug–3 Nov	10:30–5	M	T	W	·	·	S	S
9 Nov–22 Dec	11–4	·	·	·	·	·	S	S

Open Good Friday.

Bateman's

Bateman's Lane, Burwash,
East Sussex TN19 7DS

1940

Bateman's remains today as Kipling described it in 1902: 'A grey stone lichened house – AD 1634 over the door – beamed, panelled, with oak staircase all untouched and unfaked... It is a good and peaceable place, standing in terraced lawns nigh to a walled garden of old red brick and two fat-headed old oast houses with red brick stomachs and an aged silver-grey dovecot [*sic*] on top.' Much of Kipling's belongings remain as he left them. Paths wind past Kipling's 1928 Rolls-Royce, through manicured lawns and a wildflower meadow. A 17th-century working watermill stands beside the River Dudwell.

Eat, shop, stay: shop selling Kipling souvenirs and plants from the garden. Scullery bookshop specialising in pre-loved classic story books. Tea-room offering seasonal lunches, made using fresh produce from our kitchen garden, homemade cakes and light bites. Open-air seating in walled garden.

Giant gunnera at Bateman's, East Sussex, left, and the tranquil lily pond, above

Things to see and do: Indoors Explore the house as Kipling left it, the beautiful setting inspiring many of his best-known works. Seasonal talks and tours. **Outdoors** Walks, trails, storytelling and children's play area. **Dogs**: welcome on short leads in the garden and on the estate (seasonal cattle grazing).

Access:
Building **Grounds**
Parking: 30 yards.

Find out more: 01435 882302 or batemans@nationaltrust.org.uk

Bateman's		M	T	W	T	F	S	S
House								
1 Jan–1 Mar*	11–4*	**M**	**T**	**W**	**T**	**F**	**S**	**S**
2 Mar–27 Oct	11–5	**M**	**T**	**W**	**T**	**F**	**S**	**S**
28 Oct–31 Dec*	11–4*	**M**	**T**	**W**	**T**	**F**	**S**	**S**
Garden, shop and tea-room								
Open all year	10–5**	**M**	**T**	**W**	**T**	**F**	**S**	**S**

*7 January to 1 March, except February half term and 4 November to 29 November: entry to house on weekdays by guided tour only. **1 January to 15 February and 28 October to 31 December: closes 4. Closed 24 and 25 December.

Birling Gap and the Seven Sisters

near Eastbourne, East Sussex

1931

For drama, nothing beats the point where the sheer chalk cliffs of the South Downs meet the sea. One of the south coast's longest undeveloped stretches, the Seven Sisters are truly iconic. If you venture down the steps onto the beach, you can discover fascinating rock pools and the intricate wave-cut platform. The café and shop are a delightful place to start or end your peaceful downland walk. Before you explore the rare chalk heath and grassland, why not pick up a Tracker Pack or get some friendly advice from the visitor welcome team? **Note**: unstable cliff edge, stay at least 5 yards away from edge and from cliff base.

Eat, shop, stay: licensed clifftop café serving hot and cold drinks, bottled beer and wine, light lunches, cream teas and cakes. Drinks and sandwiches available to take away. Seaside shop selling gifts and seasonal items. Picnic area outside shop.

Things to see and do: rock-pooling, countryside walks and stargazing. Crowlink downland, on top of the Seven Sisters, Alfriston Clergy House and Monk's House nearby. Events and activities for all ages. **Dogs**: welcome in café, shop and on beach. Always on leads near livestock.

Access: Café Shop
Sat Nav: use BN20 0AB.
Parking: at Birling Gap.

Find out more: 01323 423197 or birlinggap@nationaltrust.org.uk

Birling Gap and the Seven Sisters	
Café and shop	
Open every day all year†	10–5*

*1 January to 16 February and 3 November to 31 December: close 4. †Closed 24 and 25 December.

Heading off for a hard day's rock-pooling at Birling Gap and the Seven Sisters in East Sussex

Bodiam Castle

Bodiam, near Robertsbridge, East Sussex TN32 5UA

1926

A brooding symbol of power for more than 700 years, the strong stone walls of Bodiam Castle rise up proudly from the peaceful river valley setting. A wide moat encircles the seemingly untouched medieval exterior. Once inside, spiral stairways, tower rooms and battlements with dizzying viewpoints are ripe for exploration. **Note**: popular with schools. Main toilets in car park. Portaloos at top of site (main season).

Eat, shop, stay: shop selling gifts and castle-themed products. Main tea-room serving homemade lunches and hot drinks. Castle View Café opposite castle entrance serving takeaway hot drinks, snacks and ice cream.

Things to see and do: **Indoors** Story of Bodiam display and film. Conservation programme revealing Bodiam's hidden collection. Bi-annual exhibition programme. **Outdoors** Trails and guided walks. Various events throughout the year.
Dogs: welcome on leads in grounds only.

Access:
Castle **Grounds**
Parking: 400 yards.

Find out more: 01580 830196 or bodiamcastle@nationaltrust.org.uk

Bodiam Castle		M	T	W	T	F	S	S
Castle								
1 Jan–1 Mar*	11–4	M	T	W	T	F	S	S
2 Mar–27 Oct	11–5	M	T	W	T	F	S	S
28 Oct–31 Dec*	11–4	M	T	W	T	F	S	S
Shop, tea-room and grounds								
Open all year**	10–5	M	T	W	T	F	S	S

*7 January to 1 March (except February half term) and 4 November to 29 November: entry to castle on weekdays by guided tour only. **1 January to 15 February and 28 October to 31 December: close 4. Closed 24 and 25 December.

Moated medieval Bodiam Castle, East Sussex

For information about getting to National Trust places, please see page 3

Bookham Commons

Church Road, Great Bookham, Surrey KT23 3LT

1923

Bookham Commons, Surrey: haven for wildlife

Enchanting ancient oak woodland, grassland plains and tranquil ponds. Listen out for tuneful nightingales and warblers in the spring and in summer look for insects hovering over the ponds. If you're lucky, you may also spot the beautiful, but elusive, purple emperor butterfly. **Note**: sorry no toilets.

Eat, shop, stay: refreshments available at Ye Olde Windsor Castle, Little Bookham and in Great Bookham village (none National Trust).

Things to see and do: bird hide and natural play area. Seasonal guided walks.
Dogs: on leads when livestock are grazing.

Access:
Sat Nav: use KT23 3LT.
Parking: at Tunnel, Mark Oak Gate and Hundred Pound Bridge car parks.

Find out more: 01306 887485 or bookhamcommons@nationaltrust.org.uk

Box Hill

Tadworth, Surrey

1914

A great place for family adventures: delving into the ancient woodland, exploring the natural play trail, finding the tower or discovering the River Mole at the Stepping Stones. On a clear day you can see for miles from the top of Box Hill, so if you're hiking up, the stunning views are well worth it. You can pick up free trail leaflets from the shepherd's hut and outside the café, or find your own way along the many footpaths.

Summer at Box Hill in Surrey, below, and in winter's icy grip, bottom

Setting out to enjoy a spot of kite-flying at Box Hill

Eat, shop, stay: the Box Hill café has indoor and outdoor seating and serves light lunches, snacks, sandwiches and cakes. The servery offers takeaway hot drinks, sandwiches and cakes as well as the famous 'revival' flapjack!

Things to see and do: home to the popular Box Hill Bugs (booking essential), borrow a children's Tracker Pack from the shepherd's hut. Guided walks and a variety of self-led trails available. **Dogs**: under close control where livestock are grazing. Assistance dogs only in café.

Access: Café Grounds
Sat Nav: use KT20 7LB (but doesn't work for all Sat Navs). **Parking**: off the Box Hill Zig Zag road (short walk to café and viewpoint).

Find out more: 01306 888793.
01306 878554 (learning and events) or
boxhill@nationaltrust.org.uk

Box Hill	
Café	
Open every day all year	10–5*

*1 January to 30 March and 28 October to 31 December: closes 4. Closed 25 December.

Chartwell

Mapleton Road, Westerham, Kent TN16 1PS

1946

Chartwell was the family home of Sir Winston Churchill, the place that brought him comfort and inspiration. Filled with treasures and personal belongings from every aspect of his life, this intimate house invites you into the private world of one of Britain's greatest leaders. Follow in the footsteps of one of the many frequent guests who are recorded in the visitor book. His studio contains the largest collection of Churchill's paintings and offers an insight into Churchill the painter. The garden reflects Churchill's love of landscape and nature, including the lakes he created. There are lots of fun things to do in our woodland area: a tree house, Donkey Jack's Caravan, swings, a bomb crater and much more to explore. **Note**: house entry by timed ticket (available on website). Chartwell can be challenging for less able.

Eat, shop, stay: café serving food inspired by Churchill's family cook – hot dishes, salads, light bites, cream teas, cakes and delicious desserts. Shop stocking Churchill memorabilia, books, garden ornaments, plants and local produce, as well as a special range of Chartwell-inspired items.

Sir Winston Churchill's family home, Chartwell in Kent, is full of his personal belongings

Things to see and do: **Indoors** New family guide. Daily talks in the studio about Sir Winston's love of painting. New exhibition displaying never-seen-before items. **Outdoors** A tree house in the woods, similar to the tree house Churchill built for his children. Guided tours of Churchill's family garden on selected days (March to October). The woodland trail offers distant views of the house and connects with the hilly 5-mile circular Weardale Walk to Emmetts Garden. Why not pick up some takeaway food from the café and enjoy a picnic on the lower lawns by the lakes? **Dogs**: welcome on short leads in the garden and estate.

Access: **Building** **Grounds**
Parking: on site.

Find out more: 01732 868381 or chartwell@nationaltrust.org.uk

Chartwell		M	T	W	T	F	S	S
House								
1 Mar–3 Nov	11:30–5*	**M**	**T**	**W**	**T**	**F**	**S**	**S**
30 Nov–15 Dec	11–3	·	·	·	·	·	**S**	**S**
Garden, exhibition, studio, shop and café								
Open all year	10–5**	**M**	**T**	**W**	**T**	**F**	**S**	**S**

*House: entry by timed ticket (available on day from visitor welcome centre); also available at least 24 hours in advance via website or by calling 0344 249 1895 (places limited).
****1 January to 3 February and 28 October to 31 December: close 4.** Studio open times vary. Everything closed 24 and 25 December.

Statue of Sir Winston and his wife, Clementine, in the garden at Chartwell

Clandon Park

West Clandon, Guildford, Surrey GU4 7RQ

1956

Clandon Park, Surrey: huge restoration project

A major restoration project is under way at Clandon Park, to breathe new life into this Palladian marvel following the fire in 2015. The house and garden will offer different types of access throughout the year, providing a unique opportunity to follow the Trust's progress as Clandon is rebuilt. **Note**: please check the website for the latest information.

Access: **Building**
Sat Nav: follow brown signs to the entrance on the A247. **Parking**: 250 yards.

Find out more: 01483 222482 or clandonpark@nationaltrust.org.uk

Clandon Park		M	T	W	T	F	S	S
Basement, ground floor and garden*								
20 Mar–3 Nov**	10–5	·	·	**W**	**T**	**F**	**S**	**S**

*Different parts of the house and wider site may be open at different times as the project progresses.
**Also open Bank Holiday Mondays.

Claremont Landscape Garden

Portsmouth Road, Esher, Surrey KT10 9JG

1949

Hidden in the heart of Surrey, this green oasis has always been a place to escape everyday life and enjoy simple pleasures. Formerly a sanctuary for the wealthiest and most influential people in the country, now everyone can enjoy this 'Capability' Brown landscape garden. The impressive turf amphitheatre offers wonderful views over the lake, and walks take in key features such as the grotto and camellia terrace. Queen Victoria loved relaxing here from a young age, and the tradition of play continues today with nine-pin bowling, play areas and our Thatched Cottage, which is full of toys and games.

Eat, shop, stay: café located outside pay barrier serving seasonal hot lunches, along with freshly made sandwiches and bakes. We have free Wi-Fi and a small shop area. The Cube kiosk by the play area also offers hot and cold drinks and snacks.

Things to see and do: events throughout the year, including children's trails and crafts during school holidays. Guided walks. Belvedere Tower open on selected dates (April to October). Boat hire, subject to availability. **Dogs**: welcome on short leads between 1 October and 30 April only.

Access: Grounds
Sat Nav: unreliable; instead follow brown signs from Cobham and Esher. **Parking**: main car park at entrance. Space limited at busy times – please use car park in West End Lane opposite.

Find out more: 01372 467806 or claremont@nationaltrust.org.uk

Claremont Landscape Garden		M	T	W	T	F	S	S
1 Jan–31 Jan	10–4	**M**	**T**	**W**	**T**	**F**	**S**	**S**
1 Feb–25 Mar	10–5	**M**	**T**	**W**	**T**	**F**	**S**	**S**
26 Mar–28 Oct	10–6	**M**	**T**	**W**	**T**	**F**	**S**	**S**
29 Oct–31 Dec	10–4*	**M**	**T**	**W**	**T**	**F**	**S**	**S**

Café and shop close 30 minutes earlier than garden.
*Closed 24 and 25 December.

Claremont Landscape Garden is a green oasis hidden in the heart of Surrey

Cobham Wood and Mausoleum

near Cobham, Kent 2014

Sitting proud in historic woodland pasture, the 18th-century Darnley Mausoleum commands stunning views across the North Kent downs. **Note**: for Sat Nav use DA12 3BS. Access to mausoleum on foot only, about 1 mile from South Lodge Barn. Mausoleum and South Lodge Barn normally open first Sunday of month, April to September, and selected other dates. Mausoleum open 12:30 to 4:30; South Lodge Barn 12 to 5.

Find out more: 01732 810378 or cobham@nationaltrust.org.uk

Denbies Hillside

near Dorking, Surrey

1963

Denbies Hillside is a dramatic chalk escarpment with panoramic views of the Surrey countryside. It's a great place to walk, picnic and watch wildlife – you may even spot chalk downland species such as the Adonis blue and chalkhill blue butterflies.

Eat, shop, stay: picnic area with benches in Steers Field.

Things to see and do: self-guided trail and spectacular views. Walk west along the North Downs Way to discover several Second World War pillboxes. Red kites, kestrels and buzzards can often be seen here.
Dogs: welcome – please keep on leads when livestock are grazing.

Access:
Sat Nav: use RH5 6SR.
Parking: at Denbies Hillside.

Find out more: 01306 887485 or denbieshillside@nationaltrust.org.uk

Ponies and Belted Galloway cattle graze the steep slopes of Denbies Hillside in Surrey

Devil's Dyke

near Brighton, West Sussex

1995

At nearly a mile long, the Dyke Valley is the longest, deepest and widest 'dry valley' in the UK. Legend has it that the Devil dug this chasm to drown the parishioners of the Weald. On the other hand, scientists believe it was formed naturally just over 10,000 years ago in the last ice age. The walls of the Iron Age hill fort can be seen when you walk around the hill, and there is a carpet of flowers and a myriad of colourful insects to discover in the valley.

Eat, shop, stay: Devil's Dyke pub (not National Trust) beside car park.

Things to see and do: self-guided walks leaflet, orienteering course map and family Discovery Packs available from information

Devil's Dyke in West Sussex, above and below, is the longest, deepest 'dry valley' in the UK

trailer (open April to September, weekends and some weekdays). Numerous bridleways offer great cycling. **Dogs**: welcome, on leads where stock grazing.

Access:
Sat Nav: use BN1 8YJ. **Parking**: on site.

Find out more: 01273 857712 or devilsdyke@nationaltrust.org.uk

Ditchling Beacon

near Ditchling, Westmeston, East Sussex

1953

Just 7 miles north of Brighton, at 248 metres above sea level, Ditchling Beacon is the highest point in East Sussex and offers panoramic views all around the summit. To the south visitors can see the sea, while to the north you look across the Weald or east-west across the Downs. The site also has the remains of an Iron Age hill fort. Situated on the South Downs Way, it makes an excellent place to start a walk heading west towards Devil's Dyke or east towards Black Cap and Lewes.

Eat, shop, stay: refreshments available from ice-cream van. Picnics welcome.

Things to see and do: great for bracing walks with amazing views on the South Downs. Traces of the rampart and ditch of the hill fort to discover. Why not visit nearby Ditchling Down? **Dogs**: welcome but must be kept on leads at all times.

The highest point in East Sussex, Ditchling Beacon, above and below, offers panoramic views

Access: P

Sat Nav: use BN6 8XG.
Parking: off Ditchling Road.

Find out more: 01323 423197 or ditchlingbeacon@nationaltrust.org.uk

East Head

near Chichester, West Sussex 1966

One of the last surviving areas of natural coastline in West Sussex, with unspoilt sand dunes and fabulous views.
Note: for Sat Nav use PO20 8AJ.
Park at West Wittering Estate car park, not National Trust (charge including members).

Find out more: 01243 814730 or easthead@nationaltrust.org.uk

Emmetts Garden

Ide Hill, Sevenoaks, Kent TN14 6BA

1965

Emmetts is a rare, stunning Edwardian garden known for its beautiful bluebells and spring colour. Summer brings the romantic rose garden, followed by vibrant autumn foliage – there is something to see all year, as well as wonderful views across the Weald of Kent that can be enjoyed from the garden and on our countryside walks. Emmetts is a garden to enjoy with friends and family, a place where you can let off steam, play games, picnic in our meadow or simply sit back and relax. **Note**: a five-year restoration scheme is under way in some areas of the garden.

Emmetts Garden in Kent, above and left: a rare and romantic Edwardian gem

Eat, shop, stay: the Old Stables serving cakes, bakes and light refreshments. Shop selling a variety of products for the home, garden and outdoors, books, souvenirs and children's toys. Venture outside to the plant area for an array of plants and garden products.

Things to see and do: **Indoors** Children's activities in the Discovery Cabin. **Outdoors** Children's trails in the school holidays, a wild play area, including swings and a tepee. Garden tours (selected days). Downloadable walks available. **Dogs**: welcome on short leads in gardens and in the wider countryside.

Access: **Grounds**
Parking: 100 yards.

Find out more: 01732 751507 or emmetts@nationaltrust.org.uk

Emmetts Garden	
Open every day all year	10–5*

*1 January to 3 February and 28 October to 31 December: closes 4. Closed 24 and 25 December.

Frensham Little Pond

Priory Lane, Frensham, Surrey GU10 3BT

1974

Frensham Little Pond, Surrey: sanctuary for wildlife

Originally created in the 11th century to supply the Bishop of Winchester with fish, the pond and surrounding area is now a sanctuary for wildlife. The heathland is a colourful mosaic of purple heathers, fragrant bright-yellow gorse and rich green bracken with many footpaths to explore. **Note**: toilet available only when café open. Swimming isn't allowed to protect the wildlife habitats.

Eat, shop, stay: Tern Café serving snacks, homemade sandwiches and cakes (outside seating only). Picnics welcome (no barbecues please).

Things to see and do: bird hide and telescope next to café. Swimming available at Frensham Great Pond only. **Dogs**: on leads from March to September and around café.

Access:
Parking: at Priory Lane corner and main car park.

Find out more: 01428 681050 (rangers) or frenshamlittlepond@nationaltrust.org.uk

Frensham Little Pond		M	T	W	T	F	S	S
Café								
4 Jan–24 Mar*	10–3	·	·	·	·	F	S	S
25 Mar–3 Nov	10–5	M	T	W	T	F	S	S
8 Nov–29 Dec**	10–3	·	·	·	·	F	S	S

*18 to 24 February: open daily, 10 to 3. **Closed 24 and 25 December.

Harting Down

Harting Down, near South Harting, West Sussex GU31 5PN 1994

A tapestry of downland with scattered scrub and woodland, rich in wildlife and steeped in history. **Note**: nearest toilets at South Harting or Uppark. Sat Nav unreliable.

Find out more: 01730 816638 or hartingdown@nationaltrust.org.uk

Hatchlands Park

East Clandon, Guildford, Surrey GU4 7RT

1945

With open fields, ancient woodland and wildflower meadows, the parkland is perfect for relaxation and exploration. Our natural adventure area, with its tree house, balance beams, willow tunnels and bug burrow, is a great place for families to get even closer to nature. Nestled in the parkland is a Georgian country house, built for naval hero Admiral Boscawen and his bluestocking wife, Fanny. The interior is the earliest documented work in an English country house by celebrated

Hatchlands Park in Surrey, below, is surrounded by meadows, woods and parkland, right

Neo-classical architect Robert Adam. Today, the ground-floor rooms display the Cobbe Collection, Europe's largest array of keyboard instruments. **Note**: only six ground-floor rooms open.

Eat, shop, stay: café in the original kitchen. Dog-friendly Coach House Café. Gift shop. Pre-loved bookshop in the Old Stable. Picnic areas.

Things to see and do: **Indoors** Guided mansion tours most Thursdays. Cellar tours (selected days). **Outdoors** Children's adventure area, courtyard garden and open-air theatre. **Dogs**: welcome under close control in the parkland and designated areas. Dog-friendly Coach House Café.

Access: [access symbols]
Building [symbols] **Grounds** [symbols]
Sat Nav: follow brown signs to main entrance on A246 (grid reference TQ06349 51580).
Parking: 300 yards.

Find out more: 01483 222482 or hatchlands@nationaltrust.org.uk

Hatchlands Park		M	T	W	T	F	S	S
House and garden								
2 Apr–3 Nov*	2–5†	·	**T**	**W**	**T**	·	·	**S**
Shop, café and park walks								
Open all year	10–5††	**M**	**T**	**W**	**T**	**F**	**S**	**S**

*Also open Bank Holiday Mondays and Fridays in August. †Garden: open 10 to 5 on house open days. ††1 January to 3 February and 4 November to 31 December: close 4. Closed 24 and 25 December.

Headley Heath

Headley Common Road, Headley Heath, Surrey KT18 6NN 1946

A wide network of tracks to explore, featuring a wonderful mosaic of heath, chalk downland and mixed woodland. **Note**: cattle grazing (please look out for notices and keep dogs on leads when nearby). Car parks at Headley Heath and Brimmer.

Find out more: 01306 885502 (rangers) or headleyheath@nationaltrust.org.uk

Hindhead Commons and the Devil's Punch Bowl

near Hindhead, Surrey

1906

Spectacular views from Hindhead Commons and uninterrupted walks to the Devil's Punch Bowl make this an unforgettable place to relax and take in some of the best countryside in the South East. Since the opening of the A3 tunnel, paths and bridleways have been reconnected and natural contours restored. Peace and calm now reign and the glorious landscape, with its carpets of purple heather in the summer and grazing Highland cattle, is there to enjoy. **Note**: car-park renovation works planned.

Eat, shop, stay: café with indoor and outdoor seating, serving drinks, hot food, sandwiches and cakes. New 'grab and go' kiosk offering takeaway options.

Things to see and do: walks leaflets available from the café and membership hut. Borrow a children's Tracker Pack at weekends to explore the wild and make the most of your visit. **Dogs**: under close control during bird-nesting season (March to October). Assistance dogs only in café.

Hindhead Commons and the Devil's Punch Bowl, Surrey, above and left: wonderful walks and views

Access:
Café and shop **Grounds**
Sat Nav: use GU26 6AB.
Parking: off the London Road.

Find out more: 01428 681050 (rangers). 01428 608771 (café) or hindhead@nationaltrust.org.uk

Hindhead Commons	
Café	
Open every day all year*	9–5**

*Closed 25 December. **1 January to 16 February and 28 October to 31 December: closes 4.

The Homewood

Portsmouth Road, Esher, Surrey KT10 9JL 1999

Patrick Gwynne's extraordinary early 20th-century family home is a masterpiece of Modernist design in the midst of a picturesque garden. **Note**: administered on behalf of the National Trust by tenant. Toilets and café at Claremont. **Access by booked tour only, via minibus from Claremont Landscape Garden**. Additional charge for tours (including members). Usually open first and third Friday and the second and fourth Saturday of every month, 1 April to 31 October. Guided tours at 10:30, 11:30, 12:30, 2 and 3 (45 minutes).

Find out more: 01372 476424 or thehomewood@nationaltrust.org.uk c/o Claremont Landscape Garden, Portsmouth Road, Esher, Surrey KT10 9JG

Ightham Mote

Mote Road, Ivy Hatch, Sevenoaks,
Kent TN15 0NT

1985

Hidden away in a secluded Kent valley is this perfectly preserved medieval moated manor house. Created in the natural landscape almost 700 years ago, Ightham Mote is built from Kentish ragstone and great Wealden oaks. While its architecture and decoration trace the development of the English country house, its owners provide the stories of a once-cherished family home, evoking a deep sense of history. In the tranquil gardens there are streams and lakes fed by natural springs, an orchard, flower borders and a cutting garden. The wider estate offers walks with secret glades and countryside views. **Note**: very steep slope from visitor reception – passenger buggy or lower drop-off available.

Eat, shop, stay: licensed café serving freshly baked produce, barista-style coffee, sandwiches, light lunches, cream teas and cakes. Free Wi-Fi. Seating indoors and outside. Takeaway kiosk open during busy periods. Picnic facilities available. Shop selling souvenirs, gifts, local products and plants.

Things to see and do: **Indoors** Introductory talks, tower tours and conservation exhibition. Quizzes. **Outdoors** Tours and walks. Events, including theatre and music. Natural play area, garden trails and themed Thursdays (school holidays) for families. **Dogs**: welcome on surrounding estate and café patio. Assistance dogs only in garden and house.

Access:
Building **Grounds**
Sat Nav: use TN15 0NU. **Parking**: 100 yards.

Find out more: 01732 810378 or ighthammote@nationaltrust.org.uk

Ightham Mote		M	T	W	T	F	S	S
House*								
1 Jan	11-3	·	**T**	·	·	·	·	·
2 Mar-27 Oct	11-5	**M**	**T**	**W**	**T**	**F**	**S**	**S**
30 Nov-31 Dec	11-3	**M**	**T**	**W**	**T**	**F**	**S**	**S**
Garden, café, exhibition and shop								
Open all year	10-5**	**M**	**T**	**W**	**T**	**F**	**S**	**S**

Estate open all year. *Partial access to house and grounds in winter, with selected rooms decorated for Christmas. **1 January to 1 March and 28 October to 31 December: close 4. Closed 24 and 25 December.

Ightham Mote in Kent: medieval perfection

Knole

Sevenoaks, Kent TN15 0RP

1946

Sitting proudly within Kent's last medieval deer park, Knole offers something for everyone. You can immerse yourself in the vast estate and follow in the footsteps of tourists who have visited Knole's show rooms for 400 years. The show rooms have reopened following a £20 million conservation project. A world-class collection of paintings and furniture awaits, improved by new lighting, displays and acquisitions. Spend the day and take in panoramic views from the top of the Gatehouse Tower, where you can also explore the life and loves of a former resident. On a short visit, take in the scale and magnificence of this 600-year-old estate by exploring the grand courtyards or wandering through the parkland, still populated by wild deer.

Eat, shop, stay: Brewhouse Café serving delicious hot and cold food, with outdoor seating available on the roof terrace. Enclosed picnic area in the park. Gift shop, plant sales and bookshop with children's area.

Things to see and do: **Indoors** Explore the vast property, including the atmospheric courtyards, Orangery, historic show rooms and tower. Join a tour of the show rooms or recently opened attics on select days of the week (subject to availability). Find out how our conservators care for the National Trust's treasures in the Knole Conservation Studio (Wednesday to Saturday). We also have an exciting programme of events all year. **Outdoors** Join a guided walk or follow the waymarked trails to explore the ancient parkland, still home to a herd of wild deer. **Dogs**: welcome in parkland/courtyards on leads. Café, shop, garden, tower, show rooms – assistance dogs only.

Access: **Show rooms** **Gatehouse Tower** **Park/garden**
Sat Nav: use TN13 1HU and follow brown signs to Sevenoaks High Street (entrance opposite St Nicholas Church). **Parking**: 60 yards. Additional parking in town centre.

Find out more: 01732 462100 or knole@nationaltrust.org.uk

Knole		M	T	W	T	F	S	S
Show rooms								
2 Mar–3 Nov*	11–5	·	T	W	T	F	S	S
Gatehouse Tower								
Open all year	11–5**	M	T	W	T	F	S	S
Café, courtyards, shop, parkland								
Open all year	10–5**	M	T	W	T	F	S	S
Conservation Studio								
2 Jan–28 Dec	11–5**	·	·	W	T	F	S	·

*Open Bank Holiday Mondays, April to August.
**November to January (inclusive): closes 4.
Closed 24 and 25 December.

Magnificent Knole, left, sits within Kent's last medieval deer park. The show rooms have all reopened, top left, following a huge conservation project, although the work never stops, below

Lamb House

West Street, Rye, East Sussex TN31 7ES

[icons] 1950

Georgian home of writers Henry James and E. F. Benson, who depicted the property in the *Mapp and Lucia* stories. Considerable conservation work was completed last year allowing us to open new rooms, including the upstairs of the house for the first time. **Note**: limited access for buggies and wheelchairs. On-going conservation work.

Eat, shop, stay: small café offering hot and cold drinks, cakes and cream teas. Outside seating available in the courtyard. Selection of James and Benson books for sale.

Things to see and do: **Indoors** More of the house open to discover, especially on the first and second floors. New interpretation throughout. **Outdoors** Inspiring and relaxing garden designed by Alfred Parsons.
Dogs: assistance dogs only.

Access: [icon] **Building** [icon] **Grounds** [icon]
Parking: no on-site parking.
Nearest car parks in Rye, not National Trust (charge including members).

Find out more: 01797 222909 or lambhouse@nationaltrust.org.uk

Lamb House		M	T	W	T	F	S	S
House and tea-room								
1 Mar–29 Oct	11–5*	**M**	**T**	·	·	**F**	**S**	**S**

*Tea-room: closes 4:30.

Leith Hill Place

Leith Hill Lane, near Coldharbour, Dorking, Surrey RH5 6LY

[icons] 1945

Childhood home of English composer Ralph Vaughan Williams, once owned by the Wedgwood family and visited by Charles Darwin. Opened to the public in 2013 for the first time in 40 years, the house is being used as a trial base for new innovations. Glorious views over the South Downs. **Note**: parking access across sloping field (often muddy).

Eat, shop, stay: small kitchen run by volunteer bakers serving hot drinks and fresh bakes. Original AGA, stone-flagged dining room and outside seating on terrace or courtyard garden. Camping at nearby Etherley Farm (not National Trust) or group stay at Henman Bunkhouse.

Things to see and do: **Indoors** Children's trails and activities. Special events, including concerts and workshops. Small museum area with Vaughan Williams's piano displayed. **Outdoors** Footpaths connect the house with the tower and rhododendron wood.
Dogs: welcome on leads in grounds and some areas of house.

Access: [icons] **House** [icon]
Courtyard garden/south terrace [icons]
Sat Nav: use RH5 6LU.
Parking: Rhododendron Wood car park, 437 yards, in Tanhurst Lane.

Find out more: 01306 711685 or leithhillplace@nationaltrust.org.uk

Leith Hill Place		M	T	W	T	F	S	S
29 Mar–27 Oct*	11–5	·	·	·	·	**F**	**S**	**S**

Open Bank Holiday Mondays. *Closed Sunday 28 July, due to RideLondon cycle race.

 For other ways to get involved go to nationaltrust.org.uk/volunteer

Leith Hill Tower and Countryside

near Coldharbour village, Dorking, Surrey

1923

Built in 1765 by Richard Hull of Leith Hill Place, the top of Leith Hill Tower is the highest point in south-east England. From here there are unbeatable views north to the high-rise buildings of London, and to the south it's possible to see the sea sparkling through Shoreham Gap. This is glorious walking country, with iconic views of the local heathland and pastoral farmland landscapes. Every season is a riot of colour – starting with the spring bluebells at Frank's Wood, the early summer colour at the Rhododendron Wood, then the stunning autumnal displays of golds and reds. **Note**: steep spiral stairs to the top of the tower; no toilet or parking at tower.

Eat, shop, stay: hot and cold food and drinks available at Leith Hill Tower (not National Trust), tea and cake available at Leith Hill Place, when open. Picnics welcome, but no barbecues please. Self-catering accommodation at Henman Bunkhouse for up to 16 people.

Things to see and do: **Indoors** Small exhibition room outlining the history of the tower. **Outdoors** Two free telescopes at top of the tower, trail leaflets covering Leith Hill Estate and seasonal guided walks available. **Dogs**: on leads on heathland (April to July).

Sat Nav: for Rhododendron Wood and Starveall Corner use RH5 6LU (height restriction barrier); for Windy Gap RH5 6LX; for Landslip RH5 6HG. **Parking**: nearest at Starveall Corner car park (not National Trust), ¾ mile (easy walking). Windy Gap car park, ¼ mile (steep steps). Landslip car park, ¾ mile (steep gradient).

Find out more: 01306 712711 or leithhill@nationaltrust.org.uk

Leith Hill	
Tower	
Open every day all year	10–3*

*Open to 5 on weekends and Bank Holidays (weather permitting). Closed 25 December.

Leith Hill Tower and Countryside in Surrey, above and below, offers glorious walks and views

Monk's House

Rodmell, Lewes, East Sussex BN7 3HF

1980

Virginia Woolf's Monk's House in East Sussex

This small 16th-century weatherboarded cottage in the village of Rodmell was the country retreat of novelist Virginia Woolf and her husband Leonard and a meeting place for the Bloomsbury Group. The garden features the room where she created her best-known works and includes cottage garden borders, orchard, allotments and ponds. **Note**: no access to Rodmell from A26.

Eat, shop, stay: gift shop selling Woolf and Bloomsbury-related products.

Things to see and do: why not try your hand at a game of bowls? One of the favoured pastimes of the Woolfs. **Dogs**: allowed in garden on leads.

Access: **Building** **Grounds**
Sat Nav: do not use – wrongly indicates access across railway crossing. **Parking**: 100 yards (2-metre height restriction barrier).

Find out more: 01273 474760 or monkshouse@nationaltrust.org.uk

Monk's House		M	T	W	T	F	S	S
3 Apr–27 Oct	1–5	·	·	**W**	**T**	**F**	**S**	**S**

House: last admission 15 minutes before closing.
Open Bank Holiday Mondays. Garden: open 12:30 to 5:30.

Nymans

Handcross, near Haywards Heath,
West Sussex RH17 6EB

1954

One of the National Trust's premier gardens, Nymans was a creative retreat for the artistic Messel family. The garden contains rare and unusual plant collections of national significance, including a stunning collection of subtly fragranced magnolias in springtime. The Rose Garden, created by Maud Messel in the 1920s, is scented by old-fashioned roses. In autumn dramatic shows of native tree colour

For information about getting to National Trust places, please see page 3

precede the winter's structural form. Discover hidden corners through stone archways, walk along tree-lined avenues, all the while surrounded by the lush countryside of the Sussex Weald. The comfortable yet elegant house, a partial ruin, reflects the personalities and stories of the talented Messel family. The adjoining woodland has plenty of opportunities to spot wildlife.

Eat, shop, stay: large shop and plant centre selling a collection of plants grown at Nymans. Hot meals served between 12 and 2:30. Light refreshments and snacks available within the garden during peak periods. Second-hand bookshop. Woodland holiday cottage.

Nymans in West Sussex, above and right: one of the National Trust's very best gardens

Agapanthus in Nymans' garden, top, and the graceful house lit by golden sun, above

Things to see and do: Indoors Messel family rooms open within the house. A small gallery shows changing exhibitions throughout the year. Freeflow visit with additional guided tours during weekdays. **Outdoors** Daily guided walks and family activities. Mobility buggy tours. Gardening and creative workshops.
Dogs: on leads only in seating area outside café. Restrictions apply in woodland.

Access: [access symbols]
House [access symbols] **Gallery** [access symbol] **Garden** [access symbols]
Parking: on site.

Find out more: 01444 405250 or nymans@nationaltrust.org.uk

Nymans								
Garden								
Open all year	10–5*	M	T	W	T	F	S	S
House and gallery**								
4 Feb–3 Nov	11–4	M	T	W	T	F	S	S

*1 January to 3 February and 4 November to 31 December: closes 4. **Gallery closed for short periods to change exhibitions. Closed 24 and 25 December.

Oakhurst Cottage

Hambledon, near Godalming, Surrey GU8 4HF 1952

Timber-framed cottage offering a rare insight into domestic life in the mid-19th century, with a traditional garden to explore. **Note**: nearest toilets and visitor facilities at Winkworth Arboretum (4 miles approximately). Open Wednesday, Thursday and weekends, 3 April to 29 September and 2 to 31 October. Admission by booked guided tour only at 2, 3 and 4 (last tour at 3 in October). Call 01483 208936 to book. Also open Bank Holiday Mondays.

Find out more: 01483 208936 (Winkworth Arboretum) or oakhurstcottage@nationaltrust.org.uk

Old Soar Manor

Plaxtol, Borough Green, Kent TN15 0QX 1947

Dating from 1290, the remaining rooms of this knight's house offer a glimpse back to the time of Edward I. **Note**: sorry no toilet or tea-room. Narrow lanes, limited off-road parking.
Open every day, apart from Friday, 1 April to 30 September, 10 to 6.

Find out more: 01732 810378 or oldsoarmanor@nationaltrust.org.uk

Owletts

The Street, Cobham, Gravesend, Kent DA12 3AP 1938

An architect's 17th-century family home with a varied history and architectural features, set within a relaxing, traditional garden.
Note: parking available. Open Sundays, 7 April to 29 September, 11 to 5.

Find out more: 01732 810378 or owletts@nationaltrust.org.uk

Petworth

Petworth, West Sussex GU28 0AE

1947

Inspired by the Baroque palaces of Europe, Petworth House is an extraordinary and surprising ancestral seat created by just one family over 900 years. The 17th-century building you see today comprises grand state rooms which form the centrepiece of your visit. Designed to display the taste, lifestyle and artistic patronage of generations, the state rooms offer an infinity of paintings and sculpture, including major works by Van Dyck, Turner, Reynolds and Gainsborough. A particular highlight is the earliest English globe in existence, dating back to 1592. This remarkable collection reflects a journey of survival and success through the Tudor Reformation, Gunpowder Plot and the Napoleonic Wars. **Note**: additional charges may apply for some events, including Winter Art Exhibition.

Eat, shop, stay: hot and cold lunches, afternoon teas and homemade cakes available in the Audit Room Café. Additional seating and takeaway refreshments available in the Servants' Hall Coffee Shop. Gift shops selling books, products inspired by the collection and locally sourced souvenirs.

Inspired by the grand Baroque palaces of Europe, Petworth in West Sussex is extraordinary

Things to see and do: **Indoors** Guided tours of the collection and behind-the-scenes areas not normally on show. Visit the Servants' Quarters to discover what life was like for those working 'below stairs'. Exhibitions all year, family trails, costumed interpretation and a festive display for the Christmas season. **Outdoors** The 283-hectare (700-acre) 'Capability' Brown deer park, a landscape masterpiece, is a space for quiet reflection offering stunning views of the South Downs National Park. You can wander through the Pleasure Grounds with its historic monuments and enjoy one of our downloadable walks. **Dogs**: under close control in Petworth Park. Assistance dogs only in Pleasure Grounds.

Access:
Building
Sat Nav: use GU28 9LR. **Parking**: on A283, 700 yards. Separate car park for Petworth deer park.

Find out more: 01798 342207 or petworth@nationaltrust.org.uk

Petworth		M	T	W	T	F	S	S
House								
1 Jan–24 Feb*	11–4	**M**	**T**	**W**	**T**	**F**	**S**	**S**
25 Feb–25 Mar*	11–5	**M**	**T**	**W**	**T**	**F**	**S**	**S**
26 Mar–31 Dec	11–5**	**M**	**T**	**W**	**T**	**F**	**S**	**S**
Pleasure Grounds, shop and café								
Open all year	10–5†	**M**	**T**	**W**	**T**	**F**	**S**	**S**
Deer park								
Open all year	8–8††	**M**	**T**	**W**	**T**	**F**	**S**	**S**

*26 January to 24 March: Winter art exhibition. Selected rooms only. Seasonal displays 30 November to 31 December. Closed 24 and 25 December. **4 November to 31 December: house closes at 4. †1 January to 3 February and 4 November to 31 December: close at 4. ††Closes 6 in winter, access via deer-park car park only. Car-park gates lock automatically.

Petworth contains many fabulous works of art, including paintings, above, by some of the most famous Old Masters. As well as being a house for entertaining, Polesden Lacey in Surrey, right, contains many world-renowned collections

Polesden Lacey

Great Bookham, near Dorking, Surrey RH5 6BD

1942

Set within the Surrey Hills Area of Outstanding Natural Beauty, Polesden Lacey was the weekend party house of incomparable socialite Margaret Greville. Surrounded by 12 hectares (30 acres) of grounds and a 566-hectare (1,400-acre) estate, there is plenty of space to explore. Discover world-renowned collections of Fabergé, maiolica and Dutch Old Masters in the 19th-century house, along with changing themes exploring Margaret's lavish parties and domestic service. The formal gardens offer colour and fragrance throughout the year, from the walled rose garden in the summer to the winter garden, designed by Graham Stuart Thomas, during colder months. Boasting colourful views that change with every season, the wider estate is also home to a vast array of wildlife, including bats and butterflies. **Note**: additional charge may apply to certain events (including members).

Eat, shop, stay: café and coffee shop offer seasonal dishes, snacks, cream teas, coffee and ice cream. Pop-up outlets open in warmer weather. Shops selling homeware, gifts, souvenirs, local crafts and plants. Second-hand bookshop in the grounds. Holiday cottage situated in formal gardens.

Things to see and do: **Indoors** Weekday morning house tours and daily introductory talks. Freeflow exploration weekday afternoons and all day weekends. Changing stories to explore throughout the year. Seasonal exhibitions. Special festive displays during December. **Outdoors** Regular garden tours. Grade II* listed gardens including formal gardens and pleasure grounds. The 566-hectare (1,400-acre) estate is a Site of Special Scientific Interest with four waymarked walks. For children there is a natural play area in the grounds, binoculars to borrow, chickens to chat to and trails during school holidays. **Dogs**: on short leads in pleasure grounds. Dog-walking guide available from visitor reception.

Access:
House **Grounds**
Sat Nav: use KT23 4PZ. **Parking**: 200 yards.

Find out more: 01372 452048 or polesdenlacey@nationaltrust.org.uk

Polesden Lacey	
Open every day all year	10–5*

*House: opens 11; weekday access by guided tour only, 11 to 12:30; freeflow from 12:30. Admission by timed ticket at certain times. Last entry one hour before closing. 1 January to 3 February and 4 November to 31 December: closes 4. Closed 24 and 25 December.

Polesden Lacey's expansive estate, below, includes formal gardens, pleasure grounds and parkland, so there is plenty of space for letting off steam or simply relaxing

Quebec House

Quebec Square, Westerham, Kent TN16 1TD

1918

The childhood home of General James Wolfe, Quebec House (above) retains much of its original charm and family feel. Interactive collections and objects belonging to Wolfe are used to explore Georgian family life and Wolfe's most celebrated victory at the Battle of Quebec in 1759.

Eat, shop, stay: second-hand books, souvenirs, special range of Quebec-themed gifts such as Mrs Wolfe's raspberry jam and a children's tricorn hat for sale in the Coach House, as well as hot and cold drinks and a selection of cakes.

Things to see and do: house guided tours at 12 and 12:30. Relive the dramatic battle to win Quebec in the exhibition. Why not explore the historic town of Westerham after visiting Quebec House? **Dogs**: welcome on short leads in the gardens.

Access:
Building **Grounds**
Parking: 80 yards in main town car park on A25 (not National Trust).

Find out more: 01732 868381 or quebechouse@nationaltrust.org.uk

Quebec House		M	T	W	T	F	S	S
27 Feb–3 Nov*	11–5	·	·	**W**	**T**	**F**	**S**	**S**
9 Nov–15 Dec	1–4	·	·	·	·	·	**S**	**S**

*House: open for tours at 12 and 12:30 bookable on the day at the Coach House; freeflow from 1. Open Bank Holiday Mondays.

Reigate Hill and Gatton Park

near Reigate, Surrey

1912

Reigate Hill commands sweeping views across the Weald to the South Downs. It's a great spot for walking, family picnics and watching wildlife. A short walk away is the 19th-century Reigate Fort. The complex is open every day and the fort buildings open for special events. To the east of Reigate Hill is Surrey Hill's hidden gem, Gatton Park, designed by Lancelot 'Capability' Brown. **Note**: areas of Gatton Park opened monthly by the Gatton Trust.

Eat, shop, stay: picnics welcome. Tea kiosk (not National Trust) at Wray Lane.

Things to see and do: walks detailed on noticeboards and downloadable from website. Spot the chalk downland species, such as the Adonis blue butterfly. Visit the B-17 plane crash memorial site, west of Reigate Fort. **Dogs**: welcome, on leads when livestock grazing.

Reigate Hill and Gatton Park, Surrey: sweeping views towards the South Downs

A sunny walk at Reigate Hill and Gatton Park

Access:
Sat Nav: use RH2 0HX. **Parking**: at Wray Lane or Margery Wood car parks.

Find out more: 01342 843036 or reigate@nationaltrust.org.uk

Reigate Hill and Gatton Park
Reigate Fort buildings open by special arrangement.

River Wey and Godalming Navigations and Dapdune Wharf

Navigations Office and Dapdune Wharf, Wharf Road, Guildford, Surrey GU1 4RR

1964

A hidden haven where you can relax and unwind on a boat trip, explore a restored barge, or enjoy scenic walks. Dapdune Wharf in Guildford brings to life stories of the historic waterway, along 20 miles of waterside towpath. A great place for children to have fun.

Note: boat trip charges, mooring and fishing fees apply to members.

Eat, shop, stay: small tea-room serving sandwiches, cakes, ice cream and drinks. Small shop with plant sales. Picnic areas at Dapdune Wharf.

Things to see and do: **Indoors** Dressing-up clothes for children. **Outdoors** Year-round events, including activities for children at Dapdune and guided walks along towpath and beyond. River Festival in September. Overnight moorings available. **Dogs**: on leads at Dapdune Wharf and lock areas; elsewhere under control.

Access:
Parking: at Dapdune Wharf.

Find out more: 01483 561389 or riverwey@nationaltrust.org.uk

River Wey and Dapdune Wharf		M	T	W	T	F	S	S
Dapdune Wharf*								
23 Mar–3 Nov	11–5**	**M**	·	·	**T**	**F**	**S**	**S**

*Open daily during local school half term and summer holidays. **20 October to 3 November: closes 4.
River trips from Dapdune Wharf, 11 to 4 (conditions permitting). Access to towpath during daylight all year.

Kayaking at River Wey and Godalming Navigations and Dapdune Wharf in Surrey

Runnymede and Ankerwycke

Egham, near Old Windsor, Surrey

1931

Seen by many as the birthplace of modern democracy, this picturesque open landscape beside the Thames was witness to King John's historic sealing of the Magna Carta more than 800 years ago. Today Runnymede and Ankerwycke offer the ideal space to enjoy ancient woodlands, countryside walks and picnics by the river, all within easy reach of the M25. Along with Lutyens' impressive Fairhaven Lodges, the peaceful landscape is also home to memorials for the Magna Carta, John F. Kennedy and Commonwealth Air Forces, making it the perfect place to remember and reflect upon important moments in world history. **Note**: mooring and fishing (during fishing season) available for additional fee (including members).

Eat, shop, stay: tea-room serving freshly baked produce, morning coffee, hot lunches and afternoon teas. Free Wi-Fi. Shop in tea-room offering Magna Carta-themed books, souvenirs and toys.

Things to see and do: seasonal programme of family events throughout the year. Explore contemporary art installations *Writ in Water* and *The Jurors*. River boat trips available with French Brothers Boat Hire (01784 439626). **Dogs**: welcome on site and in the Magna Carta tea-room. On leads near livestock.

Access: **Tea-room** **Grounds**
Sat Nav: use TW20 0AE and follow brown 'Runnymede Memorials' signs.
Parking: either side of A308 (seasonal opening).

Find out more: 01784 432891 or runnymede@nationaltrust.org.uk

Runnymede and Ankerwycke	
Tea-room	
Open every day all year	10–5*

*1 to 31 January and 29 October to 31 December: tea-room closes 3:30; 1 May to 31 August (weekends and Bank Holidays): tea-room closes 6. Car parks: locked outside opening hours. Closed 24 and 25 December.

The River Thames meanders lazily past Runnymede and Ankerwycke in Surrey

St John's Jerusalem

Sutton-at-Hone, Dartford, Kent DA4 9HQ 1943

Set within a secluded moated garden is this rare example of a 13th-century chapel built by the Knights Hospitaller. **Note**: private residence, maintained and managed by a tenant on behalf of the National Trust. Sorry no toilet or tea-room. Open Wednesdays, 3 April to 25 September, 2 to 6, and 2 to 30 October, 2 to 4.

Find out more: 01732 810378 or stjohnsjerusalem@nationaltrust.org.uk

Scotney Castle

Lamberhurst, Tunbridge Wells, Kent TN3 8JN

The medieval moated Old Scotney Castle lies in a peaceful wooded valley. In the 19th century its owner Edward Hussey III set about building a new house, partially demolishing the Old Castle to create a romantic folly, the centrepiece of his picturesque landscape. From the terraces of the new house, sweeps of rhododendrons and azaleas cascade down the slope in summer, followed by highlights of autumn leaf colour, mirrored in the moat. In the house three generations have made their mark, adding possessions and character to the homely Victorian mansion which enjoys far-reaching views out across the estate.

Scotney Castle, Kent: so much to discover both inside, left, and out in the grounds, above

Eat, shop, stay: the coach-house tea-room offers a selection of hot meals and sandwiches, as well as homemade cakes and scones. Take home your own part of Scotney with local honey, Scotney Ale and plant sales available in the shop.

Things to see and do: **Indoors** Children's trail around the house. Seasonal changing exhibitions and conservation demonstrations throughout the year. **Outdoors** Regular guided and self-led estate walks. Natural play and children's play areas. **Dogs**: welcome on leads in the garden and on the estate.

Access:
House **Grounds**
Parking: 130 yards (limited), overflow parking 440 yards.

Find out more: 01892 893820 (Infoline). 01892 893868 or scotneycastle@nationaltrust.org.uk

Scotney Castle	
Open every day all year*	10–5

*House: opens 11, closing times vary in January, February and November (please check before travelling), entry by timed ticket or guided tour. 1 January to 8 February and 4 November to 31 December: everything closes 4. Closed 24 and 25 December.

Shalford Mill

Shalford, near Guildford, Surrey GU4 8BS

1932

You can sense the evocative stories of the past in the very structure of the mill, although the machinery no longer works. The wonderful story of the Ferguson's Gang is waiting for you – eccentric young women from the 1930s, determined to save the fabric of England for the future. **Note**: sorry no toilet or refreshments. Visits by guided tour only.

Things to see and do: **Indoors** Regular guided tours, evening talks and children's events. **Outdoors** Geocaching kits available on certain Sundays. **Dogs**: assistance dogs only.

Access: **Building**
Parking: none on site. 'Blue Sky' car park available weekends (on left coming from Guildford, about 109 yards before mill).

Find out more: 01483 561389 or shalfordmill@nationaltrust.org.uk

Shalford Mill		M	T	W	T	F	S	S
7 Apr–3 Nov	11–4:30	·	·	W	·	·	·	S

Open Bank Holiday Mondays.

Shalford Mill, Surrey: history in its very fabric

Sheffield Park and Garden

Sheffield Park, Uckfield, East Sussex TN22 3QX

1954

Sheffield Park and Garden in East Sussex

Originating in the 18th century and developed by each subsequent owner, this garden of colour, perfume and sound excites your senses as you enjoy winding paths, majestic trees, ponds and dappled glades. Falls, cascades and bridges are integral to the garden design. Planting is reflected in ponds so clear that the eye is tricked into thinking up is down. Bold and grand planting has a sculptural form in winter. Spring and summer bring vibrant blooms, fragrant arbours and splashes of colour. Autumn is a blazing kaleidoscope of greens, flame-reds, burnt oranges and bright yellows, planted for their combined display. The encircling park and woodland provide opportunities for further adventure where nature thrives in riverside meadows and woods.

Eat, shop, stay: tea-room serving homemade cakes, sandwiches, hot lunches and cream teas. Takeaway refreshments and snacks in the garden (available seasonally). Shops in reception building and Coach House selling gifts, local products, gardening items and plants. Second-hand bookshop beside Coach House.

Things to see and do: events and trails in the school holidays and '50 things' self-led activities for families all year. Natural playtrail in Ringwood Toll – try den-building, balance beams, a log see-saw and much more. More than 120 hectares (300 acres) of parkland, with circular walks (just over 1 mile) of the River Ouse. Cricket matches most summer weekends. A garden for all seasons with carpets of bluebells in spring, closely followed by rhododendrons and azaleas. Waterlilies cover the lakes during summer, and autumn brings an outstanding display of colour. Walk Woods is open seasonally. Pulham Falls waterfall (12 to 1, Tuesday and Friday). **Dogs**: garden on short leads after 1:30; anytime in parkland. Off-lead in East Park.

Access:
Reception **Tea-room**
Garden
Sat Nav: please look out for brown signs when approaching property.
Parking: on site (overflow car park 600 yards in use when dry). Car park can become full during May and October.

Find out more: 01825 790231 or sheffieldpark@nationaltrust.org.uk

Sheffield Park and Garden	
Open every day all year	10–5*

*Garden: 1 January to 3 February and 4 November to 31 December closes at 4. Garden, shop and tea-room: closed 24 and 25 December.

Sheffield Park and Garden, left and below: every season brings some new delight

Sissinghurst Castle Garden

Biddenden Road, near Cranbrook, Kent TN17 2AB

1967

Sissinghurst Castle Garden in Kent

Sissinghurst Castle Garden sits within the ruin of a great Elizabethan house surrounded by the rich Kentish landscape of woods, streams and farmland. The famous garden, with its fairytale tower, is the result of the creativity of the formal design of Harold Nicolson and the lavish planting of Vita Sackville-West. The colour schemes, intimacy of the different garden 'rooms' and rich herbaceous borders are the epitome of an English garden. The wider estate, which includes a vegetable garden, lakes and rich variety of wildlife, is waiting to be explored, while our regular exhibitions tell Sissinghurst's stories and show how history and landscape have combined to shape this special place. **Note**: limited access for buggies and wheelchairs.

Eat, shop, stay: Granary restaurant serving lunch and afternoon tea made with produce from our vegetable garden (hot food available until 3). The Old Dairy, offering sandwiches, cakes and drinks. Second-hand bookshop and garden shop selling plants grown in the Sissinghurst nursery.

Things to see and do: **Indoors** Exhibitions and daily talks. The Library contains the National Trust's most significant collection of 20th-century literature, and visitors can learn how we conserve it. Daily guided tours of the South Cottage from 12 to 4 (limited availability, not open in June). **Outdoors** Welcome talks and '50 things' activities. Packs available from visitor reception to help you explore. Acres of ancient woodland and lakes. Panoramic views across the Wealden countryside. You can see animals on our working farm. Smallhythe Place, Lamb House and Stoneacre nearby.
Dogs: welcome on leads on estate. Assistance dogs only in garden and vegetable garden.

Access:
Building **Grounds**
Parking: 315 yards.

Find out more: 01580 710700 or sissinghurst@nationaltrust.org.uk

Sissinghurst Castle Garden		M	T	W	T	F	S	S
Garden								
9 Mar–31 Oct	11–5:30*	**M**	**T**	**W**	**T**	**F**	**S**	**S**
South Cottage†								
1 Jan–31 May	Tour	**M**	**T**	**W**	**T**	**F**	**S**	**S**
6 Jul–31 Dec	Tour	**M**	**T**	**W**	**T**	**F**	**S**	**S**
Shop and restaurant								
Open all year	10–5:30**	**M**	**T**	**W**	**T**	**F**	**S**	**S**
Estate								
Open all year	Dawn–dusk	**M**	**T**	**W**	**T**	**F**	**S**	**S**

*Garden: restricted access November to March; last entry 45 minutes before closing; for conservation reasons, no food, drink or buggies in garden (carriers provided). Tower open in winter. **Shop and restaurant: close 4:30 November to March. †South Cottage: closed in June; limited timed tickets. Closed 24 and 25 December.

Sissinghurst Castle Garden: the view from the tower, above, and exploring the garden, left

Slindon Estate

near Arundel, West Sussex

1950

Slindon Estate is a patchwork of woodland, downland, farmland and parkland, with an unspoilt Sussex village at its centre. Historic features cover the landscape, such as Stane Street, the Roman road from Chichester to London. Slindon has a rich and wonderfully varied wildlife with bats, badgers, butterflies and downland flowers. **Note**: sorry no toilets.

Eat, shop, stay: The Forge in Slindon village (tenant-run) stocks everything from locally baked bread, deli items, fruit and vegetables, to sandwiches, biscuits and cakes. Fresh coffee and tea, beer, light breakfasts, lunches and afternoon tea are also available.

The folly on Slindon Estate, West Sussex

Things to see and do: there are more than 25 miles of rights of way to explore on the estate, as well as the village to discover. **Dogs**: welcome under close control.

Access:
Sat Nav: use BN18 0QY for Park Lane; BN18 0SP Duke's Road; BN18 1PH Bignor Hill. **Parking**: at Park Lane, Duke's Road, Northwood Junction and Bignor Hill.

Find out more: 01243 814730 or slindonestate@nationaltrust.org.uk

Smallhythe Place

Smallhythe, Tenterden, Kent TN30 7NG

1939

Nestled among the rolling Kent countryside, the corridors of this early 16th-century cottage resonate with the vibrant spirit of its theatrical former owner, Victorian actress Ellen Terry. Bursting with memorabilia from her life-long career on stage, visitors can see unique theatrical artefacts and visit the Barn Theatre.

Eat, shop, stay: charming vintage tea-room attached to the Barn Theatre selling soup, sandwiches, cakes, as well as soft and alcoholic drinks.

Things to see and do: **Indoors** Diverse variety of plays and music performed in the Barn Theatre. **Outdoors** Open-air theatre in the garden throughout the summer. Sissinghurst Castle Garden, Lamb House and Stoneacre nearby. **Dogs**: allowed on leads in grounds.

Access:
Building **Grounds**
Parking: 50 yards (not National Trust).

Find out more: 01580 762334 or smallhytheplace@nationaltrust.org.uk

Smallhythe Place		M	T	W	T	F	S	S
6 Mar–27 Oct	11-5	·	·	W	T	F	S	S

Open Bank Holiday Mondays, 11 to 5. Tea-room: closes 30 minutes prior to house closing.

The dining room at Smallhythe Place, Kent

South Foreland Lighthouse

The Front, St Margaret's Bay, Dover, Kent CT15 5NA

1989

This historic landmark (above), dramatically situated on The White Cliffs of Dover, guided ships past the infamous Goodwin Sands and has a fascinating tale to tell. It was the first lighthouse powered by electricity and the site of the first international radio transmission. **Note**: access to lighthouse by road is not permitted. Nearest parking at White Cliffs Visitor Centre.

Eat, shop, stay: loose-leaf tea and homemade cakes served in Mrs Knott's tea-room. Shop selling ice cream, sandwiches, cold drinks and gifts.

Things to see and do: **Indoors** Tours run by knowledgeable guides. Interactive and hands-on displays. **Outdoors** Family fun with kite-flying and games. **Dogs**: in grounds only.

Access:
Lighthouse **Tea-room** **Grounds**
Parking: no onsite parking, nearest at White Cliffs (2 miles), or St Margaret's village car park (1 mile).

Find out more: 01304 853281 or southforeland@nationaltrust.org.uk

South Foreland Lighthouse		M	T	W	T	F	S	S
Lighthouse*								
25 Mar–27 Oct	11-5:30**	M	·	·	·	F	S	S
Tea-room								
2 Feb–24 Mar	11-3	·	·	·	·	·	S	S
25 Mar–27 Oct	11-5**	M	T	W	T	F	S	S

*Significant conservation work at times. Please check website for most up-to-date opening times. Open daily during local school holidays. Last tour at 5. **27 October: closes at 3.

Standen House and Garden

West Hoathly Road, East Grinstead, West Sussex RH19 4NE

1973

Nestled in the Sussex countryside with views across the High Weald, James and Margaret Beale chose an idyllic location to build their rural retreat. Designed by Philip Webb, the house is one of the finest examples of Arts and Crafts workmanship with Morris & Co. interiors and decorative art of the period. The 5-hectare (12-acre) hillside garden established by Mrs Beale is restored to its 1920s glory. Each garden room offers something for every season, from colourful spring bulbs to autumn shades. On the wider estate, footpaths lead into the woodlands and the High Weald Area of Outstanding Natural Beauty.
Note: seasonal tours to top of water tower, £2 (suggested donation).

Eat, shop, stay: Barn Café serving homemade cakes, hot lunches and cream teas (Wi-Fi). Takeaway drinks, sandwiches and ice cream. Arts and Crafts-inspired gifts in shop. Plant centre. Second-hand bookshop. Kitchen garden produce. Picnics welcome. Holiday apartment within house.

Things to see and do: Indoors Daily talks. Changing exhibitions. Family Christmas. **Outdoors** Restored garden. 10,000 spring tulips. Woodland walks. Trails (school holidays) and natural play area. **Dogs**: welcome on short leads in formal garden and woodland estate (seasonal grazing cattle).

Access:
House **Garden**
Parking: 200 yards (steep hill).

Find out more: 01342 323029 or standen@nationaltrust.org.uk

Standen House and Garden		M	T	W	T	F	S	S
House								
5 Jan–27 Jan	11–3:30	·	·	·	·	·	**S**	**S**
1 Feb–31 Dec	11–4:30*	**M**	**T**	**W**	**T**	**F**	**S**	**S**
Garden, café and shop								
Open all year	10–5**	**M**	**T**	**W**	**T**	**F**	**S**	**S**
House tours†								
1 Nov–22 Nov	11–2:30††	**M**	**T**	**W**	**T**	**F**	·	·

*November and December: closes 3:30. **January, November and December: close 4. †Admission by tour only. ††Last tour departs 2:30. Closed 24 and 25 December.

Standen House and Garden in West Sussex

Stoneacre

Otham, Maidstone, Kent ME15 8RS 1928

Medieval farmhouse surrounded by garden, orchard, rolling meadows and woodland. Home to famous designer and critic Aymer Vallance. **Note**: open Saturdays, 16 March to 21 September, 11 to 5:30. Also open Bank Holidays. Last admission one hour before closing.

Find out more: 01580 710701 or stoneacre@nationaltrust.org.uk

Uppark House and Garden

South Harting, Petersfield, West Sussex GU31 5QR

1954

High on its vantage point on the South Downs ridge, Uppark has views as far south as the Solent. Outside, the intimate garden is being gradually restored to its original 18th-century design, with plenty of space in the adjacent meadow to play and relax. Uppark's Georgian interiors (below) illustrate the comfort of life 'upstairs', in contrast to the 'downstairs' world of its servants. Highlights include one of the best examples of an 18th-century British doll's house in the country.

Uppark House and Garden, West Sussex: the grounds, above, and kitchen, right

Eat, shop, stay: café (licensed) serving breakfast, lunches and afternoon tea. Shop selling books, plants, local food and more.

Things to see and do: **Indoors** Rare 18th-century British doll's house. **Outdoors** Garden tours (April to October). Open-air theatre and music in the summer. Harting Down, Hinton Ampner and Petworth House nearby. **Dogs**: welcome on short leads in grounds only.

Access:
House **Garden**
Parking: 300 yards.

Find out more: 01730 825415 or uppark@nationaltrust.org.uk

Uppark House and Garden		M	T	W	T	F	S	S
Servants' quarters								
1 Jan–15 Feb*	11–3	M	T	W	T	F	S	S
16 Feb–3 Nov	11–4	M	T	W	T	F	S	S
9 Nov–31 Dec	11–3	M	T	W	T	F	S	S
House (ground floor only)								
2 Mar–3 Nov	12:30–4**	M	T	W	T	F	S	S
Garden, shop and café†								
Open all year	10–5	M	T	W	T	F	S	S

*Tours of servants' quarters available during winter. **Ground floor: open 11 to 4 on Bank Holidays. †1 January to 3 February and 4 November to 31 December: close at 4. Garden: limited access in winter. Everything closed 25 and 26 December.

 For information about getting to National Trust places, please see page 3

Wakehurst

Ardingly, Haywards Heath,
West Sussex RH17 6TN

1964

Wakehurst, Kew's wild botanic garden in Sussex, has more than 202 hectares (500 acres) of beautiful ornamental gardens, woodlands and a nature reserve. Internationally significant for collections, scientific research and plant conservation, you can also visit Kew's unique Millennium Seed Bank, where science and horticulture work side by side.

Note: funded and managed by the Royal Botanic Gardens, Kew.
Parking charges apply (including members).

Eat, shop, stay: Seed Café serving tea, coffee, cakes, bacon sandwiches, teacakes and soup. Redwoods Coffee Shop serving hot drinks and snacks. Stables Restaurant offering hot and cold food, plus cakes served all day. Gift shop. Plant centre (not National Trust).

Things to see and do: free daily guided tours. Seasonal festival programme, open-air theatre, lantern festival. Courses. Events all year. Natural play areas for families. Kingfisher- and badger-watching (charges apply).
Dogs: assistance dogs only.

Access:
Buildings **Grounds**
Parking: 50 yards.

Find out more: 01444 894066 or wakehurst@kew.org. kew.org

Wakehurst		M	T	W	T	F	S	S
Garden*								
1 Jan–28 Feb	10–4:30	**M**	**T**	**W**	**T**	**F**	**S**	**S**
1 Mar–31 Oct	10–6	**M**	**T**	**W**	**T**	**F**	**S**	**S**
1 Nov–31 Dec**	10–4:30	**M**	**T**	**W**	**T**	**F**	**S**	**S**

*Mansion and Millennium Seed Bank: close one hour earlier. Shop and catering closing times can vary. Shop closed Easter Sunday. UK National Trust members free (reciprocal agreements made between the Trust and other parties do not apply). The Mansion can be closed for private events, please check before you visit **Closed 24 and 25 December.

Wakehurst: Kew's Millennium Seed Bank in West Sussex

The White Cliffs of Dover

Langdon Cliffs, Dover, Kent

1968

There can be no doubt that The White Cliffs of Dover are one of this country's most spectacular natural features and have been a symbol of hope for generations. You can appreciate their beauty through the seasons by taking one of the country's most dramatic clifftop walks, which offer unrivalled views of the English Channel while savouring the rare flora and fauna found only on this chalk grassland. You can also learn more about the fascinating military history of The White Cliffs by taking a torchlit tour of Fan Bay Deep Shelter, a labyrinth of forgotten Second World War tunnels. **Note**: nearest toilets at White Cliffs. Age restrictions apply at Fan Bay.

Eat, shop, stay: shop selling gifts and outdoor goods. Coffee shop serving lunches, homemade cakes and cream teas. Both with unrivalled views of the Port of Dover. Homemade cakes, sandwiches and loose-leaf tea available in lighthouse tea-room.

Things to see and do: **Indoors** Pick up a ticket for a guided tour of the Lighthouse and Fan Bay Deep Shelter. **Outdoors** Natural play area. Spectacular viewpoints. Waymarked trail to South Foreland Lighthouse. **Dogs**: under close control at all times (animals grazing).

The White Cliffs of Dover, Kent: Fan Bay Deep Shelter, above. The iconic sweep of cliffs, below

Access: **Visitor Centre** **Fan Bay Deep Shelter** **Countryside**
Sat Nav: use CT15 5NA. **Parking**: on site, limited (please check before visiting Sundays and Bank Holidays, April to October).

Find out more: 01304 202756 or whitecliffs@nationaltrust.org.uk

The White Cliffs of Dover		M	T	W	T	F	S	S
Visitor Centre, shop and kiosk								
1 Jan–3 Feb	10–4	M	T	W	T	F	S	S
4 Feb–27 Oct	10–5*	M	T	W	T	F	S	S
28 Oct–31 Dec**	10–4	M	T	W	T	F	S	S
Fan Bay Deep Shelter								
25 Mar–27 Oct	11–3	M	·	·	·	F	S	S

*1 July to 1 September: open to 5:30.
**Closed 24 and 25 December.

Support the places you visit: please scan your member card for free parking ticket

Winkworth Arboretum

Hascombe Road, Godalming, Surrey GU8 4AD

1952

The National Trust's only arboretum was born from one man's vision and passion. Dr Wilfrid Fox used the wooded valley and its lakes as a canvas for 'painting a picture' with trees. The fruits of his labour are an award-winning collection of more than 1,000 varieties of trees and shrubs set in the picturesque Surrey Hills, offering stunning combinations of colour with every changing season. Famous for vibrant autumnal foliage and endless carpets of bluebells in spring, the azaleas, magnolias, witch hazel and snowdrops make Winkworth worth visiting all year for beautiful scenery, a picnic and fun family events. **Note**: some steep slopes; banks of lake and wetlands only partially fenced.

Eat, shop, stay: small tea-room offering freshly baked scones, cakes and light lunches.

Things to see and do: events suitable for all ages, including regular guided walks. Discover our exciting play areas and viewing platform, or relax in the boathouse and enjoy the views across the lake. **Dogs**: welcome on short leads.

Access: **Grounds**
Parking: 100 yards.

Find out more: 01483 208477 or winkwortharboretum@nationaltrust.org.uk

Winkworth Arboretum		M	T	W	T	F	S	S
1 Jan–31 Jan	10–4	**M**	**T**	**W**	**T**	**F**	**S**	**S**
1 Feb–25 Mar	10–5	**M**	**T**	**W**	**T**	**F**	**S**	**S**
26 Mar–28 Oct	10–6	**M**	**T**	**W**	**T**	**F**	**S**	**S**
29 Oct–31 Dec	10–4*	**M**	**T**	**W**	**T**	**F**	**S**	**S**

Tea-room closes 30 minutes earlier than arboretum. Car-park gates locked at closing time. *Closed 24 and 25 December.

Vibrant autumn foliage glows in the sun at Winkworth Arboretum in Surrey

Woolbeding Gardens

Midhurst, West Sussex GU29 9RR

1957

Nestling alongside the River Rother, Woolbeding Gardens is a horticultural haven where modern yet romantic planting meets sophisticated colour palettes. Elegant garden rooms and meticulous borders merge with a wooded landscape that conceals dramatic architectural follies. Ever-changing, from the seasons to the planting, every moment offers something new and picturesque. **Note**: access by park-and-ride minibus from Midhurst (booking essential).

Eat, shop, stay: Orchard Café serving barista-style coffee, speciality teas, and a selection of tempting treats. Shop selling gardening books, gifts and plants.

Things to see and do: join introductory talks and specialist Gardeners' Workshops. Enjoy the borders bursting with colour, find hidden follies waiting to be discovered and take in grand views of the countryside beyond.
Dogs: assistance dogs only.

Access:
Reception **Garden**
Parking: none available. Access by park-and-ride minibus from Midhurst (booking essential).

Find out more: 0344 249 1895 or woolbedinggardens@nationaltrust.org.uk

Woolbeding Gardens		M	T	W	T	F	S	S
25 Apr–27 Sep	10:30–4:30	·	·	·	**T**	**F**	·	·

Advance booking essential. Access by park-and-ride minibus only from Midhurst.

Woolbeding Gardens in West Sussex: an ever-changing horticultural haven

Additional countryside car parks in Kent, Surrey and Sussex

East Sussex	
Crowlink	BN20 0BA
Surrey	
Holmwood Common	RH5 4NX
Hydon's Ball and Heath	GU8 4BB
Witley and Milford Commons	GU8 5QA
Kent	
Oldbury Hill	TN15 0ET
One Tree Hill	TN15 0SN
Toys Hill	TN16 1QG

London

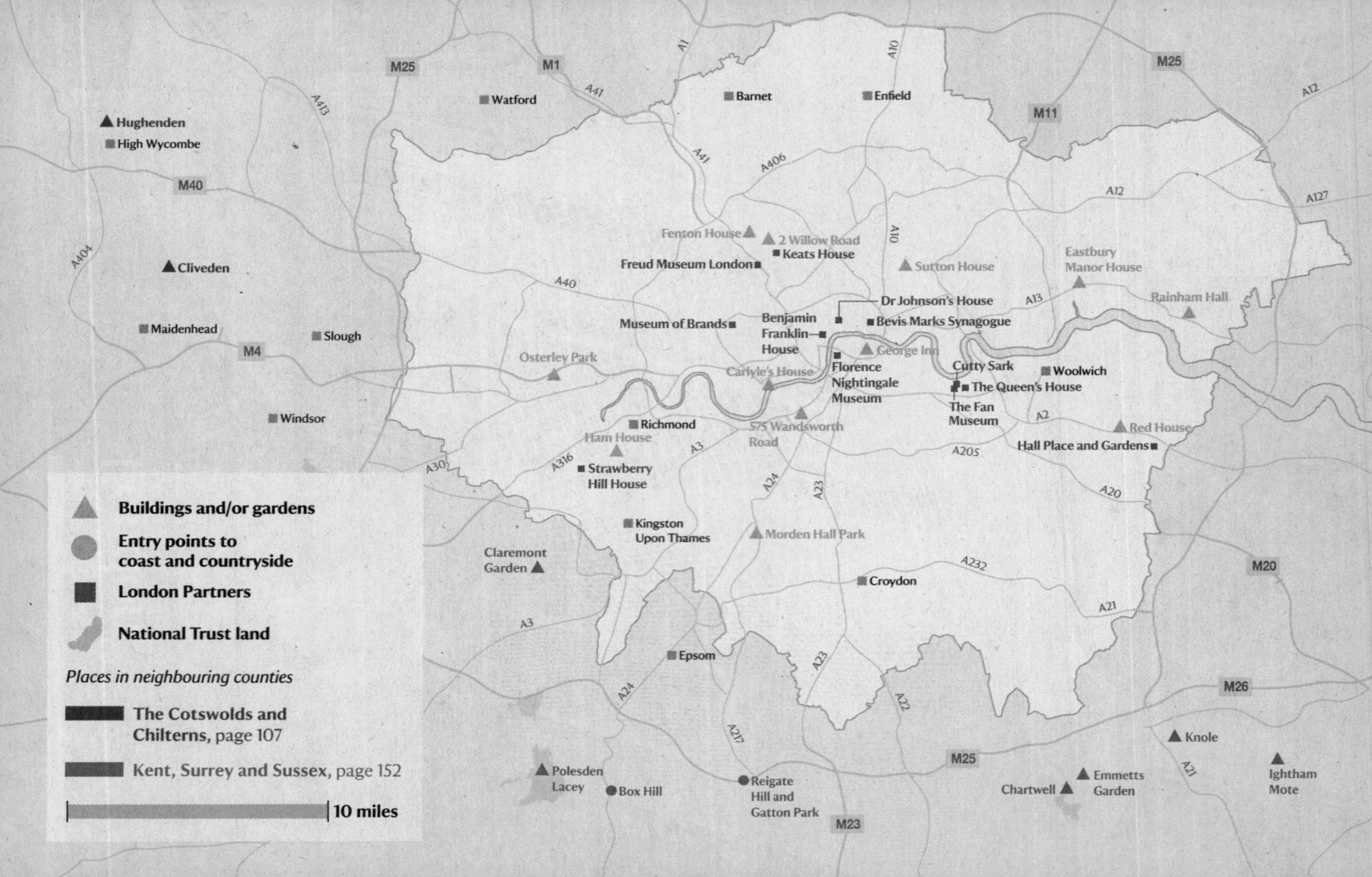
Hughenden
High Wycombe
Watford
Barnet
Enfield
Cliveden
Maidenhead
Slough
Windsor
Osterley Park
Fenton House
2 Willow Road
Keats House
Freud Museum London
Sutton House
Eastbury Manor House
Rainham Hall
Dr Johnson's House
Bevis Marks Synagogue
Museum of Brands
Benjamin Franklin House
George Inn
Carlyle's House
Florence Nightingale Museum
Cutty Sark
The Queen's House
The Fan Museum
Woolwich
Richmond
Ham House
575 Wandsworth Road
Red House
Hall Place and Gardens
Strawberry Hill House
Kingston Upon Thames
Morden Hall Park
Claremont Garden
Croydon
Epsom
Polesden Lacey
Box Hill
Reigate Hill and Gatton Park
Knole
Chartwell
Emmetts Garden
Ightham Mote
M25
M1
M11
M40
M4
M20
M26
M23
A1
A10
A41
A413
A406
A12
A127
A404
A40
A13
A2
A30
A316
A3
A205
A24
A23
A20
A232
A21
A22
A217
Buildings and/or gardens
Entry points to coast and countryside
London Partners
National Trust land
Places in neighbouring counties
The Cotswolds and Chilterns, page 107
Kent, Surrey and Sussex, page 152
10 miles

Carlyle's House

24 Cheyne Row, Chelsea, London SW3 5HL

1936

'Let no woman who values peace of soul ever dream of marrying an author!' wrote Jane Carlyle in 1837. Her amusing letters about her husband, the sage of Chelsea, their friends (including Charles Dickens), impossible servants, noisy neighbours, builders, burglars and bedbugs bring this Victorian home to hilarious life.

Access: Building Grounds
Parking: limited on street, metered (charge including members).

Find out more: 020 7352 7087 or carlyleshouse@nationaltrust.org.uk

Carlyle's House		M	T	W	T	F	S	S
2 Mar–3 Nov	11-5	·	·	**W**	**T**	**F**	**S**	**S**

Open Bank Holiday Mondays.

Victorian Carlyle's House in Chelsea: a place of literature, letters and laughter

Eastbury Manor House

Eastbury Square, Barking IG11 9SN

1918

Barely altered since it was built circa 1573, this Grade I listed Elizabethan gentry house features soaring chimneys, early 17th-century wall-paintings and an original turret staircase. Outside there is a cobbled courtyard and peaceful walled garden (above) with bee boles to explore. **Note**: managed by the London Borough of Barking and Dagenham. Some rooms are closed occasionally for functions. Special events and activities are charged at an additional cost.

Eat, shop, stay: garden tea-room (not National Trust) serving drinks, afternoon teas, sandwiches, snacks and light meals. Shop (not National Trust) selling Tudor pottery, toys, books and souvenirs.

Things to see and do: **Indoors** Exhibitions, guided tours, family trails and I-spy, talks and re-enactments. Events and holiday activities. **Outdoors** Guided tours, family trails, re-enactments and exhibitions. Special events, holiday and family activities. **Dogs**: in grounds only on leads.

Access: Building
Parking: on adjacent streets (free but limited).

Find out more: 020 8227 2942 or eastburymanor@nationaltrust.org.uk

Eastbury Manor House		M	T	W	T	F	S	S
14 Feb–13 Dec	10-4	·	·	·	**T**	**F**	·	·
31 Mar–15 Dec	11-4	·	·	·	·	·	·	**S**

House occasionally used for private bookings. Tours available on request until 2.

Fenton House and Garden

Hampstead Grove, Hampstead, London NW3 6SP

1952

This 1686 house, with views across London from Hampstead's Holly Hill, is filled with world-class collections of ceramics, paintings, textiles and musical instruments. The ever-changing horticultural gem that is the garden, includes an orchard, kitchen garden, rose garden, terraces and lawns, and never fails to delight.

Eat, shop, stay: small retail area selling local and National Trust items, garden plants and produce.

Fenton House and Garden in Hampstead: the gracious entrance, below, and garden, right

Things to see and do: **Indoors** Collections talks, exhibitions and music events. **Outdoors** Garden tours and events, including Apple Weekend. Keats House, the Freud Museum (both Trust London Partners) and 2 Willow Road are nearby. **Dogs**: assistance dogs only.

Access: **Building** **Grounds**
Parking: none on site.

Find out more: 020 7435 3471 or fentonhouse@nationaltrust.org.uk

Fenton House and Garden		M	T	W	T	F	S	S
2 Mar–3 Nov	11–5	·	·	**W**	**T**	**F**	**S**	**S**

Open Bank Holiday Mondays and selected dates in December.

George Inn

The George Inn Yard, 77 Borough High Street, Southwark, London SE1 1NH 1937

This public house, dating from the 17th century, is London's last remaining galleried inn. **Note**: leased to a private company. No table bookings (telephone for details).

Find out more: 020 7407 2056 or georgeinn@nationaltrust.org.uk

Ham House and Garden

Ham Street, Ham, Richmond TW10 7RS

1948

On the banks of the River Thames, Ham is one of London's treasure houses and gardens. With a substantial collection of 17th-century paintings, furniture and textiles, Ham reveals what life looked like during the reigns of Charles I and II. You can learn how later generations protected their heritage by caring for their ancestors' treasured heirlooms. The ongoing recreation of the 17th-century garden now features a large walled kitchen garden, an annual spring bulb display with historic tulips, a lavender parterre, a woodland wilderness garden and two meadows alongside the River Thames. **Note**: to protect fragile textiles, some rooms have low light levels.

Eat, shop, stay: the café serves lunches, teas and delicious cakes made on site using kitchen garden produce. Picnics are welcome and some tables are provided. The gift shop sells gifts for all occasions and plants, many Ham-grown.

Things to see and do: **Indoors** Art activities and trails during school holidays and weekends for families. **Outdoors** Discover more on a garden history or architecture tour. Enjoy our wildflower meadow by the Thames.
Dogs: allowed on short leads.

Ham House and Garden, Richmond, above and below: one of London's great treasure houses

Access: House Café Gardens
Sat Nav: takes you to stables on Ham Street nearby. **Parking**: none on site, nearest 380 yards (not National Trust) and on street.

Find out more: 020 8940 1950 or hamhouse@nationaltrust.org.uk

Ham House and Garden		M	T	W	T	F	S	S
House								
Open all year*	12–4	M	T	W	T	F	S	S
Garden, café and shop								
Open all year	10–5**	M	T	W	T	F	S	S

*Selected rooms only, January to March, November and December. **1 January to 3 February and 28 October to 31 December: close 4. Closed 24 and 25 December.

Morden Hall Park

Morden Hall Road, Morden, London SM4 5JD

1941

Step into this 50-hectare (125-acre) oasis and you'll soon forget you're in bustling South London. Once a private country estate, the grounds were gifted to the National Trust to become a park for all people, and have been a local treasure ever since. Peaceful tree-lined riverside paths lead to wide open meadows and a collection of historic buildings which hint at an industrial past. The 1920s rose garden is a delight for the senses in summer and a perfect picnic spot, while a stroll on the immersive wetland boardwalk gives a rare glimpse into the secretive world of waterbirds.
Note: parking for visitors to Morden Hall Park only, five-hour maximum stay (including members). Admission charges apply to some events (including members).

Eat, shop, stay: garden centre offers expert advice and sells peat-free plants grown in National Trust nurseries. The Potting Shed Café in the former kitchen garden serves hearty fare, while the Stableyard Café offers light refreshments at weekends. Second-hand bookshop with period features.

Things to see and do: **Indoors** Regular exhibitions in the Stableyard Gallery and permanent display in the Snuff Mill. **Outdoors** Open-air theatre and cinema during the summer. Family events at Easter, half terms and Christmas. Natural play area.
Dogs: welcome on leads around buildings, rose garden, playground and wetland boardwalk. Within sight elsewhere.

Access:
Snuff Mill **Café and garden centre**
Parkland
Sat Nav: use SM4 5JD and follow signs to Morden Hall Park Garden Centre.
Parking: 25 yards, next to garden centre.

Find out more: 020 8545 6850 or mordenhallpark@nationaltrust.org.uk

Morden Hall Park
Open every day all year
Potting Shed Café: open 9 to 6. Garden centre: open Monday to Saturday, 9 to 6; Sunday, 10 to 4. Rose garden and Stableyard: open 8 to 6. 1 November to 1 March: all buildings and gardens close one hour earlier, no change to garden centre Sunday opening.

Three views of Morden Hall Park, Morden: once a private country-house estate, this green haven is now enjoyed by all the community

For information about getting to National Trust places, please see page 3

Osterley Park and House

Jersey Road, Isleworth, London TW7 4RB

1949

A suburban palace caught between town and country, Osterley Park and House is one of the last surviving country estates in London. Past fields and grazing cattle, just around the lake the magnificent house awaits, presented as it would have been when it was redesigned by Robert Adam in the late 18th century for the Child family. A place for welcoming friends and clients, fashioned for show and entertaining, the lavish state apartments tell the story of a party palace. Recently returned family portraits and furniture now add a personal touch to grand rooms. Elegant pleasure gardens and hundreds of acres of parkland are perfect for whiling away a peaceful afternoon.

Eat, shop, stay: Stables Café, serving fresh seasonal dishes and homemade cakes (indoor and outdoor seating), and Brewhouse Coffee Shop (open seasonally). Gift shop, second-hand bookshop and plant sales in the Stables courtyard. Free Wi-Fi. Picnics welcome in the park and gardens.

Support the places you visit: please scan your member card for free parking ticket

Things to see and do: **Indoors** Year-round events and family activities. **Outdoors** You can stroll through colourful formal gardens, with herbaceous borders, ornamental vegetable beds and an established winter garden. With meadows, woodland and a natural play trail with rope swings and stepping stones, you can let your imagination (and the children's) run wild. Why not enjoy a game of table tennis on the front lawn or a walk around the estate, with impressive views across Middle Lake towards the 18th-century house? Family-friendly multipurpose pathways are perfect for cycling, with trail maps and suggested routes available. **Dogs**: welcome on leads in parkland, with a designated off-lead area.

Access: **House** **Shop and bookshop** **Garden**
Sat Nav: enter Jersey Road and TW7 4RD.
Parking: 400 yards.

Find out more: 020 8232 5050 or osterley@nationaltrust.org.uk

Osterley Park and House	
Open every day all year	10–5*

*House: open 11 to 12 for guided tours (places limited), freeflow 12 to 4; last entry one hour before closing; selected rooms open in winter. 1 January to 24 February and 4 November to 31 December closes 4. Closed 25 December.

Despite its setting in suburban Isleworth, magnificent Osterley Park and House feels like an estate in the depths of the country

Rainham Hall

The Broadway, Rainham, London RM13 9YN

1949

Built in 1729 for an enterprising merchant, Rainham Hall has been home to nearly 50 different inhabitants, including a *Vogue* photographer, a scientist-vicar and architectural historians. One by one, we will be bringing their stories to life, through a changing exhibition programme with a new experience this year.

Eat, shop, stay: the Stables Café serves seasonally inspired light lunches, freshly baked scones, cakes, barista coffee, teas and soft drinks. Gifts, guidebooks and postcards available.

Things to see and do: **Indoors** Our exciting exhibition programme continues with a new theme this year. Regular events, including family activities and seasonal festivities. **Outdoors** Almost 1½-hectare (3-acre) community garden.
Dogs: assistance dogs only.

Access: **House** **Café** **Garden**
Parking: 300 yards (not National Trust).

Stories come alive at Rainham Hall, Rainham

Find out more: 01708 525579 or rainhamhall@nationaltrust.org.uk

Rainham Hall		M	T	W	T	F	S	S
Stables Café and gardens								
2 Jan-29 Dec*	10-5**	·	·	**W**	**T**	**F**	**S**	**S**

Hall: a new experience opens 25 May. Please check website before visiting, as opening dates and times are subject to change. *Open Bank Holiday Mondays. Everything closed 24 to 26 December. **Gardens: in winter close dusk if earlier.

Red House

Red House Lane, Bexleyheath DA6 8JF

2003

The only house commissioned, created and lived in by William Morris, founder of the Arts and Crafts Movement, Red House (above) is a building of extraordinary architectural and social significance. An ongoing conservation project is revealing Red House's secrets, including original pre-Raphaelite wall-paintings and Morris's first decorative schemes.

Eat, shop, stay: William Morris shop housed in our Grade II* listed Coach House. Café in original kitchen serving light lunches and a selection of cakes. Picnics welcome in the orchard.

Things to see and do: **Indoors** Award-winning film installation 'A Poem of a House'. Exhibition of Philip Webb's personal effects. Wombat trails in school holidays. Guided tours. **Outdoors** Garden tours. Lawn games.
Dogs: assistance dogs only.

Access: **Building** **Grounds**
Sat Nav: use DA6 8HL – Danson Park car park.
Parking: at Danson Park, just over ½ mile. Charge at weekends and Bank Holidays (including members).

Find out more: 020 8304 9878 or redhouse@nationaltrust.org.uk

Red House		M	T	W	T	F	S	S
2 Mar-3 Nov	11-5	·	·	**W**	**T**	**F**	**S**	**S**
8 Nov-15 Dec	11-4:30	·	·	·	·	**F**	**S**	**S**

Admission by guided tour only at 11, 11:30, 12, 12:30 and 1 (booking recommended); freeflow 1:30 to 5 (4:30 in winter). Last admission 45 minutes before closing. Tea-room: last serving 4:30 (4 in winter). Open Bank Holiday Mondays.

Sutton House and Breaker's Yard

2 and 4 Homerton High Street, Hackney, London E9 6JQ

1938

For nearly 500 years Sutton House has reflected and adapted to the world around it; its identity ranging from a country house to an East London squat. Today it continues to reflect Hackney, hosting hundreds of visits from community and school groups, as well as events and weddings all year.

Eat, shop, stay: treat yourself to tea and cake in the courtyard, bookshop or among upcycled vehicles of the Breaker's Yard garden.

Things to see and do: **Indoors** Every Easter, summer, Halloween and Christmas there are new family adventures or exhibitions. The annual summer exhibition is created with artists and the local community. **Outdoors** Breaker's Yard playground. **Dogs**: assistance dogs only.

Access: **Building**
Sat Nav: use E9 6JQ. **Parking**: none on site and very limited nearby, not National Trust (charge including members).

Find out more: 020 8986 2264 or suttonhouse@nationaltrust.org.uk

Sutton House		M	T	W	T	F	S	S
6 Apr–21 Apr	12–4:30	·	·	**W**	**T**	**F**	**S**	**S**
10 Jul–22 Sep	12–4:30	·	·	**W**	**T**	**F**	**S**	**S**
19 Oct–27 Oct	12–4:30	·	·	**W**	**T**	**F**	**S**	**S**
23 Nov–22 Dec	12–4:30	·	·	**W**	**T**	**F**	**S**	**S**

Special interest tours of house available, booking essential (please see website). Open Bank Holiday Mondays.

575 Wandsworth Road

575 Wandsworth Road, Lambeth, London SW8 3JD

2010

Khadambi Asalache (1935–2006) turned this modest Grade II listed Georgian terraced house into a work of art. Featuring hand-carved fretwork throughout, the house and collections continue to inspire all who visit. Please wear or bring socks as no outdoor shoes are allowed in the house. **Note**: sorry no toilets or café. Access by booked guided tour only.

Access: **House**
Parking: none on site.

Find out more: 0344 249 1895 (bookings). 020 7622 4109 (enquiries) or 575wandsworthroad@nationaltrust.org.uk

575 Wandsworth Road		M	T	W	T	F	S	S
1 Mar–2 Nov	Tour*	·	·	·	·	**F**	**S**	·

*Access by guided tour only (approximately one hour) for up to six people (booking essential, places limited, tickets released in February, May and August).

Sutton House and Breaker's Yard, Hackney, left

2 Willow Road

Hampstead, London NW3 1TH

1994

A corner of 2 Willow Road in Hampstead

This late 1930s house, an architect's vision of the future, paints a vivid picture of the creative and social circles in which Ernö and Ursula Goldfinger moved. Today you can explore the intimate and evocative interiors, innovative designs, intriguing personal possessions and impressive 20th-century art collection. **Note**: sorry no toilet.

Eat, shop, stay: a small table in the entrance hall has property-related items available for sale.

Things to see and do: events, including late openings and tours. Fenton House nearby, as well as Keats House and the Freud Museum (both London Partners). **Dogs**: assistance dogs only.

Access: **Building**
Parking: very limited, metered on-street parking nearby (not National Trust).

Find out more: 020 7435 6166 or 2willowroad@nationaltrust.org.uk

2 Willow Road		M	T	W	T	F	S	S
2 Mar–3 Nov	11–5*	·	·	**W**	**T**	**F**	**S**	**S**

*Entry by one-hour guided tour only at 11, 12, 1 and 2 (places limited, tickets available on day at door only). Wednesday to Friday tours at 11 occasionally booked by groups. 3 to 5, self-guided viewing (timed entry when busy). Open Bank Holiday Mondays.

National Trust *Partner*

London partners

'National Trust Partner' is an exciting venture between the National Trust and a selection of small, independent heritage attractions and museums within London. The Partnership aims to bring enhanced benefits to National Trust members living in London or for those visiting the capital for a day out, helping to provide increased opportunities to explore our rich and diverse heritage.

Entry charges: 50 per cent discount for members on presentation of a valid membership card. For full visiting information (and access), please see individual National Trust Partner websites.

Benjamin Franklin House

The world's only remaining home of Benjamin Franklin, featuring a unique 'Historical Experience'.

Underground: Charing Cross or Embankment.
Train: Charing Cross.

Find out more: 020 7925 1405 or benjaminfranklinhouse.org

Cutty Sark

Nineteenth-century tea clipper, once the fastest ship of her day, meticulously preserved to tell the stories of life on board.

Overground: Cutty Sark (DLR).
Train: Greenwich.

Find out more: 020 8312 6565 or rmgenquiries@rmg.co.uk rmg.co.uk/cutty-sark

Bevis Marks Synagogue

Dated 1701, Britain's oldest surviving synagogue contains Cromwellian and Queen Anne furniture.

Underground: Liverpool Street or Aldgate.
Train: Liverpool Street.

Find out more: 020 7621 1188 or bevismarks.org.uk

Dr Johnson's House

Late 17th-century town house, once home to lexicographer and wit Samuel Johnson.

Underground: Chancery Lane or Blackfriars.
Train: Blackfriars.

Find out more: 020 7353 3745 or drjohnsonshouse.org

The Fan Museum

Unique collection of more than 4,000 fans, housed in elegant Georgian buildings.

Overground: Cutty Sark (DLR).
Train: Greenwich.

Find out more: 020 8305 1441 or thefanmuseum.org.uk

Freud Museum London

The final home of pioneering psychoanalysts Sigmund Freud and his daughter Anna.

Underground: Finchley Road.
Overground: Finchley Road & Frognal.

Find out more: 020 7435 2002 or freud.org.uk

Florence Nightingale Museum

Celebrating the life and work of the world's most famous nurse, the museum sits on the banks of the Thames opposite the Houses of Parliament.

Underground: Westminster or Waterloo.
Overground Waterloo. **Train:** Waterloo.

Find out more: 020 7188 4400 or florence-nightingale.co.uk

Hall Place and Gardens

Stunning Tudor house with magnificent gardens.

Train: Bexley.

Find out more: 01322 526574 or hallplace.org.uk

Keats House

Elegant Regency villa where the Romantic poet John Keats wrote his best-loved poems.

Underground: Hampstead or Belsize Park.
Overground: Hampstead Heath.

Find out more: 020 7332 3868 or keatshouse@cityoflondon.gov.uk

The Queen's House

Home to an internationally renowned art collection, Inigo Jones's architectural masterpiece is the first classical building in the UK. **Note**: member discount applies to guided tours.

Overground: Cutty Sark (DLR).
Train: Greenwich or Maze Hill.

Find out more: 020 8312 6608 or bookings@rmg.co.uk

Museum of Brands

Intense experience of consumer culture: journey from Victorian times to your childhood.

Underground: Ladbroke Grove.

Find out more: 020 7243 9611 or museumofbrands.com

Strawberry Hill House

Horace Walpole's beautifully restored Gothic Revival castle by the Thames in Twickenham.

Train: Strawberry Hill.

Find out more: 020 8744 1241 or strawberryhillhouse.org.uk

East of England

Dunstable Downs and the Whipsnade Estate, Bedfordshire: kite-flying heaven

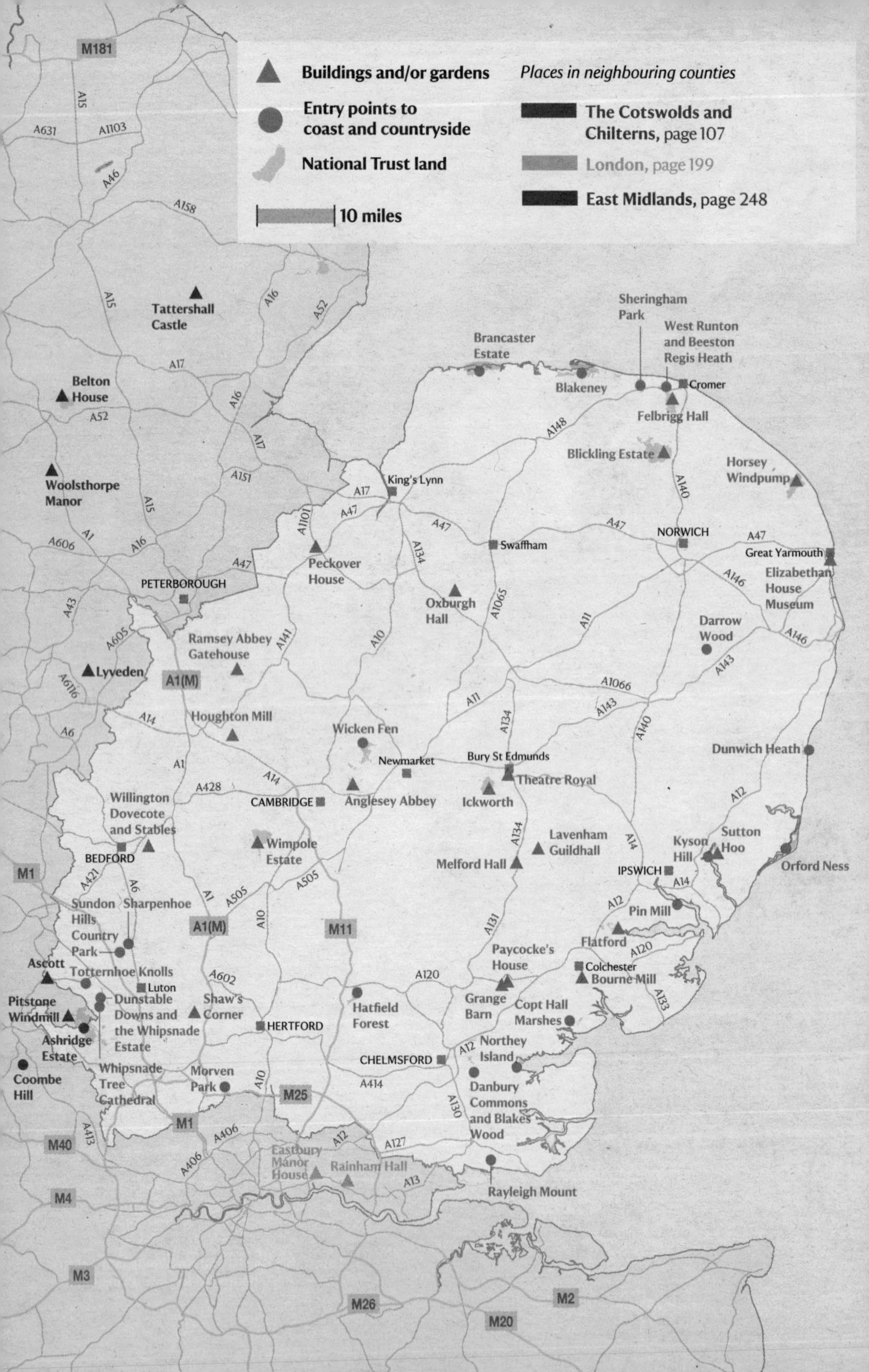
Buildings and/or gardens
Entry points to coast and countryside
National Trust land
10 miles
Places in neighbouring counties
The Cotswolds and Chilterns, page 107
London, page 199
East Midlands, page 248
Tattershall Castle
Belton House
Woolsthorpe Manor
Lyveden
Sheringham Park
West Runton and Beeston Regis Heath
Brancaster Estate
Blakeney
Cromer
Felbrigg Hall
Blickling Estate
Horsey Windpump
King's Lynn
Swaffham
NORWICH
Great Yarmouth
Elizabethan House Museum
Peckover House
Oxburgh Hall
PETERBOROUGH
Ramsey Abbey Gatehouse
Darrow Wood
Houghton Mill
Wicken Fen
Newmarket
Bury St Edmunds
Theatre Royal
Dunwich Heath
CAMBRIDGE
Anglesey Abbey
Ickworth
Willington Dovecote and Stables
BEDFORD
Wimpole Estate
Lavenham Guildhall
Melford Hall
Kyson Hill
Sutton Hoo
Orford Ness
IPSWICH
Pin Mill
Flatford
Sundon Hills Country Park
Sharpenhoe
Ascott
Totternhoe Knolls
Luton
Pitstone Windmill
Dunstable Downs and the Whipsnade Estate
Shaw's Corner
Ashridge Estate
HERTFORD
Hatfield Forest
Paycocke's House
Grange Barn
Colchester
Bourne Mill
Copt Hall Marshes
Northey Island
CHELMSFORD
Coombe Hill
Whipsnade Tree Cathedral
Morven Park
Danbury Commons and Blakes Wood
Eastbury Manor House
Rainham Hall
Rayleigh Mount
M181
A15
A631
A1103
A46
A158
A16
A52
A17
A151
A1
A606
A47
A43
A605
A6116
A1(M)
A14
A6
A428
A421
A505
A10
M11
A1101
A134
A141
A1065
A148
A140
A146
A11
A1066
A143
A12
A131
A120
A602
A133
A414
A130
M25
M1
M40
A413
A406
A127
A13
M4
M3
M26
M20
M2

Elegant Anglesey Abbey, Gardens and Lode Mill, Cambridgeshire, evokes a golden age

Anglesey Abbey, Gardens and Lode Mill

Quy Road, Lode, Cambridge, Cambridgeshire CB25 9EJ

1966

When you step into this elegant home, you journey back to a golden age of country-house living. You can discover Lord Fairhaven's extensive collection and how we care for it, then explore the domestic wing to see how the staff serving Lord Fairhaven ran his household like clockwork. The celebrated garden, with its sweeping avenues, classical statuary and flower borders, offers captivating views, vibrant colours and delicious scents whatever the season. Children can play, explore and discover nature in the Wildlife Discovery Area. A visit to the historic working watermill on beautiful Quy Water will complete your day.

Eat, shop, stay: Redwoods restaurant serving sandwiches, hot meals, teas, cakes, hot drinks. Light refreshments and snacks in gardens during peak times. Shop and plant centre selling local products and gifts. Freshly milled wholemeal flour available from the historic watermill. Second-hand bookshop.

Things to see and do: **Indoors** Hands-on activities and demonstrations in the house. **Outdoors** Self-led family activities. Weekday garden tours. **Dogs**: assistance dogs only. Downloadable dog walk in local area available.

Access:
Abbey and mill
Domestic wing **Grounds**
Parking: 50 yards (2-metre height restrictions in some areas of car park).

Find out more: 01223 810080 or angleseyabbey@nationaltrust.org.uk

Anglesey Abbey		M	T	W	T	F	S	S
Garden, restaurant, shop and plant centre								
1 Jan–30 Mar	9:30–4:30*	M	T	W	T	F	S	S
31 Mar–26 Oct	9:30–5:30*	M	T	W	T	F	S	S
27 Oct–31 Dec	9:30–4:30*	M	T	W	T	F	S	S
House								
1 Jan–30 Mar	11–4**	M	T	W	T	F	S	S
31 Mar–26 Oct	11–5**	M	T	W	T	F	S	S
27 Oct–31 Dec	11–4**	M	T	W	T	F	S	S
Lode Mill								
Open all year	10:30–3:30†	·	T	W	T	F	S	S

*Shop and plant centre: open at 10. **House: tours available before 11, last entry one hour before closing. †Lode Mill open Bank Holiday Mondays and Mondays during school holidays. Everything closed 24 to 26 December.

Ashridge Estate

near Berkhamsted, Hertfordshire

1926

This special place has been enjoyed for centuries by everyone from pilgrims to picnickers. With its rich wildlife, diverse habitats and varied history, there is plenty to uncover at Ashridge. From the scent of the bluebells in spring, glorious birdsong and spectacular views from the chalk downland of the Pitstone Hills in summer, the rutting fallow deer in autumn and crisp walks on swathes of open common in winter, Ashridge has a landscape for every season. Waymarked trails and walks leaflets available from the visitor centre. Wildwood Den natural play area for children. Climb the Bridgewater Monument for fantastic views. **Note**: toilets available only when café open.

Eat, shop, stay: our shop offers an ever-changing array of local and seasonal gifts, maps and books. The Brownlow Café (concession) serves homemade meals and snacks to eat in our outdoor courtyard.

Over the centuries, Ashridge Estate in Hertfordshire, this page and opposite, has been enjoyed by everyone from pilgrims to picnickers. Wildlife lovers also adore this special place

Things to see and do: events and children's activities throughout the year including trails, guided walks and workshops. Nearby Pitstone Windmill, also part of the Ashridge Estate, is open Sundays and Bank Holiday Mondays from 26 May to 26 August. **Dogs**: under close control at all times for the safety of wildlife and visitors.

Access:
Visitor centre **Grounds**
Sat Nav: use HP4 1LT for the visitor centre and Bridgewater Monument (points to the end of the drive). **Parking**: at visitor centre, Ivinghoe Beacon and many other parts of estate.

Find out more: 01442 851227 or ashridge@nationaltrust.org.uk

Ashridge Estate		M	T	W	T	F	S	S
Estate								
Open all year	Dawn–dusk	**M**	**T**	**W**	**T**	**F**	**S**	**S**
Visitor centre, Brownlow Café and shop*								
1 Jan–28 Feb	10–4	**M**	**T**	**W**	**T**	**F**	**S**	**S**
1 Mar–31 Oct	10–5	**M**	**T**	**W**	**T**	**F**	**S**	**S**
1 Nov–31 Dec	10–4	**M**	**T**	**W**	**T**	**F**	**S**	**S**
Bridgewater Monument (weather dependent)								
30 Mar–27 Oct	11–4	**M**	**T**	**W**	**T**	**F**	**S**	**S**

*Visitor centre, café and shop closed 24 and 25 December. Café: March to October, opens 8 and closes 6; November to February, opens 8 and closes 4. Estate may close in very high winds.

Blakeney National Nature Reserve

near Morston, Norfolk

1912

At the heart of the Norfolk Coast Area of Outstanding Natural Beauty, Blakeney National Nature Reserve boasts wide open spaces and uninterrupted views of the beautiful North Norfolk coastline. The 4-mile long shingle spit of Blakeney Point offers protection for Blakeney Harbour and provides a perfect habitat for the vast array of residential and migratory wildlife. Spectacular displays of the summer-breeding tern colony and winter-breeding grey seals will delight visitors all year round. Great for walkers, sightseers and wildlife enthusiasts alike, the internationally important reserve guarantees an inspiring and memorable visit no matter the season. **Note**: nearest toilets at Morston Quay and Blakeney Quay.

Blakeney National Nature Reserve, Norfolk: the Lifeboat House, above, and exploring, below

Eat, shop, stay: takeaway snacks, drinks and tasty treats available from our refreshment kiosk at Morston Quay. Nearby pubs and hotels (not National Trust) offering locally themed menus. Our holiday cottage, a simple lodge by Blakeney village, offers a romantic getaway for two.

Things to see and do: information centres at Morston Quay and Lifeboat House on Blakeney Point. Extensive coastal walks on the Norfolk Coast Path. Guided walks available. Ferry trips (not National Trust) to Blakeney Point.
Dogs: some restrictions apply (particularly Blakeney Point), 1 April to 15 August.

Access:
Information centre **Lifeboat House**
Sat Nav: use NR25 7BH for Morston Quay.
Parking: at Green Way Stiffkey Saltmarshes, Morston Quay and Blakeney Quay.

Find out more: 01263 740241 or blakeneypoint@nationaltrust.org.uk

Blakeney		M	T	W	T	F	S	S
Refreshment kiosk (Morston Quay)								
5 Jan–10 Feb	11–2	·	·	·	·	·	S	S
16 Feb–24 Feb	11–3	M	T	W	T	F	S	S
1 Mar–31 Oct	10–4	M	T	W	T	F	S	S
2 Nov–15 Dec	11–2	·	·	·	·	·	S	S
19 Dec–31 Dec*	11–2	M	T	W	T	F	S	S
Lifeboat House (Blakeney Point)								
30 Mar–27 Oct	Dawn–dusk	M	T	W	T	F	S	S

*Closed 25 December. Morston Information Centre open around the tides. Nature Reserve open all year.

 For information about getting to National Trust places, please see page 3

Blickling Estate

Blickling, Aylsham, Norfolk NR11 6NF

1940

You'll never forget your first sight of Blickling, as the breathtaking Jacobean mansion comes into view flanked by magnificent yew hedging. This 1,821-hectare (4,500-acre) gift to the nation was bequeathed by its visionary owner, Lord Lothian, who hoped that his former home would continue to be a place 'from which artistic endeavours go forth'. We respect this wish as our journey into contemporary art continues. This year your support is helping to tackle some of the crucial conservation work needed to protect the most significant book collection held by the National Trust and the Long Gallery that houses it. You'll see this work happening as part of your visit. **Note**: additional charges apply for some special events and experiences.

Eat, shop, stay: three cafés and a pub offering bed and breakfast (not National Trust). Large second-hand bookshop, stamp shop with extensive stock for collectors (donations welcome), gift shop, plant shop and exhibition loft. Nine holiday cottages on the estate.

Things to see and do: **Indoors** Nearly 400 years of history brought to life through contemporary art, family trails and living history performances. RAF museum with personal stories of those who served here during the Second World War. **Outdoors** The formal garden with its parterre and double borders, inspired by three centuries of history, also has a productive walled garden. Park offers waymarked cycling and walking trails (free guides). Pyramid mausoleum. Permit fishing (June to March). Changing programme throughout the year, including Easter fun, magnificent bluebells, summer music and winter lighting. Felbrigg Hall and Sheringham Park nearby. **Dogs**: welcome under close control in park and outside Farmyard café. Assistance dogs only elsewhere.

Blickling Estate in Norfolk: the breathtaking Jacobean mansion emerges from the morning mist

Access:
House **Gardens**
Parking: 400 yards.

Find out more: 01263 738030 or
blickling@nationaltrust.org.uk

Blickling Estate		M	T	W	T	F	S	S
House								
1 Jan–10 Mar	11–3:30	**M**	**T**	**W**	**T**	**F**	**S**	**S**
11 Mar–27 Oct	12–5	**M**	**T**	**W**	**T**	**F**	**S**	**S**
28 Oct–29 Nov	11–3:30	**M**	**T**	**W**	**T**	**F**	**S**	**S**
30 Nov–20 Dec	11:30–6:30	**M**	**T**	**W**	**T**	**F**	**S**	**S**
21 Dec–31 Dec*	11–3:30	**M**	**T**	**W**	**T**	**F**	**S**	**S**
Garden, shop and cafés								
1 Jan–10 Mar	10:30–4	**M**	**T**	**W**	**T**	**F**	**S**	**S**
11 Mar–27 Oct	10–5:30	**M**	**T**	**W**	**T**	**F**	**S**	**S**
28 Oct–29 Nov	10:30–4	**M**	**T**	**W**	**T**	**F**	**S**	**S**
30 Nov–20 Dec	11–7	**M**	**T**	**W**	**T**	**F**	**S**	**S**
21 Dec–31 Dec*	10:30–4	**M**	**T**	**W**	**T**	**F**	**S**	**S**
Park								
Open all year	Dawn–dusk	**M**	**T**	**W**	**T**	**F**	**S**	**S**

Last entry one hour before closing. *Closed 23, 24 and 25 December. Fishing all year, except 16 March to 15 June inclusive.

One of the cycling tracks at Blickling Estate, above, and the grand staircase, below

Support the places you visit: please scan your member card for free parking ticket

Bourne Mill

Bourne Road, Colchester, Essex CO2 8RT

1936

Picturesque watermill with working waterwheel in tranquil grounds. The ornate architecture reflects its early history as a banqueting lodge. Later the building became a fulling mill and then a flour mill. Located beside a large pond, the mill is surrounded by a delightful small garden.

Eat, shop, stay: light refreshments available. Pond-side seating area and shop selling a range of National Trust products.

Things to see and do: **Indoors** Discover how the mill works and watch the waterwheel turn. **Outside** Explore the wildlife area and see how many '50 things' activities you can do.
Dogs: welcome on leads.

Access:
Building **Grounds**
Parking: on site (very limited), or on street.

Find out more: 01206 549799 or bournemill@nationaltrust.org.uk

Bourne Mill		M	T	W	T	F	S	S
16 Feb–24 Feb	11–3	·	·	W	T	F	S	S
2 Mar–31 Mar	11–3	·	·	·	·	·	S	S
3 Apr–3 Nov	11–4	·	·	W	T	F	S	S

Open Bank Holiday Mondays, 11 to 4.

Picturesque Bourne Mill in Essex

Brancaster Estate

near Brancaster, Norfolk

1923

The Brancaster Estate comprises the beautiful endless sandy Brancaster Beach (above), perfect for summer sandcastles and winter walks, the intriguing Branodunum Roman Fort site and the traditional fishing harbour of Brancaster Staithe. The area is rich in wildlife and offers a memorable visit regardless of the time of year. **Note**: beach car park (not National Trust). Toilets at beach and harbour. Parking charges apply at Brancaster Beach (including members). Weekly and seasonal passes available.

Eat, shop, stay: stay at Brancaster Activity Centre, perfect for a large group and family getaways. Self-catering accommodation sleeping up to 48 in dorm-style bedrooms with en-suite facilities.

Things to see and do: walk along the Norfolk Coast Path and explore the coastline, taking in the panoramic views of the salt marsh across to Brancaster Harbour and Scolt Head Island National Nature Reserve beyond.
Dogs: responsible dog owners welcome. Restrictions apply on Brancaster Beach (May to September).

Access:
Sat Nav: use PE31 8AX (Beach Road); PE31 8BW (Brancaster Staithe).
Parking: Beach Road, Brancaster (not National Trust), charge including members. Limited parking at Harbour Way, Brancaster Staithe. Both subject to tidal flooding.

Find out more: 01263 740241 or brancaster@nationaltrust.org.uk

Copt Hall Marshes

near Little Wigborough, Essex 1989

Working farm on the remote and beautiful Blackwater Estuary – a fantastic birdwatching spot, important for overwintering species. **Note**: for Sat Nav use CO5 7RD. St Nicholas Church not National Trust.

Find out more: 01245 227662 or copthall@nationaltrust.org.uk

Danbury Commons and Blakes Wood

near Danbury, Essex 1953

Varied countryside, ranging from the lowland heath of Danbury Common to ancient woodland with stunning spring flowers at Blakes Wood. **Note**: sorry no toilets. Sat Nav: for Danbury Commons use CM3 4JH and for Blakes Wood use CM3 4AU. Danbury Commons main car park closes dusk.

Find out more: 01245 227662 or danbury@nationaltrust.org.uk

Darrow Wood

Darrow Green Road, Denton, Harleston, Norfolk IP20 0AY 1990

Darrow Wood is a small, hedge-enclosed, lightly wooded pasture field containing earthworks, including remains of a compact motte-and-bailey castle. **Note**: very limited roadside parking. Sorry no toilet.

Find out more: 01728 648020 (Dunwich Heath) or darrowwood@nationaltrust.org.uk

Dunstable Downs and the Whipsnade Estate, Bedfordshire, top right and right: the best picnicking and kite-flying site for miles around

Dunstable Downs and the Whipsnade Estate

near Dunstable, Bedfordshire

1928

The Downs have so much to offer all year round. The best kite-flying and picnicking site for miles around. A haven for wildlife; home to orchids, butterflies, birds and much more. Enjoy the ever-changing view from the Chilterns Gateway Centre with a refreshing drink or delicious meal. **Note**: Chilterns Gateway Centre is owned by Central Bedfordshire Council and managed by the National Trust.

Eat, shop, stay: shop selling a wide range of kites and Dunstable Downs branded products. The View Café serves light lunches, snacks, hot and cold drinks with the option to eat in or take away.

Things to see and do: events, including the annual Kite Festival in July. Nature trail and playscape in Chute Wood. Waymarked routes. History to discover and wildlife to spot.

Dogs: under close control, on leads in car parks, near livestock and ground-nesting birds.

Access: Dunstable Downs Chilterns Gateway Centre
Sat Nav: use LU6 2GY (or LU6 2TA for older equipment). **Parking**: at Dunstable Downs, off B4541, and Bison Hill off the B4540.

Find out more: 01582 500920 or dunstabledowns@nationaltrust.org.uk

Dunstable Downs		M	T	W	T	F	S	S
Chilterns Gateway Centre								
11 Feb–27 Oct	9:30–4	**M**	**T**	**W**	**T**	**F**	**S**	**S**

Closed 24 and 25 December. Hot food served up to 60 minutes before Centre closes. Entry to main car park closes 30 minutes after Centre closes.

Dunwich Heath and Beach

Dunwich, Saxmundham, Suffolk

1968

A precious landscape on the Suffolk coast, Dunwich Heath offers a true sense of being at one with nature. Located in the middle of an Area of Outstanding Natural Beauty, there is an abundance of wildlife, including rare birds such as the Dartford warbler and the mysterious nightjar. With a network of footpaths to explore, you can immerse yourself in nature with a walk on Dunwich Heath. There is also a variety of habitats, including heather heath, gorse tracks, open grassland and woodland, to discover, as well as a shingle beach at the foot of the sandy cliffs. **Note**: opening hours may be adjusted during bad weather.

Eat, shop, stay: clifftop tea-room serving breakfast, light lunches, cream teas, homemade cakes and a selection of coffees and teas. Enjoy stunning views from the lookout or warm yourself by the log burner. Gift shop selling selected National Trust bestsellers.

Dunwich Heath and Beach in Suffolk

The shingle beach at Dunwich Heath and Beach, above, and bug-hunting, left

Dunwich Heath and Beach		M	T	W	T	F	S	S
5 Jan–17 Feb	10–3	·	·	·	·	·	S	S
18 Feb–28 Feb	10–4	M	T	W	T	F	S	S
1 Mar–21 Jul	10–5	M	T	W	T	F	S	S
22 Jul–1 Sep	9:30–5	M	T	W	T	F	S	S
2 Sep–1 Nov	10–5	M	T	W	T	F	S	S
2 Nov–22 Dec	10–3	·	·	·	·	·	S	S
26 Dec–31 Dec	10–3	M	T	·	T	F	S	S

Open 1 January, 10 to 3. Opening times vary according to weather.

Things to see and do: self-guided walking trails. Heath Barn discovery centre showing wildlife footage. Children's activities, including bug-hunting, den-building, geocaching and children's trails. Special holiday team-led activities. **Dogs**: welcome. On leads on the Heath March to end of August. 'Woof' walk/beach unrestricted.

Access: Grounds
Sat Nav: use IP17 3DJ. **Parking**: on site.

Find out more: 01728 648501 or dunwichheath@nationaltrust.org.uk

Elizabethan House Museum

4 South Quay, Great Yarmouth, Norfolk NR30 2QH 1943

A 16th-century quayside home, set out to reflect day-to-day domestic life from Tudor to Victorian times. **Note**: managed by Norfolk Museums Service. Open Monday to Friday and Sundays, 1 April to 31 October, 10 to 4.

Find out more: 01493 855746 or elizabethanhouse@nationaltrust.org.uk

Felbrigg Hall, Gardens and Estate

Felbrigg, Norwich, Norfolk NR11 8PR

1969

Atmospheric Felbrigg is a place of tranquillity. The Hall, which still contains its original collection, reflects the people who shaped it. A home to eight generations, it has more than 400 years of family stories to be discovered. The Service Wing houses a temporary exhibition of five curious cabinets, by theatre designer Gary McCann. These allow visitors to view previously unseen items in a new and unique way. Set in extensive parkland, with a working walled garden and dove-house, orangery, lake and miles of estate walks, all framed by Norfolk skies, Felbrigg is the perfect place to escape and relax.

Eat, shop, stay: Squire's Pantry serving a selection of sandwiches, light meals, snacks, cakes and drinks. Jester's refreshment kiosk is open at peak times. Shop and second-hand bookshop selling a selection of gifts and plants. Eight beautiful holiday cottages on the estate.

Felbrigg Hall, Gardens and Estate, Norfolk: the atmospheric Hall, above; delicate wallpaper, left

Things to see and do: **Indoors** Introductory talks and attics and cellars tours on most days (call property to confirm on day of visit). Children's trails. **Outdoors** Events throughout the year (see website for details).

Dogs: welcome in tea-room. On leads near livestock. House, shop and gardens – assistance dogs only.

Access:
Hall **Gardens**

Sat Nav: use NR11 8PP. **Parking**: 100 yards. Electric vehicle charging point in main car park.

Find out more: 01263 837444 or felbrigg@nationaltrust.org.uk

Felbrigg Hall		M	T	W	T	F	S	S
House*								
16 Feb–29 Mar	12-3	M	T	W	T	F	S	S
30 Mar–3 Nov	12-5	M	T	W	T	F	S	S
Service Wing and garden*								
5 Jan–10 Feb	11-3	·	·	·	·	·	S	S
Service Wing*								
9 Nov–29 Dec	11-3	·	·	·	·	·	S	S
Shop and tea-room								
5 Jan–10 Feb	10-3	·	·	·	T	F	S	S
Garden, shop and tea-room								
16 Feb–29 Mar**	11-3	M	T	W	T	F	S	S
30 Mar–3 Nov**	11-5	M	T	W	T	F	S	S
4 Nov–22 Dec**	11-3	M	T	W	T	F	S	S
28 Dec–29 Dec**	11-3	·	·	·	·	·	S	S
Parkland								
Open all year	Dawn-dusk	M	T	W	T	F	S	S

*Last entry to Service Wing and house one hour before closing; Service Wing opens at 11, housing temporary 'Curious Cabinets' installation. **Shop and tea-room open at 10.

Flatford

East Bergholt, Suffolk CO7 6UL

1943

Flatford lies at the heart of the Dedham Vale Area of Outstanding Natural Beauty. This charming hamlet was the inspiration for some of John Constable's most famous paintings, including *The Hay Wain*, *Boat Building* and *Flatford Mill*. The fascinating exhibition gives you an insight into Constable's life and career whilst Bridge Cottage tells the story of the people who lived and worked at Flatford. You can explore the beautiful countryside on one of the circular walks or hire a boat and row along the River Stour. A visit to Flatford is a chance to walk in Constable's footsteps! **Note**: no public access inside Flatford Mill, Valley Farm and Willy Lott's House. £3.50 charge for guided tour (including members).

Charming Flatford, Suffolk, inspired some of John Constable's most famous paintings

Eat, shop, stay: riverside tea-room serving a tempting range of homemade cakes and light lunches. The gift shop offers quality gifts, souvenirs and Constable merchandise.

Things to see and do: volunteer guides offer short walking tours of the views which inspired John Constable (April to October only). Waymarked circular walks and family trails around Flatford. **Dogs**: welcome, but please keep dogs on leads amongst livestock.

Access:
Bridge Cottage **Grounds**
Parking: 100 yards.

Find out more: 01206 298260 or flatford@nationaltrust.org.uk

Flatford		M	T	W	T	F	S	S
1 Jan–6 Jan	10–3	·	T	W	T	F	S	S
12 Jan–10 Feb	10–3	·	·	·	·	·	S	S
16 Feb–24 Feb	10–4	M	T	W	T	F	S	S
27 Feb–31 Mar	10–4	·	·	W	T	F	S	S
1 Apr–29 Sep	10–5	M	T	W	T	F	S	S
30 Sep–3 Nov	10–4	M	T	W	T	F	S	S
6 Nov–22 Dec*	10–3	·	·	W	T	F	S	S
27 Dec–31 Dec	10–3	M	T	·	·	F	S	S

*Everything open 23 December, 10 to 3.

Grange Barn

Grange Hill, Coggeshall, Colchester, Essex CO6 1RE

1989

One of Europe's oldest timber-framed buildings, Grange Barn stands as a lasting reminder of the once-powerful Coggeshall Abbey. With oak pillars soaring up to a cathedral-like roof, bearing the weight of centuries, it was saved and restored in the 1980s. This 13th-century building has truly stood the test of time.

Eat, shop, stay: honey from Grange Barn's beehives is available to buy in season, alongside a limited range of souvenirs, second-hand books and ice cream. Coffee shop at nearby Paycocke's House and Garden. Picnics welcome.

Things to see and do: exhibition on the life and work of local woodcarver Bryan Saunders. Events during the year. Circular walk taking in Paycocke's House and Garden nearby.
Dogs: welcome on leads in grounds.

Access: Building Grounds
Parking: on site.

Find out more: 01376 562226 or grangebarncoggeshall@nationaltrust.org.uk

Grange Barn		M	T	W	T	F	S	S
16 Mar–29 Sep	11–4	**M**	**T**	**W**	**T**	**F**	**S**	**S**
30 Sep–3 Nov	11–3	**M**	**T**	**W**	**T**	**F**	**S**	**S**

Closes occasionally for private events (check before visiting).

A young visitor 'reads' about Grange Barn, Essex

Hatfield Forest

near Bishop's Stortford, Essex

1924

Hatfield Forest, Essex: one of the Red Poll cows

When Henry I established a Royal Hunting Forest here in 1100, he could little have guessed that almost a millennium later it would be the best survivor of its kind in the world. The ancient trees are managed using traditional techniques, and the forest is home to more than 3,500 species of wildlife, including fallow deer descended from the original herd. Explore the wide open plains, grazed by Red Poll cows, or enjoy the shade of the coppice woodland. With over 405 hectares (1,000 acres), there are many places for imaginative play or a spot of quiet relaxation. **Note**: to protect the forest, the best time to visit is May to September.

Eat, shop, stay: café (outdoor-only dining area) serving hot and cold refreshments, ice cream and drinks. Shop selling gifts, guidebook and maps, plus Hatfield Forest venison (when in season).

Things to see and do: you can enjoy open-air theatre, WoodFest and other events. Rowing boat hire and family activities in the summer holidays. **Dogs**: on lead near livestock, in the lake area and woodland. Always under close control.

Access:
Shell House **Forest**
Sat Nav: use CM22 6NE.
Parking: on site (limited in winter).

Find out more: 01279 874040 (Infoline). 01279 870678 or hatfieldforest@nationaltrust.org.uk

Hatfield Forest		M	T	W	T	F	S	S
Countryside and kiosk car park								
5 Jan–31 Mar	10–3	·	·	·	·	·	S	S
1 Apr–30 Sep	10–4:30	M	T	W	T	F	S	S
5 Oct–29 Dec	10–3	·	·	·	·	·	S	S
Café								
2 Jan–31 Mar	9–3	·	·	W	T	F	S	S
1 Apr–30 Sep	9–5*	M	T	W	T	F	S	S
2 Oct–29 Dec	9–3	·	·	W	T	F	S	S

Entrance car park open daily; Shell House and Elgin's car parks open April to October, 10 to 4:30, Monday to Friday, and 9 to 4:30, Saturday and Sunday (conditions permitting). *Café late opening during summer holidays. Café and internal car parks closed 25 and 26 December. Café open 1 January 2020, 10 to 2.

Many parts of Hatfield Forest are very accessible

Horsey Windpump

Horsey, Great Yarmouth, Norfolk NR29 4EE

1948

Fully restored and once again standing proud over the broadland landscape, Horsey Windpump is complete with new cap and patent sails. Explore this historic building to discover its fascinating story and the connection between man and nature. There are fantastic views over Horsey Mere and beyond from the top. **Note**: surrounded by Horsey Estate – managed by the Buxton family.

Eat, shop, stay: shop and tea-room (next to Horsey Windpump) serving snacks, drinks, tasty treats and small range of gifts. Stay in one of our converted barn holiday cottages nearby in Horsey village. Perfectly placed for exploring the Broads and Norfolk coast.

Things to see and do: great starting point for accessing the outdoors, with walking routes to Horsey Mere and the beach. Boat trips (not National Trust) across Horsey Mere (May to September). **Dogs**: welcome (on leads near wildlife and livestock).

Access:
Windpump **Grounds**
Parking: on site.

Find out more: 01263 740241 or horseywindpump@nationaltrust.org.uk

Horsey Windpump		M	T	W	T	F	S	S
16 Mar–31 Mar	10–4:30	·	·	·	·	·	S	S
1 Apr–27 Oct	10–4:30	M	T	W	T	F	S	S
2 Nov–24 Nov	10–3:30	·	·	·	·	·	S	S

Car park and toilets open all year, dawn to dusk.

Houghton Mill and Waterclose Meadows

Houghton, near Huntingdon, Cambridgeshire PE28 2AZ

1939

Historic mill in an inspiring riverside setting surrounded by meadow walks. All the family can enjoy hands-on activities in the oldest working watermill on the Great Ouse. As well as seeing milling demonstrations, you can buy flour, ground in the traditional way on our French burr millstones.

Eat, shop, stay: riverside tea-room serving snacks, cakes and scones made with our traditional stoneground flour. Freshly ground flour and gifts for sale in mill shop. Come and stay at our tranquil riverside camp/caravan site or in the new luxury camping pods.

Historic Houghton Mill and Waterclose Meadows, Cambridgeshire: still milling today

Things to see and do: **Indoors** Milling demonstrations on Sundays. Baking days. Family events. **Outdoors** Open-air theatre, activities and summer holiday events. Access to surrounding meadows via public footpaths. **Dogs**: assistance dogs only in mill; all dogs welcome in grounds on leads.

Access:
Mill **Tea-room** **Grounds**
Parking: on site.

Find out more: 01480 499990 (mill). 01480 499996 (campsite) or houghtonmill@nationaltrust.org.uk

Houghton Mill		M	T	W	T	F	S	S
Mill								
16 Mar–27 Oct	11–5	·	·	·	·	·	S	S
18 Mar–22 May	1–5	M	T	W	·	·	·	·
27 May–30 Aug	1–5	M	T	W	T	F	·	·
2 Sep–23 Oct	1–5	M	T	W	·	·	·	·
Tea-room								
4 Jan–15 Mar	10:30–3:30	·	·	·	·	F	S	S
16 Mar–27 Oct	10:30–5	M	T	W	T	F	S	S
1 Nov–22 Dec	10:30–3:30	·	·	·	·	F	S	S

Mill: open Bank Holiday Mondays and Good Friday, 11 to 5. Waterclose Meadows Caravan and Campsite (National Trust): open 15 March to 27 October (01480 499996). Car park and riverside: close 8, or dusk if earlier.

Ickworth

The Rotunda, Horringer, Bury St Edmunds, Suffolk IP29 5QE

1956

An Italianate palace in the heart of an ancient deer park. Formal gardens, pleasure grounds, rolling Suffolk landscape and woodlands invite gentle strolls or long walks, runs, bike rides and picnics. The Italianate Garden mirrors the architecture of the house and celebrates the Hervey family's passion for Italy, while also encasing an idiosyncratic Victorian stumpery, contrasting light and shade. The Rotunda is home to one of the finest silver collections in Europe, family portraits by Gainsborough and Reynolds, works by Titian and Velázquez, and Neo-classical sculpture, including Flaxman's *Fury of Athamus*. 'Below stairs', the servants' quarters recreate domestic service through the stories and memories of those who lived here. **Note**: extensive conservation works from the summer.

The Italianate Rotunda at Ickworth, Suffolk, below. Enjoying a chilly walk in the grounds, right, and exploring the house, top right

Eat, shop, stay: West Wing Café (lunch 12 to 2:30). Porter's Lodge outdoor café (dog-friendly). Squash Court Café. Gift shop and plant and garden shop. Second-hand books. Five holiday cottages. Hotel accommodation at The Ickworth (part of Luxury Family Hotel Group).

Things to see and do: **Indoors** Tours daily, house exhibitions, 1930s Servants' Quarters, cooking in the kitchen experiences and living history days, as well as children's crafts in the Gallery every school holiday. Regency furniture, Italian porcelain and paintings by Titian, Vigée Le Brun and Kauffman. Hervey family church plus bookable tours. **Outdoors** Events all year, including open-air theatre and cinema, annual Country Estate

Ickworth		M	T	W	T	F	S	S
House								
1 Jan–3 Mar*	11–3	M	T	W	T	F	S	S
4 Mar–3 Nov**	11–5	M	T	W	T	F	S	S
4 Nov–31 Dec*	11–3†	M	T	W	T	F	S	S
Gift shop and West Wing Café								
1 Jan–3 Mar	10:30–4	M	T	W	T	F	S	S
4 Mar–3 Nov	10:30–5	M	T	W	T	F	S	S
4 Nov–31 Dec	10:30–4	M	T	W	T	F	S	S
Porter's Lodge outdoor café								
Open all year	10–5	M	T	W	T	F	S	S
Plant and garden shop								
4 Mar–8 Nov	11–5	M	T	W	T	F	S	S
9 Nov–29 Dec	12–3	·	·	·	·	·	S	S
Italianate Garden								
Open all year	10:30–5:30	M	T	W	T	F	S	S

*House: weekends access by tours only; Servants' Quarters freeflow only at weekends. Last entry 2:30. Parkland, Italianate Garden, plant and garden shop and Porter's Lodge outdoor café may close earlier in winter and adverse weather. Everything closed 24 and 25 December. **Limited opening may apply due to conservation and project works. Freeflow from 12 to 4 (last entry to house at 3:15). Tours only 11 to 12 and 4 to 5. †Tours only during December weekends.

Fayre and autumn Wood Fair. Monthly speciality walks showcasing seasonal highlights, including snowdrops, walled garden produce and historic daffodils. Family activities include den-building and children's play area. **Dogs**: welcome on leads at all times. Assistance dogs only in the Italianate Garden.

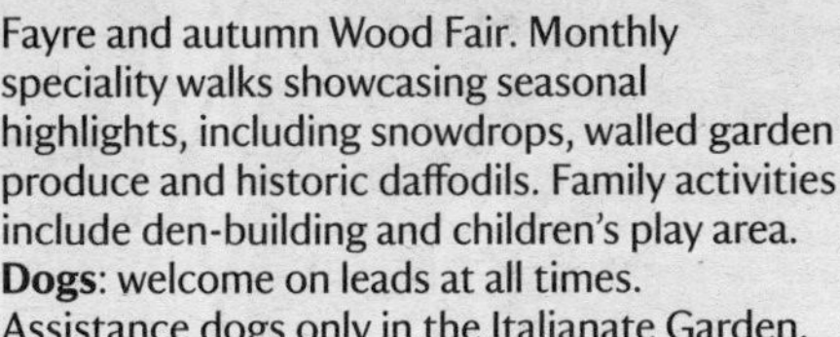

Access:
House
West Wing
Gardens/parkland

Sat Nav: may not direct you to main entrance. Access to Ickworth is through Horringer village. **Parking**: on site.

Find out more: 01284 735270 or ickworth@nationaltrust.org.uk

Kyson Hill

Broomheath, Woodbridge, Suffolk 1934

Diminutive Kyson Hill, with its grassy slopes, specimen trees and estuarine views, is a favourite destination for walking or relaxation. **Note**: sorry no toilet. Broomheath public car park, 546 yards (not National Trust). For Sat Nav use IP12 4DL. OS map reference is 197/212:TM264478.

Find out more: 01394 389700 (Sutton Hoo) or kysonhill@nationaltrust.org.uk

Lavenham Guildhall

Market Place, Lavenham, Sudbury, Suffolk CO10 9QZ

1951

The Guildhall of Corpus Christi is a remarkable medieval survivor at the centre of the village of Lavenham, remaining a constant presence over the past 500 years. When you step inside this complex of fine timber-framed buildings, you'll feel the centuries melt away. You can discover the stories of the people who have lived and worked here, their highs and lows. From religious guild to workhouse, family home to nightclub, there is more than meets the eye. After your visit, why not explore the picturesque streets of Lavenham, lined with shops, galleries and more than 320 buildings of historic interest?

Eat, shop, stay: tea-room serving light lunches, cream teas and hot and cold drinks. Shop selling local gifts, souvenirs, books and plants.

Things to see and do: **Indoors** Children's trails and dressing-up costumes. Changing exhibitions. **Outdoors** Guided walks and talks throughout the year.

Access:
Guildhall **Garden**
Parking: in village (free) – no National Trust parking. Nearest car parks at Prentice Street (200 yards, 24 spaces), use CO10 9RD, and main car park Church Street (800 yards, 86 spaces), use CO10 9SA.

Find out more: 01787 247646 or lavenhamguildhall@nationaltrust.org.uk

Lavenham Guildhall		M	T	W	T	F	S	S
4 Jan–24 Feb	11-4	·	·	·	·	**F**	**S**	**S**
1 Mar–31 Oct*	11-5	**M**	**T**	**W**	**T**	**F**	**S**	**S**
1 Nov–23 Dec**	11-4	**M**	·	·	·	**F**	**S**	**S**

*Tea-room and shop: open at 10. **6 to 8 December: museum closed for Lavenham Christmas Fair.

Feel the centuries melt away at Lavenham Guildhall in Suffolk, above and below

Melford Hall

Long Melford, Sudbury, Suffolk CO10 9AA

1960

Melford Hall has had its fair share of trials and tribulations, from being ransacked during the Civil War to being devastated by fire in 1942. It is thanks to the many generations who have left their mark that it continues to survive. This year we will concentrate on two strong women, Countess Rivers and Ulla, Lady Hyde Parker, who transformed Melford Hall in the 17th and 20th centuries respectively. It is their stories, and those of Hyde Parker family life – from naval exploits to visits from their cousin Beatrix Potter – which make this house more than mere bricks and mortar.

Eat, shop, stay: small tea-room serving light lunches, sandwiches and cream teas with seating for 45 in Park and Courtyard Rooms (additional tables outdoors). Gatehouse shop selling souvenirs, gifts, books, souvenir story books and plants.

Visitors explore the garden at Melford Hall, Suffolk, right and below

Things to see and do: **Indoors** Taster tours and talks. Spot-it quiz for children under eight. **Outdoors** Garden tours and games. Walks, talks and family events. **Dogs**: welcome on leads in car park and park walk only.

Access:
Building **Grounds**
Parking: on site.

Find out more: 01787 376395 (Infoline). 01787 379228 or melford@nationaltrust.org.uk

Melford Hall		M	T	W	T	F	S	S
3 Apr–3 Nov	12–5	·	·	**W**	**T**	**F**	**S**	**S**

House: open 12 to 1, entry by short taster tour only; freeflow from 1. Open Bank Holiday Mondays and Good Friday.

Morven Park

Great North Road, Potters Bar, Hertfordshire
1928

On the site of the original Potters Bar, these eight hectares (20 acres) of parkland were created over 150 years ago. **Note**: sorry no toilet or on-site parking. For Sat Nav use EN6 1HS.

Find out more: 01582 873663 or morvenpark@nationaltrust.org.uk

Northey Island

near Maldon, Essex 1978

A peaceful retreat in the Blackwater Estuary, important for overwintering birds, Northey is also the oldest recorded battlefield in Britain. **Note**: for Sat Nav use CM9 6PP (CM9 5JQ parking). Access by tidal causeway, please telephone in advance to check tide times and arrange permit.

Find out more: 01621 853142 or northeyisland@nationaltrust.org.uk

Orford Ness National Nature Reserve

Orford Quay, Orford, Woodbridge, Suffolk IP12 2NU

1993

Orford Ness National Nature Reserve, Suffolk, above and below: a place of ethereal beauty

Suffolk's secret coast – wild, remote, exposed. Known as the 'Island', only reached by National Trust ferry, the Ness contains the ruined remnants of a disturbing past. Ranked among the most important shingle features in the world, rare and fragile wildlife thrives where weapons, including atomic bombs, were tested and perfected. **Note**: limited tickets. Steep, slippery steps, long distances. Hazardous debris. Limited access: 'pagodas' only on tours. Charge for ferry crossing (including members).

Eat, shop, stay: shops, cafés and pubs in village (none National Trust). Fresh fish available at quay. Local smokehouses.

Things to see and do: trails lead through coastal grazing marsh and vegetated shingle habitats to the sea, taking in wildlife, ex-military testing areas, buildings and displays. **Dogs**: assistance dogs only.

Access: **Buildings** **Trails**
Sat Nav: IP12 2NU. **Parking**: at Riverside car park, Quay Street, not National Trust (charge including members), 150 yards to Trust Orford Quay office to buy ferry ticket.

Find out more: 01728 648024 (Infoline). 01394 450900 (office) or orfordness@nationaltrust.org.uk

Orford Ness		M	T	W	T	F	S	S
20 Apr–22 Jun	10–2	·	·	·	·	·	**S**	·
25 Jun–28 Sep	10–2	·	**T**	**W**	**T**	**F**	**S**	·
5 Oct–26 Oct	10–2	·	·	·	·	·	**S**	·

Access by National Trust ferry from Orford Quay. Boats cross to the Ness every 20 minutes, 10 to 2 only, returning regularly through day (last ferry back departs 5). Tickets limited, only available on day. Main visitor trail (Red Route) always available, other routes open seasonally. Also open Good Friday and Bank Holiday Sundays and Mondays (except 25 and 26 December and 1 and 2 January).

Oxburgh Hall

Oxborough, near Swaffham, Norfolk PE33 9PS

1952

Built more than 500 years ago by the Bedingfeld family, who were persecuted for their Catholic faith, Oxburgh has survived turbulent times. Just like the 6th Baronet, we're now embarking on an ambitious project to restore the roof, windows and chimneys. Inside, Victorian Gothic interiors reflect a romantic view of Oxburgh's medieval past. Discover hidden doors, a secret priest's hole and embroideries worked by Mary, Queen of Scots. The moated Hall is surrounded by gardens with seasonal interest, streams and woodland walks.

Eat, shop, stay: tea-room in old Kitchen and Servants' Hall. The Pantry is a seasonal kiosk serving light refreshments. Picnic in the grounds or area by the car park. Gift shop selling gifts, games and local products. Plant sales. Second-hand bookshop. Holiday cottage.

Three views of Oxburgh Hall, Norfolk: after a turbulent past, now all is peaceful

Things to see and do: **Indoors** Introductory talks most days, March to October. Family trails. **Outdoors** Garden tours most days, March to October. Winter weekend snowdrop walks. Children's activities, including woodland den-building area. Year-round events.
Dogs: on short leads in the gardens and countryside. Assistance dogs only indoors.

Access:
Hall **Chapel** **Garden**
Parking: on site.

Find out more: 01366 328258 or oxburghhall@nationaltrust.org.uk

Oxburgh Hall		M	T	W	T	F	S	S
House								
5 Jan–27 Jan	Tour**	·	·	·	·	·	**S**	**S**
9 Feb–8 Mar	12-3*	**M**	**T**	**W**	**T**	**F**	**S**	**S**
9 Mar–29 Sep	11-5*	**M**	**T**	**W**	**T**	**F**	**S**	**S**
30 Sep–3 Nov	11-4*	**M**	**T**	**W**	**T**	**F**	**S**	**S**
9 Nov–30 Nov	Tour**	·	·	·	·	·	**S**	**S**
7 Dec–15 Dec	11-4†	·	·	·	·	·	**S**	**S**
Garden, shop and tea-room								
5 Jan–10 Feb	11-4	·	·	·	·	·	**S**	**S**
11 Feb–8 Mar	11-4	**M**	**T**	**W**	**T**	**F**	**S**	**S**
9 Mar–29 Sep	10:30-5	**M**	**T**	**W**	**T**	**F**	**S**	**S**
30 Sep–3 Nov	10:30-4	**M**	**T**	**W**	**T**	**F**	**S**	**S**
9 Nov–21 Dec	11-4	·	·	·	·	·	**S**	**S**

*House: last entry 45 minutes before closing. **Guided tours only at 12 and 2, places limited. †Christmas event weekends, ground floor and gatehouse only. Major restoration work may affect opening hours from September.

Paycocke's House and Garden

25 West Street, Coggeshall, Colchester, Essex CO6 1NS

1924

Exquisitely carved half-timbered Tudor cloth merchant's house, with a beautiful and tranquil cottage garden. Visitors can follow the house's changing fortune and see how it was saved from demolition and restored to its former glory. You can discover five centuries of craftsmanship and conservation.

Eat, shop, stay: coffee shop serving cream teas, coffee, cakes and soft drinks (courtyard and garden). Picnics welcome. Shop selling gifts and local products. Plants for sale at our garden stall. Second-hand bookshop.

Things to see and do: **Indoors** Events all year. Children's dressing-up costumes. **Outdoors** Relax or play garden games. Why not combine with visit to nearby Grange Barn and enjoy the circular walk? **Dogs**: welcome in garden only on a lead; assistance dogs only in house.

Access: **Building** **Grounds**
Parking: at Coggeshall Grange Barn, ½ mile.

Find out more: 01376 561305 or paycockes@nationaltrust.org.uk

Paycocke's		M	T	W	T	F	S	S
16 Feb–29 Sep	11-5	**M**	**T**	**W**	**T**	**F**	**S**	**S**
30 Sep–3 Nov	11-4	**M**	**T**	**W**	**T**	**F**	**S**	**S**

Garden: open 10:30; closes as house.

Paycocke's House and Garden in Essex

Peckover House and Garden

North Brink, Wisbech, Cambridgeshire PE13 1JR

1943

While its riverside setting at Wisbech was popular among merchants, imposing Peckover House stood apart as an oasis of calm, reflecting the Quaker way of life. The Peckovers were bankers and added a specially designed wing to the house; an exhibition tells its story. This year marks the centenary of Lord Peckover's death, and we will be exploring his interests and passions, including his 'Lost Library'. The Peckovers also loved their garden; discover its delights as you explore the unexpected 0.8 hectare (2 acres) of abundance.

For information about getting to National Trust places, please see page 3

Eat, shop, stay: the Reed Barn is the ideal place for a light lunch or afternoon tea. Browse our gift shop, second-hand bookshop and our plant trolley. Stay a little longer in one of our holiday cottages – Wainman House or Coach House Loft.

Things to see and do: **Indoors** Grand piano to play, behind-the-scenes tours, handling collection, children's trails and exhibitions. **Outdoors** Garden tours and croquet/lawn games (summer). Octavia Hill's Birthplace House opposite (not National Trust). **Dogs**: assistance dogs only.

Access: [icons]
House [icons] **Garden** [icons]
Sat Nav: use PE13 1RG or PE13 2RA for nearest car parks. **Parking**: nearest at Chapel Road or Somers Road, 500 yards (not National Trust). Car parks occasionally used for town events and may not be in use – please check before journey.

Peckover House and Garden, Cambridgeshire: the kitchen stove, above, and elegant façade, left

Find out more: 01945 583463 or peckover@nationaltrust.org.uk

Peckover House and Garden		M	T	W	T	F	S	S
12 Jan–17 Feb*	12–4	·	·	·	·	·	**S**	**S**
23 Feb–7 Apr**	11–4	**M**	**T**	**W**	**T**	·	**S**	**S**
8 Apr–21 Apr†	11–5	**M**	**T**	**W**	**T**	**F**	**S**	**S**
22 Apr–30 Jun†	11–5	**M**	**T**	**W**	**T**	·	**S**	**S**
1 Jul–7 Jul†	11–5	**M**	**T**	**W**	**T**	**F**	**S**	**S**
8 Jul–20 Oct†	11–5	**M**	**T**	**W**	**T**	·	**S**	**S**
21 Oct–27 Oct†	11–4	**M**	**T**	**W**	**T**	**F**	**S**	**S**
2 Nov–17 Nov†	11–4	·	·	·	·	·	**S**	**S**
7 Dec–15 Dec††	11–4	**M**	**T**	**W**	**T**	**F**	**S**	**S**

*Garden, tea-room and shop only open. **House: open by timed tours only weekdays; freeflow at weekends. †House: open 12 to 4. ††Christmas celebration.

Pin Mill

near Chelmondiston, Suffolk 1978

A woodland and heathland restoration site. A number of footpaths from the village with panoramic views over the River Orwell. **Note**: for Sat Nav use IP9 1JW. Parking in Pin Mill village, not National Trust (charge including members), or Chelmondiston.

Find out more: 01206 298260 or pinmill@nationaltrust.org.uk

Ramsey Abbey Gatehouse

Hollow Lane, Ramsey, Huntingdon, Cambridgeshire PE26 1DH 1952

This fascinating medieval gatehouse, along with the Lady Chapel, are all that remain of the great Benedictine abbey at Ramsey. **Note**: in school grounds so no public access except on open days. Gatehouse and Lady Chapel open first Sunday of the month, April to September, 1 to 5.

Find out more: 01480 301494 or ramseyabbey@nationaltrust.org.uk

Rayleigh Mount

Rayleigh, Essex 1923

Medieval motte-and-bailey castle site, with adjacent windmill housing historical exhibition. **Note**: exhibition in windmill operated by Rochford District Council. For Sat Nav use SS6 7ED. Parking at Bellingham Lane – adjacent to main entrance (not National Trust). Gates close 2 on Saturdays. Opening times may vary, call 01268 775328 to check before visiting.

Find out more: 01284 747500 or rayleighmount@nationaltrust.org.uk

Sharpenhoe

Sharpenhoe Road, Streatley, Bedfordshire 1939

Managed as a nature reserve; archaeology, geology and nature come together to provide a stunning landscape. **Note**: sorry no toilets. For Sat Nav use LU3 3PR. Car park between Sharpenhoe and Streatley.

Find out more: 01582 873663 or sharpenhoe@nationaltrust.org.uk

Shaw's Corner

Ayot St Lawrence, near Welwyn, Hertfordshire AL6 9BX

1944

Shaw's Corner, Hertfordshire: place of inspiration

George Bernard Shaw's peaceful rural home and garden show what inspired this great playwright. Pictures and sculpture reflect his wide circle of friends in theatre and the arts. See the writing hut where he created plays which won him the Nobel Prize, an Oscar and the hearts of millions of admirers. **Note**: access roads very narrow.

Eat, shop, stay: hot drinks and cakes available from our new vintage coffee van. Ice cream and soft drinks available in garden. Small gift shop. Second-hand bookshop. Pre-1950s varieties of plants for sale.

Things to see and do: events, including open-air performances of George Bernard Shaw's plays (summer). **Dogs**: assistance dogs only.

Access:
House **Grounds**
Sat Nav: use AL6 9BX (some routes might take you through a ford and a route not signposted to Shaw's Corner). **Parking**: very limited (not suitable for large vehicles).

Find out more: 01438 821968 (Infoline). 01438 820307 or shawscorner@nationaltrust.org.uk

Shaw's Corner		M	T	W	T	F	S	S
23 Mar–27 Oct	12–5	·	·	**W**	**T**	**F**	**S**	**S**

Open Bank Holiday Mondays.

The gently undulating natural landscape of Sheringham Park, Norfolk, was used as a starting point for Repton's design

Sheringham Park

Upper Sheringham, Norfolk NR26 8TL

1987

Utilising the park's undulating landscape, Humphry Repton created views of the North Norfolk coast that can still be enjoyed today. His 1812 design stated 'Sheringham Park had more natural beauty and advantages than any place he had ever seen'. The Upcher family added an extensive rhododendron collection to Repton's design, bringing an array of colour to the wild garden in the spring. A walk around the varying habitats of the 405-hectare (1,000-acre) estate may be interrupted by the drumming of a woodpecker, the song of skylarks or the sound of a steam train travelling through the park. **Note**: Sheringham Hall is privately occupied. April to September: limited access by written appointment with leaseholder.

Eat, shop, stay: gift shop selling guidebooks, local gifts and souvenirs. Peat-free plant sales. Courtyard Café serving soup, sandwiches, cake and ice cream. A range of gluten-free food also available. Picnics welcome. Five holiday cottages on site.

Things to see and do: self-guided trails and guided walks. Climb the gazebo tower to see coastal views enjoyed since Napoleonic times. Wide-ranging events programme for families and adults. Free children's Tracker Packs. **Dogs**: welcome under control. Please keep on leads near livestock and visitor facilities.

Access:
Building **Grounds**
Parking: 60 yards. Two electric vehicle charging points in car park.

Find out more: 01263 820550 or sheringhampark@nationaltrust.org.uk

Sheringham Park		M	T	W	T	F	S	S
Park								
Open all year	Dawn–dusk	**M**	**T**	**W**	**T**	**F**	**S**	**S**
Visitor centre and Courtyard Café								
5 Jan–3 Mar	11–4	·	·	·	·	·	**S**	**S**
9 Mar–27 Oct	10–5	**M**	**T**	**W**	**T**	**F**	**S**	**S**
2 Nov–29 Dec	11–4	·	·	·	·	·	**S**	**S**

Courtyard Café opens 8:45 and visitor centre 9:30 on Saturdays. Visitor centre and Courtyard Café: open daily, 10 to 5, 16 to 24 February; 11 to 4, 27 to 31 December; open to 6, 25 to 27 May.

Sundon Hills Country Park

Harlington Road, Upper Sundon, Bedfordshire 2000

Wildlife-rich chalk grassland, beech woodland, open meadows and a picnic site with views north towards the Greensand Ridge. **Note**: sorry no toilets. For Sat Nav use LU3 3PE.

Find out more: 01582 873663 or sundonhills@nationaltrust.org.uk

Sutton Hoo

Sutton Hoo, Woodbridge, Suffolk IP12 3DJ

1998

For 1,300 years its secrets were hidden deep within a burial mound, but on the eve of the Second World War a discovery that changed history was unearthed by archaeologists at Sutton Hoo. From the sandy soil emerged the outline of a 29-yard-long ship, its timbers long since rotted away, revealed to be the ship burial of an Anglo-Saxon king, complete with exquisite gold and silver treasures. Newly designed exhibitions, breathtaking replicas, the atmospheric Royal Burial Ground with new walking route and viewing tower offering stunning views over the landscape all bring this fascinating story to life. **Note**: due to major transformation project, opening times may change (please check website before visiting).

Eat, shop, stay: café serving hot meals, snacks and cream teas with veranda looking out towards the River Deben. Gift shop. Second-hand bookshop. Three holiday apartments on the top floors of Tranmer House, all with stunning views.

Things to see and do: **Indoors** Exhibition: film, storytelling, replicas, some original treasures, guest exhibitions. Tranmer House: the history of archaeology, Discovery Room. **Outdoors** Full-scale ship sculpture, viewing tower, walks, children's trails and play area. **Dogs**: welcome on leads in reception, shop, café and walks.

Access:
Buildings **Grounds**
Parking: on site.

Sutton Hoo, Suffolk: burial mound, below, and valley, right

Find out more: 01394 389700 or suttonhoo@nationaltrust.org.uk

Sutton Hoo		M	T	W	T	F	S	S
19 Apr-27 Oct	10-5	**M**	**T**	**W**	**T**	**F**	**S**	**S**
28 Oct-23 Dec	10-4	**M**	**T**	**W**	**T**	**F**	**S**	**S**
26 Dec-31 Dec	10-4	**M**	**T**	·	**T**	**F**	**S**	**S**

Due to major transformation project, opening times may change (please check website before visiting).

Theatre Royal Bury St Edmunds

Westgate Street, Bury St Edmunds, Suffolk IP33 1QR 1974

Last surviving Regency playhouse in Britain, this Grade I listed theatre offers a vibrant drama, music, dance and comedy programme. **Note**: managed by Bury St Edmunds Theatre Management Ltd. Tours are free to National Trust Members, admission charges apply to shows.

Find out more: 01284 769505 or theatreroyal@nationaltrust.org.uk

Totternhoe Knolls

Castle Hill Road, Totternhoe, Bedfordshire 2000

The dramatic earthworks of a Norman castle rise from important chalk grassland habitat, sitting high above the surrounding landscape. **Note**: sorry no toilets. For Sat Nav use LU6 1RG.

Find out more: 01582 873663 or totternhoeknolls@nationaltrust.org.uk

West Runton and Beeston Regis Heath

near West Runton, Norfolk 1925

A lovely place to walk among heath and woods, with fine views of the North Norfolk coast. **Note**: sorry no toilets. For Sat Nav use NR27 9ND.

Find out more: 01263 820550 or westrunton@nationaltrust.org.uk

Whipsnade Tree Cathedral

Whipsnade, Dunstable, Bedfordshire 1960

Peaceful place with trees planted in shape of a medieval cathedral. Created after the First World War to commemorate fallen comrades. **Note**: dogs allowed under control. Annual service second Sunday, June. Car park open 9 to 4 (winter); 9 to 7 (summer). Sat Nav use LU6 2LQ. Donations welcome. Open daily, 1 January to 23 March and 20 October to 31 December, 9 to 4; 24 March to 19 October, 9 to 7.

Find out more: 01582 872406 or whipsnadetc@nationaltrust.org.uk

Wicken Fen National Nature Reserve

Lode Lane, Wicken, Ely, Cambridgeshire

1899

With vast skies above flowering meadows, sedge and reedbeds, Wicken Fen is a window onto a lost fenland landscape. A wealth of wildlife is at home in this important wetland, including rarities such as hen harriers and bitterns, numerous dragonflies, moths and wildfowl. The landscape feels wild, though people have managed it for years, as revealed by the fenman's yard, windpump and cottage. The Wicken Fen Vision, an ambitious landscape-scale conservation project, is opening up new areas for wildlife and for you to explore. Grazing herds of Highland cattle and Konik ponies help create a diverse range of new habitats. **Note**: some paths are subject to seasonal closure. Café building work planned January to March.

Eat, shop, stay: shop in the visitor centre selling wildlife and outdoor books, local food and crafts. Café serving light lunches and afternoon teas. Picnics welcome.

Wicken Fen National Nature Reserve in Cambridgeshire: windpump, wetland and visitors

Wicken Fen		M	T	W	T	F	S	S
Reserve, visitor centre and shop								
Open all year*	10–5**	**M**	**T**	**W**	**T**	**F**	**S**	**S**
Café								
1 Jan–17 Feb†	10–4:30	**M**	**T**	**W**	**T**	**F**	**S**	**S**
18 Feb–27 Oct†	10–5	**M**	**T**	**W**	**T**	**F**	**S**	**S**
28 Oct–31 Dec*	10–4:30	**M**	**T**	**W**	**T**	**F**	**S**	**S**

*Closed 25 December. **Access to reserve dawn to dusk; visitor centre closes dusk in winter. †Alternative to café operating January to March.

Things to see and do: explore the heart of the Fen on foot, via the Boardwalk and longer paths. Seasonal boat trips available. Cycle across the wider reserve; we hire bikes, or bring your own. **Dogs**: welcome on leads on reserve and in visitor centre.

Access:
Building **Grounds**
Sat Nav: use CB7 5XP. **Parking**: 120 yards.

Find out more: 01353 720274 or wickenfen@nationaltrust.org.uk

Willington Dovecote and Stables

Willington, Church End, near Bedford, Bedfordshire MK44 3PX 1914

These stunning remnants of Gostwick's show farm stand like two ancient warriors, the only survivors from the battle with time. **Note**: open last Sunday of month April to September, 1 to 5. Dovecote and Stables can be viewed by appointment dependent on volunteer availability, contact Judy Endersby (01234 838278).

Find out more: 01480 301494 or willingtondovecote@nationaltrust.org.uk

Wimpole Estate

Arrington, Royston, Cambridgeshire SG8 0BW

1976

A unique working estate, with an impressive mansion at its heart. Discover Wimpole's acres of parkland, miles of walks, vibrant walled kitchen garden and Home Farm. Explore the hall, where intimate rooms contrast with beautiful Georgian interiors. With its various owners driven by passion and purpose, Wimpole is both a place to escape to and a place to get involved. We continue the 3rd Earl of Hardwicke's passion for trail-blazing food production and design, celebrating the estate's past magnificence and echoing Elsie Bambridge's 20th-century revival. As owners changed, a roll-call of ingenious architects, artists and landscape designers shaped the estate. Wimpole is an 'all-year-round' place to visit, reflecting the changing seasons, with something to captivate and inspire all visitors.

Eat, shop, stay: choose from the Old Rectory Restaurant, Farm Café and Stables Café, serving produce from the walled garden and Home Farm. Stable shop with gifts and plants, Wimpole rare-breed meat, flour, apple juice and eggs. Second-hand bookshop, toy shop.

Things to see and do: **Indoors** Explore the Hall at your own pace or pop into the Gardener's Cottage to uncover our garden history.

Wimpole Estate, Cambridgeshire: the grand mansion, left and below; visitors get busy, above

Outdoors Seasonal spectaculars, including daffodils, spring blossom, June Bloom, summer parterre, herbaceous borders and autumn trees. Free guided walks in the parkland and geocaching. Daily farm activities: grooming the donkey, meeting the Shire horse, rabbits, feeding the pigs and milking the cow. Lambing time. History festival, open-air theatre, '50 things to do before you're 11¾' and Christmas events. Sporting activities, including running and walking groups, cycle and running trails. **Dogs**: welcome on leads in the park, please be mindful of livestock; assistance dogs only elsewhere.

Access:
Hall **Farm** **Gardens**
Sat Nav: entrance via A603, not A1198.
Parking: 275 yards.

Find out more: 01223 206000 or wimpole@nationaltrust.org.uk

Wimpole Estate		M	T	W	T	F	S	S
Garden, Old Rectory Restaurant and stable block								
1 Jan–15 Feb	10–4	M	T	W	T	F	S	S
16 Feb–27 Oct	10–5	M	T	W	T	F	S	S
28 Oct–31 Dec*	10–4	M	T	W	T	F	S	S
Home Farm and Farm Café								
4 Jan–15 Feb*	10:30–3:30	M	·	·	·	F	S	S
16 Feb–27 Oct	10:30–5	M	T	W	T	F	S	S
28 Oct–30 Dec*	10:30–3:30	M	·	·	·	F	S	S
Hall								
16 Feb–27 Oct**	11–5	M	T	W	T	F	S	S
Park								
Open all year	Dawn–dusk	M	T	W	T	F	S	S

*Home Farm: open 1 to 4 January and 27 to 31 December daily, 10:30 to 3:30. Estate: closes at 2, 24 December; closed 25 December; 26 December, only park and stable block (café and gift shops) open, 10 to 4. **Hall: open for tours January to February and November; freeflow for Wimpole Christmas weekends. Car park: open 7:30 to 6:30. Last entry to house one hour before closing; last orders at catering outlets 30 minutes before closing.

East Midlands

The seemingly abandoned rooms at Calke Abbey, Derbyshire, are full of discarded family treasures

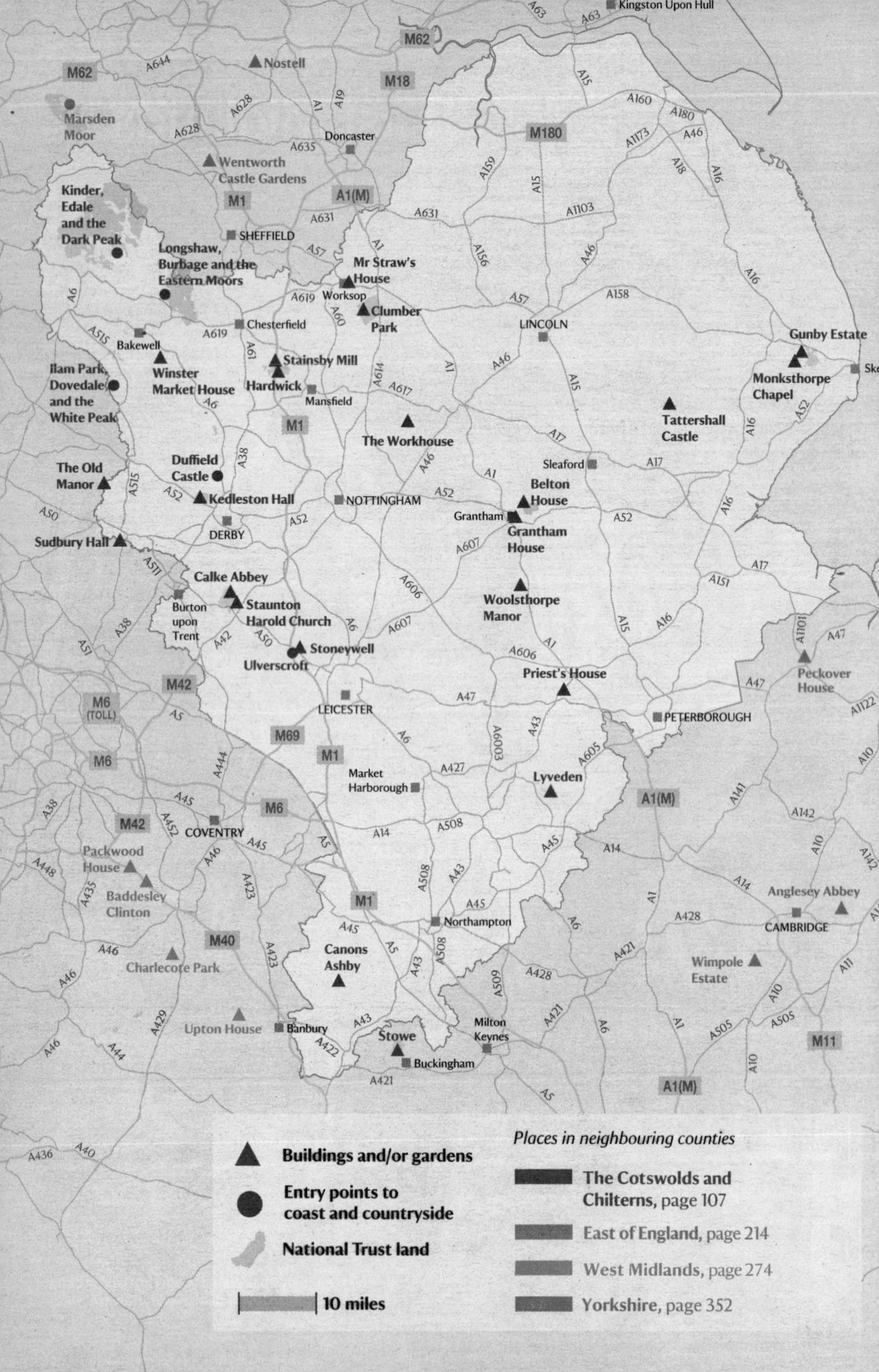
Kingston Upon Hull
M62
Nostell
M18
Marsden Moor
Doncaster
M180
Wentworth Castle Gardens
Kinder, Edale and the Dark Peak
M1
A1(M)
SHEFFIELD
Longshaw, Burbage and the Eastern Moors
Mr Straw's House
Worksop
Clumber Park
Chesterfield
LINCOLN
Bakewell
Gunby Estate
Ske
Stainsby Mill
Hardwick
Winster Market House
Ilam Park, Dovedale and the White Peak
Mansfield
Monksthorpe Chapel
Tattershall Castle
The Workhouse
Duffield Castle
Sleaford
The Old Manor
Belton House
Kedleston Hall
NOTTINGHAM
Grantham
Grantham House
DERBY
Sudbury Hall
Calke Abbey
Staunton Harold Church
Burton upon Trent
Woolsthorpe Manor
Stoneywell
Ulverscroft
Peckover House
Priest's House
M42
M6 (TOLL)
LEICESTER
PETERBOROUGH
M69
M6
Market Harborough
Lyveden
COVENTRY
Packwood House
Baddesley Clinton
Anglesey Abbey
Northampton
CAMBRIDGE
M40
Canons Ashby
Wimpole Estate
Charlecote Park
Upton House
Banbury
Stowe
Milton Keynes
Buckingham
M11
Buildings and/or gardens
Entry points to coast and countryside
National Trust land
10 miles
Places in neighbouring counties
The Cotswolds and Chilterns, page 107
East of England, page 214
West Midlands, page 274
Yorkshire, page 352

Belton House in Lincolnshire is the perfect example of a country-house estate

Belton House

Grantham, Lincolnshire

[icons] 1984

Sitting elegantly in formal gardens with views across Pleasure Grounds and an ancient deer park, Belton is often cited as being the perfect example of an English country-house estate. Although built on a relatively modest scale, it has a superlative collection of porcelain and silver, a world-renowned library, and an architectural finesse that reflects the wealth and cultured tastes of generations of the Brownlow family. In more recent times, Belton has also become a popular destination for families, with an extensive programme of activities, seasonal trails and adventure play. **Note**: entry to the mansion is by timed ticket (available to book in advance).

Eat, shop, stay: newly refurbished stables café opening this year. Hot lunches (11:30 to 2:30) include Belton's award-winning venison (seasonal). Ride Play Café and Muddy Hands kiosk for casual family dining. Large gift shop. Second-hand bookshop also offers seasonal plants.

Things to see and do: **Indoors** Learn more about Belton with themed interpretation and guided tours. The basement is open by guided tour all year. For young families, there's an indoor adventure play café (timed entry at busy times) and a discovery centre for weekend and school holiday activities. **Outdoors** Downloadable walks, seasonal trails and interpretation in the gardens and parkland. Events, including open-air cinema, theatre and autumn market. National Trust's largest outdoor adventure playground. Family-focused events during the school holidays. Christmas lights and events. Woolsthorpe Manor, home of Sir Isaac Newton, is nearby. **Dogs**: welcome in parkland and courtyards on leads.

Access:
House **Grounds**
Sat Nav: use NG32 2LW. **Parking**: on site.

Find out more: 01476 566116 or belton@nationaltrust.org.uk

Belton House		M	T	W	T	F	S	S
House*								
2 Mar–27 Oct	12:30–5	·	·	**W**	**T**	**F**	**S**	**S**
Shops, restaurant, Ride Play Café, adventure playground**								
Open all year	9:30–5:30	**M**	**T**	**W**	**T**	**F**	**S**	**S**
Basement†								
Open all year	Tour	**M**	**T**	**W**	**T**	**F**	**S**	**S**

*Timed entry to house. Last entry 4. **Close at 4 in November and December. †Volunteer-led tours (subject to availability), 11 to 3; last tour at 2 in winter. Park and gardens: open as shops and restaurant. Bellmount Woods: open daily (access from separate car park). Everything closed 25 December.

Belton House: the elegant formal gardens, above, and fun adventure playground, below

Calke Abbey

Ticknall, Derby, Derbyshire DE73 7JF

1985

With peeling paintwork and overgrown courtyards, Calke Abbey tells the story of the dramatic decline of a country-house estate. Faded garden buildings and a redundant kitchen garden hint at former fortunes, while inside a vast collection tells tales of an eccentric family who never threw anything away and who sought isolation from the world. The long drive through hidden parkland, expansive estate and secluded house in the hollow create moments for reflection and retreat. The historic and fragile habitats of Calke Park and its National Nature Reserve await discovery, together with the limeyards, ancient trees and ponds. **Note**: opening this year, new visitor facilities at Calke Explore – the start for outdoor adventures.

Eat, shop, stay: breakfast and main meals served daily in the restaurant with light refreshments available in the café at weekends and peak times. Barbecue offers estate-reared burgers (peak times). Large shop selling seasonal gifts, plants and local food. Five holiday cottages.

The faded grandeur of Calke Abbey in Derbyshire, above and below, tells a tale of dramatic decline

The many cycling trails at Calke Abbey suit all abilities, from scooters to top-of-the-range bikes

Things to see and do: **Indoors** House taster visit every morning; full house open from 12:30 (timed-ticket entry). Stableyards, garden outbuildings and underground tunnels reveal the isolation of Calke Abbey and the people who lived and worked here. Family activities in Squirt's Stable during weekends and school holidays (February to October). **Outdoors** Productive working garden and seasonal highlights, such as lambing and a rare surviving auricula theatre. Cycling and waymarked walks, including the Tramway Trail. Family activities and Tracker Packs for exploring outdoors. Children's play areas. Broad events programme, including food and craft fairs, open-air cinema and themed tours and talks. Stoneywell is nearby. **Dogs**: welcome on leads in parkland and stableyards; assistance dogs only in house and garden.

Access:
House Stables Grounds
Sat Nav: use DE73 7JF. **Parking**: on site.

Find out more: 01332 863822 or calkeabbey@nationaltrust.org.uk

Calke Abbey		M	T	W	T	F	S	S
Calke Park National Nature Reserve†								
Open all year	7:30–7	**M**	**T**	**W**	**T**	**F**	**S**	**S**
House*								
2 Mar–3 Nov	11–5	**M**	**T**	**W**	**T**	**F**	**S**	**S**
Garden**								
2 Jan–22 Dec	10–5	**M**	**T**	**W**	**T**	**F**	**S**	**S**
Stables, restaurant and shop**								
Open all year	10–5	**M**	**T**	**W**	**T**	**F**	**S**	**S**

†Closes dusk, if earlier; closed 25 December. *House: taster visit, 11 to 12:30, then open fully by timed ticket. **Garden, stables, restaurant and shop: close at 5 when house is open, March to October; at 4 all other times. Everything closed 25 December.

Canons Ashby

near Daventry, Northamptonshire NN11 3SD

1981

Ancient and peaceful, Canons Ashby is far removed from today's bustling lifestyle. Medieval canons built their priory near the small village of Ashby, but the Dissolution left a curiously truncated church and the village was lost, leaving nothing but mounds in the landscape. Nearby, the Elizabethan Dryden family built their home, making few changes during their 450 years of occupation. Victorian Sir Henry Dryden's curiosity led him to record the detail of the mansion, its unusual blend of architectural styles, mysterious wall-paintings, plasterwork and fine furnishings. Outside, lush gardens, parkland and ancient church offer space for tranquil contemplation. **Note**: admission may be by timed tickets on busy days.

Eat, shop, stay: Stables tea-room and pretty tea garden offering light meals and freshly baked treats. Coach House shop selling home and garden gifts and Canons Ashby homegrown plants. Well-stocked second-hand bookshop.

Canons Ashby, Northamptonshire: the kitchen, below, and lush garden, right

Things to see and do: **Indoors** Discovery trails for families in the house. **Outdoors** Parkland and garden walks all year. Family activities and trails available throughout the year. Garden games and natural play available. **Dogs**: welcome on leads in car park, paddock, tea garden and parkland only.

Access:
House **Church** **Grounds**
Parking: 218 yards.

Find out more: 01327 861900 or canonsashby@nationaltrust.org.uk

Canons Ashby		M	T	W	T	F	S	S
Tea-room, garden, shop, priory church and parkland*								
1 Jan–2 Jan*	10-3	·	T	W	·	·	·	·
4 Feb–31 Mar*	10-3:30	M	T	W	T	F	S	S
1 Apr–3 Nov	10-5	M	T	W	T	F	S	S
4 Nov–22 Dec*	10-3:30	M	T	W	T	F	S	S
27 Dec–31 Dec*	10-3	M	T	·	·	F	S	S
House*								
4 Feb–1 Mar*	11-3	M	T	W	·	F	S	S
2 Mar–31 Mar*	11-3	M	T	W	T	F	S	S
1 Apr–3 Nov	11:30-4	M	T	W	T	F	S	S
9 Nov–1 Dec*	11-3	·	·	·	·	·	S	S
2 Dec–22 Dec*	11-3	M	T	W	T	F	S	S

*Garden and house: some areas may close in winter for conservation work. House: last entry 2:30 in February, March, November and December and 3:30, April to October; closes dusk if earlier. Timed tickets may operate at certain times.

Clumber Park

Worksop, Nottinghamshire S80 3BE

1946

Carved out of the ancient forest of Sherwood, a space of playfulness and pleasure on a grand scale was created by the Dukes of Newcastle. Clumber Park is true to its spirit as a place of recreation, with 20 miles of cycle routes and 1,537 hectares (3,800 acres) of parkland, woodland and heathland to explore. The beauty of the Gothic Revival chapel, with its original stained-glass windows, reveals a rich historic past. The Pleasure Grounds frame the magnificent lake, making a perfect place to stroll or picnic. The Walled Kitchen Garden, with its National Collection of Rhubarb, provides a variety of fruit and vegetables to the café, and there are colourful herbaceous borders during the summer.

Eat, shop, stay: café and garden tea-house serving hot meals, snacks, cream teas and a children's menu. Barbecue and pizza oven (peak times). Large gift shop and plant sales. Second-hand bookshop; cycle hire, servicing and sales. Picnics welcome and designated barbecue site.

Things to see and do: **Indoors** Year-round activities for all ages and interests, including art, history and wildlife exhibitions at the Discovery Centre. The glasshouse and Museum of Gardening Tools at the Walled Kitchen Garden and Clumber chapel – a cathedral in miniature. **Outdoors** Seasonal highlights include the spring bluebells, rhododendrons and apple blossom, late-summer-flowering heathers and autumn tree colour. During your visit, tick off some of the '50 things to do before you're 11¾'. There are many downloadable walks, woodland play areas, a cycle hire centre and many outdoor activities.
Dogs: welcome, some restrictions apply. Indoor refreshment area for dog walkers. Downloadable guide.

Support the places you visit: please scan your member card for free parking ticket

Clumber Park, Nottinghamshire: exploring the garden, above, and the Pleasure Grounds, left and below

Access:
Buildings **Grounds**
Parking: 250 yards.

Find out more: 01909 476592 or clumberpark@nationaltrust.org.uk

Clumber Park		M	T	W	T	F	S	S
Park								
Open all year	7–7	**M**	**T**	**W**	**T**	**F**	**S**	**S**
Visitor facilities, café, shop, kitchen garden and chapel*								
1 Jan–30 Mar**	10–4	**M**	**T**	**W**	**T**	**F**	**S**	**S**
31 Mar–26 Oct**	10–5	**M**	**T**	**W**	**T**	**F**	**S**	**S**
27 Oct–31 Dec**	10–4	**M**	**T**	**W**	**T**	**F**	**S**	**S**

Park: open until dusk in summer. 31 March to 27 October: visitor facilities (café, shop, Walled Kitchen Garden, chapel, cycle hire centre, garden tea-house, Discovery Centre and woodland play park) close at 6 at weekends and Bank Holidays. Open daily, except 25 December.
*Chapel: 14 January to 17 March, closed for conservation.
**Café: opens at 9. Last cycle hire two hours before closing.

Duffield Castle

Duffield, Derbyshire 1899

Site of one of England's largest medieval castles – you can see its foundations, imagine the stories and savour the views. **Note**: sorry no toilets. Steep steps. For Sat Nav use DE56 4DW.

Find out more: 01332 842191 or duffieldcastle@nationaltrust.org.uk

Grantham House

Castlegate, Grantham, Lincolnshire NG31 6SS 1944

Handsome town house, one of the oldest buildings in Grantham, with a riverside walled garden. **Note**: the opening arrangements for Grantham House are undergoing change this year. For information about visiting please call the team at Belton House on 01476 566116.

Find out more: 01476 566116 (Belton House) or granthamhouse@nationaltrust.org.uk

Gunby Estate, Hall and Gardens

Gunby, Spilsby, Lincolnshire PE23 5SS

1944

The Massingberd family home from 1700 until 1967, Gunby Hall still feels cherished and lived-in. Exploring three floors, you can easily imagine you'll bump into one of the family at any moment. Enjoy garden colour whatever the season: abundant spring flowers, summer roses, autumn borders and plentiful fruit and vegetables. **Note:** building works all year.

Gunby Estate, Hall and Gardens, Lincolnshire, above

Eat, shop, stay: courtyard tea-room offering small selection of cakes and packaged sandwiches. Well-stocked second-hand bookshop. Small gift shop, seasonal plants and produce. Choose from three holiday cottages: The Old Rectory and Whitegates Cottage in Bratoft or Orchard Cottage, nestled in the gardens.

Things to see and do: events throughout year, from open-air theatre to Rose and Apple Days. Public footpaths run across the wider historic park and estate: ask for directions and maps at admissions. **Dogs**: welcome on leads in the gardens, courtyard tea-room terrace and grounds.

Access: **House** **Grounds**
Sat Nav: may misdirect – entrance is off roundabout (not beyond or before).
Parking: on site.

Find out more: 01754 890102 or gunbyhall@nationaltrust.org.uk

Gunby Estate		M	T	W	T	F	S	S
House*								
9 Mar–27 Oct	11–5	**M**	**T**	**W**	·	·	**S**	**S**
Gardens and tea-room**								
9 Mar–27 Oct	11–5	**M**	**T**	**W**	**T**	**F**	**S**	**S**

*House: last admission one hour before closing (on busy days admission may be by timed ticket).
**Tea-room: last service 4:30. May close dusk, or earlier.

Gunby Hall Estate: Monksthorpe Chapel

Monksthorpe, near Spilsby, Lincolnshire PE23 5PP 2000

Monksthorpe Chapel, dated 1701, was made to look like a barn to avoid detection and features a rare open-air baptistry. **Note**: chapel open daily, 9 March to 27 October, 11 to 5. Grounds open every day all year, 11 to 5. Access by key, obtained from Gunby Hall tea-room (£20 refundable deposit required).

Find out more: 01754 890102 or monksthorpe@nationaltrust.org.uk

Hardwick

Doe Lea, Chesterfield, Derbyshire S44 5QJ

1959

Wending its way through parkland scattered with ancient oaks, Hardwick's steep drive offers tantalising glimpses of the Hall's turrets, which bear the initials of an indomitable lady. Bess of Hardwick had the vision, the wealth and the sheer audacity to construct a house that still takes people's breath away today. Built as a testament to the wealth and taste of Bess, the house contains a collection of objects and textiles fine enough to grace any room in any palace in Europe. You can wander through the

With its turrets and many glittering windows, Hardwick, Derbyshire, is still as striking as when it was built

herb-scented gardens, with their seasonal delights and surprises, then explore the beautiful parkland and discover the duck decoy and ice house in the lower park. **Note**: Old Hall owned by the National Trust and administered by English Heritage (01246 850431).

Eat, shop, stay: Great Barn Restaurant serving hot meals, seasonal specials (made using garden produce) and cakes. Stables shop and garden shop with many plants propagated in Hardwick's nursery. Picnic areas. Three holiday cottages (sleeping two, six and 12).

Things to see and do: **Indoors** Seasonal events, including Easter and Christmas.

Outdoors Open-air films during the summer and themed tours and talks. You can see the garden highlights, including the stumpery and herbaceous borders. There are also walking trails around the estate and surrounding countryside. Family woodland trail and fun family activities during all school holidays. Stainsby Mill is nearby. **Dogs**: welcome on leads in stableyard, park and car park. Assistance dogs only in gardens.

Access:
Hall **Restaurant** **Garden**
Sat Nav: use S44 5RW.
Parking: 600-space car park.

Find out more: 01246 850430 or hardwick@nationaltrust.org.uk

One of the exquisite tapestries at Hardwick

Hardwick		M	T	W	T	F	S	S
Hall								
16 Feb-31 Mar	11-4	·	·	**W**	**T**	**F**	**S**	**S**
3 Apr-3 Nov[1]	11-5	·	·	**W**	**T**	**F**	**S**	**S**
23 Nov-22 Dec[2]	11-3	·	·	**W**	**T**	**F**	**S**	**S**
Garden								
1 Jan-31 Mar	10-5	**M**	**T**	**W**	**T**	**F**	**S**	**S**
1 Apr-3 Nov*	9-6	**M**	**T**	**W**	**T**	**F**	**S**	**S**
4 Nov-31 Dec	10-4	**M**	**T**	**W**	**T**	**F**	**S**	**S**
Restaurant and shop†								
1 Jan-31 Mar	9-5	**M**	**T**	**W**	**T**	**F**	**S**	**S**
1 Apr-3 Nov	9-6	**M**	**T**	**W**	**T**	**F**	**S**	**S**
4 Nov-31 Dec	9-5	**M**	**T**	**W**	**T**	**F**	**S**	**S**
Park								
Open all year	Dawn-dusk	**M**	**T**	**W**	**T**	**F**	**S**	**S**

[1]Hall: also open Bank Holiday Mondays; [2]Christmas opening: ground and middle floors only open. *Garden: last entry at 5. †Shop: opens at 10. Closed 25 December.

Hardwick Estate: Stainsby Mill

Doe Lea, Chesterfield, Derbyshire S44 5RW

1976

Hardwick Estate: Stainsby Mill, Derbyshire

A fully operational Victorian flour mill giving an insight into the workplace of a 19th-century miller. There has been a mill on this site for hundreds of years, providing flour for the local villages and the Hardwick Estate. Flour is ground regularly showing the cogs and machinery in action. **Note**: nearest toilets and refreshments at Hardwick Hall.

Eat, shop, stay: you can learn more about the mill from our guides and pick up recipes to try at home. Restaurant and gift shop at nearby Hardwick Hall.

Things to see and do: why not start your day at Stainsby Mill, with its children's trail and activity sheets? Visitors are welcome to have a go grinding flour on the hand quern.
Dogs: welcome on leads in Hardwick Park.

Access: **Building** **Grounds**
Parking: limited on-road parking (not National Trust).

Find out more: 01246 850430 or stainsbymill@nationaltrust.org.uk

Hardwick Estate: Stainsby Mill		M	T	W	T	F	S	S
16 Feb-24 May*	10-4	·	·	**W**	**T**	**F**	**S**	**S**
25 May-21 Jul*	10-5	·	·	**W**	**T**	**F**	**S**	**S**
24 Jul-1 Sep	10-5	**M**	**T**	**W**	**T**	**F**	**S**	**S**
4 Sep-3 Nov	10-4	·	·	**W**	**T**	**F**	**S**	**S**

*Open Bank Holiday Mondays, 10 to 4.

Ilam Park, Dovedale and the White Peak

Ilam, Ashbourne, Derbyshire

1934

The Stepping Stones at Dovedale lead to a riverside walk through the National Nature Reserve full of caves and pinnacles, rich in wildlife and fossils. A 1½-mile walk across fields links Dovedale and Ilam Park, a tranquil parkland nestled beneath steep-sided hills on the bank of the River Manifold. The park is dotted with majestic mature trees and offers views across to the rugged backdrop of Thorpe Cloud and Bunster Hill. A 1-mile circular parkland route makes this a popular choice for families and dog walkers. **Note**: Ilam Hall is let to the Youth Hostel Association. Dovedale car park is privately owned and there is also a charge for toilets.

Eat, shop, stay: tea-room at Ilam Park, with views towards Dovedale. Peak season accessible grab-and-go in stableyard. Shops at Ilam Park and Dovedale Barn offering maps, gifts and information. Stay at Ilam bunkhouse or at one of two holiday cottages at Wetton Mill.

Things to see and do: summer play across the river in Hinkley Hollow. Summer school holiday activities. See the orchard area developing beside the tea-room. Free Monday and Friday walks all year (no booking needed). **Dogs**: under close control; on leads spring and summer (ground-nesting birds), and near livestock.

Access: Tea-room **Shop and visitor centre** **Ilam Park** **Sat Nav**: use DE6 2AZ. **Parking**: at Ilam Park 119:132507 and Dovedale, not National Trust (charge including members).

Find out more: 01335 350503 or peakdistrict@nationaltrust.org.uk

Ilam Park		M	T	W	T	F	S	S
Dovedale Barn								
13 Apr–29 Sep	11–5	**M**	**T**	**W**	**T**	**F**	**S**	**S**
Tea-room and shop*								
1 Jan–15 Feb	10:30–4	**M**	**T**	**W**	**T**	**F**	**S**	**S**
16 Feb–3 Nov	10:30–5	**M**	**T**	**W**	**T**	**F**	**S**	**S**
4 Nov–31 Dec	10:30–4	**M**	**T**	**W**	**T**	**F**	**S**	**S**

*Shop: opens 11. Tea-room and shop: closed 24 and 25 December. Ilam bunkhouse: open all year (0344 335 1296). Darfar and Redhurst holiday cottages: available to let all year (0344 800 2070). Ilam Hall: available for overnight accommodation via the Youth Hostel Association (01335 350212).

Hiking at Ilam Park, Dovedale and the White Peak in Derbyshire

Riverside walk at Kedleston Hall in Derbyshire

Kedleston Hall

near Quarndon, Derby, Derbyshire DE22 5JH

1987

Be inspired by a living celebration of architecture, painting and sculpture – a true 'temple of the arts' – as envisioned by the celebrated architect Robert Adam. Experience the ambitious grandeur of this lavishly decorated 1760s show palace, lived in over the centuries by the Curzon family. Discover the treasures of the Eastern Museum, a collection amassed by Lord Curzon while he travelled through Asia and during his service as the Viceroy of India. The mansion is set among 332 hectares (820 acres) of landscape parkland and Pleasure Grounds, which are perfect for walks, picnics, wildlife-spotting and ancient tree-hunting. **Note**: the medieval All Saint's Church is cared for and managed by the Churches Conservation Trust.

Eat, shop, stay: Old Kitchen restaurant serves breakfasts, hot and cold lunches, cakes and ice cream. Refreshments available from kiosk at peak times. Plant sales, second-hand bookshop and gift shop. Luxury Park House holiday cottage sits on the edge of Kedleston Park.

Things to see and do: **Indoors** Explore the striking State Floor and the collections within the Eastern Museum. **Outdoors** Waymarked walks with a hermitage on the long walk. Talks and tours. Family crafts and activities. **Dogs**: welcome within the grounds on leads.

Access:
Ground floor **State floor** **Grounds**
Sat Nav: for main entrance use DE22 5JD. **Parking**: 200 yards.

Find out more: 01332 842191 or kedlestonhall@nationaltrust.org.uk

Kedleston Hall		M	T	W	T	F	S	S
Park and Pleasure Grounds								
1 Jan–15 Feb	10–4	M	T	W	T	F	S	S
16 Feb–3 Nov	10–6	M	T	W	T	F	S	S
4 Nov–31 Dec	10–4	M	T	W	T	F	S	S
Hall								
16 Feb–22 Feb*	11–4	M	T	W	T	F	S	S
23 Feb–20 Oct	11–5	M	T	W	T	·	S	S
21 Oct–3 Nov	11–4	M	T	W	T	·	S	S
4 Nov–30 Dec	11–3	M	·	·	·	F	S	S
Restaurant and shop								
1 Jan–15 Feb	10–3:30	M	T	W	T	F	S	S
16 Feb–3 Nov	10–5	M	T	W	T	F	S	S
4 Nov–31 Dec	10–3:30	M	T	W	T	F	S	S

*Ground floor only. Hall: 11 to 12, entry by guided tour only (places limited). Open Good Friday. Everything closed 25 December and occasionally for events.

Kinder, Edale and the Dark Peak

near Hope Valley, Derbyshire

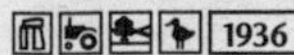

The Dark Peak, including Kinder, the Vale of Edale and along the Snake moors to the Derwent edges, offers exhilarating walks across heather moors, high gritstone edges and monumental windswept tors. Stories and wild nature abound amid the ancient peat bogs and quiet wooded cloughs. You can follow the route of the 1932 Mass Trespass onto Kinder Scout National Nature Reserve, retracing the steps of those early champions of access to wild places. Alternatively, a short walk up the steps of Mam Tor rewards you with panoramic views from this ancient hilltop fortress. **Note**: nearest toilets in villages and visitor centres (not Trust) at Ladybower Reservoir, Edale and Castleton.

Eat, shop, stay: Dalehead Bunkhouse offers group accommodation in a stone-built farmhouse deep in the Edale Valley.

Things to see and do: downloadable walking and cycling routes. **Dogs**: on leads near livestock and throughout spring and summer (ground-nesting bird breeding season).

Parking: at Mam Nick National Trust car park 110:SK124832. Also non-National Trust parking at Edale, Castleton, Bowden Bridge, Hayfield, Sett Valley, Hayfield and Upper Derwent Valley (charge including members).

Find out more: 01433 670368 or peakdistrict@nationaltrust.org.uk

Kinder, Edale and the Dark Peak

Welcome shelters open all year: Lee Barn (110:SK096855), Dalehead (110: SK101843) and Edale End (SK161864) in the Edale Valley; South Head (SK060854) above Hayfield; Grindle Barns above Ladybower Reservoir (SK189895). Mam Nick car park (SK123832) and Dalehead Bunkhouse (0344 335 1296) open all year.

Kinder, Edale and the Dark Peak in Derbyshire, below, and Longshaw, Burbage and the Eastern Moors, Derbyshire, right

 For information about getting to National Trust places, please see page 3

Longshaw, Burbage and the Eastern Moors

Longshaw, near Sheffield, Derbyshire

1931

A countryside haven on Sheffield's doorstep, Longshaw, Burbage and the Eastern Moors has a network of footpaths and bridleways you can explore within a typical Peak District landscape of skies and silhouettes. Here you'll find long views, with scooping shapes of rocks and hills and gorges where water tumbles through ancient woods and over mossy boulders. A diverse range of wildlife lives peacefully here among abandoned millstones and packhorse routes of the past. The designed landscape around Longshaw Lodge, a former grouse-shooting estate, offers a warm and friendly starting point for your adventure. **Note**: National Trust/RSPB manage Eastern Moors for Peak District National Park; Burbage for Sheffield County Council.

Eat, shop, stay: Longshaw café serving snacks and dishes made using produce plucked straight from the kitchen garden. Shop selling outdoor and wildlife-themed products, maps and guides. White Edge Lodge, an old gamekeeper's house, is now available as holiday accommodation.

Things to see and do: accessible woodland walks, natural play, bridleways and waymarked walks. Kitchen garden behind tea-room. Regular trails, outdoor activity and nature conservation-themed Muck In events. Free guided walks (Wednesdays and Sundays). **Dogs**: on leads near livestock and throughout spring and summer (ground-nesting bird breeding season).

Access: **Café and shop** **Moorland Discovery Centre** **Grounds**
Sat Nav: use S11 7TZ (follow brown signs).
Parking: at Woodcroft car park (110: 266800), Wooden Pole and Haywood for Longshaw and at Curbar Gap, Birchen Edge and Shillito Wood for the Eastern Moors. Additional car parks at Surprise View and Burbage, not National Trust (charge including members).

Find out more: 01433 631757 (Longshaw). 0114 289 1543 (Eastern Moors) or peakdistrict@nationaltrust.org.uk

Longshaw, Burbage, Eastern Moors		M	T	W	T	F	S	S
Tea-room and shop								
1 Jan–15 Feb	9:30–4	M	T	W	T	F	S	S
16 Feb–3 Nov	9:30–5	M	T	W	T	F	S	S
4 Nov–31 Dec	9:30–4	M	T	W	T	F	S	S

Closed 24 and 25 December. White Edge Lodge: available as holiday cottage all year (0344 800 2070). Longshaw Lodge: not open to public.

Lyveden

Harley Way, near Oundle,
Northamptonshire PE8 5AT

[icons] 1922

Deep in the Northamptonshire countryside lies a mysterious garden. Begun by Sir Thomas Tresham in 1595 but never completed, Lyveden stands as testament to his Catholicism. Persecuted for his religious beliefs, Tresham sought solace and contemplation in the creation of his gardens. Moats, terraces and spiral mounts surround an enigmatic building rich in religious symbolism. The restored orchard and wildflower meadows add to the peace and tranquillity of the setting. The full extent of Tresham's symbolic design remains unexplained to this day. Our audio tour reveals the intriguing story behind Tresham's design and the ultimate fate of his garden.

Eat, shop, stay: small traditional Northamptonshire cottage tea-room, serving light bites, cakes and cream teas. Ice cream available from visitor reception. Picnics welcome.

Things to see and do: free audio tour. Children's activities in the Family Den. Numerous public footpaths and bridleways within easy reach for exploring further afield.
Dogs: welcome on leads only.

Access: [icons] **Building** [icon] **Grounds** [icon]
Parking: 100 yards.

Find out more: 01832 205158 or lyveden@nationaltrust.org.uk

Lyveden		M	T	W	T	F	S	S
5 Jan–24 Feb	10:30–3:30	·	·	·	·	·	**S**	**S**
1 Mar–3 Nov	10:30–5*	**M**	**T**	**W**	**T**	**F**	**S**	**S**
9 Nov–29 Dec	10:30–3:30	·	·	·	·	·	**S**	**S**

*Tea-room: last orders 4. Last audio guide issued one hour before closing.

Mysterious Lyveden in Northamptonshire

Mr Straw's House

5–7 Blyth Grove, Worksop,
Nottinghamshire S81 0JG

1990

Inside Mr Straw's House, Nottinghamshire

Within the Sanderson-papered walls of this middle-class home, the family lived thriftily, installing few modern conveniences since 1923. A large and intriguing collection of everyday objects and personal papers has survived alongside traces of the occasional indulgence. The lovingly tended garden and orchard include a cacti collection and fruit trees. **Note**: entrance is by timed ticket only (these must be bought in advance).

Eat, shop, stay: small shop selling a range of souvenirs, plants, jams, books and gifts. Tea and coffee area.

The modest exterior of Mr Straw's House

Things to see and do: changing displays, family activities, events and guided town walks all year. **Dogs**: assistance dogs only.

Access: Warwick Villa, 5 Blyth Grove Endcliffe Villa, 7 Blyth Grove Gardens
Parking: on site, in orchard opposite property.

Find out more: 01909 482380 or
mrstrawshouse@nationaltrust.org.uk

Mr Straw's House		M	T	W	T	F	S	S
5 Mar–2 Nov*	Tour	·	**T**	**W**	**T**	**F**	**S**	·

*Admission by timed ticket (please telephone in advance to book). Last timed ticket at 4. Guided tours 10 to 12:30, freeflow from 12:30. Closed Good Friday.

The Old Manor

Norbury, Ashbourne, Derbyshire DE6 2ED
1987

An idyllic medieval hall featuring a rare king post and well-preserved Tudor door, set within beautiful gardens and peaceful countryside. **Note**: parking limited (cars only). Open Friday, 22 March to 25 October, 11 to 1, and Saturday, 23 March to 26 October, 1 to 3. Next to National Trust holiday house, please respect the occupants' privacy.

Find out more: 01283 585337 or
oldmanor@nationaltrust.org.uk

Priest's House, Easton on the Hill

38 West Street, Easton on the Hill, near Stamford, Northamptonshire PE9 3LS 1966

Delightful small late 15th-century building, with interesting local architecture and museum exploring Easton on the Hill's industrial and mining heritage. **Note**: open daily, 10 to 5. Unmanned. Access from neighbouring keyholders (details on property noticeboard).

Find out more: 01832 205158 or
priestshouse2@nationaltrust.org.uk

Staunton Harold Church

Staunton Harold Estate, Ashby-de-la-Zouch, Leicestershire LE65 1RW 1954

A rare and imposing church built in 1653, with a landscape lake and rolling wooded hills as its backdrop. **Note**: nearest toilet 500 yards (not National Trust). Parking not National Trust; Staunton Harold Estate (charge including members). Open weekends, 6 April to 3 November, and Wednesday to Sunday, 5 June to 1 September, 1 to 4:30. Also open Good Friday and Bank Holidays. Services are normally held Easter to December, first and third Sundays.

Find out more: 01332 863822 or stauntonharold@nationaltrust.org.uk

Stoneywell

Whitcroft's Lane, Ulverscroft, Leicestershire LE67 9QE

2012

Zigzagging from its rocky outcrop, Stoneywell is the realisation of one man's Arts and Crafts vision within a family home. Original furniture and family treasures fill the cottage's quirky rooms and, outside, every turn conjures childhood memories of holiday excitement – one way to the fort, another to the woods beyond. **Note**: booking essential (including members).

Stoneywell, Leicestershire, inside and out

Eat, shop, stay: Stables tea-room (for use by booked visitors only) serving light lunches, homemade cakes, and cream and scones. Small range of gifts, seasonal plants and second-hand books available. Picnics welcome in grounds.

Things to see and do: **Indoors** Guided tours, events and family activities reveal stories of life at Stoneywell. **Outdoors** The garden and woodland are great for exploring, with seasonal highlights, including daffodils, bluebells and rhododendrons. **Dogs**: assistance dogs only.

Access:
Stables **Cottage** **Gardens**
Parking: for booked visitors only.

Find out more: 01530 248040 (Infoline). 01530 248048 (bookings) or stoneywell@nationaltrust.org.uk

Stoneywell		M	T	W	T	F	S	S
1 Feb–30 Nov	Tour	**M**	**T**	**W**	**T**	**F**	**S**	**S**

Sudbury Hall and the National Trust Museum of Childhood

Sudbury, Ashbourne, Derbyshire DE6 5HT

1967

A complete day out, with two unique experiences in one location. The Hall has one of the most surprising, light and beautiful long galleries in England and is the result of George Vernon's aspirations to create a perfect new home. Enjoy the way the magnificent interiors, including exuberant plasterwork and Grinling Gibbons woodcarving, breathe the spirit of the Restoration through their fineness, delicacy and touches of humour. The museum is a place of fun and fascination for all ages. You can discover about childhood from the Victorian period to the present day; send your little one up a chimney, play with our hands-on toys and games and experience the Victorian Schoolroom.

Eat, shop, stay: tea-room serving light lunches and homemade cakes. Gift shop, plant sales, sweets, ice cream, toys and second-hand bookshop all situated in the stable yard area. Picnics welcome in the grounds.

Things to see and do: **Indoors** Hands-on toys in the museum and family crafts during most school holidays. Volunteer-led tours, subject to availability. **Outdoors** Trails and fun activities for all the family during most school holidays. Spot wildlife by the lake. Younger visitors can have great adventures in the woodland play area.

Sudbury Hall and the National Trust Museum of Childhood, Derbyshire: magnificent interior

Looking at old toys at Sudbury Hall and the National Trust Museum of Childhood, top, and the south front, above

Access:
Hall **Museum** **Grounds**
Parking: 500 yards.

Find out more: 01283 585337 or sudburyhall@nationaltrust.org.uk

Sudbury Hall		M	T	W	T	F	S	S
Hall, museum, tea-room and shop*								
4 Jan–11 Feb	11–4	**M**	·	·	·	**F**	**S**	**S**
15 Feb–4 Nov	11–5	**M**	**T**	**W**	**T**	**F**	**S**	**S**
8 Nov–30 Dec	11–4	**M**	·	·	·	**F**	**S**	**S**

*Hall: 11 to 1 access limited and by guided tour (subject to availability). Check before visiting for details. Tea-room and shop: open 10:30.

Tattershall Castle

Sleaford Road, Tattershall, Lincolnshire LN4 4LR

1925

Rising proudly from the flat Lincolnshire fens, Tattershall Castle was designed to display wealth, position and power. Built by Lord Ralph Cromwell, Treasurer of England, the Great Tower is one of the earliest and finest surviving examples of English medieval brickwork. Dramatically saved from being dismantled and exported, the castle and its huge Gothic fireplaces were restored from ruin by Lord Curzon of Kedleston between 1912 and 1914. Imagine the splendour of this once-palatial private residence as you wander through the vast echoing chambers. Ascend the spiral staircase from basement to battlements and take in spectacular views of the countryside. **Note**: access to the tower via a spiral staircase only (149 steps). Loose gravel paths throughout.

Eat, shop, stay: Guardhouse shop selling gifts, plants, souvenirs, second-hand books and a limited catering offer (hot and cold drinks, wrapped cakes and ice cream). Picnics welcome in the grounds.

 For other ways to get involved go to nationaltrust.org.uk/volunteer

Things to see and do: **Indoors** Multimedia guides (adult and family versions), children's trails, medieval games. **Outdoors** Year-round events for all ages and interests, including Easter Hunt, re-enactment weekends, open-air theatre and themed Christmas events.
Dogs: welcome on leads in the grounds only. Some events may have restrictions.

Access: Castle
Parking: 150 yards from entrance. Height restrictions apply, maximum 2.4 metres.

Find out more: 01526 342543 or tattershallcastle@nationaltrust.org.uk

Tattershall Castle		M	T	W	T	F	S	S
16 Feb–3 Nov	11–5	**M**	**T**	**W**	**T**	**F**	**S**	**S**
9 Nov–24 Nov	11–3*	·	·	·	·	·	**S**	**S**

Last entry one hour before closing. Last multimedia guide issued one hour before closing. Some rooms in the Great Tower may temporarily close for weddings. *May close earlier due to light levels.

Ulverscroft Nature Reserve

near Copt Oak, Loughborough, Leicestershire 1945

Nestled in the ancient Charnwood Forest, the heathland and woodland habitats of Ulverscroft support a rich variety of wildlife.
Note: assistance dogs only. Sorry no toilet. For Sat Nav use LE67 9QE. Limited parking along Whitcroft's Lane adjacent to the reserve. Access by permit only from The Secretary, Leicestershire and Rutland Wildlife Trust, The Old Mill, 9 Soar Lane, Leicester, LE3 5DE (0116 262 9968). Please allow a week to receive permit.

Find out more: 01332 863822 or ulverscroftnaturereserve@nationaltrust.org.uk

Winster Market House

Main Street, Winster, Matlock, Derbyshire DE4 2DJ 1906

A small listed 16th-century Market House with displays upstairs – the first Derbyshire place acquired by the National Trust, costing £50.
Note: Winster Market House is unstaffed. Open daily, 13 April to 3 November, 11 to 5.

Find out more: 01335 350503 or winstermarkethouse@nationaltrust.org.uk

Tattershall Castle, Lincolnshire, rises proudly above the fens, left. A colourful window, above

Woolsthorpe Manor

Water Lane, Woolsthorpe by Colsterworth, near Grantham, Lincolnshire NG33 5PD

1943

The world changed here. Isaac Newton, mathematician, scientist, thinker, craftsman, was born and grew up at Woolsthorpe Manor, doing much of his most important scientific work before he was 26. Sent home from Cambridge by the plague during 1665–7, he experimented obsessively, laying foundations for a groundbreaking scientific revolution. Here he split sunlight into colours with a prism and an apple fell from a tree to inspire his theory of gravity. Newton's genius still resonates through our world and for more than 300 years people have come to walk in his footsteps and be inspired by his story. **Note**: potential building works and changes to opening pattern – please check before you visit.

Eat, shop, stay: Newton's Barn coffee shop. Small shop in ticket office with local and Newton-specific gifts.

Woolsthorpe Manor in Lincolnshire was the birthplace and home of Isaac Newton

Things to see and do: **Indoors** Hands-on Science Centre and family activities. Science fairs and volunteer-led 'Tales from Woolsthorpe' and 'pop-up' science. Film. Family events. **Outdoors** The apple tree which inspired Newton's theory of gravity. **Dogs**: welcome in car park only.

Access: **Grounds** **House** **Science Centre**
Parking: 50 yards.

Find out more: 01476 860338 or woolsthorpemanor@nationaltrust.org.uk

Woolsthorpe Manor
Opens early March. Please visit website for details of opening times.

The Workhouse, Southwell

Upton Road, Southwell,
Nottinghamshire NG25 0PT

2002

Walking up the paupers' path towards The Workhouse, it is easy to imagine how the Victorian poor might have felt as they sought refuge here. This austere building, the most complete workhouse in existence, was built in 1824 as a place of last resort for the destitute. Its architecture was influenced by prison design, and its harsh regime became a blueprint for workhouses throughout the country. The stories of people who lived and worked here over the years help tell the history of the building's evolution and prompt reflection on how society has tackled social welfare through time. **Note**: please expect some disruption as we embark on our creative presentation and building works programme.

Eat, shop, stay: café offering hot drinks, soup, sandwiches, cakes and snacks. Shop selling gifts, ice cream and traditional toys. Picnic benches in the garden.

Things to see and do: **Indoors** 'Re-imagining The Workhouse' updates our story through art, music, photography and innovative technology. Regular activities, including living history days, family events and exhibitions. **Outdoors** Recreated Victorian vegetable garden. **Dogs**: assistance dogs only in house and garden. Dogs on leads in front field.

Access:
Workhouse **Firbeck**
Grounds
Sat Nav: use NG25 0QB. **Parking**: 200 yards.

Find out more: 01636 817260 or theworkhouse@nationaltrust.org.uk

The Workhouse, Southwell		M	T	W	T	F	S	S
23 Apr–3 Nov	12–5*	**M**	**T**	**W**	**T**	**F**	**S**	**S**

*Café: open 10:30 to 4. Guided tour of the outside and other buildings at 11 (places limited, book on arrival only). House: open Bank Holidays from 11; last admission one hour before closing; may close earlier due to light levels.

The austere façade of The Workhouse, Southwell, Nottinghamshire, left, greeted many a pauper. The recreated vegetable garden below

West Midlands

A pause for bubbles on the lawn in front of Berrington Hall in Herefordshire

M56
A537
A6
A619
Chesterfield
Bakewell
A55
A54
M6
A51
Congleton
Hardwick
A494
A483
A41
Little Moreton Hall
Ilam Park, Dovedale and the White Peak
Mansfield
Biddulph Grange Garden
A534
Crewe
A523
Wrexham
Erddig
A49
M1
A515
A38
A6
STOKE-ON-TRENT
A5
A525
Chirk Castle
A34
Kedleston Hall
A41
Downs Banks
A50
A52
A495
Stone
DERBY
Oswestry
Sudbury Hall
A51
A49
A53
A442
A483
Calke Abbey
A5
A513
Stafford
Shugborough Estate
A518
A6
A38
Shrewsbury
Attingham Park
A449
A42
Welshpool
A458
Letocetum Roman Baths and Museum
Sunnycroft
M6 (TOLL)
A46
Town Walls Tower
Powis Castle
Cronkhill
M54
Moseley Old Hall
M42
A444
Benthall Hall
Tamworth
Wightwick Manor
WOLVERHAMPTON
Morville Hall
M69
A49
A5
Carding Mill Valley and the Long Mynd
Wilderhope Manor
Bridgnorth
M5
M6
BIRMINGHAM
Dudmaston
Birmingham Back to Backs
A45
M6
Kinver Edge
A456
Clent Hills
A452
COVENTRY
Knowles Mill
Kidderminster
M42
A46
A45
M45
Rosedene
Packwood House
Baddesley Clinton
A456
A448
Croft Castle
Berrington Hall
The Firs
A423
Warwick
A44
Leominster
Hanbury Hall
Wichenford Dovecote
Hawford Dovecote
A46
Coughton Court
A422
A423
Charlecote Park
A4112
Kinwarton Dovecote
WORCESTER
Farnborough Hall
Stratford upon Avon
A49
A417
Brockhampton
A44
Canons Ashby
Cwmmau Farmhouse
Greyfriars' House
A438
A4103
Middle Littleton Tithe Barn
A429
Upton House
A438
Banbury
The Weir Garden
Croome
Evesham
Hidcote
HEREFORD
The Fleece Inn
A465
A49
A46
Snowshill Manor
M50
M40
Chipping Norton
A479
A40
Stow-on-the-Wold
A40
A44
A34
A436
M5
A40
A417
A429
A40
A48
Buildings and/or gardens
Entry points to coast and countryside
National Trust land
10 miles
Places in neighbouring counties
The Cotwolds and Chilterns, page 107
East Midlands, page 248
North West, page 306
Wales, page 390

Attingham Park

Atcham, Shrewsbury, Shropshire SY4 4TP

1947

Attingham inspires a sense of beauty, space and awe. From the moment you enter the gates, views open across the 200-year-old parkland to the Shropshire Hills and the impressive mansion emerges against silhouettes of cedar trees. The house, which sits at the heart of the Lord Berwicks' estate, is an example of classical design and Italian influence. Outside, cattle graze and fallow deer roam, shaded woodland glades of historic trees offer peace and shade, while the red-brick organic walled garden is a place of order, productivity and horticulture. The accessible paths around the parkland are perfect for walks, running or exploring the 1,619-hectare (4,000-acre) estate. Full of life and locally loved, there's something for everyone all year round.

Eat, shop, stay: hot food, light meals and afternoon tea are available from the main café (open daily). Greedy Pig kiosk in the Field of Play. Stables shop selling walled-garden produce, plants and venison (in season). Second-hand bookshop. Ismore Coppice Campground nearby.

Things to see and do: **Indoors** Relaxed visit to three floors of the mansion, including basement servants' quarters (selected days). Daily themed tours. Attingham Christmas in December (booking essential). 2019 National Portrait Gallery exhibition (selected dates). **Outdoors** Led walks and talks (selected days), run routes, Field of Play, natural play trail, river walks (1 to 4 miles), pleasure grounds, ice house, bothy and historic stables to explore. Seasonal spectaculars include snowdrops, bluebells, summer blossom and autumn tree colour. Year-round events for all ages and interests, including family trails, deer-park safaris, annual classic car rally and open-air film and theatre evenings. Sunnycroft is nearby in Wellington. **Dogs**: welcome, some restrictions apply. Dog-walkers' guide available. Assistance dogs only in buildings.

It is impossible not to be awestruck by the sheer beauty of Attingham Park in Shropshire

Access: [icons]
Mansion [icons] **Café** [icon] **Grounds** [icons]
Parking: 25 to 200 yards.

Find out more: 01743 708123 (Infoline). 01743 708162 or attingham@nationaltrust.org.uk

Attingham Park		M	T	W	T	F	S	S
Park, Field of Play, Carriage House Café and Stables shop[1]								
1 Jan–15 Feb	8–5*	M	T	W	T	F	S	S
16 Feb–24 May	8–6	M	T	W	T	F	S	S
25 May–1 Sep	8–7	M	T	W	T	F	S	S
2 Sep–3 Nov	8–6*	M	T	W	T	F	S	S
4 Nov–31 Dec	8–5*	M	T	W	T	F	S	S
Walled Garden								
Open all year	9–5*	M	T	W	T	F	S	S
Mansion								
4 Jan–10 Feb†	11–3	·	·	·	·	F	S	S
16 Feb–3 Nov	11–4:30	M	T	W	T	F	S	S
30 Nov–23 Dec††	10–3:30	M	T	W	T	F	S	S

[1]Carriage House Café opens 9 and Stables shop opens 10; both close one hour before park, except 30 November to 29 December when close 4:30. †Entry by tour (booking required). †† Entry by timed ticket (booking required). *Dusk if earlier. Field of Play kiosk open 13 April to 1 September from 11 weekends and daily during Shropshire school holidays (weather permitting). 24 December: mansion closed; site closes 3. Everything closed 25 December.

Attingham Park Estate: Cronkhill

near Atcham, Shrewsbury, Shropshire SY5 6JP 1947

Delightful picturesque Italianate hillside villa designed by Regency architect John Nash, with beautiful views across the Attingham Estate. **Note**: house ground floor, garden and stables open as part of visit. Property contents belong to tenant. Open Friday and Sunday, 10 and 12 May, 5 and 7 July as well as 13 and 15 September, 11 to 4 (admission by booked timed tickets).

Find out more: 01743 708162 or cronkhill@nationaltrust.org.uk

Attingham Park's impressive classical façade, left, clearly shows its Italian influence, while the design of moated Baddesley Clinton in Warwickshire, right, bears witness to more varied and eclectic architectural styles

Attingham Park Estate: Town Walls Tower

Shrewsbury, Shropshire SY1 1TN 1930

This last remaining 14th-century watchtower sits on what were once the medieval fortified, defensive walls of Shrewsbury. **Note**: sorry no toilet or car parking and 40 extremely steep, narrow steps to top floor. Open weekends, 27 and 28 April, 8 and 9 June, 17 and 18 August, 5 and 6 October, 10:30 to 3:30 (admission by booked timed ticket).

Find out more: 01743 708162 or townwallstower@nationaltrust.org.uk

Baddesley Clinton

Rising Lane, Baddesley Clinton, Warwickshire B93 0DQ

[icons] 1980

The magic of Baddesley Clinton comes from its secluded, timeless setting deep within its own parkland. From refuge to haven, this atmospheric moated manor house has been a sanctuary since the 15th century. Discover Baddesley's late medieval, Tudor and 20th-century histories and uncover its stories, from hiding persecuted Catholics in its priest's holes, to the history of the Ferrers family who lived at Baddesley for more than 500 years. This year find out about some of Baddesley's strong female characters and their intriguing stories.

The peaceful gardens include fish pools, walled garden and a lakeside walk, perfect for a tranquil stroll.

Eat, shop, stay: Barn Restaurant serving hot meals, drinks and snacks and The Stables offering light refreshments, hot drinks and ice cream. Picnics welcome. Shop selling seasonal gifts, local foods and plants. Second-hand bookshop.

Things to see and do: **Indoors** Discover Baddesley's story, from medieval farmstead to modest Georgian status symbol and Victorian retreat. Seasonal children's trails. House dressed for Christmas throughout December. **Outdoors** Natural play around the estate all year. Outdoor games in school holidays. Welcome talks and garden tours, plus walking trails around the estate and surrounding countryside. Packwood House and Coughton Court are nearby. **Dogs**: welcome on leads in car park and estate public footpaths. Assistance dogs only beyond visitor reception.

Access:
Building **Grounds**
Parking: 100 yards.

Find out more: 01564 783294 or baddesleyclinton@nationaltrust.org.uk

Baddesley Clinton		M	T	W	T	F	S	S
Baddesley Clinton								
1 Jan–15 Feb	9–4*	**M**	**T**	**W**	**T**	**F**	**S**	**S**
16 Feb–3 Nov	9–5*	**M**	**T**	**W**	**T**	**F**	**S**	**S**
4 Nov–31 Dec	9–4*	**M**	**T**	**W**	**T**	**F**	**S**	**S**

19 to 22 April: admission by bookable tickets only, limited (including members). *House: opens 11, admission by timed ticket (not bookable). 7 January to 15 February and 4 to 29 November: weekdays admission to house by guided tour (not bookable). Closed 24 and 25 December.

Atmospheric Baddesley Clinton, above and right, has offered sanctuary since the 15th century

Benthall Hall

Broseley, Shropshire TF12 5RX

1958

Within this fine stone house, discover the history of the Benthall family from the Saxon period to the present day. Outside, the garden includes a beautiful Restoration church, a restored plantsman's garden with pretty crocus displays in spring and autumn, and an old kitchen garden.

Eat, shop, stay: tea-room serving drinks, cakes and ice cream.

Things to see and do: **Indoors** Informative guides, children's trail. **Outdoors** Elizabethan skittle alley. Circular walks through the park and woodland. **Dogs**: in park and woodland only.

Access:
House **Church**
Parking: 100 yards.

Find out more: 01952 882159 or benthall@nationaltrust.org.uk

Benthall Hall		M	T	W	T	F	S	S
2 Feb–24 Feb	1-4*	·	·	·	·	·	**S**	**S**
2 Mar–30 Oct	1-5*	·	**T**	**W**	·	·	**S**	**S**

Open Bank Holiday Mondays and Good Friday. Tea-room: last orders 30 minutes before house closes. *Garden and church: open and close 30 minutes earlier and later than stated times, apart from February when open at 1.

Benthall Hall, Shropshire: fine stone house

Berrington Hall

near Leominster, Herefordshire HR6 0DW

1957

Standing proud and strong, this fine Georgian mansion sits within 'Capability' Brown's final garden and landscape. In the house are jewel-like interiors, designed by Henry Holland and home to the Harley, Rodney and Cawley families. Upstairs you can see a dress fit for a king and explore an artistic response to Ann Bangham, wife of first owner Thomas Harley. Discover the Walled Garden and Pleasure Grounds restoration project, with a visit to the Georgian-inspired Look!Look!Look! pavilion, by artists Heather and Ivan Morison, then follow the parkland walk to experience Brown's design.

Berrington Hall, Herefordshire: the east front, above, and elegant staircase, left

Eat, shop, stay: shop selling gifts, local products and preserves made from our fruit. Tea-room serving lunches, afternoon tea and cakes, made using produce from the garden. Stables café, open on busy days selling 'grab and go' fare. Triumphal Arch holiday cottage for a longer stay.

Things to see and do: **Indoors** Exhibitions and costume collection. Family trails, games and dressing up. Servants' quarters. **Outdoors** Stables, welcome centre and walled garden. Relax by the lake. Children's den-building and play area. Waymarked walks. **Dogs**: welcome on leads in parkland and in parts of garden.

Access:
Building **Grounds**
Parking: 30 yards.

Find out more: 01568 615721 or berrington@nationaltrust.org.uk

Berrington Hall		M	T	W	T	F	S	S
1 Jan	10–4	·	T	·	·	·	·	·
5 Jan–10 Feb	10–4	·	·	·	·	·	S	S
16 Feb–3 Nov	10–5	M	T	W	T	F	S	S
9 Nov–22 Dec	10–4	·	·	·	·	·	S	S
27 Dec–31 Dec	10–4	M	T	·	·	F	S	S

Mansion and shop open at 11. Last admission one hour before closing. **Gardens, parkland and Stables café: open 5:30 to 8:30 on Saturdays only in August.**

Biddulph Grange Garden

Grange Road, Biddulph, Staffordshire ST8 7SD

[icon] 1988

Biddulph Grange Garden is a remarkable survival, a formal Victorian horticultural masterpiece and a quirky, playful paradise full of intrigue and surprise. Created by its visionary owner, James Bateman, the garden and Geological Gallery express his attempts to reconcile his religious convictions with his passion for botany and geology. His plant and fossil collections come from all over the world – a visit takes you on a journey from an Italian terrace to an Egyptian pyramid, via a Himalayan glen and Chinese garden, hidden by tunnels, hedges and rockwork. The collection includes rhododendrons, Wellingtonias and the oldest golden larch in Britain. **Note**: there are 400 steps in the garden.

Eat, shop, stay: self-service tea-room with indoor and outdoor seating. Gift shop. Plant centre selling a range of plants and trees, including species you will see growing in the garden. Picnic area in the paddock beside the car park.

Things to see and do: talks in the Geological Gallery, introductory talks available and guided tours by arrangement. Programme of activities and events for visitors of all ages throughout the year. **Dogs**: assistance dogs only in garden.

Access: [icons] **Garden** [icon]
Parking: 50 yards.

Find out more: 01782 517999 or biddulphgrange@nationaltrust.org.uk

Biddulph Grange Garden		M	T	W	T	F	S	S
1 Jan–15 Feb	10–3:30	**M**	**T**	**W**	**T**	**F**	**S**	**S**
16 Feb–8 Mar	10–4:30	**M**	**T**	**W**	**T**	**F**	**S**	**S**
9 Mar–31 May	10–5:30	**M**	**T**	**W**	**T**	**F**	**S**	**S**
1 Jun–29 Sep	9–5:30	**M**	**T**	**W**	**T**	**F**	**S**	**S**
30 Sep–25 Oct	10–5:30	**M**	**T**	**W**	**T**	**F**	**S**	**S**
26 Oct–3 Nov	10–4:30	**M**	**T**	**W**	**T**	**F**	**S**	**S**
4 Nov–31 Dec	10–3:30	**M**	**T**	**W**	**T**	**F**	**S**	**S**

Closes dusk if earlier. Closed 25 and 26 December.

Biddulph Grange Garden, Staffordshire: this quirky, playful paradise is full of intrigue and surprise

Birmingham Back to Backs

55-63 Hurst Street/50-54 Inge Street, Birmingham, West Midlands B5 4TE

2004

Birmingham Back to Backs in the West Midlands

Immerse yourself in the life of residents at Birmingham's last surviving court of back to backs. The evocative tour will give you an insight into how people lived from the 1840s to 1970s. With privies, coal fires, candlelight and cramped spaces, you'll get a real taste of back-to-back life. **Note**: booking essential. Eight flights of steep, winding stairs. Ground-floor tours available. Sorry no café.

Eat, shop, stay: traditional sweetshop selling childhood favourites and a small gift shop. Vintage holiday cottages (booked via National Trust Holidays).

Things to see and do: events all year.

Access: **Building**
Parking: nearest at Arcadian Centre, Bromsgrove Street, Hurst Street (none National Trust).

Find out more: 0121 666 7671 (booking line). 0121 622 2442 (office) or backtobacks@nationaltrust.org.uk

Birmingham Back to Backs		M	T	W	T	F	S	S
29 Jan–22 Dec	Tour	·	**T**	**W**	**T**	**F**	**S**	**S**

Admission by timed, guided tour only (booking essential). Closed 2 to 5 September. Open Bank Holiday Mondays (but closed next day). Term-time tours from 1: Tuesdays, Wednesdays and Thursdays. Last tour times vary in winter due to low light levels.

Brockhampton

Bringsty, near Bromyard, Herefordshire WR6 5TB

1946

More than 600 years ago the Dumbleton family built this moated manor house tucked away in a Herefordshire valley. Find out about the lives of the people who called this place home from the 15th to the 20th centuries and discover how what was once a grand medieval hall, with prestigious gatehouse, slowly transformed into a humble home for farmers. The house is surrounded by orchards and sits next to an ancient ruined chapel. In the wider estate there are six walks through a farming landscape with designed parkland, hidden dingles, gushing streams and wild woodlands waiting to be discovered. **Note**: challenging terrain with extremely steep slopes and muddy areas.

Eat, shop, stay: Old Apple Store tea-room serves light lunches, tea and cakes. Granary shop selling plants, gifts and local produce, with kiosk serving takeaway drinks and snacks. Both open all year. Second-hand bookshop.

Three holiday cottages – sleeping three, five and 10.

Things to see and do: **Indoors** Year-round family activities – meet characters from history, historical demonstrations and re-enactments. **Outdoors** Event days, school holiday family trails and games. Natural play trail, orienteering and waymarked walks. Picnics welcome. **Dogs**: welcome on leads outdoors (caution near livestock). Dog waste bins in car parks.

Access:
Building **Grounds**
Parking: 100 yards and 1 mile.

Find out more: 01885 482077 or brockhampton@nationaltrust.org.uk

Brockhampton		M	T	W	T	F	S	S
Estate								
Open all year	10-5	**M**	**T**	**W**	**T**	**F**	**S**	**S**
House, Granary shop and Old Apple Store tea-room*								
5 Jan-10 Feb	10-4**	·	·	·	·	·	**S**	**S**
16 Feb-3 Nov	10-5**	**M**	**T**	**W**	**T**	**F**	**S**	**S**
9 Nov-29 Dec	10-4**	·	·	·	·	·	**S**	**S**

*House, grounds, Granary shop and Old Apple Store tea-room close 30 minutes before estate. **House and Granary shop open 11.

Brockhampton, Herefordshire: built 600 years ago, this moated manor lies tucked away in a remote valley

Carding Mill Valley and the Long Mynd

near Church Stretton, Shropshire

1965

At Carding Mill Valley you are suddenly in the heart of wild countryside. Here families can enjoy playing in the stream, a variety of walks and exploring. From the valley, head up to the top of the Long Mynd and be rewarded with views of Shropshire and beyond.

Eat, shop, stay: Chalet Pavilion tea-room and roof terrace in Carding Mill Valley serving hot lunches, afternoon teas, drinks and ice cream. Shop selling gifts, souvenirs, maps and pond nets.

Things to see and do: courses and family-friendly events all year. Free walks cards available in Carding Mill Valley.
Dogs: on a lead and under close control (grazing livestock and ground-nesting birds).

Access: **Building**
Sat Nav: use SY6 6JG. **Parking**: 50 yards.

Find out more: 01694 725000 or cardingmill@nationaltrust.org.uk

Carding Mill Valley		M	T	W	T	F	S	S
Tea-room								
1 Jan-15 Feb	10-4	**M**	**T**	**W**	**T**	**F**	**S**	**S**
16 Feb-3 Nov	10-5	**M**	**T**	**W**	**T**	**F**	**S**	**S**
4 Nov-31 Dec*	10-4	**M**	**T**	**W**	**T**	**F**	**S**	**S**
Shop								
1 Jan	11-4	·	**T**	·	·	·	·	·
5 Jan-10 Feb	10-4	·	·	·	·	·	**S**	**S**
16 Feb-3 Nov	11-5**	**M**	**T**	**W**	**T**	**F**	**S**	**S**
4 Nov-31 Dec*	11-4**	**M**	**T**	**W**	**T**	**F**	**S**	**S**

*Tea-room and shop: closed 25 December. **Shop: opens 10 at weekends.

Charlecote Park

Wellesbourne, Warwick,
Warwickshire CV35 9ER

1946

Charlecote Park was already in its middle age when Elizabeth I arrived 450 years ago, entering through the gatehouse and on to the welcoming red-brick mansion, just as you will today. A family home for more than eight centuries, it is a place of surprising treasures, with collections reflecting the tastes of the Lucy family, lifestyle and varied fortunes. Imagine the hum of activity of a working estate in the domestic 'below-stairs' spaces and in the laundry room and brewhouse in the courtyard. In the stables see the family's carriage collection, while in the parkland Jacob sheep and fallow deer roam across the 'Capability' Brown landscape, a haven for wildlife in which you can picnic and play, walk and wander.

Eat, shop, stay: variety of catering facilities across the site, serving a range of meals and snacks. Servants' Hall gift shop sells a range of Charlecote specific, locally sourced produce and seasonal plant sales. Picnics welcome. Stay at Turret holiday flat (sleeps six).

Things to see and do: **Indoors** Hands-on activities bring the Victorian kitchen to life. You can explore the carriage houses, brewhouse, laundry and tack room and learn more in the introductory gatehouse room. The house is festively decorated during December. **Outdoors** Why not take a walk through the wider parkland? There are guided walks, talks and seasonal trails for all ages. **Dogs**: welcome on a short lead at all times (designated areas only).

Access:
Building **Grounds**
Parking: 300 yards.

Find out more: 01789 470277 or charlecotepark@nationaltrust.org.uk

Charlecote Park		M	T	W	T	F	S	S
Park and garden								
1 Jan–15 Feb	9–4†	M	T	W	T	F	S	S
16 Feb–31 Mar	9–5†	M	T	W	T	F	S	S
1 Apr–3 Nov	9–6	M	T	W	T	F	S	S
4 Nov–31 Dec	9–4†	M	T	W	T	F	S	S
House**								
16 Feb–3 Nov[1]	11–3:30[2]	M	T	W	T	F	S	S
9 Nov–24 Nov	11–3:30[2]	·	·	·	·	·	S	S
30 Nov–22 Dec	11–3:30[2]	M	·	·	·	F	S	S
23 Dec–31 Dec	11–3:30[2]	M	T	·	T	F	S	S
Tea-room and shop*								
1 Jan–31 Mar	9–4	M	T	W	T	F	S	S
1 Apr–3 Nov	9–5	M	T	W	T	F	S	S
4 Nov–31 Dec	9–4	M	T	W	T	F	S	S

*Shop: opens 10:30. [1]House: Wednesdays by guided tours only (places limited); [2]Admission by timed tickets. †Park and garden: close dusk if earlier. Everything closed 25 December. **Some projects may impact on house availability.

Charlecote Park, Warwickshire: clockwise from above, examining an antique globe in the Library, the house in winter and the Great Hall

Clent Hills

near Romsley, Worcestershire

1959

A snowy scene in the Clent Hills, Worcestershire

Set on the edge of Birmingham and the Black Country, this green oasis with panoramic views is the perfect place for a refreshing walk or a picnic on a sunny day. Families can create their own adventures – building dens, hunting for geocaches or simply getting closer to nature. **Note**: nearest facilities at Nimmings Wood entrance.

Eat, shop, stay: café (not National Trust) at Nimmings Wood car park serving light meals and refreshments.

Things to see and do: regular guided rambles and family activities. Natural play area and play trail. **Dogs**: welcome, but please be considerate to other visitors.

Access:
Sat Nav: use B62 0NL for Nimmings Wood entrance. **Parking**: at Nimmings Wood; additional parking at Adam's Hill and Walton Hill.

Find out more: 01562 887912 or clenthills@nationaltrust.org.uk

Clent Hills
Nimmings Wood car park: open 8:30 to 5 (to 4 from 1 November to 31 March). Closed 25 December.

Coughton Court

Alcester, Warwickshire B49 5JA

1946

Coughton has been home to the Throckmorton family for more than 600 years. Facing persecution for their Catholic faith, they were willing to risk everything. You can discover their story and find out about a family's ingenuity, resilience and resolve, including their link to the infamous Gunpowder Plot. Coughton is very much a family home with an intimate feel. The Throckmorton family still live here and they created and manage the gardens, including a riverside walk, bog garden and beautiful display of roses in the walled garden.

Eat, shop, stay: Coughton Café serving lunch and teas. Drinks and ice cream available from the Stableyard Coffee Bar. Coach House shop selling local food and seasonal gifts. Throckmorton family plant sales. Second-hand bookshop.

Coughton Court, Warwickshire: inside and out

Things to see and do: Indoors Children's trail. Outdoors Wide selection of talks. Walking trails around the estate and surrounding countryside. Natural play and outdoor games. Baddesley Clinton and Packwood nearby.
Dogs: welcome on leads in car park and public footpaths. Assistance dogs only in gardens.

Access:
House **Grounds**
Parking: 150 yards.

Find out more: 01789 400777 or coughtoncourt@nationaltrust.org.uk

Coughton Court		M	T	W	T	F	S	S
House, shop, café and grounds*								
1 Mar-31 Mar**	11-4	·	·	·	T	F	S	S
3 Apr-21 Jul	11-5	·	·	W	T	F	S	S
23 Jul-1 Sep	11-5	·	T	W	T	F	S	S
4 Sep-29 Sep	11-5	·	·	W	T	F	S	S
3 Oct-3 Nov	11-4	·	·	·	T	F	S	S

*Walled garden: opens at 12. **Grounds closed. Open Bank Holiday Mondays. Everything closed for private Throckmorton family days on 15 June, 27 July, 14 and 15 September. Admission to the house by timed entry ticket, not bookable.

Croft Castle and Parkland in Herefordshire, right, has many compelling 20th-century stories to tell

Croft Castle and Parkland

Yarpole, near Leominster, Herefordshire HR6 9PW

1957

This intimate house became the Croft family home before the Domesday Book. The castle has many compelling 20th-century stories to uncover, including Croft during the war years and some of its remarkable women. The interiors, styled by Thomas Farnolls Pritchard, also tell an 18th- and 19th-century tale. Relax in the walled garden, complete with vineyard and glasshouse, take the dog for a stroll to the Iron Age hill fort, exploring the historic parkland, wood pasture and many ancient trees along the way. Discover new views and walks with the revival and restoration of the Fishpool Valley in the Picturesque style.

Eat, shop, stay: tea-room (licensed) serving food made using garden produce – hot lunches, cakes and ice cream. Children's lunchboxes and half portions. Shop selling gifts, plants, home and garden products. Second-hand bookshop. Picnic area. Garden and Ambrey holiday cottages for a longer stay.

Things to see and do: **Indoors** Games, interactive memorabilia and dressing up. **Outdoors** Family activities, living history, open-air theatre, seasonal events. Natural and castle-inspired play areas. Walks, dog-walking, bird hide, information barn and orienteering. **Dogs**: welcome on leads in gardens, parkland and glazed area of tea-room only.

Access:
Castle **Grounds**
Sat Nav: use HR6 0BL. **Parking**: 100 yards.

Find out more: 01568 780246 or croftcastle@nationaltrust.org.uk

Croft Castle and Parkland		M	T	W	T	F	S	S
Tea-room, garden, shop and parkland								
1 Jan	10-4	·	**T**	·	·	·	·	·
27 Dec-31 Dec	10-4	**M**	**T**	·	·	**F**	**S**	**S**
Castle, tea-room, garden, shop and parkland								
5 Jan-10 Feb	10-4	·	·	·	·	·	**S**	**S**
16 Feb-3 Nov	10-5	**M**	**T**	**W**	**T**	**F**	**S**	**S**
9 Nov-22 Dec	10-4	·	·	·	·	·	**S**	**S**

Castle and shop: open 11. Play area: open as parkland.

Detail of an ornately painted screen at Croft Castle and Parkland, below. Right, the stately mansion at Croome, Worcestershire, and Chinese Bridge, opposite

Croome

near High Green, Worcester, Worcestershire WR8 9DW

1996

There's more than meets the eye at Croome. A secret wartime airbase, now a visitor centre and museum, was once a hub of activity for thousands of people. Outside is the grandest of English landscapes, 'Capability' Brown's masterful first commission, with commanding views over the Malverns. The parkland, nearly lost but now restored, is great for walks and adventures with a surprise around every corner. At the heart of the park lies Croome Court, once home to the Earls of Coventry. The 6th Earl was an 18th-century trendsetter, and today Croome follows his lead using artists and craftspeople to tell the story of its eclectic past in inventive ways. Explore four floors of the mansion, perfect for making new discoveries. **Note**: Walled Gardens, privately owned (admission charge towards their restoration, including members), open days throughout the year.

Eat, shop, stay: 1940s-style restaurant, gift shop, Gardener's Bothy plant shop and second-hand bookshop at the Visitor Centre. Kitty Fisher's Coffee House serving light lunches in Croome Court's basement.

There is so much to do at Croome, with acres of parkland to explore, top, and something fascinating at every turn within the house, above

Things to see and do: **Indoors** Contemporary exhibitions, including select pieces from the collection and creative installations. All four floors of the house are open, some areas by guided tour. RAF Defford Museum at the Visitor Centre. **Outdoors** Acres of parkland to explore. Regular guided tours of the park and outer eye-catcher open days. Special family trails around park every school holiday. RAF-themed playground, natural play area and bird hide close to the Visitor Centre. Walled Gardens to explore. **Dogs**: welcome on short fixed leads. Assistance dogs only in house, RAF museum, restaurant and shop.

Access:
House **Park**
Sat Nav: follow signs from main road, not Sat Nav. **Parking**: on site.

Find out more: 01905 371006 or croome@nationaltrust.org.uk

Croome		M	T	W	T	F	S	S
House and RAF Museum								
1 Jan–15 Feb	11–4	**M**	**T**	**W**	**T**	**F**	**S**	**S**
16 Feb–3 Nov	11–4:30	**M**	**T**	**W**	**T**	**F**	**S**	**S**
4 Nov–31 Dec*	11–4	**M**	**T**	**W**	**T**	**F**	**S**	**S**
Park, restaurant and shop								
1 Jan–15 Feb	10–4	**M**	**T**	**W**	**T**	**F**	**S**	**S**
16 Feb–3 Nov	10–5	**M**	**T**	**W**	**T**	**F**	**S**	**S**
4 Nov–31 Dec*	10–4	**M**	**T**	**W**	**T**	**F**	**S**	**S**

*Everything closed 24 and 25 December.

Cwmmau Farmhouse

Brilley, Whitney-on-Wye, Herefordshire HR3 6JP 1965

A charming 17th-century timbered farmhouse with many original features and stunning views across Herefordshire. **Note**: open daily, 21 to 27 June, 11:30 to 4:30.

Find out more: 01568 780246 or cwmmaufarmhouse@nationaltrust.org.uk

Downs Banks

Washdale Lane, Oulton Heath, near Stone, Staffordshire 1950

A little wilderness of woodlands and heath, with easy access walks, in the heart of the Midlands. **Note**: sorry no toilets. Some steep paths.

Find out more: 01889 880160 or downsbanks@nationaltrust.org.uk

Dudmaston

Quatt, near Bridgnorth, Shropshire WV15 6QN

1978

Stretching across 1,214 hectares (3,000 acres) of ancient woodland and park, Dudmaston is a working estate with a family home at its heart. Steeped in history but shaped by modern tastes and radical thinking, it is a delightful collision of unexpected contrasts. From the picturesque dingle, to the remarkable pieces by Moore and Matisse in the galleries, art has always found a home here. Discover modern sculpture in the garden or find a tranquil spot to take in the views over the pool. Explore the wider estate all year, with walks from Comer Woods, Hampton Loade and Sawmill. **Note**: the family home of Mr and Mrs Mark Hamilton-Russell.

Eat, shop, stay: Orchard Tea-room offering lunches and homemade cakes. A seasonal ice-cream parlour and takeaway snacks from the Apple Store. Seasonal food outlet in Comer Woods. Gift shop selling locally sourced items and plants. Second-hand bookshop. Holiday cottage and bunkhouse for rent.

Things to see and do: **Indoors** Historical family rooms, as well as modern, Spanish and botanical art collections, with guided art tours. **Outdoors** Garden tours, woodland playground and year-round walking and cycling trails. **Dogs**: welcome on leads in parkland and orchard. Assistance dogs only in the garden and indoor spaces.

The tranquil garden at Dudmaston, Shropshire, above, and welcoming Library, below

Access:
Building **Grounds**

Parking: Dudmaston Hall car park (seasonal) and pay and display car parks in Comer Woods, Hampton Loade and the Sawmill.

Find out more: 01746 780866 or dudmaston@nationaltrust.org.uk

Dudmaston		M	T	W	T	F	S	S
Park, tea-room, shop and second-hand bookshop								
16 Feb–24 Feb*	11–4	·	·	·	·	·	S	S
17 Mar–28 Mar	11–4:30	M	T	W	T	·	·	S
1 Apr–30 Sep	11–5	M	T	W	T	·	·	S
1 Oct–31 Oct	11–4	M	T	W	T	·	·	S
2 Nov–1 Dec	11–4	·	·	·	·	·	S	S
Galleries								
17 Mar–31 Oct	12:30–4	M	T	W	T	·	·	S
Hall and galleries								
1 Apr–30 Sep	12:30–4:30	M	T	W	T	·	·	S
Garden**								
17 Mar–31 Oct	11:30–4:30	M	T	W	T	·	·	S

No entry to the car park before opening time.
*Restricted park access – Dingle walks only.
**1 April to 30 September: garden closes at 5.

Farnborough Hall

Farnborough, near Banbury, Warwickshire OX17 1DU 1960

Carolean house with exquisite plasterwork and grand stairway. Set in landscaped gardens with a mile-long terrace walk and parkland views. **Note**: occupied and administered by the Holbech family. Open Wednesday and Saturday, 3 April to 28 September, 2 to 5:30. Also open 5 and 6 May.

Find out more: 01295 670266 (option six) or farnboroughhall@nationaltrust.org.uk

The Firs – Birthplace of Edward Elgar

Crown East Lane, Lower Broadheath, Worcester, Worcestershire WR2 6RH

2017

Family treasures tell the story of Sir Edward Elgar's humble beginnings in the family cottage. Learn more about Elgar's inspiration in the modern Visitor Centre (three exhibition spaces). Outside, the cottage garden is the perfect place to sit and reflect on the life of this great composer and his works.

The Firs – Birthplace of Edward Elgar, Worcestershire: the kitchen, above, and garden, below

Eat, shop, stay: tea-room with outdoor courtyard dining area serving soup, hotpots, seasonal food, cakes and scones freshly baked throughout the day. Shop selling gifts, plants, books and Elgar-related souvenirs. Second-hand bookshop. Picnics welcome.

Things to see and do: 'All you need to write a symphony' exhibition. Live music performances and lectures throughout the year. **Dogs**: assistance dogs only in cottage/indoor tea-room. Dog-friendly site with outdoor courtyard dining area.

Access: **Garden** **Visitor centre** **Cottage**
Parking: on site.

Find out more: 01905 333330 or thefirs@nationaltrust.org.uk

The Firs		M	T	W	T	F	S	S
4 Jan–31 Oct	10–5	**M**	**T**	**W**	**T**	**F**	**S**	**S**
1 Nov–30 Dec	10–4	**M**	**T**	**W**	**T**	**F**	**S**	**S**

Closed 24 and 25 December.

The Fleece Inn

Bretforton, near Evesham, Worcestershire WR11 7JE 1978

Medieval half-timbered longhouse, now a traditional village inn, with barn and orchard. Known for folk music, Morris dancing and asparagus. **Note**: open daily, 10 to 11 (reduced opening 25 December).

Find out more: 01386 831173 or fleeceinn@nationaltrust.org.uk

Greyfriars' House and Garden

Friar Street, Worcester,
Worcestershire WR1 2LZ

1966

Set in the heart of historic Worcester, this timber-framed house (below), built in the 1490s, reflected the fortunes of its surroundings for centuries until it was rescued and carefully restored by the Matley-Moores. Now you can explore 500 years of history through the lens of an unusual brother and sister.

Eat, shop, stay: light refreshments served on the garden terrace, indoor seating available in colder weather. Small gift shop and second-hand bookshop.

Things to see and do: **Indoors** Themed events throughout the year, including house tours. Children's trails. **Outdoors** Garden games and geocaching. **Dogs**: welcome in garden.

Access: House
Parking: none on site, nearest at nearby St Martins Gate, King Street and Cathedral Plaza car parks, not National Trust (charge including members).

Find out more: 01905 23571 or greyfriars@nationaltrust.org.uk

Greyfriars		M	T	W	T	F	S	S
12 Feb-30 Mar*	11-4**	·	T	W	T	F	S	·
2 Apr-26 Oct*	11-5**	·	T	W	T	F	S	·
29 Oct-14 Dec*	11-4**	·	T	W	T	F	S	·

*This year we are trialling Sunday opening (please call for details). **House: taster tours only from 11 to 1, tour places allocated on arrival; freeflow access from 1. Open Bank Holiday Mondays.

Hanbury Hall

School Road, Hanbury, Droitwich Spa,
Worcestershire WR9 7EA

1953

The breathtakingly lavish Painted Staircase at Hanbury Hall in Worcestershire

A country retreat in the heart of Worcestershire. The house and garden, originally a stage-set for summer parties, offer a glimpse into life at the turn of the 18th century. Don't miss the original wall-paintings by Sir James Thornhill; full of drama and politics, they show the birth of Georgian society. The original formal gardens, designed by George London, have been faithfully recreated and complement the relaxed later gardens, with orangery, orchards and walled garden. If you venture further afield, our walks will help you find George London's visionary Semicircle in the parkland – the beginning of the landscape movement.

Eat, shop, stay: Servants' Hall tea-room serving meals and cakes made using seasonal Hanbury-grown produce. Chambers tea-room serving traditional afternoon teas. Plants and produce from the walled garden for sale. Make Hanbury a home from home in one of two holiday cottages.

Things to see and do: spend perfect days picnicking and playing on sweeping lawns, surrounded by rolling Worcestershire countryside. For those seeking a more adventurous day, enjoy estate walks or 10k runs through the parkland. **Dogs**: welcome on leads in parkland and in the stableyard. Assistance dogs only in gardens.

Access:
Building **Grounds**
Parking: 150 yards.

Find out more: 01527 821214 or hanburyhall@nationaltrust.org.uk

Hanbury Hall		M	T	W	T	F	S	S
House								
2 Jan–28 Feb*	11–4†	M	T	W	T	F	S	S
1 Mar–3 Nov	11–5	M	T	W	T	F	S	S
4 Nov–31 Dec*	11–4	M	T	W	T	F	S	S
Park, garden and tea-room								
1 Jan–28 Feb*	10–4	M	T	W	T	F	S	S
1 Mar–31 Dec*	9–5**	M	T	W	T	F	S	S

*Closed 23 and 24 January; 24 and 25 December.
**Closes 5 or dusk if earlier. †January and February: trialling new ways of opening house (please call for details).

Hanbury Hall, above, was originally built as little more than a stage-set for summer parties. Opposite, Kinver Edge and the Rock Houses, Staffordshire

Hawford Dovecote

Hawford, Worcestershire WR3 7SG 1973

Picturesque dovecote, which has survived virtually unaltered since the late 16th century, retaining many nesting boxes. **Note**: sorry no toilet or tea-room. Please park carefully to one side of lane. Open daily, dawn to dusk.

Find out more: 01527 821214 or hawforddovecote@nationaltrust.org.uk

Kinver Edge and the Rock Houses

Holy Austin Rock Houses, Compton Road, Kinver, near Stourbridge, Staffordshire DY7 6DL

1917

At the Holy Austin Rock Houses, inhabited until the 1960s, discover how a community of people carved themselves homes deep into the rock of this imposing sandstone ridge. A walk in the surrounding woodland of Kinver Edge leads to open heath buzzing with wildlife, offering dramatic views across three counties.

Eat, shop, stay: quirky tea-room inside a rock house with a woodburning stove, serving homemade savoury food, cakes and drinks. Seating outside with views across the surrounding countryside. Small shop and second-hand bookshop.

Things to see and do: **Indoors** Traditional toys, rag-rugging and free tours weekdays in term-time. **Outdoors** Natural play-trail, more rock houses tucked away in the woods and an Iron Age hill fort. Family events year-round.
Dogs: welcome on leads within gardens of Rock Houses and countryside. Assistance dogs only inside.

Access: Restored Rock Houses Tea-room and toilets Gardens
Sat Nav: use DY7 6DL for Rock Houses.
Parking: for the Rock Houses park in lay-by on Compton Road or in the overflow car park on Kingsford Lane. For the wider countryside, either park in lay-by on Comber Road or in the car park with toilets on Kingsford Lane.

Find out more: 01384 872553 or kinveredge@nationaltrust.org.uk

Kinver Edge and the Rock Houses		M	T	W	T	F	S	S
16 Feb–4 Nov	11-4	M	·	·	T	F	S	S
9 Nov–15 Dec	11-4	·	·	·	·	·	S	S

Open every day during local school holidays. Gardens and tea-room open to 4:30.

Kinwarton Dovecote

Kinwarton, near Alcester, Warwickshire B49 6HB 1958

Rare 14th-century circular dovecote with metre-thick walls, hundreds of nesting holes and original rotating ladder. **Note**: sorry no toilet. Limited parking (not National Trust). Open daily, 1 March to 3 November, 9 to 6.

Find out more: 01789 400777 or kinwartondovecote@nationaltrust.org.uk

Knowles Mill

Dowles Brook, Bewdley, Worcestershire DY12 2LX 1938

Dating from the 18th century, the mill retains much of its machinery, including the frames of an overshot waterwheel. **Note**: Mill Cottage not open to visitors (please respect resident's privacy). Sorry no toilets/tea-room. No parking at Mill Cottage. Open daily, dawn to dusk.

Find out more: 01527 821214 or knowlesmill@nationaltrust.org.uk

Letocetum Roman Baths and Museum

Watling Street, Wall, near Lichfield, Staffordshire WS14 0AW 1934

Open-air remains of a once-important Roman staging post and settlement, including *mansio* (Roman inn) and bathhouse. **Note**: in the guardianship of English Heritage. Baths accessible all year, dawn to dusk. Museum open last weekend of month, March to October. Additional openings during August and for some Bank Holidays.

Find out more: 0370 333 1181 (English Heritage) or letocetum@nationaltrust.org.uk

Middle Littleton Tithe Barn

Middle Littleton, Evesham, Worcestershire WR11 8LN 1975

The largest and finest restored 13th-century tithe barn in the country. **Note**: sorry no toilets. Open daily, 1 April to 31 October, 2 to 5 (guided tours available).

Find out more: 01905 371006 or middlelittleton@nationaltrust.org.uk

Morville Hall

Morville, near Bridgnorth, Shropshire WV16 5NB 1965

Elizabethan gem with a Georgian makeover. Enchanting gardens spill down to the Mor Brook against the backdrop of Shropshire hills. **Note**: property contents are a mix of items on loan and tenant's own. Open Friday and Saturday, 10 and 11 May, 14 and 15 June, 12 and 13 July, 13 and 14 September, 12 to 5. Dower House gardens opened independently by Dr K. Swift on Sundays, Wednesdays and Bank Holiday Mondays, 1 April to 30 September (telephone 01746 714407 for details).

Find out more: 01746 780866 (Dudmaston Hall) or morvillehall@nationaltrust.org.uk

Moseley Old Hall

Moseley Old Hall Lane, Fordhouses, Wolverhampton, Staffordshire WV10 7HY

1962

This atmospheric farmhouse, built circa 1600, holds many secrets. Charles II hid here after escaping the 1651 Battle of Worcester. Inside, a log fire crackles as 17th-century domestic life surrounds you. Outside, explore the walled

Moseley Old Hall, Staffordshire: the knot garden

garden, containing herbs and vegetables, the orchard and knot garden. Beyond is King's Walk Wood.

Eat, shop, stay: tea-room serving soup and seasonal specials. Cakes and scones baked throughout the day. New accessible kiosk offering range of light refreshments. Shop selling gifts and plants. Second-hand bookshop.

Things to see and do: Indoors Specialist talks, tours and interactive demonstrations recreating 17th-century life all year. **Outdoors** Children's activities, including two-level tree hide, den-building, rope swings, trails and activity packs. Wightwick Manor nearby. **Dogs**: welcome on leads in garden and grounds.

Access: **House** **Tea-room** **Garden and woodland**
Parking: on site.

Find out more: 01902 782808 or moseleyoldhall@nationaltrust.org.uk

Moseley Old Hall		M	T	W	T	F	S	S
14 Feb-15 Mar	10-4	M	T	W	T	F	S	S
16 Mar-3 Nov	10-5	M	T	W	T	F	S	S
4 Nov-23 Dec	10-4	M	·	·	·	F	S	S

House: opens 11; entry on Bank Holiday weekends and very busy times by timed ticket; February, March, November and December: access to top floor may be limited for safety; last entry one hour before closing.

 For information about getting to National Trust places, please see page 3

Packwood House

Packwood Lane, Lapworth,
Warwickshire B94 6AT

1941

Surrounded by beautiful gardens and countryside, Packwood was described by a guest in the 1930s as 'a house to dream of, a garden to dream in'. Lovingly restored at the beginning of the 20th century by Graham Baron Ash, you can discover the detail behind the man, his passion for collecting and his collection. The gardens include brightly coloured, 'mingled style' herbaceous borders, famous sculpted yews and an 18th-century gentleman's kitchen garden.

Eat, shop, stay: Garden Kitchen café serving hot food, sandwiches, cakes and snacks. Catering trailer open during busy periods. Shop selling gifts, local foods and plants, many grown on site. Picnics welcome by the lake and in the picnic area by car park.

Things to see and do: **Indoors** Children's trail. **Outdoors** Welcome and garden talks, countryside walks and natural play. Baddesley Clinton and Coughton Court nearby. Areas of the gardens may be closed, please call before travelling. **Dogs**: welcome in car park, park footpaths and café terrace. Assistance dogs only in gardens.

Access:
House **Grounds**
Parking: 150 yards.

Discovering Packwood House in Warwickshire

Packwood House: sculpted yews in the garden

Find out more: 01564 782024 or packwood@nationaltrust.org.uk

Packwood House		M	T	W	T	F	S	S
1 Jan–15 Feb	9-4†	M	T	W	T	F	S	S
16 Feb–3 Nov	9-5*	M	T	W	T	F	S	S
4 Nov–31 Dec	9-4†	M	T	W	T	F	S	S

19 to 22 April: admission by bookable tickets only, limited (including members). House: admission by timed ticket (not bookable). *House, formal gardens and gift shop: open at 11. †House, formal gardens and gift shop: open 11 to 4 (access to house may be by guided tour), last entrance to house at 3. Closed 24 and 25 December.

Rosedene

Victoria Road, Dodford, near Bromsgrove,
Worcestershire B61 9BU 1997

Restored 1840s cottage with an organic garden and orchard, illustrating the mid-19th-century Chartist Movement. **Note**: available to hire as a 'back to basics' holiday cottage. Admission by guided tour on the first Sunday of month, March to December (booking essential).

Find out more: 01527 821214 or rosedene@nationaltrust.org.uk

Shugborough Estate

Milford, near Stafford, Staffordshire ST17 0XA

1966

Join us on a journey as we revive and reunite the Shugborough Estate over the coming years. Home to the Anson family since 1624 and with a legacy of exploration and innovation, it was once described as 'a perfect paradise'. You can explore sweeping parkland, where historic breeds of cattle and sheep graze freely, visit ancient woodland, wander through a landscape peppered with monuments and discover Park Farm, created at the cutting-edge of agricultural reforms. In the Georgian mansion, unearth prized treasures and experience life 'below stairs', then enter a world of glamour and royalty in the apartment of Patrick Lichfield, 5th Earl and fashion photographer.

Eat, shop, stay: delicious treats and meals on offer at the mansion tea-room and Park Farm café. Why not visit the shop or plant centre and pick up the perfect gift or take home some produce from the walled garden?

Things to see and do: **Indoors** There are stories of adventure, travels and triumphs to discover in the mansion. **Outdoors** New estate walks to explore and wonderful views from the Triumphal Arch to enjoy plus explorers' wood natural play area for children. **Dogs**: on leads in formal gardens and parkland.

Access:
Building **Grounds**
Parking: 25 yards from reception.

Find out more: 01889 880160 or shugborough@nationaltrust.org.uk

Shugborough Estate, Staffordshire, clockwise from right: rapt visitors, delicate statuary in the garden and the River Sow meanders through the parkland, passing the Georgian mansion

Support the places you visit: please scan your member card for free parking ticket

Shugborough Estate		M	T	W	T	F	S	S
Park, gardens and Park Farm*								
1 Jan–31 Mar	9–4	**M**	**T**	**W**	**T**	**F**	**S**	**S**
1 Apr–3 Nov	9–6	**M**	**T**	**W**	**T**	**F**	**S**	**S**
4 Nov–31 Dec	9–4	**M**	**T**	**W**	**T**	**F**	**S**	**S**
Servants' quarters								
16 Feb–3 Nov	11–4:30	**M**	**T**	**W**	**T**	**F**	**S**	**S**
30 Nov–22 Dec	11–4:30	**M**	**T**	**W**	**T**	**F**	**S**	**S**
Mansion and Lichfield apartment**								
18 Mar–3 Nov	11–4:30	**M**	**T**	**W**	**T**	**F**	**S**	**S**
30 Nov–22 Dec†	11–3	**M**	**T**	**W**	**T**	**F**	**S**	**S**
Mansion tea-room and shop								
1 Jan–31 Mar	10–3:30	**M**	**T**	**W**	**T**	**F**	**S**	**S**
1 Apr–3 Nov	10–5	**M**	**T**	**W**	**T**	**F**	**S**	**S**
4 Nov–31 Dec	10–4	**M**	**T**	**W**	**T**	**F**	**S**	**S**

*Walled garden and visitor reception: open as park, gardens and Park Farm. **Lichfield apartment entry by timed ticket only. Closed 25 December. †Mansion only open 30 November to 22 December, Lichfield apartment closed in December.

Sunnycroft

200 Holyhead Road, Wellington, Telford, Shropshire TF1 2DR

1999

Hidden down an avenue of towering redwoods is this miniature country estate in the middle of suburbia. This rare survival of a Victorian red-brick villa is a time capsule of a self-sufficient way of life. Sunnycroft is a family home that envelopes you in times past. **Note**: in February and March some parts of house may be closed due to re-wiring project.

Eat, shop, stay: small tea-room in house, with doors leading onto the veranda, serving light lunches, cakes, scones and slices, ice cream and drinks. Picnics welcome on lawn. Shop in the historic kitchen selling gifts, seasonal plants, produce and second-hand books.

Things to see and do: **Indoors** Introductory talks, guided tours, workshops, family activities and trails reveal the stories of life at Sunnycroft. **Outdoors** Family trails, garden games on lawn, seasonal events and garden tours. **Dogs**: welcome on leads in grounds only.

Access: Building Grounds
Sat Nav: use TF1 2DP (exit seven from M54).
Parking: 150 yards.

Find out more: 01952 242884 or sunnycroft@nationaltrust.org.uk

Sunnycroft		M	T	W	T	F	S	S
16 Feb–24 Feb	10:30–4	M	T	·	·	F	S	S
2 Mar–31 Mar	10:30–4	·	·	·	·	·	S	S
1 Apr–3 Nov	10:30–5	M	T	·	·	F	S	S
30 Nov–23 Dec	10:30–4	M	T	·	·	F	S	S

House: last admission one hour before closing. Last service in tea-room 30 minutes before closing. Entry by timed tickets.

Upton House and Gardens

near Banbury, Warwickshire OX15 6HT

1948

Upton House, purchased in 1927 by the 2nd Viscount Bearsted, has been remodelled and is ready to welcome its new owners, staff and guests. This year Upton invites you to a special 'at home' with Lord and Lady Bearsted. See the modern age arrive with the Bearsteds' renovations; discover how they created a made-to-measure home to showcase a world-class art and porcelain collection, including works by Bosch, Stubbs and El Greco. Every ideal home needs a spectacular garden. Lady Bearsted's passion for plants is revealed with spring bulbs, herbaceous planting and kitchen garden – all reflected in the Mirror Pool.

Eat, shop, stay: restaurant (licensed) serving lunches and freshly baked cakes; gluten-free and vegetarian options always available. Shop selling gifts, plants and mementoes of your visit. Second-hand bookshop. Two holiday cottages; one with 1930s décor and one overlooking the gardens.

Things to see and do: **Indoors** New servants' rooms, topical house tours, world-class art and porcelain collection, changing exhibitions, activities and workshops. **Outdoors** Woodland walk, quiet orchard space, seasonal planting schemes, garden chats and events.
Dogs: assistance dogs only.

Access:
House and gallery **Grounds**
Sat Nav: follow brown signs to car park once you arrive at postcode location.
Parking: 300 yards.

Find out more: 01295 670266 or uptonhouse@nationaltrust.org.uk

Upton House and Gardens		M	T	W	T	F	S	S
Gardens, restaurant and shop*								
1 Jan–2 Jan	12–4	·	T	W	·	·	·	·
5 Jan–3 Feb	12–4	·	·	·	·	·	S	S
9 Feb–3 Nov	11–5	M	T	W	T	F	S	S
4 Nov–22 Dec	12–4	M	·	·	·	F	S	S
26 Dec–31 Dec	12–4	M	T	·	T	F	S	S
House**								
5 Jan–3 Feb	12–4	·	·	·	·	·	S	S
9 Feb–3 Nov	1–5	M	T	W	T	F	S	S
4 Nov–22 Dec	12–4	M	·	·	·	F	S	S

*November to March: gardens open by winter walk only.
**Timed tickets operate daily. 9 February to 3 November: themed tours 11 to 1, places limited.

Upton House and Gardens, Warwickshire, below, was made-to-measure to showcase world-class art and porcelain collections. Right, springtime at The Weir Garden in Herefordshire

The Weir Garden

Swainshill, Hereford, Herefordshire HR4 7QF

1959

Whatever the season, the natural beauty of this riverside garden is completely captivating. During spring, the ground beneath the ancient trees is carpeted with bulbs; then, in summer, a picnic by the river while watching the wildlife is irresistible. Autumn brings an abundance of seasonal produce in the walled garden.
Note: sturdy footwear recommended.

Eat, shop, stay: self-service tea and coffee available. Picnics welcome.

Things to see and do: events, including walks and talks. Historical secrets to discover, from giant fish to Roman remains. Natural play area and family trails during school holidays.
Dogs: assistance dogs only (dogs allowed in car park).

Access: **Grounds**
Parking: on site.

Find out more: 01981 590509 or theweir@nationaltrust.org.uk

The Weir Garden		M	T	W	T	F	S	S
13 Jan–27 Jan	10:30–4	·	·	·	·	·	S	S
28 Jan–3 Nov	10:30–4:30	M	T	W	T	F	S	S
9 Nov–15 Dec	10:30–4	·	·	·	·	·	S	S

Wichenford Dovecote

Wichenford, Worcestershire WR6 6XY 1965

Small but striking 17th-century half-timbered dovecote at Wichenford Court. **Note**: no access to Wichenford Court (privately owned). Sorry no toilet or tea-room. Please consider local residents when parking. Open every day all year, dawn to dusk.

Find out more: 01527 821214 or wichenforddovecote@nationaltrust.org.uk

Wightwick Manor and Gardens

Bridgnorth Road, Wolverhampton, West Midlands WV6 8BN

1937

A place where liberal dreams for the future mix with a love for unfashionable art. The Mander family's political ideals inspired them to share their home and fill it with art for the nation to enjoy. Their belief in social activism, the right to roam, fairness for their employees and confronting fascism combines with a home bursting with works by the greatest artists of the pre-Raphaelites and Arts and Crafts movement. A house of colour and comfort; a garden of yew and roses; and a gallery of De Morgan treasures – the legacy of one remarkable family and their friends.

Wightwick Manor and Gardens, West Midlands, this page and opposite. This comfortable house was built by a family with dreams of a more egalitarian future

Eat, shop, stay: specialist shop selling William Morris and Arts and Crafts-inspired ranges with plant centre. Tea-room serving breakfast, light lunches, sandwiches and sweet treats.

Things to see and do: **Indoors** World-class art collection, interactive servants' rooms, specialist talks and tours available all year. Malthouse gallery with De Morgan Collection exhibition. **Outdoors** Natural woodland play areas, family orienteering and trails.
Dogs: welcome on leads in garden.

Access:
Manor **Malthouse**
Gardens
Parking: entrance off A454.

Find out more: 01902 761400 (Infoline) or wightwickmanor@nationaltrust.org.uk Wightwick Bank, Wolverhampton, West Midlands WV6 8EE

Wightwick Manor and Gardens		M	T	W	T	F	S	S
1 Jan–15 Mar*	10–4**	**M**	**T**	**W**	**T**	**F**	**S**	**S**
16 Mar–27 Oct	10–5**	**M**	**T**	**W**	**T**	**F**	**S**	**S**
28 Oct–31 Dec	10–4**	**M**	**T**	**W**	**T**	**F**	**S**	**S**

*House: reduced number of rooms open in January, February and March. **House: opens 11, entry by tour only 11 to 12; freeflow from 12. Shop and gallery: open 10:30. Last entry to house one hour before closing. Closed 25 and 26 December.

Wilderhope Manor

Longville, Much Wenlock, Shropshire TF13 6EG 1936

Charming Elizabethan manor house with commanding views across a secluded valley with many original features inside and lovely walks outside. **Note**: Youth Hostel, access may be restricted. Open Sunday, 6 January to 31 March, 6 October to 29 December and Wednesday, 7 April to 29 September, 2 to 4.

Find out more: 01694 771363 (Hostel Warden YHA) or wilderhope@nationaltrust.org.uk

Additional countryside car parks in the West Midlands

Ignore Sat Nav when close and follow signs

Hawksmoor	ST10 3AW
Comer Wood (Dudmaston)	WV15 6DU
Wenlock Edge	
Much Wenlock	TF13 6DH
Presthope	TF13 6DQ

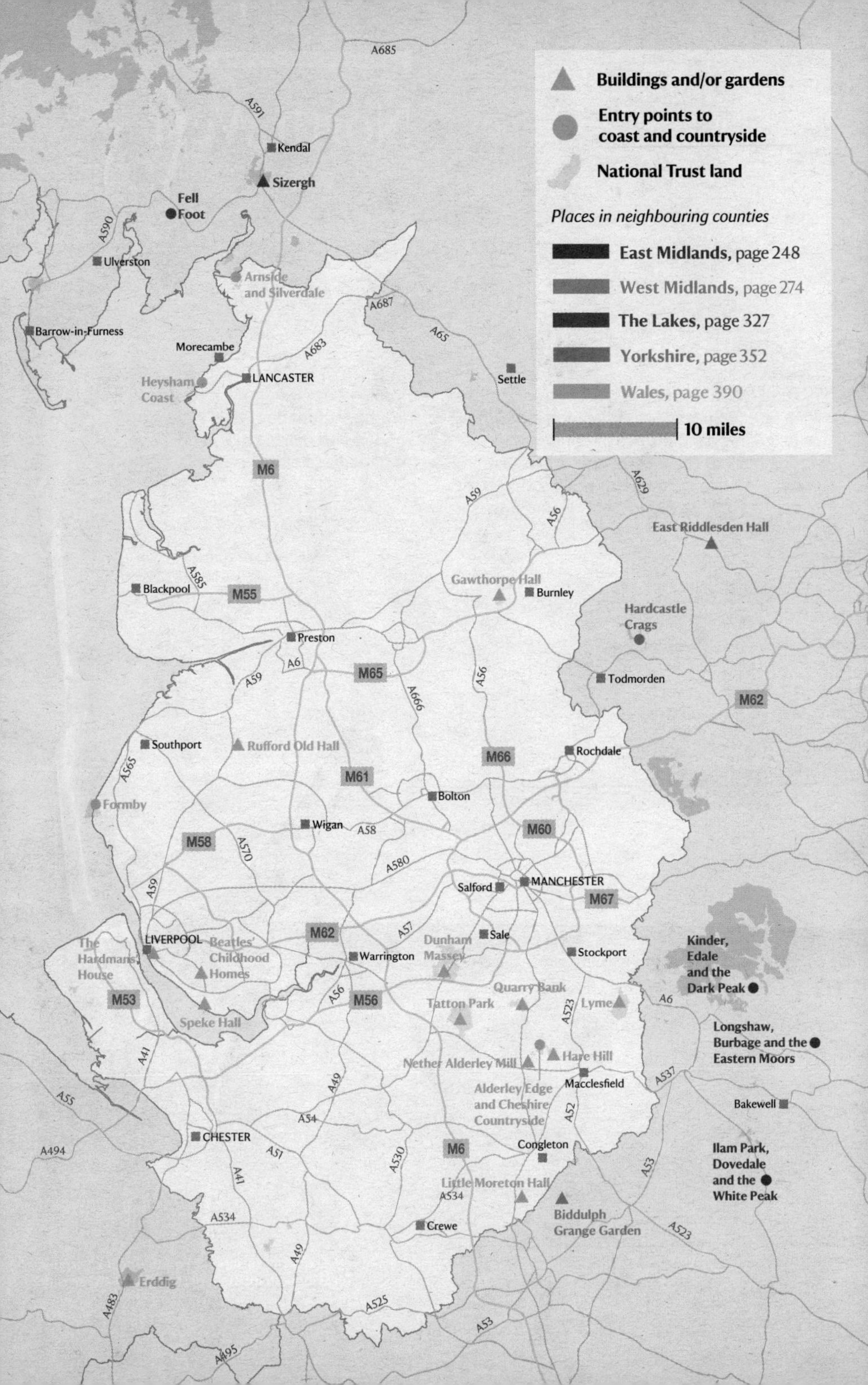

Buildings and/or gardens
Entry points to coast and countryside
National Trust land
Places in neighbouring counties
East Midlands, page 248
West Midlands, page 274
The Lakes, page 327
Yorkshire, page 352
Wales, page 390
10 miles
A685
A591
Kendal
Sizergh
Fell Foot
A590
Ulverston
Arnside and Silverdale
Barrow-in-Furness
Morecambe
A687
A65
A683
Settle
Heysham Coast
LANCASTER
M6
A629
A59
A56
East Riddlesden Hall
A585
Blackpool
M55
Gawthorpe Hall
Burnley
Hardcastle Crags
Preston
A6
M65
A59
A666
A56
Todmorden
M62
Southport
Rufford Old Hall
A565
M66
Rochdale
M61
Bolton
Formby
Wigan
A58
M60
M58
A570
A580
A59
Salford
MANCHESTER
M67
M62
A57
Sale
LIVERPOOL
The Hardmans' House
Beatles' Childhood Homes
Warrington
Dunham Massey
Stockport
Kinder, Edale and the Dark Peak
A6
M53
Speke Hall
A56
M56
Tatton Park
Quarry Bank
A523
Lyme
Longshaw, Burbage and the Eastern Moors
Nether Alderley Mill
Hare Hill
A41
A49
Macclesfield
A537
A55
Alderley Edge and Cheshire Countryside
Bakewell
A54
A52
A494
CHESTER
A51
A530
M6
Congleton
A53
Ilam Park, Dovedale and the White Peak
A41
Little Moreton Hall
A534
A534
Biddulph Grange Garden
Crewe
A523
A49
Erddig
A483
A525
A53
A495

North West

Sunshine and wide expanses of sand at Formby, near Liverpool:
ideal ingredients for a perfect day at the seaside

Alderley Edge and Cheshire Countryside

Nether Alderley, Macclesfield, Cheshire

1946

The dramatic red sandstone escarpment of Alderley Edge has far-reaching views over the Cheshire Plain and towards the Peak District. Numerous paths meander through open pasture and mature pine and beech woodland. It's a Site of Special Scientific Interest because of its geology and history of copper mining dating back to the Bronze Age, and is also known for its wizard myth, which inspired the novel *The Weirdstone of Brisingamen*. There's more Cheshire countryside to explore: Bickerton, Bulkeley and Helsby Hills on the Sandstone Ridge, Thurstaston Common on the Wirral, and The Cloud and Mow Cop on the Staffordshire border. **Note**: toilets at Alderley Edge car park only.

Eat, shop, stay: Alderley Edge: Wizard Tea-room and Wizard Inn (neither National Trust). Ice-cream van (when weather is fine, not National Trust). Picnic area close to car park.

Things to see and do: guided walks exploring the industrial archaeology, geology and legends of Alderley Edge. Waymarked walking routes. Three orienteering courses. Ancient copper mine tours by Derbyshire Caving Club, twice a year. **Dogs**: welcome under close control; on leads near livestock and ground-nesting birds.

Access: Grounds
Sat Nav: for Alderley Edge use SK10 4UB; for Mow Cop ST7 3PA; for Bickerton SY14 8LN.
Parking: at Alderley Edge, Mow Cop ST7 3PA and Bickerton SY14 8LN (plus roadside elsewhere).

Find out more: 01625 584412 or alderleyedge@nationaltrust.org.uk

Alderley Edge	
Car park	
Open every day all year	8–5*

*1 April to 27 October, closes at 8.

The dramatic red stone escarpment at Alderley Edge in Cheshire

Arnside and Silverdale

near Arnside, Cumbria

1929

With a wildlife-rich landscape of limestone pavement, grassland, woodland and meadow, this coastal countryside has miles of footpaths and views over Morecambe Bay. Arnside Knott and Eaves Wood are home to butterflies and flowers; Jack Scout's cliffs are perfect for watching the setting sun or migrant birds passing through.

Eat, shop, stay: variety of small shops, galleries and cafés in and around Arnside and Silverdale villages (none National Trust). Nearest National Trust café at Sizergh.

Things to see and do: viewpoint with toposcope (landmark orientation map) a short walk uphill from Arnside Knott car park. Stroll to Silverdale cove or follow the Silverdale village heritage walk. **Dogs**: welcome under close control (on leads where stock grazing).

Sat Nav: use LA5 0BP for Arnside Knott; LA5 0UG for Eaves Wood (Silverdale), both nearby. **Parking**: at Arnside Knott (signposted from Arnside Promenade) and Eaves Wood, Silverdale. Also in Silverdale village (not National Trust).

Find out more: 01524 701178 or arnsidesilverdale@nationaltrust.org.uk

Peaceful Arnside in Cumbria

The Beatles' Childhood Homes

Woolton and Allerton, Liverpool

2002

A combined tour to Mendips and 20 Forthlin Road, the childhood homes of John Lennon and Paul McCartney, is the only way to see inside the houses where The Beatles met, composed and rehearsed many of their earliest songs. You can walk through the back door into the kitchen and imagine John's Aunt Mimi cooking him his tea, or stand in the spot where Lennon and McCartney composed 'I Saw Her Standing There'. The custodians take you on a trip down memory lane in these two atmospheric houses, so typical of Liverpool life in the 1950s. **Note**: handbags, cameras and recording equipment must be left in secure facilities at both houses. Access is by minibus tour only, departing from Liverpool city centre and Speke Hall (times vary, booking essential). Admission charges apply to all, including members.

Eat, shop, stay: you can buy guidebooks with your tour ticket. Refreshments are available at Jurys Inn, Liverpool (not National Trust) and at Speke Hall's Home Farm Restaurant.

Things to see and do: take a tour and step back in time to the 1950s and 60s to discover more about the birth of The Beatles.

Access: **Building**
Parking: numerous car parks near collection point (not National Trust) for tours from city centre, or at Speke Hall for tours departing from there.

Find out more: 0151 427 7231 (booking line) or thebeatleshomes@nationaltrust.org.uk

The Beatles' Childhood Homes		M	T	W	T	F	S	S
2 Mar–2 Jun	Tour*	·	·	**W**	**T**	**F**	**S**	**S**
3 Jun–27 Oct	Tour*	**M**	**T**	**W**	**T**	**F**	**S**	**S**
30 Oct–24 Nov	Tour*	·	·	**W**	**T**	**F**	**S**	**S**

*Admission by guided tour only. Times and pick-up locations vary (please visit website or call for details and tickets).

The Beatles' Childhood Homes, Liverpool: 20 Forthlin Road, left and two views of the simple kitchen at Mendips

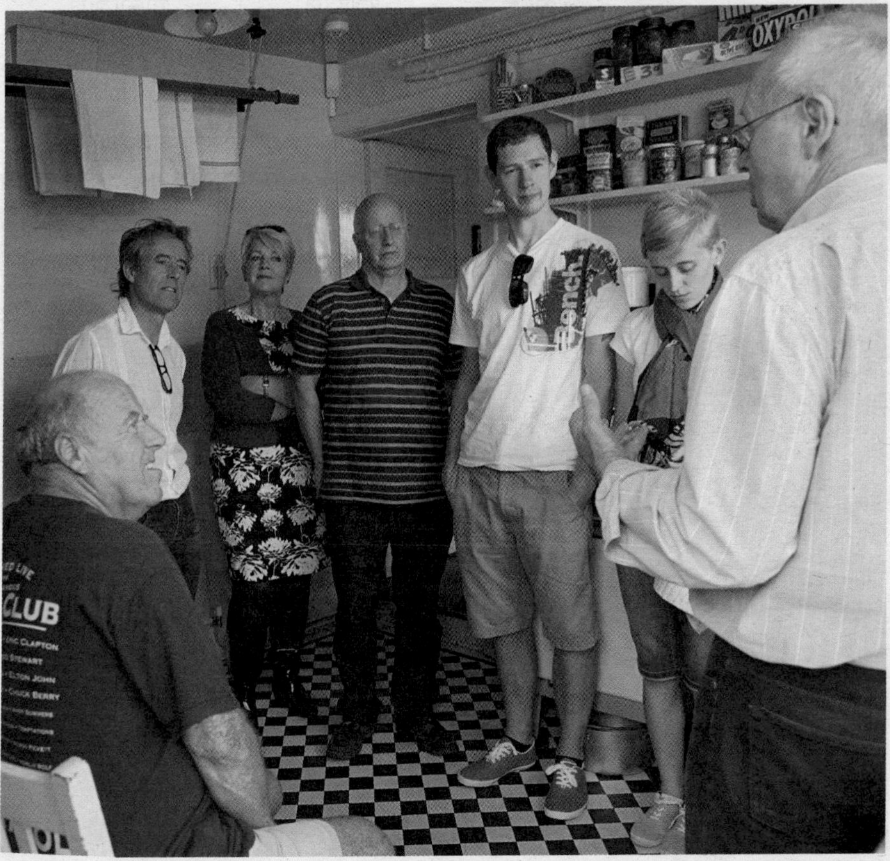

Dunham Massey

Altrincham, Greater Manchester WA14 4SJ

1976

A green haven surrounded by a wall of red brick, Dunham Massey park is at the heart of a 1,200-hectare (3,000-acre) estate. The ancient deer park is home to birds and insects and has the largest collection of veteran trees in the North West. Wild fallow deer can be seen among the tree-lined avenues. In the house, selected rooms reveal stories about the family and workers, while others show what it takes to look after a diverse collection and archive. The gardens include one of the UK's largest winter gardens, a rose garden, water features and swathes of planting which are colourful all year. The stables and 400-year-old mill are also open as part of this working estate. **Note**: everyone requires a house and garden ticket, including members (available from reception on the day).

Eat, shop, stay: large shop selling food, locally sourced gifts and a wide range of plants. Stamford Café with indoor and outdoor seating, Stables Restaurant serving hot lunches and the Parlour offering drinks and snacks, including ice cream (hours vary).

Things to see and do: **Indoors** At least one free guided tour of the house every day. Turn on the waterwheel and see the old sawmill in action. **Outdoors** Seasonal garden highlights include snowdrops, daffodils, bluebells, tulips, roses and hydrangeas. Guided tours and routes for walks, runs and cycling on the wider estate (cycling in the deer park for under-fives only). Events all year, including open-air theatre and cinema, family activities during school holidays and Christmas celebrations. **Dogs**: on leads in the deer park. Assistance dogs only in the house and garden.

Access:
House **Garden and park**
Parking: 200 yards.

Find out more: 0161 942 3989 (Infoline). 0161 941 1025 or dunhammassey@nationaltrust.org.uk

Dunham Massey		M	T	W	T	F	S	S
Garden, café, restaurant, shop and stables								
1 Jan–8 Feb	10:30–4*	M	T	W	T	F	S	S
9 Feb–3 Nov	10:30–5*	M	T	W	T	F	S	S
4 Nov–31 Dec**	10:30–4*	M	T	W	T	F	S	S
House and mill†								
23 Mar–3 Nov	11–5††	M	T	W	·	·	S	S
Park								
1 Jan–8 Feb	8–6	M	T	W	T	F	S	S
9 Feb–3 Nov	8–8	M	T	W	T	F	S	S
4 Nov–31 Dec	8–6	M	T	W	T	F	S	S

*Garden: closes dusk if earlier. Café, restaurant and shop: open 10. Restaurant: closes one hour earlier. **Garden, café, restaurant, shop and stables: closed 20 November and 25 December. Stables: open 11. †House: 9 February to 22 March, partly open for special guided tours (book on the day). ††House: closes dusk, if earlier; last entry one hour before closing. Mill: open 12 to 4.

Dunham Massey, Greater Manchester, clockwise from above: the grand house sits at the heart of an unspoilt walled park, the Butler's Pantry and golden autumn colour

Formby

near Formby, Liverpool

1967

Everyone can enjoy Formby, near Liverpool

Formby has 3 miles of shifting sands and dynamic dunes. Sea views over Liverpool Bay to the hills of North Wales can be enjoyed from the wide sandy beaches. Footprint trails that are 5,000 years old sometimes reappear as the sea erodes ancient mudflats. Take a pinewood walk and look for red squirrels or follow the Asparagus Trail or Ravenmeols Heritage Trail. Formby is a place for simple pleasures: a family day out, healthy exercise, fresh air and relaxation, or a seaside picnic in the perfect spot. Choose between two coastal car parks at Victoria Road and Lifeboat Road. **Note**: toilets open at Victoria Road when car park is staffed. Sorry none at Lifeboat Road.

Eat, shop, stay: a favourite place for picnics. Ice cream, soft drinks, coffee and confectionery available from mobile vans (not National Trust). New food offers being trialled at Lifeboat Road. Safe barbecue area at the family picnic site at Victoria Road.

Things to see and do: self-guided trails, including the Formby Asparagus Trail and the Ravenmeols Heritage Trail. Guided walks. Circular and longer walks linked to the Sefton Coastal Path. Orienteering and geocaching. **Dogs**: on leads on Squirrel Walk and under close supervision elsewhere.

Access: **Grounds**
Sat Nav: use L37 1LJ for Victoria Road car park; L37 2EB for Lifeboat Road. **Parking**: on site (long traffic queues in summer).

Find out more: 01704 878591 or formby@nationaltrust.org.uk

Formby		M	T	W	T	F	S	S
Car park								
1 Jan–3 Feb	9–4	**M**	**T**	**W**	**T**	**F**	**S**	**S**
4 Feb–24 Mar	9–4:45	**M**	**T**	**W**	**T**	**F**	**S**	**S**
25 Mar–29 Sep	9–5:15	**M**	**T**	**W**	**T**	**F**	**S**	**S**
30 Sep–24 Nov	9–4:45	**M**	**T**	**W**	**T**	**F**	**S**	**S**
25 Nov–31 Dec	9–4	**M**	**T**	**W**	**T**	**F**	**S**	**S**

Closed 25 December.

Constantly on the move, the miles of shifting sands at Formby are backed by dynamic dunes

 For information about getting to National Trust places, please see page 3

Gawthorpe Hall

Burnley Road, Padiham, near Burnley, Lancashire BB12 8UA

1972

This Elizabethan house, in the heart of urban Lancashire, has extravagant 19th-century interiors by Sir Charles Barry (of Houses of Parliament and 'the real *Downton Abbey*' fame). The Hall displays textiles from the Gawthorpe Textile Collection. Outside, you can enjoy the garden and woodland walks.
Note: financed and run in partnership with Lancashire County Council.

Eat, shop, stay: tea-room serving sandwiches, cakes, scones and hot and cold drinks. Second-hand books.

Things to see and do: **Indoors** 17th-century panelling in drawing room. Guided tours, talks and exhibitions. Events throughout the year, including Victorian Christmas. **Outdoors** Open-air theatre in July, events and family activities. **Dogs**: welcome under close control in grounds.

Access:
Building **Grounds**
Sat Nav: use BB12 8SD then follow brown signs. **Parking**: 150 yards, narrow access road (passing places).

Find out more: 01282 771004 or gawthorpehall@nationaltrust.org.uk

Gawthorpe Hall		M	T	W	T	F	S	S
Hall and tea-room								
27 Mar–3 Nov	12-5*	·	·	**W**	**T**	**F**	**S**	**S**
Grounds								
Open all year	8-7	**M**	**T**	**W**	**T**	**F**	**S**	**S**

Hall and tea-room: open Bank Holidays. *Tea-room: open 11, last orders 4:30. Opening times subject to change.

The Hardmans' House

59 Rodney Street, Liverpool, Merseyside L1 9ER

2003

Discover Liverpool's best kept secret and step inside a true time capsule – the home and studio of a 1950s society photographer. The handsome Georgian house, both glamorous workplace and modest, cluttered home for Edward Chambré Hardman and his talented wife Margaret, is packed with vintage treasures and fascinating photography. **Note**: admission by guided tour only (booking advised). Entrance on Pilgrim Street at rear of property.

Eat, shop, stay: small shop selling unique photographic prints, postcards, guidebooks and hot drinks. The nearest café (not National Trust) is just a short walk away at the Anglican Cathedral.

Things to see and do: tours (book your place to avoid disappointment). Family trail. Virtual tour of the house. Special interest walking tours available.

Access: **Building**
Parking: none on site. Car parks at Anglican Cathedral and Slater Street, not National Trust (charge including members).

Find out more: 0151 709 6261 or thehardmanshouse@nationaltrust.org.uk

The Hardmans' House		M	T	W	T	F	S	S
13 Mar–26 Oct	11-3:30	·	·	**W**	**T**	**F**	**S**	·

Admission by timed ticket only, booking advisable (places limited). Open Bank Holiday Mondays.

Hare Hill

Over Alderley, Macclesfield, Cheshire SK10 4PY

1978

Hare Hill is a place to refresh the senses and the soul. Set within tenanted farmland, this wooded garden is full of twists, turns and surprises, wooden hares, hidden paths and ponds. At its heart is the walled white garden, offering an oasis of tranquillity.

Eat, shop, stay: refreshments at weekends and Bank Holidays only (not National Trust). Picnics welcome in the garden. Small shop in car park and plants for sale. Information room with second-hand books available for a small donation.

Hare Hill, Cheshire: the walled garden, right, and exploring one of the many hidden paths, below

Things to see and do: you can discover the history and planting of Hare Hill in new guides. Families can spot all the hares and borrow a nature pack to explore the garden.
Dogs: assistance dogs only in garden.

Access: **Grounds**
Sat Nav: use SK10 4PY to take you 109 yards west of car park. **Parking**: on site.

Find out more: 01625 829973 or harehill@nationaltrust.org.uk

Hare Hill		M	T	W	T	F	S	S
16 Feb–3 Nov	10:30–5	**M**	**T**	**W**	**T**	**F**	**S**	**S**

Car park closes at 5.

Heysham Coast

Heysham, near Morecambe, Lancashire 1996

A sandstone headland with a beautiful walk through grassland and woodland, passing a ruined Saxon chapel and unusual rock-cut graves. **Note**: nearest facilities in village (not National Trust); park in the main village car park. For Sat Nav use LA3 2RW.

Find out more: 01524 701178 or heysham@nationaltrust.org.uk

Little Moreton Hall

Congleton, Cheshire CW12 4SD

1938

While modern life rushes by on the busy road outside, Little Moreton Hall, surrounded by its moat, survives as a Tudor fantasy, transporting you back to another time. Built to impress by craftsmen's hands more than 500 years ago, the Hall has a unique quirky charm and homely feel. With its crooked walls and uneven floors, it seems so resilient yet still so fragile. Outside there's a manicured knot garden and borders with herbs and vegetables used in Tudor times. This remarkable survivor inspires you to reflect on the ups and downs of a simpler way of life.

Eat, shop, stay: Little Tea-room (with outdoor seating) and Mrs Dale's Tea-room serving delicious homemade food made in the on-site bakery. Ice-cream kiosk (open on sunny days) and large shop in the car park selling gifts, plants and local products.

Things to see and do: **Indoors** Free guided tours and family trails. Tudor displays and activities most days. Costumes to try on. **Outdoors** Open-air theatre in summer and Tudor festivals throughout the year. **Dogs**: on leads in car park and front lawn only.

Access:
Hall **Reception**
Grounds
Parking: 100 yards.

Find out more: 01260 272018 or littlemoretonhall@nationaltrust.org.uk

Little Moreton Hall		M	T	W	T	F	S	S
Hall, garden, tea-room and shop								
30 Mar-3 Nov*	11-5**	·	·	**W**	**T**	**F**	**S**	**S**
29 Nov-15 Dec	11-4**	·	·	·	·	**F**	**S**	**S**
Shop								
9 Nov-24 Nov	12-4	·	·	·	·	·	**S**	**S**

Open Bank Holiday Mondays. *3 to 28 April, 22 May to 2 June, 24 July to 1 September and 23 October to 3 November: open daily. **Upper floors may close early if light levels are poor.

Leave the 21st century behind at Little Moreton Hall, Cheshire, and step back into Tudor times

Lyme

Disley, Stockport, Cheshire SK12 2NR

1947

If you had to conjure up the ultimate grand English country house, you might picture something like Lyme. The glorious mansion, which sits in 570 hectares (1,400 acres) of deer park, with far-reaching views across Manchester and the Cheshire Plain, was the much-loved home of the Legh family for more than 600 years. Its lavish interiors reflect the life of a great estate, from its earliest beginnings to its Regency heyday, when Thomas Legh brought Lyme back to its full glory. You may recognise Lyme as 'Pemberley' from the BBC adaptation of *Pride and Prejudice*, starring Colin Firth. Lyme's ever-changing gardens, with the Reflection Lake, Orangery and Rose Garden, are ideal places to stroll and relax. **Note**: facility improvements taking place, please check before visit. Partly financed by Stockport Metropolitan Borough Council.

Clockwise from below: with stately interiors and a glorious mansion, Lyme, Cheshire, epitomises the grand English country house, now open to all

Eat, shop, stay: choice of café and tea-rooms serving snacks and lunches. Salting Room Tea Parlour and Garden offers afternoon tea (booking essential). Timber Yard shop for gardening/outdoors products. Gift and book shop. East Lodge holiday cottage in deer park with wide views.

Things to see and do: **Indoors** We're celebrating the tenth anniversary of the Lyme Missal (considered the single most important printed book in the National Trust's collection) being returned to the Library with a year of activities. Have a go at dressing up in period costume, experience the beautiful sounds of Lyme's harp or try your hand at playing billiards. **Outdoors** Regular Saturday parkruns. Variety of levels of orienteering routes. Self-led woodland and moorland walks. Adventurous play in Crow Wood Playscape for five-to-12 year olds. Events throughout the year, including Easter trails, summer holiday activities, Halloween and Christmas celebrations.

Dogs: under close control in park; leads near livestock and vehicles; selected days in garden.

Access:
House **Garden**
Sat Nav: use SK12 2NR. **Parking**: 200 yards.

Find out more: 01663 762023 or lyme@nationaltrust.org.uk

Lyme		M	T	W	T	F	S	S
House								
16 Feb–30 Mar	11–4	**M**	**T**	·	·	**F**	**S**	**S**
31 Mar–3 Nov*	11–5	**M**	**T**	·	·	**F**	**S**	**S**
22 Nov–23 Dec**	11–3	**M**	·	·	·	**F**	**S**	**S**
Garden, shop and tea-rooms								
1 Jan–15 Feb	11–3†	**M**	**T**	**W**	**T**	**F**	**S**	**S**
16 Feb–3 Nov	11–5†	**M**	**T**	**W**	**T**	**F**	**S**	**S**
4 Nov–21 Nov	11–3†	**M**	**T**	**W**	**T**	**F**	**S**	**S**
22 Nov–31 Dec	10–3†	**M**	**T**	**W**	**T**	**F**	**S**	**S**
Estate								
1 Jan–30 Mar	8–6††	**M**	**T**	**W**	**T**	**F**	**S**	**S**
31 Mar–26 Oct	8–8††	**M**	**T**	**W**	**T**	**F**	**S**	**S**
27 Oct–31 Dec	8–6††	**M**	**T**	**W**	**T**	**F**	**S**	**S**
Timber Yard shop and café[1]								
1 Jan–30 Mar	10–4	**M**	**T**	**W**	**T**	**F**	**S**	**S**
31 Mar–26 Oct	10–5	**M**	**T**	**W**	**T**	**F**	**S**	**S**
27 Oct–31 Dec	10–4	**M**	**T**	**W**	**T**	**F**	**S**	**S**

House: last entry one hour before closing. *Open Thursdays June to August. **Parts of house open for Christmas events; also open 24 December. †Garden: opens 10:30; also open 24 December. ††Gates locked at closing. [1]Building works planned to start early autumn. Everything closed 25 December.

Nether Alderley Mill

Congleton Road, Nether Alderley, Macclesfield, Cheshire SK10 4TW

 1950

Concealed under the long sloping roof of this medieval building is a fully restored, working corn mill. You can take a guided tour inside to spot centuries-old graffiti and discover more about the life of a miller. Watch as the waterwheels turn, powering the huge millstones that grind the flour. **Note**: view by guided tour only. Uneven floor, steep stairs and low ceilings throughout. Limited parking.

Eat, shop, stay: small range of souvenirs available, along with flour produced in the mill. Sorry no toilets or food outlets. Nearest National Trust facilities at nearby Alderley Edge.

Things to see and do: demonstrations show how the working machinery turns grain into flour. Find out about the restoration work carried out in the 20th century.

Access: Mill
Parking: limited.

Find out more: 01625 527468 or netheralderleymill@nationaltrust.org.uk

Nether Alderley Mill		M	T	W	T	F	S	S
4 Apr–6 Oct	1–4:30	·	·	·	**T**	·	**S**	**S**

Access by guided tour (book on arrival). Last tour 3:45.

Medieval Nether Alderley Mill in Cheshire

Quarry Bank

Styal, Wilmslow, Cheshire SK9 4LA

1939

Quarry Bank, Cheshire: the restored glasshouse, above, contrasts with the huge mill buildings, right

In the early years of the Industrial Revolution, the tranquillity of the river valley at Quarry Bank gave way to the clatter and bustle of an industrial community at work. The people here, from the mill-owning Greg family in Quarry Bank House to the workers living in Styal village and the Apprentice House, were at the cutting edge during a time of great change. You can see the heritage machinery in action in the mill and discover what working life was like for the men, women and children toiling 10 hours a day. Uncover the very different lives led by the mill owners by walking through their gardens and estate and exploring their elegant family home.

Eat, shop, stay: mill and garden shops selling gifts, including fabric and glass cloths produced in the mill. Mill café serving hot lunches and afternoon tea. Garden café offering light lunches and snacks. Drinks and ice cream available from Stables Ice Cream Parlour. Picnic areas.

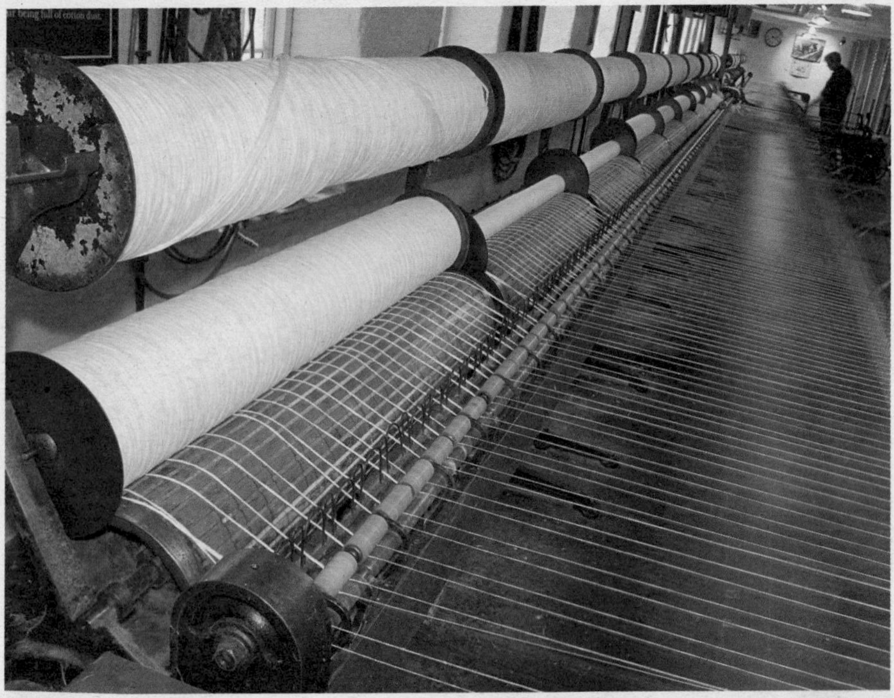

Things to see and do: **Indoors** Guided tours of the Apprentice House and the two-up-two-down worker's cottage in Styal village bring you closer to the home lives of the mill workers and the community that they built together. Exhibitions and events throughout the year reveal different strands of life at Quarry Bank. Limited availability for tours. **Outdoors** Wander through the colourful gardens and explore the restored glasshouse, where exotic plants and fruit are grown. You can walk through the woodland and follow the path of the winding River Bollin. Families will enjoy the natural play in Chapel Woods and playing Pooh sticks on the bridges. **Dogs**: welcome under close control on estate. On leads in garden, mill yard and meadow.

Access:
Mill **Gardens and estate**
Quarry Bank House/Apprentice House
Parking: on site.

Find out more: 01625 527468 or quarrybank@nationaltrust.org.uk

Quarry Bank		M	T	W	T	F	S	S
1 Jan–6 Jan	10:30–4	·	T	W	T	F	S	S
12 Jan–8 Feb	10:30–4	·	·	W	T	F	S	S
9 Feb–3 Nov	10:30–5	M	T	W	T	F	S	S
6 Nov–22 Dec	10:30–4	·	·	W	T	F	S	S
26 Dec–31 Dec	10:30–4	M	T	·	T	F	S	S
Estate								
Open all year*	8–6	M	T	W	T	F	S	S

Garden: closes dusk if earlier. Everything closed 7 to 11 January for maintenance. *Closed 25 December. Open daily 1 to 5 January 2020.

The mill at Quarry Bank, above, was once full of clatter and bustle. Today visitors can enjoy the peace, right

Rufford Old Hall

200 Liverpool Road, Rufford, near Ormskirk, Lancashire L40 1SG

1936

This black-and-white Tudor building, with its contrasting mellow red-brick Jacobean wing, hunkers in the low-lying mosslands of south-west Lancashire. More than 500 years old, this family home has many stories to tell about the intriguing Hesketh who used to live here, and a Great Hall that might make your jaw drop! Children can get closer to nature with bug hunting and wild art kits, and you can unwind in the Victorian-style garden and grounds with colourful seasonal displays, from carpets of bluebells in spring to golden leaves in autumn.

Eat, shop, stay: you can experience local tastes with Lancashire tea in the Victorian tea-room. The shop offers special treats, including Lancashire sauce, Lancashire crisps and plenty of gifts to keep memories of Rufford Old Hall alive.

Things to see and do: **Indoors** Daily house talks and seasonal children's trail. Christmas events. **Outdoors** Guided garden tours. Events, including open-air theatre. Seasonal family trails and games. **Dogs**: welcome on leads in the courtyard and woodland only.

Access:
Building **Grounds**
Parking: on site.

Find out more: 01704 821254 or ruffordoldhall@nationaltrust.org.uk

Rufford Old Hall		M	T	W	T	F	S	S
16 Feb–7 Apr	11–4	M	T	W	·	·	S	S
8 Apr–21 Apr	11–5	M	T	W	T	F	S	S
22 Apr–26 May	11–5	M	T	W	·	·	S	S
27 May–2 Jun	11–5	M	T	W	T	F	S	S
3 Jun–28 Jul	11–5	M	T	W	·	·	S	S
29 Jul–1 Sep	11–5*	M	T	W	T	F	S	S
2 Sep–20 Oct	11–5	M	T	W	·	·	S	S
21 Oct–30 Oct	11–5	M	T	W	T	F	S	S
2 Nov–1 Dec	11–4	·	·	·	·	·	S	S
5 Dec–15 Dec	11–4	·	·	·	T	F	S	S

*Shop and tea-room: open 10:30. Car park: closes 30 minutes after closing. Tudor Great Hall occasionally closed until 1 for weddings, check website before visit.

Rufford Old Hall, Lancashire: visitors enjoying the garden with the iconic Tudor building behind

Speke Hall

Speke, Liverpool L24 1XD

1944

Almost 500 years ago, the Norris family replaced a medieval manor house on the banks of the River Mersey with the very latest in Tudor architecture. The iconic black-and-white Hall has seen centuries of turbulent history but was sympathetically restored in Victorian times as a cosy home. Surrounded by tranquil gardens and semi-ancient woodland, it's a slice of the past in the urban surroundings of Liverpool. Drive through the gates and leave the 21st century behind as you enter a peaceful world where you can be as restful or as active as you choose. The grounds are full of things to discover, from spring carpets of daffodils and bluebells to a Victorian-themed maze and natural woodland play trails.

Eat, shop, stay: Home Farm Restaurant serving regional specialities, including Scouse and Wet Nelly. Stable Tea-room offering hot drinks and homemade cakes. Locally sourced gifts, as well as plants and books available in the shop.

Things to see and do: **Indoors** Discover the Arts and Crafts restoration of the Hall and original William Morris wallpaper. Take a costumed guided tour. Try your hand at billiards. Solve a tricky family trail. **Outdoors** Wander through the formal gardens and discover the recently restored Secret Garden.

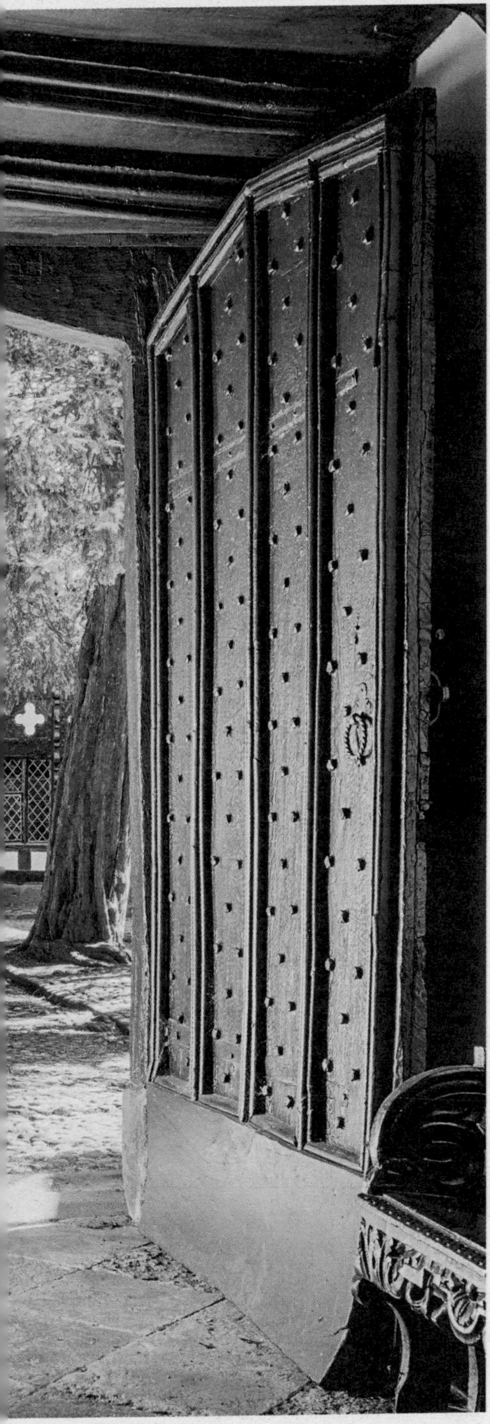

Explore and spot wildlife, whatever the weather, with a coastal or woodland walk. Families can enjoy the formal play area, woodland play area and Childe of Hale play trail. Events throughout the year, with family activities every school holidays and seasonal events such as Tudor May Day, open-air theatre in summer, Christmas weekends and festive music evenings. **Dogs**: welcome on leads in the woodland and on signed estate walks.

Access:
Hall **Grounds**
Parking: on site.

Find out more: 0151 427 7231 or spekehall@nationaltrust.org.uk

Speke Hall		M	T	W	T	F	S	S
House								
16 Feb–21 Jul	11–5*	·	·	**W**	**T**	**F**	**S**	**S**
23 Jul–1 Sep	11–5*	·	**T**	**W**	**T**	**F**	**S**	**S**
4 Sep–3 Nov	11–5*	·	·	**W**	**T**	**F**	**S**	**S**
29 Nov–15 Dec	11–4*	·	·	·	·	**F**	**S**	**S**
Gardens, catering and retail								
Open all year†	10:30–5**	**M**	**T**	**W**	**T**	**F**	**S**	**S**

*House: entry before 12:30 by guided tour only (tickets available from reception on day); 16 February to 10 March, entry by guided tour. **Shop: opens 11. †12 March, 19 November and 24 to 26 December: everything closed. Access and closing times vary in winter (check at reception on arrival).

Striking Speke Hall, Liverpool, left and opposite, has witnessed centuries of turbulent history. Today, visitors can enjoy total tranquillity, below

Tatton Park

Knutsford, Cheshire WA16 6QN

1960

Tatton Park is a grand country estate set in 400 hectares (1,000 acres) of historic deer park. The Egerton family acquired an impressive collection of fine art, books and furnishings that can be seen in the Neo-classical mansion, which also houses the servants' quarters. There is a medieval Old Hall and 20 hectares (50 acres) of award-winning gardens, including a 100-year-old Japanese Garden. The farm recently received a £1.3 million grant from the Heritage Lottery Fund to open buildings and tell the story of Tatton's food production over the centuries, with new guided tours, demonstrations and rare-breed animals. **Note**: financed and managed by Cheshire East Council. £7 park vehicle entry and charges for Old Hall, farm (50% discount), tours and special events, including Christmas and RHS Flower Show, apply to members.

Tatton Park, Cheshire: the Japanese garden, above, and farm

Eat, shop, stay: self-service Stables Restaurant and award-winning Gardener's Cottage offering afternoon tea. Speciality shops include the Housekeeper's Store, selling local and estate-reared meat and produce. Gift, garden, farm and tuck shops. None of the shops or places to eat are National Trust.

Things to see and do: **Indoors** You can visit the mansion, Old Hall, farm, shops and restaurants. Learning activities and events. **Outdoors** Gardens, parkland, farm, adventure playground and stableyard. Events and learning activities. **Dogs**: on leads: farm; under close control: parkland. Assistance dogs only: buildings and gardens.

Access:
Mansion **Grounds**
Sat Nav: use WA16 6SG.
Parking: park vehicle entry charge £7 (including National Trust members).

Find out more: 01625 374400 or tatton@cheshireeast.gov.uk tattonpark.org.uk

Tatton Park		M	T	W	T	F	S	S
Parkland								
1 Jan–29 Mar	10–5	·	T	W	T	F	S	S
30 Mar–27 Oct	10–7	M	T	W	T	F	S	S
29 Oct–31 Dec	10–5	·	T	W	T	F	S	S
Mansion*								
30 Mar–27 Sep	1–5	·	·	W	T	F	S	S
2 Oct–3 Nov	12–4	·	·	W	T	F	S	S
Farm**								
5 Jan–24 Mar	11–4	·	·	·	·	·	S	S
30 Mar–27 Oct	12–5	·	T	W	T	F	S	S
28 Oct–3 Nov	11–4	M	T	W	T	F	S	S
9 Nov–29 Dec	11–4	·	·	·	·	·	S	S
Gardens								
1 Jan–29 Mar	10–4	·	T	W	T	F	S	S
30 Mar–3 Nov	10–6†	M	T	W	T	F	S	S
5 Nov–31 Dec	10–4	·	T	W	T	F	S	S
Shops and restaurants								
1 Jan–29 Mar	12–4††	·	T	W	T	F	S	S
30 Mar–27 Oct	11–5††	M	T	W	T	F	S	S
29 Oct–31 Dec	12–4††	·	T	W	T	F	S	S

*Mansion: also open Bank Holiday Mondays and for Christmas event. **Farm: also open 1 January, 18 to 22 February and Bank Holiday Mondays; closed during July RHS Flower Show. †Gardens: close 4, 28 October to 3 November. ††Restaurants: open 10. Old Hall special opening arrangements and charge. Parkland, mansion, farm and garden last entry one hour before closing. Everything closed 25 December.

The Lakes

A cycling adventure by Windermere in Cumbria

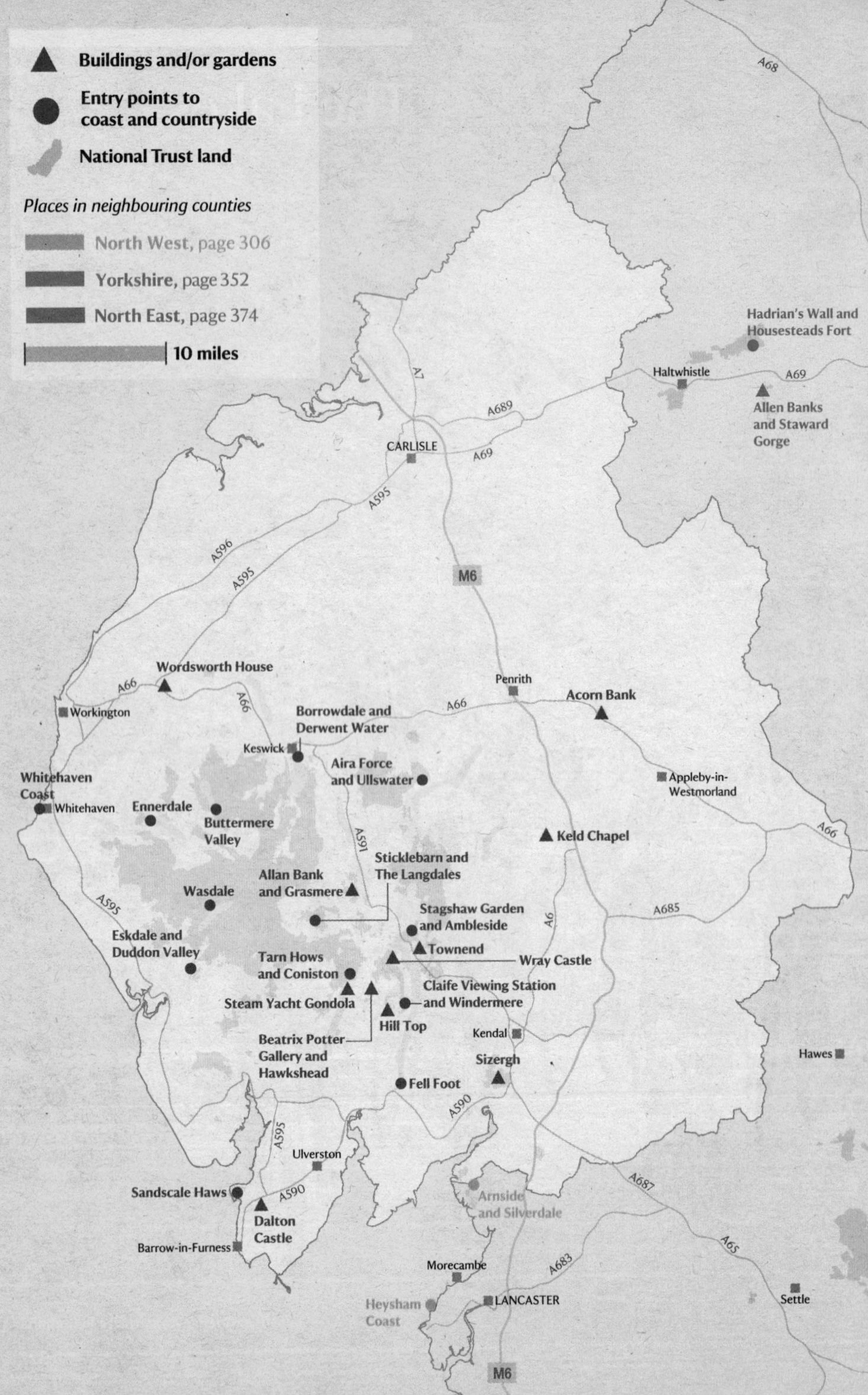

Buildings and/or gardens
Entry points to coast and countryside
National Trust land
Places in neighbouring counties
North West, page 306
Yorkshire, page 352
North East, page 374
10 miles
A68
Hadrian's Wall and Housesteads Fort
Haltwhistle
A69
A7
A689
Allen Banks and Staward Gorge
CARLISLE
A69
A595
A596
A595
M6
Wordsworth House
A66
A66
Penrith
Acorn Bank
A66
Workington
Borrowdale and Derwent Water
Keswick
Aira Force and Ullswater
Appleby-in-Westmorland
Whitehaven Coast
Whitehaven
Ennerdale
Buttermere Valley
A591
Keld Chapel
A66
Sticklebarn and The Langdales
Allan Bank and Grasmere
Wasdale
A595
Stagshaw Garden and Ambleside
A685
A6
Townend
Wray Castle
Eskdale and Duddon Valley
Tarn Hows and Coniston
Claife Viewing Station and Windermere
Steam Yacht Gondola
Hill Top
Kendal
Beatrix Potter Gallery and Hawkshead
Sizergh
Hawes
Fell Foot
A590
A595
Ulverston
A687
Sandscale Haws
A590
Arnside and Silverdale
Dalton Castle
A65
Barrow-in-Furness
Morecambe
A683
LANCASTER
Settle
Heysham Coast
M6

Acorn Bank

Temple Sowerby, near Penrith,
Cumbria CA10 1SP

1950

At the heart of the Eden Valley, with views to the Lake District and Howgill Fells, Acorn Bank is a tranquil haven with a rich history. The walled gardens shelter a medicinal herb garden and traditional orchards, as well as herbaceous borders, stone steps and a lily-filled pond. Woodland walks reveal a half-hidden story of gypsum mining and a working medieval watermill. The estate surrounds a 17th-century sandstone manor, once owned by indomitable writer Dorothy Una Ratcliffe. This unfurnished house is partially open to visitors, with a guided tour being the best way to explore the stories of its past. **Note**: some paths may be closed after wet weather.

Eat, shop, stay: tea-room with outdoor tables. Home-grown garden produce to buy. Shop selling plants, flour milled on site and local products. Second-hand bookshop in house. Enjoy the estate after hours at Sandwath and Bank Wood, spacious holiday apartments sleeping two to three.

With its manor house, left, and gardens, above, Acorn Bank in Cumbria offers a tranquil haven. There are also woodland walks on the estate

Things to see and do: you can see the watermill running most weekends during summer. Woodland trails. Wild play area and secret pixie houses hidden in the woodland for children to discover. Bird hide. **Dogs**: welcome in the woodland. Assistance dogs only in the gardens and house.

Access: **Watermill** **House** **Grounds**
Parking: large car park.

Find out more: 017683 61893 or acornbank@nationaltrust.org.uk

Acorn Bank		M	T	W	T	F	S	S
16 Feb–27 Oct	10–5*	**M**	**T**	**W**	**T**	**F**	**S**	**S**
28 Oct–29 Dec**	10–4*	**M**	**T**	**W**	**T**	**F**	**S**	**S**

*Tea-room: opens 30 minutes later and closes 30 minutes earlier. House: partially open; guided tours available (places limited). **Closed 25 and 26 December.

Aira Force and Ullswater

near Watermillock, Penrith, Cumbria

1906

Aira Force is a showcase for the power and beauty of nature; a place to escape the ordinary. Rainwater runs from the fells into Aira Beck and thunders over the falls in one 65-foot drop. Yet Aira Force is more than an impressive waterfall. Weave your way from Ullswater lakeshore to Gowbarrow summit, passing ancient woodlands, towering Himalayan firs and landscaped glades and you can enjoy views across Ullswater and spot rare red squirrels. Why not start your day in Glenridding, arriving by boat and taking in the Ullswater Valley sights along the way, then stroll back along the lakeshore? **Note**: boat rides on Ullswater operated by Ullswater 'Steamers' (not National Trust).

Eat, shop, stay: tea-room serving light lunches, cakes, ice cream and hot and cold drinks. Shop selling gifts, ice cream, souvenirs and maps. Takeaway kiosk serving hot drinks and snacks. Picnics welcome.

Things to see and do: red squirrel trail and natural play area. Arrive early for your best chance of spotting a red squirrel. Canoe at Glencoyne Bay or walk to Gowbarrow summit for panoramic views. **Dogs**: welcome on leads.

Access:

Sat Nav: use CA11 0JS for Aira Force; CA11 0NQ for Glencoyne Bay. **Parking**: at Aira Force, Aira Force High Cascades, Aira Force Park Brow and Glencoyne Bay.

Find out more: 017684 82067 or ullswater@nationaltrust.org.uk

Aira Force and Ullswater	
Tea-room and shop	
Open every day all year*	10:30–4

*Closed 22 to 26 December. Opening times may vary during low season.

Escape from the ordinary at Aira Force and Ullswater, Cumbria: a showcase for nature's beauty

Allan Bank and Grasmere

near Ambleside, Cumbria LA22 9QB

1920

Make yourself at home at Allan Bank, where views of Grasmere's valley unfold from picture windows and woodland grounds. Once home to National Trust founder Canon Rawnsley, it's now only partially decorated and not your typical National Trust experience. You can watch red squirrels as you read by the fire or walk the woodland paths, draw and paint, tuck into a picnic in the house or garden or help yourself to a cup of tea. Secret hideaways, such as the Victorian viewing tunnel, create an air of mystery. It's the perfect place to relax, reflect and be inspired. **Note**: limited accessible parking only on site. Follow directions on foot from The Inn at Grasmere.

Eat, shop, stay: tea and coffee for a donation; picnics welcome indoors and outside. Church Stile shop in Grasmere selling unusual gifts, local books and maps in Grade II listed 17th-century building.

Things to see and do: **Indoors** Crafts room, board games, children's activities. Read the papers or borrow a book from the library. Binoculars for wildlife spotting. **Outdoors** Deckchairs, kitchen garden, woodland trail, wild play area. **Dogs**: welcome on leads indoors and out.

Access: **House**
Sat Nav: use LA22 9TA for nearest car park.
Parking: nearest in village, not National Trust (charge including members).

Find out more: 015394 35143 or allanbank@nationaltrust.org.uk

Allan Bank and Grasmere		M	T	W	T	F	S	S
Allan Bank								
9 Feb–24 Feb	10:30–4	**M**	**T**	**W**	**T**	**F**	**S**	**S**
1 Mar–29 Mar	10:30–4	·	·	·	·	**F**	**S**	**S**
30 Mar–3 Nov	10:30–5	**M**	**T**	**W**	**T**	**F**	**S**	**S**
8 Nov–15 Dec	10:30–4	·	·	·	·	**F**	**S**	**S**
Grasmere shop								
1 Jan–6 Jan	10:30–4		**T**	**W**	**T**	**F**	**S**	**S**
16 Feb–31 Dec*	10:30–4	**M**	**T**	**W**	**T**	**F**	**S**	**S**

*Grasmere shop: closed 24 and 25 December; opening times may vary during low season.

The relaxed house, left, and wooded grounds, below, of Allan Bank in Cumbria

Beatrix Potter Gallery and Hawkshead

Main Street, Hawkshead, Cumbria LA22 0NS

1947

The Beatrix Potter Gallery is housed in a quirky 17th-century building which was once the office of Beatrix's solicitor husband. If you've ever been charmed by Beatrix's endearing characters, you can take a closer look at her miniature masterpieces inside and find out more about her life beyond the books. A new exhibition of her original artwork, illustrations and letters explores the enduring popularity of Beatrix's tales. The quaint Hawkshead village makes the perfect base for exploring the countryside that inspired Beatrix and many other famous poets, writers and artists. **Note**: nearest toilets 300 yards in main village car park (not National Trust).

Beatrix Potter Gallery and Hawkshead, Cumbria: the gallery façade, right, and interior, below

Eat, shop, stay: gallery shop selling Beatrix Potter items. Hawkshead corner shop stocks local products. Refreshments available at pubs and cafés in Hawkshead (none National Trust). Stay in nearby holiday cottages Summer House or Rose Castle, or camp at Low Wray.

Things to see and do: **Indoors** Original Beatrix Potter artwork on display. **Outdoors** Choice of walking routes, including a new path to Hill Top. The Courthouse nearby has an interesting history (collect key from shop). **Dogs**: assistance dogs only in gallery.

Access: Gallery
Parking: 300 yards, not National Trust (charge including members).

Find out more: 015394 36355 (gallery). 015394 36471 (shop) or beatrixpottergallery@nationaltrust.org.uk

Beatrix Potter Gallery/Hawkshead		M	T	W	T	F	S	S
Gallery								
16 Feb–3 Nov	10:30–4	M	T	W	T	F	S	S
Hawkshead shop								
16 Feb–3 Nov	10:30–5	M	T	W	T	F	S	S
4 Nov–22 Dec	10:30–4	M	T	W	T	F	S	S

At busy periods, timed entry system in operation. Medieval Hawkshead Courthouse: open 30 March to 27 October (access by key from National Trust shop in Hawkshead).

Borrowdale and Derwent Water

near Keswick, Cumbria

1902

From the lakeshore at Crow Park, just a few minutes' walk from the centre of the busy Lakeland town of Keswick, there are far-reaching views across Derwent Water, dotted with small islands and surrounded by a skyline of dramatic fells. In the distance, Castle Crag sits between the lake and upper Borrowdale, where scenic drives, traditional hamlets and waymarked walks await. Nine car parks in the valley make it easy to access some of Lakeland's most photographed views at Friar's Crag, Ashness Bridge and Bowder Stone, as well as walks along the River Derwent, which flows from its source in Borrowdale to the lake, sometimes shallow and crystal clear, often fast-flowing, fed by cascading falls and forces.

Note: charges apply to members on Force Crag Mine and Derwent Island House open days.

Eat, shop, stay: Keswick lakeside shop offers local knowledge to help you plan your visit, plus souvenirs, cold drinks and ice cream. There are tenant-run cafés at Watendlath and Rosthwaite. Watendlath Bothy (sleeps six) and Millbeck Towers (sleeps 12) provide perfect holiday bases.

Things to see and do: Seatoller car park is a good starting point for the Castle Crag circular walk or for heading into the high fells. Great Wood's waymarked walks take you along lakeshore paths or up into the protected Atlantic oakwoods, guide you on a gentle climb to Ashness Bridge or join the 10-mile round Derwent Water walk. If you're looking for something more unusual, our 4x4 can take you to Force Crag Mine, and rafted canoes are provided to get you to Derwent Island House – both places only open for five days each year, so booking ahead is essential. **Dogs**: very welcome, but please keep them under close control at lambing time.

The lakeshore of Derwent Water in Cumbria

Access: **Derwent Island**
Force Crag Mine **Derwent Water foreshore**
Sat Nav: use CA12 5DJ for Keswick lakeside shop and CA12 5XN for Seatoller (at foot of Honister Pass). **Parking**: at Great Wood, Ashness Bridge, Surprise View, Watendlath, Kettlewell, Bowder Stone, Rosthwaite, Seatoller and Honister Pass.

Find out more: 017687 74649 or borrowdale@nationaltrust.org.uk

Borrowdale and Derwent Water		M	T	W	T	F	S	S
Shop and visitor centre								
5 Jan–10 Feb	10–4	·	·	·	·	·	**S**	**S**
11 Feb–27 Oct	10–5	**M**	**T**	**W**	**T**	**F**	**S**	**S**
28 Oct–1 Dec	10–4	**M**	·	·	·	**F**	**S**	**S**
7 Dec–29 Dec	10–4	·	·	·	·	·	**S**	**S**

Shop and visitor centre: open weekends, 4 January to 9 February 2020. For open days at Derwent Island House and Force Crag Mine, check 'What's on' page online.

Borrowdale and Derwent Water: cairn on Castle Crag looking down on the village of Rosthwaite

Buttermere Valley

near Cockermouth, Cumbria

1935

The dramatic Buttermere Valley encompasses the lakes of Buttermere, Crummock Water (above) and Loweswater, all offering easy low-level lakeshore walks and access onto the higher surrounding fells. Buttermere's 4½-mile round-the-lake path takes in shingle beaches, cascading waterfalls and a hand-cut Victorian tunnel, perfect for family adventures. **Note**: toilets at Buttermere village only (not National Trust).

Eat, shop, stay: pubs and cafés in Buttermere and Loweswater hamlets (none National Trust). You can stay in comfort at Watergate Farm, with fishing, swimming and walking from your doorstep, or choose simplicity at Holme Wood Bothy, a camping barn on Loweswater's shore.

Things to see and do: Buttermere and Crummock Water are Special Areas of Conservation. The whole valley is great for wildlife-spotting and picnics; look out for deer, red squirrels, birds, fish and otters. **Dogs**: welcome throughout the valley (under close control at lambing time please).

Access: Lakeshore path
Sat Nav: use CA13 9UZ for Buttermere; CA13 0RT for Crummock Water; CA13 0RU for Loweswater. **Parking**: at Honister Pass, Buttermere village, Rannerdale, Cinderdale, Lanthwaite Green, Lanthwaite Wood near Crummock Water and Maggie's Bridge at Loweswater.

Find out more: 017687 74649 or buttermere@nationaltrust.org.uk

Claife Viewing Station and Windermere West Shore

near Far Sawrey, Cumbria LA22 0LW

1962

Perched on the tranquil west shore of Windermere, just minutes from the Bowness ferry, Claife Viewing Station was built in the 1790s for the first tourists to the Lake District. Today, you can enjoy the same panoramic views of the lake from the platform, framed by coloured glass. Afterwards sit under the fairy lights in the courtyard or cosy up in the café by the fire. If you're feeling active, there are 4 miles of lakeside path towards Wray Castle to explore, or stroll through the landscape that inspired Beatrix Potter as you head towards Hill Top and Hawkshead village. **Note**: toilets at nearby Ferry House. Passenger boats operated by Windermere Lake Cruises; car ferry council-run.

Claife Viewing Station and Windermere West Shore, Cumbria: inside the Viewing Station

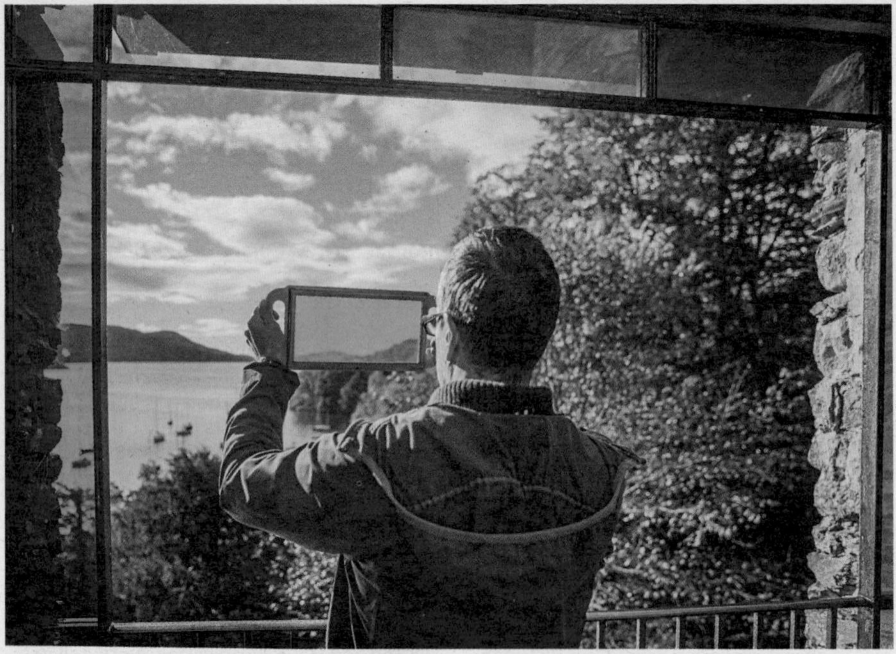

Claife Viewing Station and Windermere West Shore: the Viewing Station, top, and lakeshore

Eat, shop, stay: café in the courtyard beneath the viewing station serving light lunches, drinks and cakes (not National Trust). Picnics welcome on the lakeshore or in picnic area. Stay at High or Low Strawberry Gardens, with England's largest lake on your doorstep.

Things to see and do: the platform offers a unique viewpoint over Windermere – bring your camera or sketchbook and be inspired. Walk or cycle along the lakeshore path or paddle in the water. **Dogs**: welcome under close control.

Access: Viewing Station Café

Sat Nav: use LA22 0LP for Ash Landing; LA22 0LR Harrowslack; LA22 0JH Red Nab (all nearby). **Parking**: at Ash Landing and Harrowslack for Claife Viewing Station and Windermere west shore. Red Nab is further north along the lakeshore, close to Wray Castle.

Find out more: 015394 41456 or claife@nationaltrust.org.uk

Dalton Castle

Market Place, Dalton-in-Furness, Cumbria LA15 8AX 1965

Standing proud in Dalton town centre, this impressive 14th-century tower was once the manorial courthouse of Furness Abbey. **Note**: opened on behalf of the National Trust by the Friends of Dalton Castle. Parking in Dalton town centre (not National Trust). Open Saturday, 30 March to 28 September, 2 to 5.

Find out more: 015395 60951 or daltoncastle@nationaltrust.org.uk

Ennerdale

Cleator, Cumbria

1927

Peaceful, yet dramatic, Ennerdale is home to the UK's largest wildland partnership – Wild Ennerdale. A horseshoe of rugged fells surrounds a narrow forested valley where Galloway cattle roam free and the untamed River Liza flows. The views widen across Ennerdale Water, which is circled by lakeshore paths and beaches. **Note**: nearest toilets at Ennerdale Bridge (not National Trust).

Eat, shop, stay: three hostels in the valley. Two pubs and B&Bs in nearby Ennerdale Bridge as well as the Ennerdale Centre with The Gather Café and Shop (none National Trust).

Things to see and do: accessible Ennerdale Views trail starts from Bleach Green. Bowness Knott is the gateway to miles of traffic-free walking and cycling through wildlife and archaeology. 6½-mile walk around the lake. **Dogs**: very welcome, but please keep under close control near livestock.

Access: Ennerdale Centre
Bleach Green lakeshore
Sat Nav: use CA23 3BA for Ennerdale Bridge; CA23 3AU for Bowness Knott; CA23 3AS for Bleach Green. **Parking**: at Bowness Knott and Bleach Green (not National Trust).

Find out more: 017687 74649 or ennerdale@nationaltrust.org.uk

Dramatic, yet peaceful, Ennerdale in Cumbria

Eskdale and Duddon Valley

Eskdale, near Ravenglass; Duddon Valley, near Broughton in Furness, Cumbria

1926

Eskdale (above) is a valley of contrasts. Upper Eskdale leads to the high mountains, including Scafell and Bowfell; the valley floor has meandering riverside and woodland paths, including the Eskdale Trail, for walkers and cyclists. Across high mountain passes lies the Duddon Valley, with meadows, woodlands, mountains, hill farms and rivers.

Eat, shop, stay: pubs at Eskdale Green, Boot and Seathwaite; shops at Eskdale Green, Boot and Ulpha; café and shop at Dalegarth station (none National Trust). Bird How and Thrang holiday cottages are cosy countryside retreats with walks from their front doors.

Things to see and do: walks from 'La'al Ratty' railway running through Eskdale. Woodland and riverside paths in the Duddon Valley. Upland walks to Harter Fell and Seathwaite Tarn. Hardknott Roman Fort (English Heritage). **Dogs**: well-behaved dogs welcome. Please follow local and seasonal guidance.

Access:
Parking: in lay-bys, along roadsides and at some small village car parks (not National Trust).

Find out more: 019467 26064 or eskdaleandduddon@nationaltrust.org.uk

Fell Foot

Newby Bridge, Windermere, Cumbria

[icons] 1948

Sitting on the southern tip of Windermere with views across the lake to the mountains, Fell Foot is a family-friendly park for playing, exploring and getting out on the water. Extensive lawns roll down to the water, providing an ideal spot for picnics in the summer. The park's network of paths and easy lake access make this the perfect place for running, paddling, swimming, or simply strolling along the lakeshore and taking in the Lakeland views. The newly open Fell Foot Active Base sitting on the water's edge has state-of-the-art changing facilities and a clubhouse overlooking the lake, offering a comfortable, accessible way to enjoy water sports on the lake for both seasoned pros and beginners. **Note**: facility improvements under way; building work possible. Additional charges (including members) for use of new changing and launch facilities and for rowing boats, canoes and kayaks (for hire mid-April to October).

Eat, shop, stay: Boathouse Café serving hot and cold drinks, soup, snacks, homemade cakes and pastries. Selection of children's toys, gifts, maps, picnic rugs and seasonal goods available in the Boathouse Shop. Picnics welcome on the lawns.

Things to see and do: seasonal rowing boat hire (weather permitting) and canoe/kayak hire (at weekends and during school holidays). New Fell Foot Active Base with changing and launch facilities. Toddler playground, wild play area and lake access with 'beach' for paddling. Regular activities including weekly parkrun, Nordic walking, yoga and open-water swimming. There are also quiet spots and an easy meadow walk, with wild flowers, butterflies and birds to spot. You can get the ferry from Fell Foot across to Lakeside, where you can join a Windermere Lake Cruise or hop on a steam train (neither National Trust). **Dogs**: welcome on leads.

Access: [icons]
Sat Nav: use LA12 8NN.
Parking: two large car parks on site.

Find out more: 015395 31273 or fellfoot@nationaltrust.org.uk

Fell Foot		M	T	W	T	F	S	S
1 Jan–15 Mar	9–5*	M	T	W	T	F	S	S
16 Mar–27 Oct	8–6**	M	T	W	T	F	S	S
28 Oct–31 Dec	9–5*	M	T	W	T	F	S	S

Fell Foot is undergoing building conservation work, so opening times may vary (check before visit). Closed 25 December. *Catering and retail: open 10 to 4. **Catering and retail: open 10 to 5. Catering: opens 9 on Saturdays. Boat hire available, 16 March to 27 October (weather permitting).

The lake and surrounding park at Fell Foot in Cumbria, below and right, are heaven for lovers of the great outdoors – whether watersports or a simple stroll is your passion

Hill Top

Near Sawrey, Hawkshead, Ambleside, Cumbria LA22 0LF

1944

Beatrix Potter's beloved farmhouse Hill Top was her sanctuary as well as a source of inspiration for her much-loved children's tales. Stroll through the quaint village of Near Sawrey and through the colourful garden and you may recognise scenes and landmarks from Beatrix's illustrations along the way. Filled with her personal possessions, from traditional Lakeland furniture to trophies for her prize-winning Herdwick sheep, the house is just as she left it when it came into the Trust's care in 1944. Today, we're continuing Beatrix's work to look after the Lake District in a changing world. **Note**: house entry by timed ticket – during busy periods there may be a wait.

Eat, shop, stay: shop selling Beatrix Potter collectables, including items exclusive to Hill Top, drinks and ice creams. Refreshments available at Sawrey House Hotel or Tower Bank Arms (not National Trust). Stay at High or Low Strawberry Gardens on Windermere's west shore.

Inside Hill Top in Cumbria, below, and the garden, above: Beatrix Potter's sanctuary

Things to see and do: visit the Beatrix Potter Gallery in nearby Hawkshead (2 miles) to see Beatrix's original artwork. Walk to Moss Eccles Tarn (1 mile) where Beatrix and her husband went boating. **Dogs**: allowed in garden on short leads. Assistance dogs only in house.

Access: **House** **Shop** **Garden**
Parking: limited and for visitors to Hill Top only.

Find out more: 015394 36269. 015394 36801 (shop) or hilltop@nationaltrust.org.uk

Hill Top		M	T	W	T	F	S	S
House, shop and garden*								
16 Feb–23 May**	10–4:30	**M**	**T**	**W**	**T**	·	**S**	**S**
25 May–1 Sep	10–5	**M**	**T**	**W**	**T**	**F**	**S**	**S**
2 Sep–3 Nov**	10–4:30	**M**	**T**	**W**	**T**	·	**S**	**S**
Shop and garden								
9 Nov–22 Dec	10:30–3:30	·	·	·	·	·	**S**	**S**

*House: entry by timed ticket (places limited), free entry to garden and shop. **Shop and garden also open Fridays; house opens some Fridays during school holidays (check before visit).

Keld Chapel

Keld Lane, Shap, Cumbria CA10 3NW 1918

Tucked away in east Cumbria, this rustic 16th-century stone Chapel was once the chantry for Shap Abbey. **Note**: sorry no facilities. For Sat Nav use CA10 3NW. Open every day all year, dawn to dusk (for key, please see notice on Chapel door).

Find out more: 017683 61893 or keldchapel@nationaltrust.org.uk

Sandscale Haws National Nature Reserve

near Barrow-in-Furness, Cumbria 1984

This beach has wild, grass-covered dunes and Lakeland mountain views; it's the perfect habitat for rare wildlife, including natterjack toads. **Note**: for Sat Nav use LA14 4QJ. Welcome hut serving light refreshments. Red Hut open daily, 1 March to 31 October, and weekends, 2 November to 29 December, 10 to 4.

Find out more: 01229 462855 or sandscalehaws@nationaltrust.org.uk

Sizergh

Sizergh, near Kendal, Cumbria LA8 8DZ

1950

This imposing house, still home to the Strickland family who built it, stands proud at the gateway to the Lake District. With 750 years of history, it has many tales to tell. Inside, there's impressive wood panelling, while the Inlaid Chamber is one of the best examples of Elizabethan craftsmanship, with its elaborate woodwork and plasterwork. The house is surrounded by gardens and a 647-hectare (1,600-acre) estate. With wetland, limestone pastures, orchards and semi-natural woodland, it's home to a wide variety of wildlife, including the rare hawfinch. There's also a unique limestone rock garden, where the colours change with the seasons – its timeless atmosphere makes this the perfect place to relax. **Note**: some opening restrictions apply. Separate admission charges may apply for tours or special events.

Clipped yews in the garden at Sizergh, Cumbria, with the imposing house glimpsed beyond

Eat, shop, stay: contemporary licensed café serving drinks, meals, snacks and cakes. Shop selling local products, home accessories, gifts, toys and plants. Strickland Arms pub (tenant-run) nearby. You can make Sizergh your holiday destination and stay at rustic Holeslack Farmhouse or Courtyard Cottage.

Things to see and do: **Indoors** Exhibitions and guided tours. Elizabethan carved furniture and panelling. Important collection of portraits of members of the exiled Stuart court. **Outdoors** Working organic kitchen garden with bees and hens. Sizergh is home to four National Collections of Hardy Ferns, some showcased in the stumpery. The orchard features more than 50 apple varieties, some rare and some local. A walk through Brigsteer Wood leads to a newly created wetland area and bird hide at Park End Moss. There's a network of footpaths in the wider estate, along with guided walks and orienteering. Children can enjoy a natural play trail. **Dogs**: welcome on estate footpaths (on leads where stock is grazing). House/garden: assistance dogs only.

Access:
Building **Grounds**
Sat Nav: use LA8 8DZ. **Parking**: 250 yards. Parking for cars and bikes only.

Find out more: 015395 60951 or sizergh@nationaltrust.org.uk

Sizergh		M	T	W	T	F	S	S
House*								
16 Mar–27 Oct	12–3:30	·	**T**	**W**	**T**	**F**	**S**	**S**
Garden, café and shop								
1 Jan–6 Jan**	10–4	·	**T**	**W**	**T**	**F**	**S**	**S**
19 Jan–15 Mar**	10–4	**M**	**T**	**W**	**T**	**F**	**S**	**S**
16 Mar–27 Oct	10–5	**M**	**T**	**W**	**T**	**F**	**S**	**S**
28 Oct–31 Dec**	10–4	**M**	**T**	**W**	**T**	**F**	**S**	**S**
Estate								
Open all year	9–6†	**M**	**T**	**W**	**T**	**F**	**S**	**S**

*House: guided tours (excluding Saturdays) at 11 and 11:20 (places limited, £1 per person). **Garden: areas subject to closure. †Estate: 1 January to 15 March and 28 October to 31 December, closes 4:30. Car park: open as estate. Closed 25 December.

The impressive drawing room at Sizergh

Stagshaw Garden and Ambleside

near Windermere, Cumbria

1927

On the edge of Windermere, Stagshaw Garden bursts into life with azaleas and rhododendrons. Rising behind, Skelghyll Woods are home to Cumbria's tallest trees; in front, Jenkin's Field is great for a lakeshore picnic and paddle. A mile north, the town of Ambleside, on Windermere's northern tip, has many attractions. **Note**: Ambleside Roman Fort (see below) owned by English Heritage, run by the National Trust.

Eat, shop, stay: plenty of places to eat and drink in Ambleside (none National Trust). Nearest National Trust pub at Sticklebarn, Langdale. National Trust shop in Grasmere, 4 miles.

Things to see and do: Bridge House, Ambleside's smallest building, built on a bridge over a beck. Tall Tree Trail at Skelghyll Woods. The remains of Ambleside Roman Fort (free) on Ambleside's edge. Townend nearby. **Dogs**: welcome on leads.

Access: **Bridge House** **Stagshaw Garden**
Sat Nav: use LA22 0HE for Stagshaw Garden and Skelghyll Woods; LA22 9AN for Bridge House. **Parking**: small car park at Stagshaw Garden. Several car parks in Ambleside, not National Trust (charge including members).

Find out more: 015394 46402 or stagshawgarden@nationaltrust.org.uk

Stagshaw Garden		M	T	W	T	F	S	S
Stagshaw Garden*								
Open all year	Dawn–dusk	**M**	**T**	**W**	**T**	**F**	**S**	**S**
Bridge House								
30 Mar–3 Nov	11:30–4:15	**M**	**T**	**W**	**T**	**F**	**S**	**S**

*Stagshaw Garden is at its best April to July.

Steam Yacht Gondola

Coniston Pier, Lake Road, Coniston, Cumbria LA21 8AN

1980

This steam yacht was rebuilt by the National Trust from the original 1859 *Gondola*: today's passengers can experience the nostalgia of a steam-driven cruise on Coniston Water as enjoyed by the Victorians. Based on the design of a Venetian 'Burchiello' boat, Steam Yacht Gondola cuts silently through the water, with the carved figurehead of Sid the golden sea serpent at the bow of her streamlined hull. You can explore the boat, watch the steam engine in action at close quarters, and listen to the crew's commentary on Gondola's long history on the lake and her association with *Swallows and Amazons*. **Note**: cruises depart from Coniston Pier (subject to weather conditions). Sorry no toilet on scheduled sailings. Steam Yacht Gondola (a member of National Historic Ships Fleet) is very costly to run. Charges for members with 10% discount on scheduled round-trip cruises.

Eat, shop, stay: small shop on board selling souvenirs. Gift experiences available online. Bluebird Café at Coniston Pier and coffee house/restaurant at Brantwood (neither National Trust). Rose Castle Cottage above Tarn Hows is a perfect base for ramblers, or camp at Hoathwaite.

Rebuilt by the National Trust, Steam Yacht Gondola cruises on Cumbria's Coniston Water

Steam Yacht Gondola on Coniston Water

Things to see and do: 'Steam and Cream' and 'Engineer for the Day' gift experiences. Grand Victorian Circular Tour package for small groups. Guided and downloadable walks from Gondola's jetties. Private charters available. **Dogs**: welcome in outside areas only.

Access: [icons] Gangway [icons]
Parking: at Coniston Pier, 50 yards, not National Trust (charge including members).

Find out more: 015394 32733 or sygondola@nationaltrust.org.uk Booking Office, The Hollens, Grasmere, Cumbria LA22 9QZ

Steam Yacht Gondola		M	T	W	T	F	S	S
Head of Lake Cruise								
1 Apr–31 Oct	11–11:45	M	T	W	T	F	·	·
1 Apr–31 Oct	12–12:45	M	T	W	T	F	·	·
1 Apr–31 Oct	1–1:45	M	T	W	T	F	S	S
30 Mar–27 Oct	2:30–3:15	·	·	·	·	·	S	S
30 Mar–27 Oct	3:30–4:15	·	·	·	·	·	S	S
Full Lake Cruise								
1 Apr–31 Oct	2:30–4:15	M	T	W	T	F	·	·
Walkers/Full Lake Cruise								
30 Mar–27 Oct	11–12:45	·	·	·	·	·	S	S

All sailings depart Coniston Pier. You can 'hop off/hop on' at other piers: Monk Coniston and Parkamoor, plus Lake Bank and Brantwood (not National Trust). Cruises subject to weather conditions.

Sticklebarn and The Langdales

near Ambleside, Cumbria

[icons] 1925

The barn-turned-pub, Sticklebarn, sits at the heart of the Langdales: with fresh food, real ale and roaring fires, this is the perfect place to relax after a day on the fells. The great Lakes guidebook author, Alfred Wainwright, said 'no mountain profile arrests and excites the attention more than that of the Langdale Pikes'. With miles of walking, cycling and climbing routes, they're a natural playground. The ambitious can tackle the dramatic peaks, but it's not all about high-level scrambling. The route around Blea Tarn is easily accessible, with views of Little and Great Langdale. Nearby High Close Estate and Arboretum offers 4.5 hectares (11 acres) of tranquillity with over 100 years of history and trees from around the globe.

Eat, shop, stay: Sticklebarn serves freshly prepared hot food and a range of drinks, including Cumbrian real ales. Outdoor eating on the terrace. Café at High Close. Camping options at Great Langdale Campsite or stay at Silverthwaite cottage (sleeps eight) in Langdale valley.

Sticklebarn and The Langdales, Cumbria: after a day on the fells, right, the cosy pub calls, below

Things to see and do: **Indoors** Sticklebarn is the perfect place to relax in all weather: read a book by the fire, play a board game, watch a family movie in the Hayloft or simply catch up over a drink. **Outdoors** Walking and climbing in the Lakeland fells. Guided gyhll scrambling and rock climbing from Great Langdale Campsite. Off-road cycle trail from Skelwith Bridge to Sticklebarn. Take a riverside ramble from Elterwater (below) or explore the tree trail at High Close. Finish your day on the terrace at Sticklebarn with occasional live music. Sleep under the stars at Great Langdale Campsite. **Dogs**: welcome on leads indoors and out.

Access: **Sticklebarn**
Sat Nav: use LA22 9JU for Sticklebarn; LA22 9PG for Blea Tarn; LA22 9HP for Elterwater; LA22 9HJ for High Close Estate. **Parking**: at Stickle Ghyll, Old Dungeon Ghyll, Blea Tarn, Elterwater village and High Close Estate.

Find out more: 015394 37356 (Sticklebarn) or sticklebarn@nationaltrust.org.uk

Sticklebarn and The Langdales		M	T	W	T	F	S	S
Sticklebarn*								
25 Jan–31 Mar	11–9†	M	T	W	T	F	S	S
1 Apr–3 Nov	11–10:30†	M	T	W	T	F	S	S
4 Nov–31 Dec**	11–9†	M	T	W	T	F	S	S
Great Langdale Campsite††								
Open all year		M	T	W	T	F	S	S

*Sticklebarn: open 1 January, 11 to 10:30.
**Closed 24 and 25 December; 31 December open 11 to 1 in the morning. †Bar: open till 11, Fridays and Saturdays. ††For detailed opening times and bookings please visit ntlakescampsites.org.uk or call 015394 32733.

Tarn Hows and Coniston

near Coniston, Cumbria

1930

Tarn Hows and Coniston in Cumbria

Tarn Hows offers an accessible walk for all the family. The circular 1¾-mile path through this 19th-century man-made landscape showcases ever-changing scenery and views of the Lakeland fells, making it a favourite with walkers of all abilities. Arrive early or late for a meditative moment among mountain views. **Note**: toilets in main car park. Mobility scooters free to hire (donations welcome). Livestock grazing.

Eat, shop, stay: ice-cream van on site most days during summer. Picnics welcome. National Trust shop in Hawkshead. Plenty of pubs and cafés in nearby Coniston and Hawkshead (none National Trust). Find a quiet countryside retreat at Rose Castle holiday cottage.

Things to see and do: you can make the most of your visit with a leisurely Steam Yacht Gondola cruise across Coniston Water, then walk through Monk Coniston Hall's grounds to Tarn Hows. **Dogs**: welcome on leads and under close control.

Access: **Grounds**
Sat Nav: nearest postcode is LA22 0PP. Follow road signs for Tarn Hows from Coniston or Hawkshead Hill. **Parking**: on site at Tarn Hows, also at Glen Mary nearby. Parking available in Coniston (not National Trust).

Find out more: 015394 41456 or tarnhows@nationaltrust.org.uk

Tarn Hows and Coniston		M	T	W	T	F	S	S
Tarn Hows								
Open all year	Dawn–dusk	**M**	**T**	**W**	**T**	**F**	**S**	**S**
Hoathwaite Campsite*								
5 Apr–16 Sep		**M**	**T**	**W**	**T**	**F**	**S**	**S**

*For detailed opening times and bookings please visit ntlakescampsites.org.uk or call 015394 32733.

Townend

Troutbeck, Windermere, Cumbria LA23 1LB

1948

A cosy farmhouse near Windermere brimming with character. Home to the Browne family for 400 years, Townend is full of intricately carved furniture and rare books, including 44 that are the only remaining copies in the world.

Experience life in the 18th century and spend time in the cottage garden. **Note**: unfortunately we cannot take card payments.

Eat, shop, stay: picnics welcome. Tea-room in Troutbeck village (not National Trust).

Things to see and do: **Indoors** Guided tours at 11 and 12 (places limited). 'A Taste of Townend' living history cooking demonstrations on Thursdays. Children's trail. **Outdoors** Garden trail for children. Traditional games.
Dogs: welcome in the garden.
Assistance dogs only in the house.

Access: **Building** **Grounds**
Parking: 300 yards.

Find out more: 015394 32628 or townend@nationaltrust.org.uk

Townend		M	T	W	T	F	S	S
16 Mar–27 Oct	1–5*	.	.	**W**	**T**	**F**	**S**	**S**

*Guided tours at 11 and 12 (places limited). Open Bank Holiday Mondays. May close early due to poor light.

Brimming with character, Townend in Cumbria, boasts intricately carved furniture and rare books

Wasdale

near Gosforth, Cumbria

1920

In the shadow of England's highest mountains lies Wasdale. From the tops of Illgill Head and Whin Rigg the screes sweep down to create ever-changing reflections in Wastwater below. Great Gable stands at the head of the valley with Scafell Pike nearby. This is a mountain landscape for hill-walking, climbing and exploring. Towards the southern end of the lake and Nether Wasdale, winding paths weave through woodland and along the water's edge, giving a gentler aspect to the valley. Planning ahead will give you the best experience: check the weather and prepare well, and enjoy your day on the fells. **Note**: limited toilet facilities (building work to improve facilities is expected to start later this year).

Eat, shop, stay: with numerous camping options – tents, campervans and pods – and cosy cottages, Wasdale is a perfect place for digital-detox holidays. Campsite shop. Pub and shop at Wasdale Head; pubs in Nether Wasdale and Santon Bridge (none National Trust).

Things to see and do: walking and climbing in England's highest mountains. Lakeside, riverbank and woodland rambles. Wild swimming and paddling in Wastwater and rivers. Herdwick sheep graze in fields and on fellsides. **Dogs**: well-behaved dogs welcome. Follow local and seasonal guidance. Keep dogs on leads near livestock.

Hiking in Wasdale, Cumbria, left, and enjoying a night under canvas, above

Sat Nav: use CA20 1EX. **Parking**: at Lake Head CA20 1EX; Overbeck CA20 1EX (limited space); Nether Wasdale CA20 1ET (limited space).

Find out more: 019467 26064 or wasdale@nationaltrust.org.uk

Wasdale
Wasdale Campsite*
Open every day all year

*For detailed opening times and bookings please visit ntlakescampsites.org.uk or call 015394 32733.

Whitehaven Coast

Whitehaven, Cumbria 2008

This post-industrial coastline is teeming with wildlife. Enjoy clifftop walks, the Georgian harbour and views to the Isle of Man. **Note**: sorry no toilets. For Sat Nav use CA28 9BG for clifftop car park and CA28 7LY for Whitehaven Harbour.

Find out more: 017687 74649 or whitehavencoast@nationaltrust.org.uk

Wordsworth House and Garden

Main Street, Cockermouth, Cumbria CA13 9RX

1938

Step back to the 1770s at the childhood home and garden that inspired William to become a poet. Hands-on rooms give a feel for middle-class Georgian life – there's even a rope bed to try. Costumed servants cook in the kitchen, gossip and tell tales on selected days in term-time and throughout school holidays. Guided and audio tours reveal the happiness and heartache experienced by the Wordsworth household, while in the cellar, their 'ghosts' share personal stories. Two new exhibitions, 'This Land is Our Land' and 'Under Northern Skies', explore our love of landscape and the fragility of the natural environment.

Eat, shop, stay: browse through Wordsworth and local souvenirs in the shop. Tea and scones make the perfect end to a visit. Picnics welcome. Second-hand books for sale.

Things to see and do: replica costumes, toys and games. Evocative and atmospheric animations related to the Wordsworths showing in some rooms. Holiday activities. A relaxing spot, the garden has heritage flowers, vegetables and trees. **Dogs**: on leads in front garden only. Free dog biscuits.

Access:
Building **Grounds**
Parking: in town-centre car parks, none National Trust (charge including members). Please note long-stay car park signposted as coach park, 300 yards, Wakefield Road.

Find out more: 01900 820884 (Infoline). 01900 824805 or wordsworthhouse@nationaltrust.org.uk

Wordsworth House and Garden		M	T	W	T	F	S	S
9 Mar–27 Oct	11–5*	M	T	W	T	·	S	S

*Last entry to house one hour before closing (timed tickets may operate on busy days). Open selected Fridays in holidays (please telephone for information).

Young visitors have fun letting off steam at Wordsworth House and Garden in Cumbria

Wray Castle

Low Wray, Ambleside, Cumbria LA22 0JA

1929

Standing on the west shore of Windermere, this dramatic Gothic Revival castle was built in the 1840s by a retired couple from Liverpool. With wide views of the Lake District hills, it's easy to imagine why they chose this striking spot. Since then, the castle has had many uses, and it came to the Trust without its original contents, providing rooms for family adventures and interactive spaces to explore its story. We're continually learning about Wray's past, and this year we're looking at the impact the castle had on the surrounding area since it was built. You can join a daily talk or tour to discover the latest findings, then explore the castle, grounds, parkland and lakeshore at your leisure. **Note**: steep walk from jetty if arriving by boat. Limited car parking.

Eat, shop, stay: Kitchen Court Café serving hot and cold drinks, sandwiches, soup and cakes. Indoor picnic room. Shop selling family games, gifts and souvenirs. Camp or glamp next door at Low Wray Campsite or stay in one of the holiday cottages nearby.

Arriving in style at Wray Castle in Cumbria, above, and the dramatic Gothic Revival castle, below

Things to see and do: Indoors Explore the family-friendly rooms upstairs, including the Peter Rabbit Adventure, dressing up and castle-building. Talks, tours and activities shed light on the castle's enigmatic past, architecture and the surrounding landscape. **Outdoors** Take a boat from Ambleside or Brockhole to the castle's jetty (sailings by Windermere Lake Cruises). Explore the grounds, parkland and woods. Tackle the play trail with tree house and rope swings. Find the shingle beach, climb up Latterbarrow hill or take the lakeshore path to Claife Viewing Station (4 miles). There are picnic benches in front of the castle or choose your own spot within the grounds. **Dogs**: welcome on short leads and under close control within grounds; assistance dogs only indoors.

Access: [access symbols] Castle [access symbols]
Parking: restricted car parking. Please come by boat, bike or boot to avoid disappointment.

Find out more: 015394 33250 or wraycastle@nationaltrust.org.uk

Wray Castle		M	T	W	T	F	S	S
Castle								
16 Feb–29 Mar	10–4	**M**	**T**	**W**	**T**	**F**	**S**	**S**
30 Mar–3 Nov	10–5	**M**	**T**	**W**	**T**	**F**	**S**	**S**
9 Nov–1 Dec	10–4	·	·	·	·	·	**S**	**S**
Grounds								
Open all year	Dawn–dusk	**M**	**T**	**W**	**T**	**F**	**S**	**S**
Low Wray Campsite*								
29 Mar–3 Nov		**M**	**T**	**W**	**T**	**F**	**S**	**S**

*For detailed opening times and bookings please visit ntlakescampsites.org.uk or call 015394 32733.

Additional countryside car parks in The Lakes

Borrowdale and Derwent Water

Great Wood	CA12 5UP
Kettlewell	CA12 5UN
Ashness Bridge	CA12 5UN
Surprise View	CA12 5UU
Watendlath	CA12 5UW
Bowder Stone	CA12 5XA
Rosthwaite	CA12 5XB
Seatoller	CA12 5XN

Buttermere Valley

Buttermere Village	CA13 9UZ
Cinderdale	CA13 9UY
Honister Pass	CA12 5XN
Lanthwaite Green	CA13 9UY
Lanthwaite Wood	CA13 0RT
Maggie's Bridge	CA13 0RU

Ullswater

Glencoyne Bay	CA11 0NQ
High Cascades	CA11 0JY
Park Brow	CA11 0JY

Wasdale

Lake Head	CA20 1EX
Overbeck	CA20 1EX
Nether Wasdale	CA20 1ET

The Langdales

Blea Tarn	LA22 9PG
Old Dungeon Ghyll	LA22 9JY
Stickle Ghyll	LA22 9JU
Elterwater	LA22 9HP
High Close	LA22 9HJ

Coniston

Glen Mary	LA21 8DP

Windermere West Shore

Red Nab	LA22 0JH
Harrowslack	LA22 0LR
Ash Landing	LA22 0LP

Beningbrough Hall, Gallery and Gardens

Beningbrough, York, North Yorkshire YO30 1DD

1958

From the wealthy teenager who inherited the estate to the Hall's use as an RAF billet, Beningbrough has been shaped by the many people who lived here and is still evolving today. The architecture and collections on the ground floor tell the story of a country house, while the Saloon Galleries host changing exhibitions of contemporary and traditional artwork in partnership with the National Portrait Gallery. In the interactive spaces on the top floor, explore how art is made and have a go yourself. The garden is also enjoying a revival. Alongside lawns, formal gardens, herbaceous borders and a walled kitchen garden, look out for the Pergola, one in a series of planned new gardens by international designer Andy Sturgeon.

Eat, shop, stay: the Walled Garden Restaurant serves hot lunches, sandwiches and snacks. You can choose from plants and extensive home and garden ranges in the shop. A holiday apartment above the Victorian laundry provides exclusive out-of-hours access to the gardens.

Beningbrough Hall, Gallery and Gardens, North Yorkshire: art, history and gardens come together

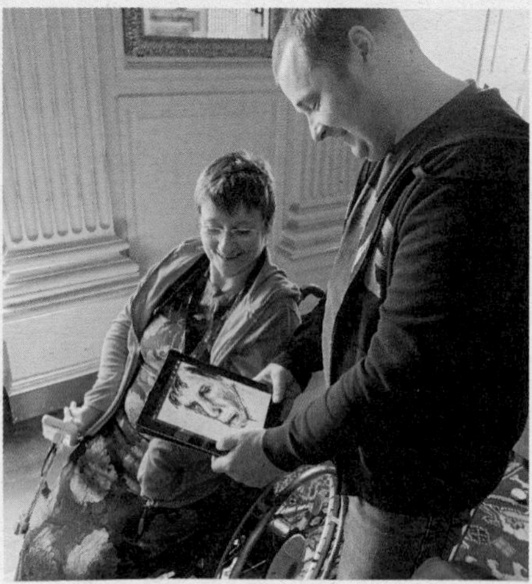

Explore and get creative at Beningbrough Hall, Gallery and Gardens, above left and right

Things to see and do: **Indoors** You can get creative in the hands-on spaces and discover history and portraiture from a new perspective. Dress up and sit for your own virtual 18th-century portrait. Glimpse servant life in the Victorian laundry. There's a programme of family and adult activities throughout the year. **Outdoors** Get off the beaten track on riverside paths or walk through the woodland glades. Relax in the garden, with seasonal colour from snowdrops, crocuses and daffodils in spring to dahlias, pumpkins and apples in autumn, or pause to enjoy the parkland views. Families can let off steam in the wilderness play area. **Dogs**: welcome on non-extendable leads in the garden and parkland.

Access: Stable block Hall Gardens
Parking: on site.

Find out more: 01904 472027 or beningbrough@nationaltrust.org.uk

Beningbrough Hall		M	T	W	T	F	S	S
5 Jan–24 Feb	11–3:30*	·	·	·	·	·	S	S
26 Feb–3 Mar	11–3:30*	·	T	W	T	F	S	S
5 Mar–31 May	10:30–5**	·	T	W	T	F	S	S
1 Jun–31 Aug	10:30–5**	M	T	W	T	F	S	S
1 Sep–3 Nov	10:30–5**	·	T	W	T	F	S	S
9 Nov–22 Dec†	11–3:30	·	·	·	·	·	S	S
26 Dec–29 Dec†	11–3:30	·	·	·	T	F	S	S

Open Bank Holidays, except 25 December. *Hall: parts closed, remaining areas open 11:30. **Hall: open 11:30 to 4. Shop: opens 12. †Hall: major conservation work planned, Hall may be closed on selected days, any accessible areas open at 11:30.

Braithwaite Hall

East Witton, Leyburn, North Yorkshire DL8 4SY 1941

Grand 17th-century tenanted farmhouse in the heart of Coverdale, close to the River Cover and surrounded by farmland and woodland. **Note**: sorry, no toilet. Parts of the Hall are open in June, July and August (by arrangement in advance with the tenant).

Find out more: 01969 640287 or braithwaitehall@nationaltrust.org.uk

Bridestones, Crosscliff and Blakey Topping

near Pickering, North Yorkshire 1944

On the North York Moors, the Bridestones are geological wonders – rock formations with moorland views, woodland walks and grassy valleys. **Note**: nearest toilets at Staindale Lake car park. For Sat Nav use YO18 7LR. Road access is via Dalby Forest Drive starting 2½ miles north of Thornton le Dale: toll charges payable (including members) to Forestry Commission.

Find out more: 01723 870423 or bridestones@nationaltrust.org.uk

Brimham Rocks

Summerbridge, Harrogate, North Yorkshire HG3 4DW

1970

These eye-catching rocks have been sculpted by 320 million years of ice, wind and continental movement, creating strange shapes and geological curiosities. With names such as the Dancing Bear and Blacksmith's Anvil, they look just like you'd imagine. With climbs and hidden spaces, the rocks are a natural playground while the panoramic views across Nidderdale have inspired people for centuries. You can explore the wide open moorland, which provides a rare habitat for wildlife including internationally important plants. Brimham is a great place for walkers, climbers, nature spotters and picnickers, as well as families looking for the freedom to explore.
Note: nearest toilets 600 yards from car park.

Eat, shop, stay: grab a coffee, sausage roll or slice of cake from the kiosk. Picnic benches, with additional indoor seating at visitor centre. The shop stocks a range of items, including locally made bilberry jam.

Things to see and do: regular guided walks, photography, orienteering, events, family activities, geocaching and climbing days. An exhibition at the visitor centre tells the story of the rocks and the on-going conservation work.
Dogs: welcome on leads.

Access:
Visitor centre/shop **Countryside**
Parking: on site.

Find out more: 01423 780688 or brimhamrocks@nationaltrust.org.uk

Brimham Rocks		M	T	W	T	F	S	S
Countryside								
Open all year	Dawn–dusk*	M	T	W	T	F	S	S
Visitor centre, shop and kiosk								
1 Jan–6 Jan	11-4	·	T	W	T	F	S	S
12 Jan–10 Feb**	11-3	·	·	·	·	·	S	S
16 Feb–24 Mar†	11-4	M	T	W	T	F	S	S
30 Mar–3 Nov	10:30–4:30	M	T	W	T	F	S	S
9 Nov–22 Dec	11-4	·	·	·	·	·	S	S
23 Dec–31 Dec††	11-4	M	T	W	T	F	S	S

*Main gate: closes 9, or dusk if earlier. **Shop: closed 12 January to 10 February. †Visitor centre, shop and kiosk: 9 to 24 March opening times may vary. ††Visitor centre, shop and kiosk: closed 24 and 25 December. Open 1 to 5 January 2020.

Brimham Rocks in North Yorkshire: sculpted by millions of years of wind and ice

East Riddlesden Hall

Bradford Road, Riddlesden, Keighley, West Yorkshire BD20 5EL

1934

Hundreds of years ago this West Yorkshire manor was a thriving farming estate. Today the house tells tales of the ambition, success and failure of those who lived and worked here. The Great Barn displays 400-year-old markings of proud craftsmen. The gardens can be enjoyed at any time of the year, and seasonal highlights include the scented herb border in spring, cottage garden flowers in summer and trees laden with apples, pears and figs in autumn. The play area, mud-pie kitchen and den-building corner give families the opportunity to enjoy outdoor natural play.

Eat, shop, stay: a converted bothy is home to a shop selling gifts, books, homeware, gardenware, plants and ice cream. On the first floor the tea-room sells seasonal light meals, sandwiches, cakes and drinks. Accessible tables on the ground floor. Outdoor picnics welcome.

Things to see and do: **Indoors** Plasterwork ceilings, textiles, furniture and objects to handle inside the house. Great Barn with ancient oak beams. **Outdoors** Intimate gardens to relax in, bird hide and natural play areas.

Dogs: welcome on lower fields and riverside. Assistance dogs only in house and gardens.

Access:
House, shop and tea-room **Gardens**
Parking: 250 yards.

Find out more: 01535 607075 or eastriddlesden@nationaltrust.org.uk

East Riddlesden Hall		M	T	W	T	F	S	S
House, tea-room, shop and garden								
16 Feb–24 Feb	10:30–4:30	**M**	**T**	**W**	**T**	·	**S**	**S**
2 Mar–17 Mar	10:30–4:30	·	·	·	·	·	**S**	**S**
18 Mar–3 Nov*	10:30–4:30	**M**	**T**	**W**	**T**	·	**S**	**S**
Tea-room and shop								
9 Nov–22 Dec	10:30–3:30	·	·	·	·	·	**S**	**S**

Tea-room: last entry 15 minutes before closing.
*Open Good Friday.

East Riddlesden Hall, West Yorkshire, above and below: ambition, success and failure

 For information about getting to National Trust places, please see page 3

Fountains Abbey and Studley Royal Water Garden

near Ripon, North Yorkshire HG4 3DY

1983

Deep within the Skell Valley lies Fountains Abbey and Studley Royal, a World Heritage Site waiting to be explored. Humans have tamed and teased the valley's wild waters over hundreds of years, creating an expansive landscape with imposing Abbey ruins and sweeping Georgian water garden. Cistercian monks chose this place to establish Fountains Abbey in 1132, and the walls echo with centuries-old stories. Follow the riverside path to Studley Royal, a playful water garden designed by visionaries John and William Aislabie in the 18th century. You can spend a day among statues, follies and cascades before venturing beyond the lake to Studley Royal deer park, with its ancient lime tree avenues and red, fallow and sika deer.

Eat, shop, stay: restaurant serving specials and Sunday lunch. Lighter bites at Mill Café and Studley Tea-room with lake views/terrace. Picnics welcome. Shop with gardening section. Fourteen holiday cottages, including a waterside lodge and apartment inside Fountains Hall.

Things to see and do: **Indoors** You can grind your own flour and watch the water flow at the mill made by the monks. Uncover the Abbey's history in Porter's Lodge or try medieval crafts in Swanley Grange. Find out about the 1930s Settlers Society at Fountains Hall and admire St Mary's Church, a Victorian Gothic masterpiece in the deer park. **Outdoors** Kids can scramble in the wooden play area and whizz along the zip wire. The orchard and herb garden are great for exploring. There are miles of walks in the deer park and Water Garden. Free guided tours and shuttle bus across estate. **Dogs**: welcome on leads. Fresh water bowls and dog-friendly eating areas outside restaurant and tea-room.

Fountains Abbey and Studley Royal Water Garden, North Yorkshire: the imposing Abbey ruins

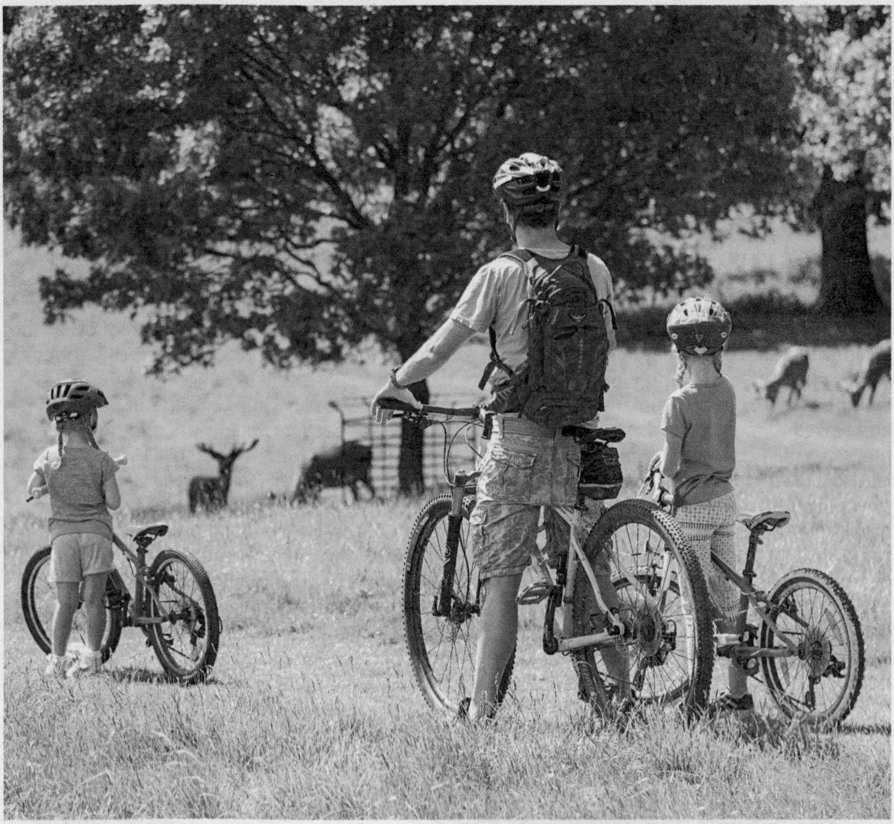

Access:

Fountains Abbey **Fountains Hall**

Water Garden

Parking: on site at visitor centre (two electric vehicle charging points), West Gate car park and Studley Lakeside.

Find out more: 01765 608888 or fountainsabbey@nationaltrust.org.uk

Fountains Abbey		M	T	W	T	F	S	S
Abbey and Water Garden, visitor centre restaurant, shop								
1 Jan–3 Mar*	10–5**	**M**	**T**	**W**	**T**	**F**	**S**	**S**
4 Mar–27 Oct	10–6**	**M**	**T**	**W**	**T**	**F**	**S**	**S**
28 Oct–31 Dec*	10–5**	**M**	**T**	**W**	**T**	·	**S**	**S**
Deer park								
Open all year	6–6	**M**	**T**	**W**	**T**	**F**	**S**	**S**

Last admission one hour before closing. *Closed Fridays in January, plus 1 February, 24 and 25 December. **Visitor centre restaurant and shop close one hour earlier. Check opening times before visit for Fountains Hall, mill, tea-rooms, Studley Royal shop and St Mary's Church.

There are miles of paths to explore at Fountains Abbey and Studley Royal Water Garden

Goddards House and Garden

27 Tadcaster Road, Dringhouses, York, North Yorkshire YO24 1GG

1984

Discover the Terry family's story and confectionery history (think Chocolate Orange) at their former house and garden. Goddards is a cherished oasis where you can imagine living at a gentler pace. A warm Arts and Crafts building full of memories, you're invited to make yourself at home in the drawing room with a sherry or indulge your nostalgic side by remembering your favourite Terry's sweets in the 'factory rooms'. Outside, the Terry chocolate factory clock tower can be spotted from the paddock orchard. You can take your time and meander through garden 'rooms', exploring fragrant borders and hidden corners.

Eat, shop, stay: lunch is served in the Terry's dining room. You can take coffee or afternoon tea in the drawing room, or tuck into a slice of chocolate-orange cake on the terrace, enjoying views of the Arts and Crafts garden.

Things to see and do: **Indoors** Curl up by the fire on chilly days. Family trails and nostalgic displays of chocolate boxes, remembering old favourites. **Outdoors** Beautifully restored Arts and Crafts garden with outdoor games. **Dogs**: welcome on leads in the garden.

Access:
House **Garden**
Sat Nav: enter 27 Tadcaster Road, Dringhouses, York, not postcode. **Parking**: accessible parking only on site (small car park is used by staff and volunteers). Please use city centre car parks (1 to 2 miles) or park on Knavesmire Road (off A1036) by York racecourse, 1 mile.

Find out more: 01904 771930 or goddards@nationaltrust.org.uk

Goddards		M	T	W	T	F	S	S
1 Mar–3 Nov	10:30–5	·	·	**W**	**T**	**F**	**S**	**S**
14 Nov–15 Dec	10:30–4	·	·	·	**T**	**F**	**S**	**S**

Open Bank Holiday Mondays.

Arts and Crafts Goddards House and Garden in North Yorkshire: relaxing on the lawn

Hardcastle Crags

near Hebden Bridge, West Yorkshire

1950

This picturesque valley has more than 160 hectares (400 acres) of ancient woodland with tumbling streams, waterfalls and deep ravines. It's a great place to walk, with over 25 miles of footpaths. It's also home to the northern hairy wood ant and internationally rare waxcap grasslands. Seasonal highlights include carpets of sweet-smelling bluebells in late spring, golden leaves in autumn and rare, delicate frost flowers in winter. Gibson Mill, a former cotton mill and Edwardian entertainment emporium, tells the story of the valley during the past 200 years, with interactive displays and dressing up. **Note**: steep paths, rough terrain. Toilets and café at Gibson Mill, 1 mile from car parks.

Eat, shop, stay: café serving drinks, light lunches and cakes, with log burner in cooler weather. Outdoor ice-cream parlour during summer months. Shop selling walking trails, books, gifts and sweets. Stay longer at one of the two holiday cottages.

Things to see and do: **Indoors** Find out about the mill's history and the local area. See 'off the grid' technology and occasional exhibitions. **Outdoors** Walking trails, guided walks, picnics, wildlife and family activities. **Dogs**: welcome under close control, including in café. On leads near livestock.

Access: **Mill**
Sat Nav: for Midgehole car park use HX7 7AA; Clough Hole car park HX7 7AZ. **Parking**: at Midgehole car park, 1 mile to Gibson Mill, or Clough Hole car park, ¾ mile (steep walk).

Find out more: 01422 844518 (weekdays). 01422 846236 (weekends) or hardcastlecrags@nationaltrust.org.uk

Hardcastle Crags		M	T	W	T	F	S	S
Gibson Mill and Weaving Shed Café								
1 Jan–6 Jan	11–3	·	**T**	**W**	**T**	**F**	**S**	**S**
12 Jan–17 Feb	11–3	·	·	·	·	·	**S**	**S**
18 Feb–24 Feb	11–3	**M**	**T**	**W**	**T**	**F**	**S**	**S**
2 Mar–17 Mar	11–3	·	·	·	·	·	**S**	**S**
18 Mar–3 Nov	11–4	**M**	**T**	**W**	**T**	**F**	**S**	**S**
9 Nov–22 Dec	11–3	·	·	·	·	·	**S**	**S**
23 Dec–31 Dec	11–3	**M**	**T**	·	**T**	**F**	**S**	**S**

With tumbling streams, waterfalls, woods and ravines, Hardcastle Crags, West Yorkshire, offers endless adventures – on two legs or four

Maister House

160 High Street, Hull, East Yorkshire
HU1 1NL 1966

A merchant family's tale of fortune and tragedy is intertwined with the intriguing history of the 18th-century Maister House. **Note**: staircase and entrance hall only on show. Sorry no toilet. Due to a change in circumstances we are unable to confirm opening arrangements at the time of going to print. Please visit website for opening details.

Find out more: 01904 472027 (Beningbrough Hall) or maisterhouse@nationaltrust.org.uk

Marsden Moor

Marsden, Huddersfield, West Yorkshire

This Site of Special Scientific Interest, with views across the South Pennines and Peak District, has more than 2,300 hectares (5,700 acres) of countryside to explore. Regular guided walks will take you along miles of footpaths to favourite viewpoints, where you can spot wildlife and rare plants. **Note**: sorry, no toilet.

Marsden Moor, West Yorkshire: miles of footpaths, viewpoints and wildlife

Eat, shop, stay: cafés and pubs in Marsden village (none National Trust). Plant sales every Friday in spring and summer, with home-grown plants, handmade recycled wooden planters and wildlife homes. Christmas trees on sale at weekends in December.

Things to see and do: walking leaflets and guided walks all year. Friday plant sales in spring/summer. Due to ground-nesting birds please keep to footpaths. **Dogs**: welcome on leads, livestock roaming and ground-nesting birds (1 March to 31 July).

Access: Information Room
Sat Nav: use HD7 6DH for the Information Room, guided walks, plant sales and Marsden village, HD3 3FT for Buckstones and HD9 4HW for Wessenden Head.
Parking: Marsden village (not National Trust), Buckstones and Wessenden Head.

Find out more: 01484 847016 or marsdenmoor@nationaltrust.org.uk

Marsden Moor	
Information Room	
Open every day all year*	9–5

*Closed 25 December.

Middlethorpe Hall Hotel, Restaurant and Spa

Bishopthorpe Road, York,
North Yorkshire YO23 2GB

2008

Middlethorpe Hall is a country house just outside York, built of mellow red brick during the reign of William III in 1699 and set in eight hectares (20 acres) of gardens. Furnished with antiques and paintings, Middlethorpe still has the look and feel of a well-kept manor house. The comfortable bedrooms are complemented by elegant public rooms, including the drawing room and wood-panelled dining room, where imaginative meals are served. The gardens include a rose garden, a walled garden and a meadow leading to a tree-ringed lake. In the spa, which has a small gym, indoor swimming pool and sauna, the trained therapists use Aromatherapy Associates products.
Note: access is for guests staying at the hotel, using the spa or enjoying luncheon, afternoon tea and dinner. Children over the age of six welcome.

Find out more: 01904 641241.
01904 620176 (fax) or info@middlethorpe.com
middlethorpe.com

Moulton Hall

Moulton, Richmond,
North Yorkshire DL10 6QH 1966

Elegant 17th-century tenanted manor house with a beautiful carved staircase, set in a pretty garden with stone paths and borders.
Note: sorry no toilet. Visit by arrangement in advance with the tenant (please give as much notice as possible).

Find out more: 01325 377227 or
moultonhall@nationaltrust.org.uk

Mount Grace Priory, House and Gardens

Staddle Bridge, Northallerton,
North Yorkshire DL6 3JG 1953

Explore the well-preserved ruins of a medieval priory set in woodland, with pretty gardens and Arts and Crafts-style manor house.
Note: managed by English Heritage; National Trust members free, except on event days. Open weekends, 5 January to 17 February and 2 November to 29 December, 10 to 4; open daily, 18 February to 24 February, 10 to 4; 1 April to 30 September, 10 to 6 and 1 to 31 October, 10 to 5; open Wednesday to Sunday, 27 February to 31 March, 10 to 4.

Find out more: 01609 883494 or
mountgracepriory@nationaltrust.org.uk

Nostell

Doncaster Road, Nostell, near Wakefield,
West Yorkshire WF4 1QE

1954

Built to impress in the 18th century, Nostell is one of the great treasure houses in the north of England. Generations of the Winn family employed the best architects, craftsmen and artists to create a showcase for fashionable design. Discover interiors by influential

Nostell, West Yorkshire: one of the north of England's great treasure houses, right, and its estate, below

With world-class collections and Robert Adam interiors, Nostell is truly inspirational

architect Robert Adam, a world-class collection of furniture, textiles and wallpaper supplied by Thomas Chippendale, priceless paintings, a Georgian doll's house and a rare John Harrison clock. Home to wildlife including swans, kingfishers and bats, the surrounding 121-hectare (300-acre) estate includes parkland, lakes, a working kitchen garden and the tranquil Menagerie Garden.
With displays of snowdrops, daffodils and bluebells, woodland cycle trails and all-weather paths, you can find new things to see and do in every season.

Eat, shop, stay: Courtyard Café serving hot food and refreshments. Shop selling gifts, souvenirs and plants. Second-hand bookshop and kiosk offering snacks and drinks open at peak times. Picnics welcome in the park and gardens.

Things to see and do: **Indoors** You can find out more about Nostell's collections through temporary exhibitions and events or learn a new skill in artist-led sessions for adults. Families can follow the house trail and make masterpieces in the Workshop every school holiday. **Outdoors** Explore the parkland paths by bike, foot, scooter or wheelchair, or practise your twists and turns on the cycle-only trails. Children can go wild with led activities every school holiday and enjoy nature-spotting, geocaching, den-building and the outdoor play area all year. **Dogs**: assistance dogs only in gardens/house. Under close control, on leads when requested, in park.

Access:
House **Grounds**
Parking: 650 yards.

Find out more: 01924 863892 or nostell@nationaltrust.org.uk

Nostell		M	T	W	T	F	S	S
House*								
2 Mar–3 Nov	11–4	·	·	W	T	F	S	S
7 Dec–22 Dec	11–3	·	·	·	·	·	S	S
Gardens, shop and café								
1 Jan–1 Mar	10–4	M	T	W	T	F	S	S
2 Mar–3 Nov	10–5	M	T	W	T	F	S	S
4 Nov–31 Dec	10–4	M	T	W	T	F	S	S
Parkland								
Open all year	7–7**	M	T	W	T	F	S	S

*House: check additional opening arrangements before visit. Open Bank Holidays. **Parkland: last entry 6, or dusk if earlier. Closed 25 December.

Nunnington Hall

Nunnington, near York,
North Yorkshire YO62 5UY

1953

A welcoming house and garden in a picturesque Yorkshire setting, Nunnington Hall has centuries of stories. Find out about the Fife family, owners of the Hall in the 1920s, or the scandals and rise and fall of Lord Preston during the 17th century. In the attic, you'll discover the Carlisle Collection, regarded by many as the finest collection of miniature rooms, complete with tiny books, instruments and artwork. Outdoors, wildflower meadows bloom in the organic garden in spring, the lawn is perfect for relaxing and picnicking by the river in summer, and the orchards are bursting with produce in autumn.

Eat, shop, stay: waitress-service licensed tea-room in the main part of the house, serving snacks, meals, cakes and scones. Outdoor garden kiosk (open during peak times) with seating next to the River Rye. Shop on the third floor, selling gifts and souvenirs.

Things to see and do: **Indoors** 'Carlisle Collection' of miniature rooms, touring art exhibitions, conservation in action and events throughout the year. **Outdoors** Organic gardens, orchard and wildflower meadows. Garden games, giant chess and croquet. **Dogs**: welcome on leads in the garden and tea garden.

Access: **Building** **Grounds**
Parking: on site.

Find out more: 01439 748283 or nunningtonhall@nationaltrust.org.uk

Nunnington Hall		M	T	W	T	F	S	S
9 Feb–8 Mar	10:30–4	·	T	W	T	F	S	S
9 Mar–31 May	10:30–5	·	T	W	T	F	S	S
1 Jun–8 Sep	10:30–5	M	T	W	T	F	S	S
10 Sep–3 Nov	10:30–5	·	T	W	T	F	S	S
15 Nov–15 Dec	10:30–4	·	·	·	·	F	S	S

Last entry 45 minutes before closing. Open Mondays during school holidays and Bank Holiday Mondays.

Welcoming Nunnington Hall in North Yorkshire

Ormesby Hall

Ladgate Lane, Ormesby, near Middlesbrough, Redcar & Cleveland TS3 0SR

1962

Sitting in a calm green lung in urban Middlesbrough, this Georgian house is full of stories that are far from peaceful. The Pennyman family home tells tales of divorce, bankruptcy, love, revolutionary theatre, military service and royal connections from the past 300 years, up to the last owners, traditional Jim and socialist Ruth. Together they opened their doors to war refugees, artists, a prime minister and the local community. The formal and spring gardens offer an escape among the seasonal flowers, such as daffodils and tulips. The acres of parkland are great for exploring and spotting wildlife along the way.

Eat, shop, stay: Pennyman Pantry Tea-room serving barista-style coffee and a range of hot and cold drinks, soup, sandwiches, light lunches, cakes and scones. New shop selling National Trust products, children's toys and plants. Second-hand bookshop. Picnics welcome in the garden.

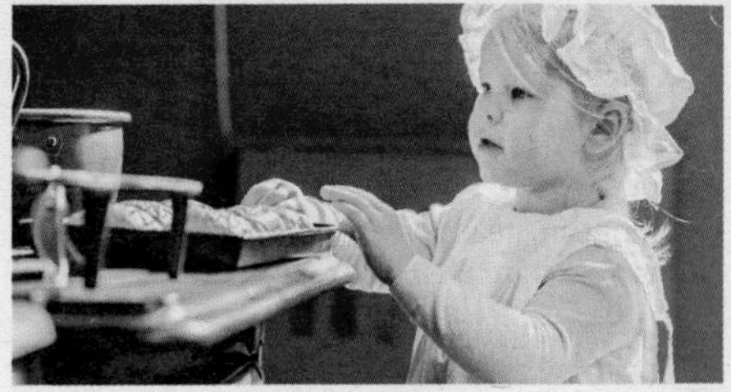

Things to see and do: **Indoors** Victorian kitchen and laundry, model railway layouts, family room and activities during school holidays. **Outdoors** Natural wild play area, mud pie kitchen, '50 things' trail, garden games and croquet. **Dogs**: welcome on leads in garden, courtyards and parkland. Assistance dogs only in house.

Access:
House **Grounds**
Parking: 200 yards.

Find out more: 01642 324188 or ormesbyhall@nationaltrust.org.uk

Ormesby Hall		M	T	W	T	F	S	S
10 Feb–4 Apr	11–4	**M**	**T**	**W**	**T**	·	·	**S**
7 Apr–3 Nov	11–5	**M**	**T**	**W**	**T**	·	·	**S**
23 Nov–30 Dec*	12–6	**M**	·	·	·	·	**S**	**S**

Last entry one hour before closing. *Closed 23 December.

Ormesby Hall, Redcar & Cleveland, above and below: a green oasis in an urban setting

Rievaulx Terrace, North Yorkshire: the Ionic Temple

Rievaulx Terrace

Rievaulx, Helmsley, North Yorkshire YO62 5LJ

1972

Designed to impress, Rievaulx Terrace was created by the Duncombe family in the 18th century and still feels just as grand and tranquil today. Enjoy a peaceful woodland walk out onto the terrace with views of Rievaulx Abbey. Look up inside the Ionic Temple to see the beautifully painted ceiling. **Note**: no access from Rievaulx Terrace to Rievaulx Abbey (managed by English Heritage).

Eat, shop, stay: packed snacks, ice cream and hot and cold drinks available. Picnics welcome. Shop selling gifts and souvenirs.

Things to see and do: furnished Ionic Temple opens at set times throughout the day. Natural play area. Family trails and activities, including den-building, rope swing, balance beam, log-scotch, quoits and stepping stones.
Dogs: welcome on leads.

Access: Visitor centre Temples Grounds
Parking: 100 yards.

Find out more: 01439 798340 (summer). 01439 748283 (winter) or rievaulxterrace@nationaltrust.org.uk

Rievaulx Terrace		M	T	W	T	F	S	S
2 Mar–27 Sep	10–5	M	T	W	T	F	S	S
28 Sep–3 Nov	10–4	M	T	W	T	F	S	S

Last entry one hour before closing.

Roseberry Topping

near Newton-under-Roseberry, North Yorkshire 1985

Affectionately known as 'Yorkshire's Matterhorn', Roseberry Topping has woodland walks and wildlife on its slopes, and views from its summit. **Note**: nearest parking at Newton-under-Roseberry, not National Trust (charge including members). Nearest toilets also in this car park. For Sat Nav use TS9 6QR.

Find out more: 01723 870423 or roseberrytopping@nationaltrust.org.uk

Treasurer's House, York

Minster Yard, York, North Yorkshire YO1 7JL

1930

Tucked behind York Minster, Treasurer's House is not as it first appears. In 1897 it was bought by Frank Green, the grandson of a wealthy industrialist, and by 1900 he had transformed it at great speed into an elaborately decorated town house, ready for the visit of Edward VII. Hear about Frank's life and find out how he saved Treasurer's House and changed it from a ramshackle collection of buildings into the grand show home we see today. The award-winning garden is an oasis of calm and offers unrivalled views of York Minster, making it an ideal place to relax.

Eat, shop, stay: Below Stairs Café serves morning coffee, lunch and a variety of cakes. Around the corner on Goodramgate, the Trust's large high-street shop sells a wide selection of gifts. Stay a little longer in Minstergate, the city-centre holiday apartment.

Things to see and do: family trails. Hard-hat tours into the cellar (over fives), the site of York's most famous ghost story, and town house tours (both on selected days). The house is decorated for Christmas.
Dogs: welcome in the garden on leads.

Access: House Garden
Parking: nearest at Lord Mayor's Walk (not National Trust). Park and ride from city outskirts recommended.

Find out more: 01904 624247 or treasurershouse@nationaltrust.org.uk

Treasurer's House		M	T	W	T	F	S	S
1 Apr–3 Nov*	11–4:30	M	T	W	T	F	S	S
9 Nov–21 Dec	11–4:30	M	T	W	T	F	S	S

*On selected days access is by guided tour only.

Treasurer's House in York, North Yorkshire: the tranquil garden, above, and intriguing collections, below

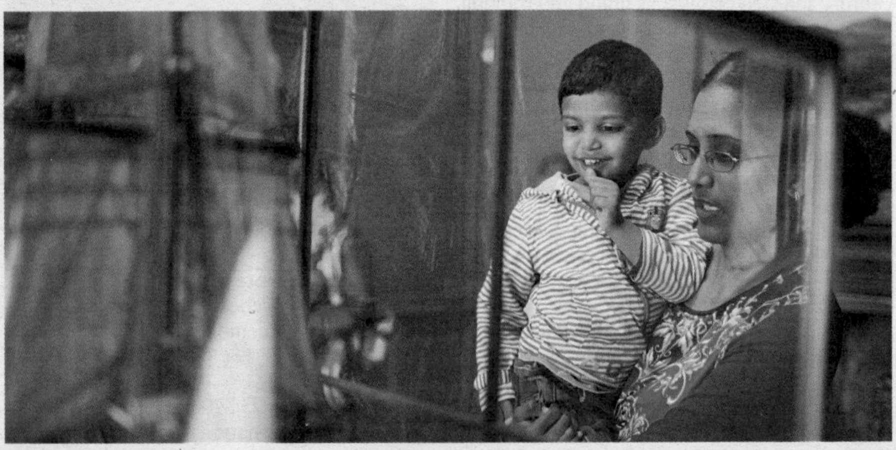

Wentworth Castle Gardens

Lowe Lane, Stainborough, Barnsley, South Yorkshire S75 3EN

2018

Working together with Barnsley Council and Northern College, this estate, rooted in rivalry, will now provide a space to bring people together. Royal diplomat Thomas Wentworth was outraged when a cousin inherited his family home in 1695, and was determined to outdo him, creating this place once known as 'the finest garden in England'. Today it is South Yorkshire's only Grade I registered landscape, with acres of parkland and gardens to explore. There are surprises along every avenue, including a castle that is not what it seems. **Note**: house closed to visitors as it houses Northern College, which offers residential adult education courses.

Eat, shop, stay: café serving light meals, cakes and refreshments. Shop selling gifts and souvenirs. Kiosk offering snacks and drinks open at peak times. Picnics welcome in the parkland and gardens.

Things to see and do: Victorian conservatory, flower garden and fernery, as well as 200 hectares (500 acres) of parkland to explore. Adventure play area for families. **Dogs**: welcome on leads in the gardens and parkland.

Access:
Long Barn **Grounds**
Sat Nav: use S75 3EN. **Parking**: on site.

Find out more: 01226 776040 or wentworthcastlegardens@nationaltrust.org.uk

Wentworth Castle Gardens
Wentworth Castle Gardens is due to open in the summer (please check before visiting for confirmation of dates/times).

Wentworth Castle Gardens, South Yorkshire

Wentworth Woodhouse

Cortworth Lane, Wentworth, Rotherham, South Yorkshire S62 7TQ 2017

Large 18th-century country house, saved for the nation by Wentworth Woodhouse Preservation Trust, which is working to restore it. **Note**: operated by Wentworth Woodhouse Preservation Trust. National Trust members receive 50 per cent discount on all tours. Admission to house and garden by booked guided tour only (call for details). Shop and café open on tour days.

Find out more: 01226 351161 or info@wentworthwoodhouse.org.uk

Yorkshire Coast

near Ravenscar, North Yorkshire

1976

The coastline from Saltburn to Filey has sea views, clifftop walks, cycling routes and sandy bays with excellent rock-pooling and fossil-hunting. You can get ideas to make the most of your visit at Ravenscar Visitor Centre and there's a coastal exhibition at the Old Coastguard Station, Robin Hood's Bay.

Eat, shop, stay: the Old Coastguard Station shop sells gifts, books, maps and toys. Ravenscar Visitor Centre offers a limited selection of drinks and snacks. With sea views, the holiday cottages at Ravenscar and Robin Hood's Bay are great places to stay.

Yorkshire Coast, North Yorkshire: after a long walk, above, don't miss the Old Coastguard Station, left

Things to see and do: **Indoors** Exhibitions at the Old Coastguard Station. **Outdoors** Family events, geocaching, wildlife activities and guided walks from Ravenscar and the Old Coastguard Station. **Dogs**: welcome, on leads around livestock and most events. Old Coastguard Station: assistance dogs only.

Access: **Old Coastguard Station**
Sat Nav: for Ravenscar use YO13 0NE.
Parking: on roadside at Ravenscar. Pay and display at Saltburn, Runswick Bay and Robin Hood's Bay, not National Trust (charge including members).

Find out more: 01723 870423 or yorkshirecoast@nationaltrust.org.uk

Yorkshire Coast		M	T	W	T	F	S	S
Old Coastguard Station and Ravenscar Visitor Centre								
1 Jan–6 Jan	10–4	·	**T**	**W**	**T**	**F**	**S**	**S**
12 Jan–17 Feb	10–4	·	·	·	·	·	**S**	**S**
23 Feb–3 Mar	10–4	**M**	**T**	**W**	**T**	**F**	**S**	**S**
9 Mar–3 Nov	10–5	**M**	**T**	**W**	**T**	**F**	**S**	**S**
9 Nov–22 Dec	10–4	·	·	·	·	·	**S**	**S**
27 Dec–31 Dec	10–4	**M**	**T**	·	·	**F**	**S**	**S**

Yorkshire Dales

North Yorkshire

1946

The Yorkshire Dales is a great place to relax and explore the great outdoors. Take in the limestone landscape with its drystone walls and barns, fields of sheep and cows, and wildflower meadows and pastures. You can walk along the boardwalk at the National Nature Reserve at Malham Tarn and explore the river and woodland valleys of Upper Wharfedale on foot or by bike. Further north, Hudswell Woods has over 5 miles of footpaths through ancient woodlands and there are peaceful spots along the River Swale to enjoy a picnic or perhaps skim a stone. **Note**: nearest toilets located at National Park Centre car parks or council car park (Hudswell Woods).

Eat, shop, stay: tea-rooms, shops, pubs and facilities in Buckden and Malham villages (none National Trust). Stay at The Old Smithy (sleeps two) or Town Head Barn Bunkhouse (sleeps 13) in Buckden, or Darnbrook Cottage (sleeps five) on Malham Moor.

Things to see and do: accessible boardwalk and tramper for hire at Malham Tarn. Walking routes and cycling trails. Events, including exhibitions at the Orchid House, Malham Tarn, and Town Head Barn in Malham village.
Dogs: welcome on leads (livestock roaming).

Access: **Town Head Barn** **Grounds**
Sat Nav: use BD23 5JA for Upper Wharfedale; BD24 9PT for Malham Tarn; DL10 4TJ for Hudswell Woods. **Parking**: for Upper Wharfedale use car parks in Kettlewell and Buckden, not National Trust (charge including members). For Malham Tarn, either off-road at Waterhouses or at Watersinks car park. For Hudswell Woods use Round Howe car park, not National Trust (charge including members).

Find out more: 01729 830416 or yorkshiredales@nationaltrust.org.uk

Totally immerse yourself in nature's glory in the Yorkshire Dales, North Yorkshire

North East

Puffin-watching on the unspoilt Farne Islands, Northumberland

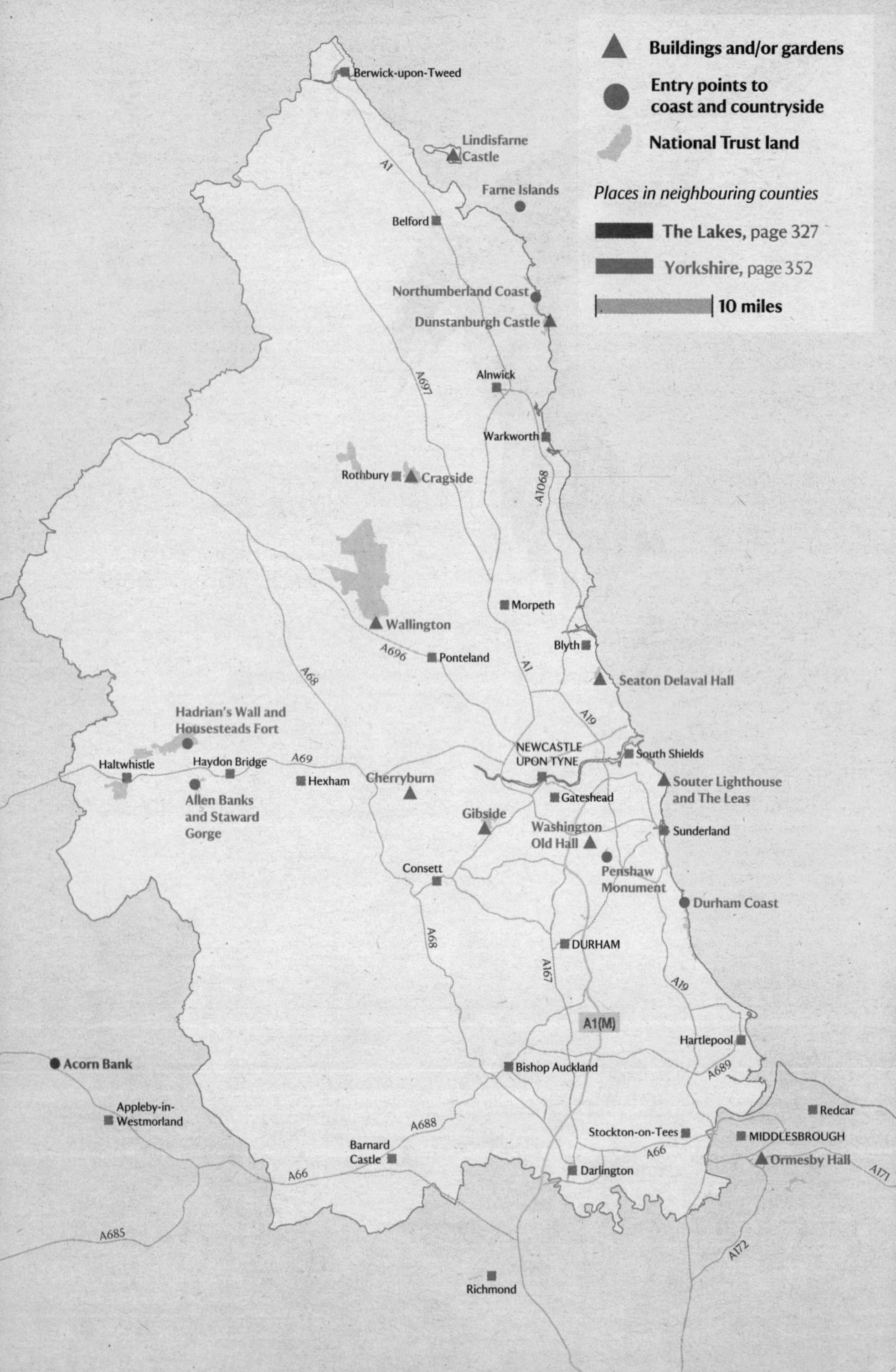

Buildings and/or gardens
Entry points to coast and countryside
National Trust land
Places in neighbouring counties
The Lakes, page 327
Yorkshire, page 352
10 miles
Berwick-upon-Tweed
Lindisfarne Castle
A1
Farne Islands
Belford
Northumberland Coast
Dunstanburgh Castle
A697
Alnwick
Warkworth
A1068
Rothbury
Cragside
Morpeth
Wallington
Blyth
A696
Ponteland
A1
Seaton Delaval Hall
A68
A19
Hadrian's Wall and Housesteads Fort
NEWCASTLE UPON TYNE
South Shields
Haltwhistle
Haydon Bridge
A69
Hexham
Cherryburn
Souter Lighthouse and The Leas
Gateshead
Allen Banks and Staward Gorge
Gibside
Washington Old Hall
Sunderland
Penshaw Monument
Consett
Durham Coast
A68
DURHAM
A167
A19
A1(M)
Hartlepool
Acorn Bank
Bishop Auckland
A689
Appleby-in-Westmorland
Redcar
A688
Stockton-on-Tees
MIDDLESBROUGH
Barnard Castle
A66
Ormesby Hall
A66
Darlington
A171
A685
A172
Richmond

Allen Banks and Staward Gorge

near Ridley Hall, Bardon Mill, Hexham, Northumberland NE47 7BP

1942

Allen Banks and Staward Gorge, Northumberland

With its deep gorge created by the River Allen, this 250-hectare (617-acre) site is the ideal backdrop for an outdoor adventure. It is the largest area of ancient semi-natural woodland in Northumberland, with miles of waymarked walks and paths up to treetop views, and is home to wildlife and fungi. **Note**: site suffered severe storm damage in 2015 – please check for open sections before visiting.

Eat, shop, stay: picnics welcome in the woodland. Picnic benches by the car park. Sorry no refreshments on site; hot and cold drinks, sandwiches and snacks available at nearby Housesteads Fort.

Things to see and do: woodland walks and wildlife to spot, including red squirrels, deer and over 70 species of bird. Medieval pele-tower, man-made ornamental tarn and restored summerhouse in the woodland. **Dogs**: welcome under close control.

Access:
Sat Nav: postcode directs to Ridley Hall – turn left at Ridley Hall gates for Allen Banks car park. **Parking**: at Allen Banks.

Find out more: 01434 321888 or allenbanks@nationaltrust.org.uk

Cherryburn

Station Bank, Mickley, Stocksfield, Northumberland NE43 7DD

1991

Set in a tranquil garden with views across the Tyne Valley, this unassuming Northumbrian farmstead (below) was the birthplace of celebrated artist and naturalist Thomas Bewick. Cherryburn is still surrounded by the natural world that inspired his work. Explore the museum with Bewick's pioneering wood engravings and meet the farm animals.

Eat, shop, stay: books and a selection of Bewick prints from original blocks to buy. Cosy café selling hot and cold drinks, snacks, scones and ice cream. Picnics welcome in the garden.

Things to see and do: **Indoors** Printing demonstrations, temporary art installations and museum. **Outdoors** Cottage garden with deckchairs. Family trail and activities; mini wild-play area. Paddock walk and farmyard with animals (seasonal).
Dogs: welcome on short leads in garden and grounds (animals in farmyard).

Access: **Birthplace** **Café and museum** **Grounds**
Sat Nav: some misdirect, follow brown signs.
Parking: on site.

Find out more: 01661 843276 or cherryburn@nationaltrust.org.uk

Cherryburn		M	T	W	T	F	S	S
16 Feb–5 Apr	11-4	M	T	W	T	F	S	S
6 Apr–29 Sep	11-5	M	T	W	T	F	S	S
30 Sep–3 Nov	11-4	M	T	W	T	F	S	S

Cragside

Rothbury, Morpeth, Northumberland NE65 7PX

1977

Cragside, Northumberland: the façade and interior of the magnificent Arts and Crafts house, above and right, and exploring the rocky grounds, below

Trip the light fantastic to the home where modern living began. Cragside was the first house in the world to be lit by hydroelectricity, making it a wonder of the Victorian age. What started as a modest country retreat for engineer and inventor William Armstrong and his wife Margaret became the most technologically advanced house of its time with every home comfort imaginable, as well as being an Arts and Crafts masterpiece. Outside, Lord and Lady Armstrong were equally ambitious with the garden and grounds, engineering the landscape and experimenting with plants on a massive scale. Rocky crags, tumbling water, open lakes, towering North American conifers and great drifts of rhododendrons create changing scenery. **Note**: challenging terrain and distances outside, stout footwear essential.

Eat, shop, stay: tea-room serving hot meals, sandwiches, handmade treats and cream teas. Kiosks at the house and play area. Shop selling souvenirs, gifts, local food, crafts and plants. Two holiday cottages in the formal garden, plus bunkhouse sleeping up to 16 people.

Things to see and do: **Indoors** Armstrong's Victorian home packed full of ingenious gadgets and a large collection of British art and furniture. Exhibitions, Victorian baking demonstrations, behind-the-scenes events and family activities throughout the year. **Outdoors** Rugged landscape with colourful rhododendron displays, trickling burns and huge rock garden, along with engineering features, including an Archimedes' Screw, Iron Bridge and Power House. Six-mile carriage drive through woodland and numerous footpaths, with walks for all abilities. Intimate formal garden with seasonal planting and views across Northumberland. Family highlights include a labyrinth, adventure play area, den-building, barefoot walk and Young Engineers' Zone. Free shuttle bus between main features. **Dogs**: welcome outdoors on leads.

Access:
House **Visitor centre** **Estate**
Sat Nav: may try and bring you through exit. Please follow brown signs to main entrance. **Parking**: nine car parks on estate.

Find out more: 01669 620333 or cragside@nationaltrust.org.uk

Cragside		M	T	W	T	F	S	S
Gardens and woodland								
1 Jan–15 Feb	10-3*	**M**	**T**	**W**	**T**	**F**	**S**	**S**
16 Feb–3 Nov	10-5*	**M**	**T**	**W**	**T**	**F**	**S**	**S**
4 Nov–31 Dec†	10-3*	**M**	**T**	**W**	**T**	**F**	**S**	**S**
House								
5 Jan–17 Feb	11-3**	·	·	·	·	·	**S**	**S**
18 Feb–3 Nov	11-5**	**M**	**T**	**W**	**T**	**F**	**S**	**S**
9 Nov–29 Dec	11-3**	·	·	·	·	·	**S**	**S**

*Last admission at gate one hour before closing. Carriage Drive closes at 5:30, or sunset if earlier. **House: last entry one hour before closing; there may be queues at busy times. †Everything closed 24 and 25 December.

 For other ways to get involved go to nationaltrust.org.uk/volunteer

Dunstanburgh Castle

Craster, Alnwick, Northumberland NE66 3TT
1961

This castle ruin occupies a dramatic position on the Northumberland coastline, a mile from Craster and towering over Embleton Bay. **Note**: managed by English Heritage. National Trust members admitted free. Sorry no toilets – closest at Craster car park. Parking at Craster pay-and-display car park, not National Trust (charge including members). Call English Heritage on 01665 576231 or visit english-heritage.org.uk for opening times. Closed 1 January and 24 to 26 December.

Find out more: 01665 576231 or dunstanburghcastle@nationaltrust.org.uk

Durham Coast

between Seaham and Horden, County Durham

1987

Rocky headlands, sheltered bays, rare magnesian limestone grasslands and wildlife-rich wooded valleys characterise this coastline, part of Durham's Heritage Coast. The 'black beaches' of the coal-mining days have been cleaned up; clifftop paths look over a revitalised coastal landscape you can now explore. **Note**: nearest toilets at Seaham.

Eat, shop, stay: shops and cafés at Seaham, Easington Colliery and Horden (none National Trust).

Things to see and do: guided walks, rock-pooling and wildlife events. The Durham Coast Half Marathon has become a popular annual sporting event. **Dogs**: welcome, including at most events. Must be on leads around livestock.

Sat Nav: use SR7 7PS for Nose's Point car park (not National Trust) near Seaham. **Parking**: Nose's Point near Seaham, Easington Colliery and Horden (none National Trust).

Find out more: 01723 870423 or durhamcoast@nationaltrust.org.uk

Farne Islands

Northumberland

1925

Get really close to nature. An exhilarating boat trip takes you into the world of 23 seabird species during nesting season and offers unrivalled close-ups of thousands of puffins, Arctic terns and guillemots (May to July). Each autumn, more than 2,000 grey seal pups are born on the islands. **Note**: Inner Farne island: basic toilets; easy-access boardwalk. Staple island: sorry no toilets; challenging, slippery terrain. Access by boat from Seahouses (not National Trust), charge applies (including members). Please show membership cards at harbour trailer (no facility to check membership validity).

Eat, shop, stay: shop in Seahouses selling a wide range of items, including local produce and puffin products. Small shop in Inner Farne Visitor Centre selling some souvenirs. You can stay in one of five cottages at nearby Low Newton and Holy Island.

 For information about getting to National Trust places, please see page 3

Things to see and do: wildlife-spotting paradise. Bring a hat – terns will dive-bomb! On Inner Farne: St Cuthbert's Chapel, with vibrant stained glass, Victorian lighthouse and small visitor centre. Lindisfarne Castle and Northumberland coast nearby. **Dogs**: sorry, not allowed (including assistance dogs) due to extremely sensitive nature of resident wildlife.

Access: Inner Farne [access symbol] Staple Island [access symbol]
Sat Nav: use NE68 7RQ.
Parking: in Seahouses, not National Trust (charge including members).

Find out more: 01665 721099 (Seahouses shop). 01289 389244 (Lindisfarne Castle) or farneislands@nationaltrust.org.uk

Farne Islands		M	T	W	T	F	S	S
Inner Farne Island								
30 Mar–30 Apr	10–5	M	T	W	T	F	S	S
1 May–31 Jul	1:15–5:30	M	T	W	T	F	S	S
1 Aug–3 Nov	10–5	M	T	W	T	F	S	S
Staple Island								
1 May–31 Jul	10–1:30	M	T	W	T	F	S	S
Shop								
3 Jan–28 Feb	11–4	·	·	W	T	F	S	S
1 Mar–30 Jun	10–5	M	T	W	T	F	S	S
1 Jul–31 Aug	10–5:30	M	T	W	T	F	S	S
1 Sep–31 Oct	10–5	M	T	W	T	F	S	S
1 Nov–31 Dec*	10–4	M	T	W	T	F	S	S

Landings on Inner Farne and Staple Island only. Landings on both islands are subject to rangers' discretion to ensure visitor safety and bird welfare. *Seahouses shop: closed 25 and 26 December.

Gibside

near Rowlands Gill, Gateshead, Tyne & Wear NE16 6BG

[symbols] 1974

A Georgian garden forged in an industrial past. Gibside is one of the few surviving 18th-century designed landscapes and was created with two things in mind: spectacular views and 'wow' moments. The estate, commissioned by coal baron George Bowes, offers a glimpse into the past and the dramatic story of heiress Mary Eleanor Bowes. Escape the hustle and bustle of modern life within 243 hectares (600 acres) of gardens, woodland and countryside – perfect for wildlife-spotting. There's also an impressive chapel, restored stable block and grand ruin to discover. Explore for longer on Friday and Saturday evenings during summer.

Eat, shop, stay: café. Shop selling garden and outdoor products, plants, books, cards and gifts. Carriage House Coffee Shop and Renwick's second-hand bookshop in stables courtyard. Bunkhouse with group accommodation at stables and glamping at yurt village. Refreshment kiosk at play area (weekends/holidays).

Gibside, Tyne & Wear: plenty of 'wow' moments

Things to see and do: **Indoors** Columned chapel (above) with unique three-tier pulpit. Find out about Gibside's history and wildlife at the stables. **Outdoors** Miles of footpaths. Wildlife-spotting. Guided walks and events. Play areas. **Dogs**: welcome on leads. Assistance dogs only in Strawberry Castle play area.

Access: **Stables** **Chapel** **Garden**
Parking: 382 yards from café and shop (uphill walkway).

Find out more: 01207 541820 or gibside@nationaltrust.org.uk

Gibside		M	T	W	T	F	S	S
Garden, woodlands and café*								
1 Jan–28 Feb	10–4†	M	T	W	T	F	S	S
1 Mar–20 Oct**	10–6†	M	T	W	T	F	S	S
21 Oct–31 Dec	10–4†	M	T	W	T	F	S	S
Chapel								
5 Jan–24 Feb	10–4						S	S
1 Mar–20 Oct	10–5	M	T	W	T	F	S	S
26 Oct–29 Dec	10–4	.	.	.	.	.	S	S

*Garden, woodlands and café: open 9:30 at weekends.
**3 May to 14 September: close 9, Fridays and Saturdays.
†Café: closes one hour earlier. Everything closed 24 and 25 December.

Hadrian's Wall and Housesteads Fort

near Bardon Mill, Hexham, Northumberland NE47 6NN

1930

A UNESCO World Heritage Site, Hadrian's Wall is the Roman Empire's best preserved outpost in northern Europe. Sitting on the Whin Sill escarpment, this epic structure joins together geology and human engineering. The surrounding countryside offers invigorating walks and dramatic landscapes while the fort provides insights into Roman soldiers' lives. **Note**: fort is National Trust-owned, English Heritage-managed and is a half-mile uphill walk from visitor centre. Car park is run by Northumberland National Park Authority, parking charges apply (including members).

Eat, shop, stay: visitor centre offering sandwiches, snacks, ice cream and drinks. Shop selling books, cards, gifts, souvenirs and plants. Picnics welcome. Three holiday cottages, ideal for walkers and stargazers.

Things to see and do: well-preserved fort, and museum (not National Trust) with dressing up and video presentation. Walk along the wall to Milecastle 37 and Sycamore Gap. Play area. Events, including rock climbing and stargazing. **Dogs**: welcome on leads.

Access: **Visitor centre** **Museum**
Sat Nav: can misdirect, please follow brown signs. **Parking**: at Housesteads, Steel Rigg and Cawfields, not National Trust (charge including members).

Find out more: 01434 344525 or housesteads@nationaltrust.org.uk

Hadrian's Wall and Housesteads Fort
Housesteads Fort: open daily, except some days over Christmas; opening hours vary by season (please check before visiting).

Hadrian's Wall and Housesteads Fort in Northumberland: a World Heritage Site

 Support the places you visit: please scan your member card for free parking ticket

Lindisfarne Castle

Holy Island, Berwick-upon-Tweed, Northumberland TD15 2SH

1944

Lindisfarne Castle, one of the UK's most iconic castles, presides over Holy Island, reached by a tidal causeway. Once a Tudor fort, it was converted into a holiday home for *Country Life* editor Edward Hudson by architect Sir Edwin Lutyens in 1903. A year on from a major conservation project, you can experience the castle through a new exhibition. Without furniture, the stripped-back spaces are atmospheric and revealing, and there'll be new things to discover throughout the season. Beyond the castle, you can explore the summer-flowering Gertrude Jekyll walled garden and Victorian lime kilns, and visit the National Trust shop. **Note**: unfurnished rooms. Limited toilet facilities. Island accessed by tidal causeway – check safe crossing times.

Eat, shop, stay: shop in the village with a large range of homeware and gardenware. There are two holiday cottages on the island: Lutyens-designed St Oswald's with castle views (dog-friendly) and Glen House in the village. Refreshments in the village (not National Trust).

Things to see and do: **Indoors** Lutyens' architecture to explore. **Outdoors** Panoramic views from Upper Battery. Castle Point walk. Sheltered walled garden filled with vegetables, herbs and colourful flowers. Farne Islands (boats from Seahouses) nearby.
Dogs: welcome on leads in the grounds. Assistance dogs only in castle.

Access: **Castle** **Lime kilns**
Parking: at main island car park, 1 mile, not National Trust (charge including members). Intermittent locally operated shuttle bus service (not National Trust).

Find out more: 01289 389244 or lindisfarne@nationaltrust.org.uk

Lindisfarne Castle		M	T	W	T	F	S	S
Castle								
13 Feb–3 Nov	10–5*	**M**	**T**	**W**	**T**	**F**	**S**	**S**
Garden								
Open all year		**M**	**T**	**W**	**T**	**F**	**S**	**S**

*Opening times vary due to tides, usually 10 to 3 or 11 to 5 (check before visiting).

Iconic Lindisfarne Castle in Northumberland

Northumberland Coast

Northumberland

1935

From Lindisfarne to Druridge Bay, there are wide open skies and miles of sandy beaches. You'll find pretty fishing villages, castles, delicate dune plants, wildlife and deserted beaches with excellent rock pools. Look out for seals, dolphins, wading shorebirds and nesting terns at Long Nanny Estuary on Beadnell Bay. **Note**: public car parks only (charge including members).

Eat, shop, stay: shops on Holy Island and in Seahouses. Cafés, pubs and shops in nearby towns and villages (none National Trust). Holiday cottages with coastal views: two on Holy Island; three at Low Newton, including in the fisherman's square at Newton-by-the-Sea.

Miles of sandy beaches characterise the Northumberland Coast, above and below

Things to see and do: little tern breeding colony at Long Nanny (June to August), access from High Newton. Events, '50 things' activities, wildlife-spotting. Bird hides at Newton Pool. Farne Islands and Lindisfarne Castle nearby. **Dogs**: welcome, some local restrictions may apply. On leads around/at Long Nanny shorebird site.

Sat Nav: for Low Newton use NE66 3EH; Druridge Bay NE61 5EG; St Aidan's Dunes NE68 7SH. **Parking**: limited at Druridge Bay. Also at Holy Island, Seahouses, Beadnell, Newton-by-the-Sea and Craster, none National Trust (charge including members).

Find out more: 01665 576874 or northumberlandcoast@nationaltrust.org.uk

Penshaw Monument

near Penshaw, Tyne & Wear DH4 7NJ 1939

This Wearside landmark can be seen from miles around, but the temple is worth closer inspection for views and walks. **Note**: sorry no toilets. Walking routes nearby. Tours to the top of the monument on Saturdays, Sundays and Bank Holidays, 6 April to 29 September.

Find out more: 0191 416 6879 or penshaw.monument@nationaltrust.org.uk

Seaton Delaval Hall

The Avenue, Seaton Sluice,
Northumberland NE26 4QR

2009

Dramatic Seaton Delaval Hall was designed by Sir John Vanbrugh (Castle Howard, Blenheim Palace) and home to the flamboyant Delaval family. In an age famous for extremes of behaviour, they were the most notorious of all Georgian partygoers and pranksters. The Central Hall bears the scars of fierce fires, which almost condemned it to ruin 200 years ago. This year we'll be turning the place upside down in true Delaval style when we start a major project. It won't be an ordinary visit; we'll stay open so that you can see the conservation work as it happens.
Note: major restoration project under way, please check the latest information on opening arrangements before you visit.

Eat, shop, stay: small café serving drinks, snacks and sweet treats. Refreshments are also served from the summerhouse in fine weather. Shop in the welcome building selling souvenirs, gifts and plants.

Things to see and do: **Indoors** Discover Vanbrugh's architecture, including stables, Central Hall with fire-damaged interior and original statues. Ongoing conservation work. **Outdoors** Formal gardens, walks and coastal landscape. Events and activities.
Dogs: welcome on leads outdoors.

Access: Hall **Stables** **Grounds**
Parking: 500 yards.

Find out more: 0191 237 9100 or seatondelavalhall@nationaltrust.org.uk

Seaton Delaval Hall		M	T	W	T	F	S	S
16 Feb–3 Nov	10–5*	·	·	·	T	F	S	S
7 Nov–29 Dec**	10–3*	·	·	·	T	F	S	S

*Last admission 45 minutes before closing.
**Closed 26 December. Major restoration project under way (please check latest opening arrangements before visiting).

The Central Hall at Seaton Delaval Hall, Northumberland: come and see conservation in action

Souter Lighthouse and The Leas

Coast Road, Whitburn, Sunderland, Tyne & Wear SR6 7NH

1990

Souter Lighthouse and The Leas, Tyne & Wear: vivid red hoops, above, and rock-pool fun, right

Climb the 76 steps to the top of the first lighthouse in the world designed and built to be lit by electricity and look out over the bracing North Sea. The Engine Room and Keeper's Cottage give a flavour of life in a working lighthouse. To the north stretches The Leas, dotted with wildflower meadows containing bee orchids, yellow rattle and red clover. To the south is Whitburn Coastal Park, cared for by our rangers and great for wildlife: its nature reserve provides water and rest for birds making their way across the sea and along the coast. **Note**: Whitburn Coastal Park owned by South Tyneside Council, leased and managed by the National Trust.

Eat, shop, stay: Lighthouse Café serving light lunches, soup, cakes and refreshments. Local dishes Panackelty and Singin' Hinnies are a must-try. Shop stocking coastal gifts and Souter souvenirs. Picnic area. Extend your visit and stay in the picturesque, clifftop Lighthouse Keeper's cottages.

Things to see and do: events and activities, including seashore safaris, bug-hunting, nature walks, birdwatching, holiday crafts and car-boot sales. Self-led family activity packs available. Play area. Foghorn demonstrations. Wildlife and sensory gardens. **Dogs**: welcome on leads outdoors.

Access:
Building **Grounds**
Parking: on site.

Find out more: 0191 529 3161 or souter@nationaltrust.org.uk

Souter Lighthouse and The Leas		M	T	W	T	F	S	S
Lighthouse								
2 Feb–3 Nov	11–5	**M**	**T**	**W**	**T**	**F**	**S**	**S**
4 Nov–1 Dec	11–4	**M**	**T**	**W**	**T**	**F**	**S**	**S**
Café and shop*								
5 Jan–27 Jan	10–4	·	·	·	·	·	**S**	**S**
2 Feb–3 Nov	10–5**	**M**	**T**	**W**	**T**	**F**	**S**	**S**
4 Nov–1 Dec	10–4	**M**	**T**	**W**	**T**	**F**	**S**	**S**
7 Dec–22 Dec	10–4	·	·	·	·	·	**S**	**S**

*Shop: opens 11. **Café: closes 6, July and August.

Wallington

Cambo, near Morpeth,
Northumberland NE61 4AR

1941

Wallington is a 5,260-hectare (13,000-acre) working estate gifted to you by Sir Charles Philips Trevelyan, socialist MP and 'illogical Englishman'. The woodland gardens are full of wildlife and ancient trees; you can visit the hide to spot red squirrels or take the river walk where you may see otters or crayfish. There are lots of walks, or you can explore the estate using the family-friendly cycle trail. The three outdoor play spaces capture the spirit of the adventurous Trevelyan children. Throughout the year the walled garden and Edwardian conservatory are bursting with colour. The Trevelyans' informal home is full of treasured collections and curiosities: make yourself at home and find out about this unconventional family.

Eat, shop, stay: Clocktower Café offers hot and cold refreshments throughout the day. The seasonal kiosks in the courtyard, walled garden and West Wood serve drinks and snacks. Wide range of gifts for sale in the shops and plant centre. Bunkhouse accommodation available.

Things to see and do: **Indoors** Soak up the atmosphere in the Trevelyans' home and admire the pre-Raphaelite paintings around the Central Hall, showing the history of Northumberland. Regular activities, including conservation in action, cookery demonstrations, family activities in the indoor play space and Christmas events in December.

Wallington, Northumberland: the stone dragon heads, above, and Owl House and Edwardian conservatory, below

Outdoors Enjoy heady fragrances in the Edwardian conservatory in the walled garden. Seasonal displays of snowdrops and crocuses. Choose from one of the many walks; there are miles and miles of footpaths and trails to explore. Family-friendly Dragon Cycle Trail, wildlife hide, adventure playground, play train and fort. Regular guided walks and family activities during school holidays. **Dogs**: welcome on leads outdoors and on all walks.

Access:
House
Garden and grounds
Parking: on site.

Find out more: 01670 773600 or wallington@nationaltrust.org.uk

Wallington		M	T	W	T	F	S	S
Walled garden, woodland and estate*								
Open all year	10-dusk	M	T	W	T	F	S	S
House								
16 Feb-27 Oct	12-5	M	T	W	T	F	S	S
28 Oct-3 Nov	12-4	M	T	W	T	F	S	S
23 Nov-22 Dec	10-7:30**	·	·	·	·	F	S	S
Shops and café								
1 Jan-15 Feb	10:30-4:30	M	T	W	T	F	S	S
16 Feb-27 Oct	10:30-5:30	M	T	W	T	F	S	S
28 Oct-31 Dec†	10:30-4:30††	M	T	W	T	F	S	S

*Walled garden: closes 7 in summer; 4 in winter.
**House: opens 4:30 on Fridays and closes 4 on Sundays.
†Shops and café: closed 24 to 26 December. ††Shops and café: 23 November to 22 December, close at 7:30 on Fridays and Saturdays. Café: last orders 30 minutes before closing.

The Dragon Cycle Trail at Wallington, left, and exploring the intricate knot garden, right, at Washington Old Hall, Tyne & Wear

Washington Old Hall

The Avenue, Washington Village, Washington, Tyne & Wear NE38 7LE

1956

A little gem with a big story. This is the original medieval home of George Washington's ancestors: without Washington Old Hall the capital of the US wouldn't have that name. The small manor house overlooks tranquil gardens and a 'nuttery' – a haven for nature and wildlife (and humans wanting quiet).

Eat, shop, stay: café serving a selection of soups, cakes, homemade scones, and hot and cold drinks. Small seating areas indoors and outside. Small shop selling books, children's toys, confectionery, jams, local beers and ciders.

Things to see and do: **Indoors** 17th-century hall, tenement rooms and new exhibition about chef Robert May's 1664 cookbook. Christmas events including the Green Man. **Outdoors** Bird hide, mini play area, Fourth of July ceremony. **Dogs**: welcome on leads in garden only.

Access:
Building **Grounds**
Parking: on site (additional unrestricted parking on The Avenue).

Find out more: 0191 416 6879 or washingtonoldhall@nationaltrust.org.uk

Washington Old Hall		M	T	W	T	F	S	S
Hall and gardens								
9 Feb-31 Mar	10-4	M	T	W	T	F	S	S
1 Apr-20 Oct	10-5	M	T	W	T	F	S	S
21 Oct-30 Nov	10-4	M	T	W	T	F	S	S
1 Dec-23 Dec	12-6	M	T	W	T	F	S	S
Café								
9 Feb-30 Nov	10-4	M	T	W	T	F	S	S
1 Dec-23 Dec	12-6	M	T	W	T	F	S	S

Cymru Wales

Blue skies and crisp snow at the popular
Brecon Beacons in Powys

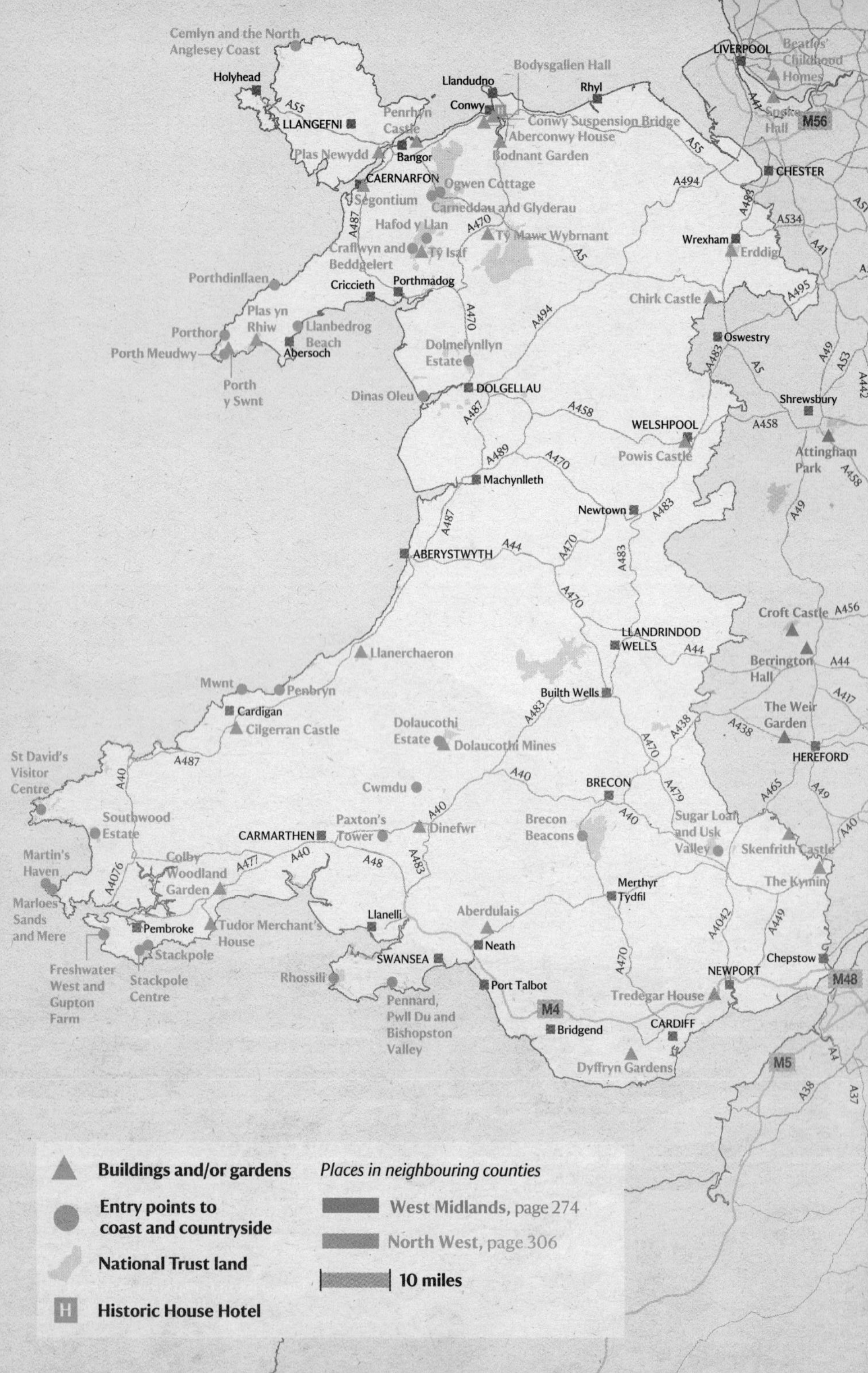

Cemlyn and the North Anglesey Coast
Holyhead
A55
LLANGEFNI
Penrhyn Castle
Llandudno
Bodysgallen Hall
Conwy
Conwy Suspension Bridge
Aberconwy House
Bodnant Garden
Rhyl
LIVERPOOL
Beatles' Childhood Homes
Speke Hall
M56
A41
A55
CHESTER
Plas Newydd
Bangor
CAERNARFON
Segontium
Ogwen Cottage
Carneddau and Glyderau
A487
Hafod y Llan
A470
Tŷ Mawr Wybrnant
Craflwyn and Beddgelert
Tŷ Isaf
A5
A494
A483
A51
A534
Wrexham
Erddig
A41
Porthdinllaen
Criccieth
Porthmadog
Plas yn Rhiw
Llanbedrog Beach
Porthor
Porth Meudwy
Abersoch
Porth y Swnt
A470
A494
Chirk Castle
A495
Oswestry
A483
A5
A49
A53
A442
Dolmelynllyn Estate
Dinas Oleu
DOLGELLAU
A487
A458
Shrewsbury
A458
WELSHPOOL
Attingham Park
Powis Castle
A489
A470
A458
Machynlleth
Newtown
A483
A49
A487
ABERYSTWYTH
A44
A470
A483
A470
Croft Castle
A456
LLANDRINDOD WELLS
A44
Llanerchaeron
Berrington Hall
A44
Mwnt
Penbryn
Builth Wells
A417
Cardigan
Cilgerran Castle
The Weir Garden
A483
Dolaucothi Estate
Dolaucothi Mines
A438
A438
A470
HEREFORD
St David's Visitor Centre
A40
A487
A40
BRECON
A479
A465
A49
Cwmdu
Southwood Estate
A40
Paxton's Tower
Dinefwr
CARMARTHEN
A40
Brecon Beacons
Sugar Loaf and Usk Valley
Skenfrith Castle
A40
Martin's Haven
Colby Woodland Garden
A477
A40
A48
A483
A4076
The Kymin
Marloes Sands and Mere
Merthyr Tydfil
Aberdulais
Tudor Merchant's House
Pembroke
Llanelli
A4042
A449
Stackpole
Neath
Freshwater West and Gupton Farm
Stackpole Centre
SWANSEA
A470
Chepstow
Rhossili
NEWPORT
Port Talbot
M48
Pennard, Pwll Du and Bishopston Valley
Tredegar House
M4
Bridgend
CARDIFF
Dyffryn Gardens
M5
A4
A38
A37
Buildings and/or gardens
Entry points to coast and countryside
National Trust land
Historic House Hotel
Places in neighbouring counties
West Midlands, page 274
North West, page 306
10 miles

Aberconwy House

Castle Street, Conwy LL32 8AY

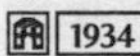 1934

This is the only medieval merchant's house in Conwy to have survived the turbulent history of the walled town over seven centuries. Furnished rooms and helpful volunteers bring different periods in its history alive. **Note**: nearest toilets 50 yards. Steps to all parts of property.

Eat, shop, stay: gift shop.

Things to see and do: Easter events.
Dogs: assistance dogs only.

Access: Building
Parking: none on site.

Mae'r wybodaeth sydd yn y llawlyfr hwn am feddiannau'r Ymddiriedolaeth Genedlaethol yng Nghymru ar gael yn Gymraeg o Swyddfa'r Ymddiriedolaeth Genedlaethol, Tŷ Tredegar, Casnewydd, NP10 8YW, neu drwy e-bostio wa.customerenquiries@nationaltrust.org.uk Am fwy o fanylion ewch i nationaltrust.org.uk/handbook-welsh

Find out more: 01492 592246 or aberconwyhouse@nationaltrust.org.uk

Aberconwy House		M	T	W	T	F	S	S
House								
7 Mar–3 Nov	10–5	**M**	**T**	**W**	**T**	**F**	**S**	**S**
9 Nov–22 Dec	11–4	·	·	·	·	·	**S**	**S**
Shop								
2 Jan–28 Feb	10–5	·	**T**	**W**	**T**	**F**	**S**	**S**
1 Mar–31 Dec	10–5	**M**	**T**	**W**	**T**	**F**	**S**	**S**

Shop: closed 25 and 26 December plus 1 January 2020.

Aberconwy House in Conwy: turbulent history

Aberdulais

Aberdulais, Neath, Neath Port Talbot SA10 8EU

1980

Archaeology has uncovered the secrets of industries in days gone by at Aberdulais – one of Britain's oldest tin works. When you wander through the site, you'll find yourself at the very heart of the earliest industry in Britain. You'll discover how Aberdulais played its part in shaping the world as we know it today. Water was the power behind all of the industries at Aberdulais; take in the sound of the waterfall, see the majestic waterwheel turning, while the turbine is busy converting this energy into electricity to power the site. **Note**: waterwheel and turbine subject to water levels and conservation work.

Eat, shop, stay: Old Schoolhouse tea-room serving light lunches, soup, cakes and refreshments. Gift shop, plants and second-hand bookshop.

Things to see and do: programme of activities throughout the year, including exhibitions, talks and tours as well as seasonal events such as Easter and Victorian Christmas. **Dogs**: welcome on leads and inside buildings. Assistance dogs only in the Schoolhouse tea-room.

Access: Grounds Stable and Tin Exhibition Turbine House
Sat Nav: follow brown signs. **Parking**: 50 yards.

Find out more: 01639 636674 or aberdulais@nationaltrust.org.uk

Aberdulais		M	T	W	T	F	S	S
5 Jan–10 Feb	10:30–3	·	·	·	·	·	S	S
16 Feb–3 Mar	10:30–4	M	T	W	T	F	S	S
4 Mar–12 Apr	10:30–3	M	T	W	T	F	S	S
13 Apr–28 Apr	10–5	M	T	W	T	F	S	S
29 Apr–24 May	10:30–4	M	T	W	T	F	S	S
25 May–2 Jun	10–5	M	T	W	T	F	S	S
3 Jun–21 Jul	10:30–4	M	T	W	T	F	S	S
22 Jul–1 Sep	10–5	M	T	W	T	F	S	S
2 Sep–25 Oct	10:30–3	M	T	W	T	F	S	S
26 Oct–3 Nov	10:30–4	M	T	W	T	F	S	S
8 Nov–22 Dec	11–3	·	·	·	·	F	S	S

Tea-room: opening times vary (call for details).

Discover how Aberdulais in Neath Port Talbot, above and below, shaped today's world

Bodnant Garden

Tal-y-Cafn, near Colwyn Bay, Conwy LL28 5RE

1949

A Grade I listed garden in Snowdonia's foothills, home to historic plant collections, with breathtaking mountain views. The garden was established in 1874 by Victorian entrepreneur Henry Pochin, and five generations of the family have transformed the Conwy Valley hillside with rare trees and shrubs from around the world. Since 1949 the 32-hectare (80-acre) garden has been nurtured in collaboration with the National Trust. Enjoy formal Italianate terraces with roses, herbaceous beds and parterres, as well as informal shrub borders, woods and meadows, and riverside dells with waterfalls and towering conifers. Every season brings new delights – magnolias and rhododendrons in spring, roses and water lilies in summer, followed by rich leaf colour in autumn and frosted winter landscapes.

Bodnant Garden, Conwy: sitting in the foothills of Snowdonia, the views are simply breathtaking

Two views of Bodnant Garden. There are new delights to enjoy every season

Eat, shop, stay: two tea-rooms, as well as two open-air refreshment kiosks. Picnic areas. Shop. Neighbouring garden centre and craft units (not National Trust).

Things to see and do: events all year, including guided walks with a gardener, family trails and holiday activities for families. **Dogs**: welcome daily October to end March; also Wednesday evenings, April to end September.

Access: Grounds
Parking: 150 yards. Electric vehicle charging point opposite café.

Find out more: 01492 650460 or bodnantgarden@nationaltrust.org.uk

Bodnant Garden		M	T	W	T	F	S	S
1 Jan–28 Feb	10–4	**M**	**T**	**W**	**T**	**F**	**S**	**S**
1 Mar–30 Apr*	10–5	**M**	**T**	**W**	**T**	**F**	**S**	**S**
1 May–30 Jun*	9–5	**M**	**T**	**W**	**T**	**F**	**S**	**S**
1 Jul–31 Oct*	10–5	**M**	**T**	**W**	**T**	**F**	**S**	**S**
1 Nov–31 Dec**	10–4	**M**	**T**	**W**	**T**	**F**	**S**	**S**

Pavilion tea-room: open from 9 daily. *Garden: open to 8 on Wednesdays, April to end September. **Garden and tea-room: closed 24 to 26 December.

Bodysgallen Hall Hotel, Restaurant and Spa

The Royal Welsh Way, Llandudno, Conwy LL30 1RS

2008

This Grade I listed 17th-century house, set within 89 hectares (220 acres) of parkland, has the most spectacular views towards Conwy Castle and Snowdonia. The romantic gardens, which have won awards for their restoration, include a rare parterre filled with sweet-smelling herbs, as well as several follies, a cascade, walled garden and formal rose gardens. Beyond, the hotel's parkland offers miles of stunning walks and views to the coastline. **Note**: access is for paying guests of the hotel, including for luncheon, afternoon tea and dinner, and the spa. Children over the age of six welcome.

Find out more: 01492 584466.
01492 582519 (fax) or info@bodysgallen.com
bodysgallen.com

Brecon Beacons

Powys

1947

The Brecon Beacons have captivated visitors for hundreds of years with their soaring peaks, including southern Britain's highest mountain Pen y Fan. From the popular mountaintops to the tranquil valleys, lush farmland to ancient woodland, they are perfect for hill-walking and exploring. Not forgetting South Wales's highest waterfall, Henrhyd Falls, which plunges 90 feet into the wooded Graig Llech Gorge, a haven for rare mosses and ferns. In contrast, you can discover the vast remote moorlands of Abergwesyn Commons in the heart of Wales or ramble over the Begwns with panoramic views of the Brecon Beacons. **Note**: disruption possible at Pont ar Daf due to redevelopment of car park.

Things to see and do: **Indoors** Dan y Gyrn bunkhouse in the Tarell Valley near Pen y Fan.

Loved by walkers, below, the soaring peaks of the Brecon Beacons, Powys, are captivating

Outdoors Why not visit nearby Aberdulais to explore the tin works and waterfall? **Dogs**: welcome on leads.

Sat Nav: use LD3 8NL. **Parking**: main car park at Pont ar Daf, off A470; alternatives not all National Trust.

Find out more: 01874 625515 or brecon@nationaltrust.org.uk

Carneddau and Glyderau

Nant Ffrancon, Bethesda, Gwynedd

1951

This 8,498-hectare (21,000-acre) mountainous area includes Cwm Idwal National Nature Reserve, renowned for its geology and Arctic-Alpine plants, such as the rare Snowdon lily. There are nine tenanted upland farms here and nine peaks over 3,000 feet, including the famous Tryfan, where Edmund Hilary trained for his ascent of Everest. The area is home to a variety of wildlife, including otters, feral ponies and rare birds, such as ring ouzel and twite. The 60 miles of footpaths attract more than 500,000 walkers each year, while the bleak, photogenic landscapes have proved popular with artists. **Note**: mountainous and difficult terrain – please come well equipped and check the weather. Charges apply in the National Park car parks.

Eat, shop, stay: food kiosk on site (not National Trust). Ranger base, as well as a warden centre run in partnership with Snowdonia National Park and Natural Resources Wales. There are two holiday cottages in Dyffryn Mymbyr and one near Llyn Ogwen.

Things to see and do: you can walk to Cwm Idwal and enjoy dramatic mountain views, following in the footsteps of Charles Darwin (who 'discovered' glaciation here). Visit Ogwen ranger base for more information. **Dogs**: on a lead at all times.

Sat Nav: use LL57 3LZ. **Parking**: at Ogwen Lake (not National Trust).

Find out more: 01248 605739 or carneddau@nationaltrust.org.uk

Carneddau and Glyderau in Gwynedd: home to wild ponies, left, and perfect for hiking

Cemlyn and the North Anglesey Coast

Cemaes Bay, Anglesey

1971

Part of Anglesey's Area of Outstanding Natural Beauty, the north-west coast has a ruggedly beautiful coastline of rocks, small bays and headlands and is a delight for walkers. Cemlyn is a North Wales Wildlife Trust Nature Reserve and a Site of Special Scientific Interest. Renowned for its breeding colony of Sandwich, common and Arctic terns, Cemlyn Bay is a hive of seabird activity in spring and summer. Headland paths offer dramatic land and seascapes during autumn and winter. The brackish lagoon is separated from the sea by a remarkable shingle ridge. **Note**: nearest toilets in Cemaes Bay, 3 miles (not National Trust).

Things to see and do: numerous footpaths and downloadable walks to help you explore. Events, including pram walks and walking festival. Summer fair at Swtan, a restored whitewashed cottage nearby (LL65 4EU). **Dogs**: welcome under control near livestock.

Sat Nav: use LL67 0DY.
Parking: at Bryn Aber car park, Cemlyn.

Find out more: 01248 714795 or cemlyn@nationaltrust.org.uk

Cemlyn and the North Anglesey Coast, Anglesey: a shingle ridge separates the sea from a lagoon

Chirk Castle

Chirk, Wrexham LL14 5AF

1981

Completed by Marcher Lord Roger Mortimer in 1310, Chirk is the last Welsh castle from the reign of Edward I still inhabited today. You can explore medieval towers and dungeons, visit the 17th- and 18th-century rooms of the Myddelton family home, including the historic laundry, and discover the story of influential 20th-century tenant and polymath Lord Howard de Walden. The prized gardens contain clipped yews, herbaceous borders and rock gardens. A terrace gives stunning views over the Cheshire and Shropshire plains, while the large estate, divided by King Offa's Dyke, provides habitat for rare invertebrates, wild flowers and veteran trees.

Eat, shop, stay: café serving hot and cold food, drinks and cakes. Seasonal kiosk at Home Farm selling hot and cold drinks and snacks. Gift shops in Home Farm and courtyard, with plant sales and second-hand books. Two holiday cottages on the estate.

Things to see and do: **Indoors** Medieval fortress and dungeon, Myddelton family home, Servants' Hall and Victorian laundry to explore. **Outdoors** There are the formal gardens and a 194-hectare (480-acre) estate to discover.
Dogs: welcome on leads. Assistance dogs only in formal gardens and Pleasure Ground wood.

Chirk Castle, Wrexham: from gardens to dungeons, there is something for everyone

Access:
State rooms **Adam's Tower**
Gardens
Parking: at Home Farm by ticket office, 200 yards (steep hill) to castle. Two electric vehicle charging points at Home Farm.

Find out more: 01691 777701 or chirkcastle@nationaltrust.org.uk

Chirk Castle		M	T	W	T	F	S	S
Estate								
Open all year	7-7	M	T	W	T	F	S	S
Garden, Adam's Tower, shop and café								
2 Feb-3 Nov	10-4*	M	T	W	T	F	S	S
9 Nov-24 Nov	10-4	·	·	·	·	·	S	S
30 Nov-22 Dec	10-4	M	T	W	T	F	S	S
State rooms								
2 Feb-8 Mar**	11-4	M	T	W	T	F	S	S
9 Mar-3 Nov†	12-4*	M	T	W	T	F	S	S
9 Nov-24 Nov††	11-4	·	·	·	·	·	S	S
30 Nov-22 Dec	11-4	M	T	W	T	F	S	S

*Open until 5, April to September. **East wing only. Timed tickets available on the day (places limited). †Guided tours: 11:15 and 11:30 (places limited). ††Guided access only, timed tickets available on day (places limited).

Cilgerran Castle

near Cardigan, Pembrokeshire SA43 2SF 1938

13th-century castle overlooking the Teifi Gorge – the perfect location to repel attackers. Walk the walls and admire the stunning views. **Note**: in the guardianship of Cadw – Welsh Government's historic environment service. Dogs welcome on leads. Open daily, 2 January to 31 March, 10 to 4; 1 April to 31 October, 10 to 5; 1 November to 31 December, 10 to 4 (closed 24 to 26 December).

Find out more: 01239 621339 or cilgerrancastle@nationaltrust.org.uk

Colby Woodland Garden

near Amroth, Pembrokeshire SA67 8PP

1980

Colby Woodland Garden, Pembrokeshire

A short walk from the beach, this hidden wooded valley, with its secret garden and industrial past, is a place for play. There are fallen trees to climb, rope swings and playful surprises everywhere. Spring brings bluebells, camellias, rhododendrons and azaleas, while the walled garden gives year-round colour, peace and seclusion. There are woodland walks,

Colby Woodland Garden: year-round interest

meandering streams and ponds with stepping stones and log bridges in the wildflower meadow, and the whole valley teems with wildlife. Fun learning activities and exploration packs are available, and there are picnic and campfire spots in the meadow and free games to borrow. **Note**: sorry, house not open.

Eat, shop, stay: shop, plant sales and second-hand books. Bothy tea-room (concession). Picnics welcome. Three holiday cottages nearby.

Things to see and do: have fun with rope swings, pond-dipping and natural play. Children's exploration packs and games equipment available from the shop. Seasonal activities include Easter trails, wildlife walks and holiday events. **Dogs**: welcome on leads in woodland garden and meadow.

Access:
Grounds
Parking: 50 yards.

Find out more: 01834 811885 or colby@nationaltrust.org.uk

Colby Woodland Garden		M	T	W	T	F	S	S
Woodland and walled gardens*								
7 Jan–15 Feb	10-3	M	T	W	T	F	S	S
16 Feb–3 Nov	10-5	M	T	W	T	F	S	S
4 Nov–23 Dec	10-3	M	T	W	T	F	S	S
Shop								
16 Feb–3 Nov	10-5	M	T	W	T	F	S	S
Tea-room								
6 Apr–3 Nov	10-4:30	M	T	W	T	F	S	S

*Car park and bothy exhibition open as woodland and walled gardens. Closed 24 to 31 December.

Conwy Suspension Bridge

Conwy LL32 8LD

1965

Graceful Conwy Suspension Bridge, Conwy

Designed in the 1820s by Thomas Telford, this graceful bridge with its beautifully restored tiny toll-keeper's house has stunning views over the Conwy Estuary. Kept open by a husband and wife at a time when trade and travel brought Conwy to life, it never closed, whatever the weather. **Note**: sorry no toilet.

Eat, shop, stay: why not bring a picnic to enjoy on the grassed area?

Things to see and do: superb views of the river and castle. '50 things' activities for families and games. **Dogs**: allowed.

Access: **Building** **Grounds**
Parking: none on site.

Find out more: 01492 573282 or conwybridge@nationaltrust.org.uk

Conwy Suspension Bridge
Suspension bridge open from 7 March to 3 November. Toll House opening times available at Aberconwy House (01492 592246).

Craflwyn and Beddgelert

near Beddgelert, Gwynedd

1994

The 81-hectare (200-acre) Craflwyn Estate is set in the heart of beautiful Snowdonia, within a landscape steeped in history and legend. There's a network of paths and woodland walks to explore and tumbling waterfalls to discover. At Craflwyn you can learn about the Princes of Gwynedd, before venturing up to nearby Dinas Emrys, legendary birthplace of the red dragon of Wales. Within a couple of miles of Craflwyn, there are great walks for all abilities – from a village stroll at pretty Beddgelert to the rugged Fisherman's Path down the spectacular Aberglaslyn Pass. **Note**: Craflwyn Hall is run and managed by HF Holidays (surrounding land open to the public).

Tumbling waterfalls and rushing torrents characterise Craflwyn and Beddgelert, Gwynedd

Eat, shop, stay: picnics welcome at Craflwyn. Local crafts on offer in Tŷ Isaf shop in Beddgelert. The village also has a selection of restaurants, cafés, taverns and hotels (not National Trust). Holiday cottage, chalet and campsite at Hafod y Llan.

Things to see and do: you can learn about Prince Llywelyn's legendary faithful hound by visiting Gelert's Grave. Children's adventure packs, maps and guides available from Tŷ Isaf shop in the centre of the village. **Dogs**: welcome, but on a lead near livestock.

Sat Nav: use LL55 4NG. **Parking**: in Craflwyn.

Find out more: 01766 510120 or craflwyn@nationaltrust.org.uk

Cwmdu

Llandeilo, Carmarthenshire 1991

Georgian terrace with pub, post office, chapel and vestry. Representing a rural Welsh village of the past. **Note**: pub and shop run by community. For Sat Nav use SA19 7DY. Inn open Wednesday to Saturday, 2 January to 28 December, 7 to 11. Shop and post office open Tuesday to Saturday, 2 January to 28 December, 9:30 to 1:30 (close 12:30 on Saturdays). Restaurant open selected Saturdays.

Find out more: 01558 685088 or cwmdu@nationaltrust.org.uk

Dinas Oleu

near Barmouth, Gwynedd 1895

Our beginnings are rooted on this gorse-clad hill, the first place to be donated in 1895 by Mrs Fanny Talbot. **Note**: some steep rocky terrain and steps to reach the top. Nearest parking in town, not National Trust (charge including members).

Find out more: 01341 440238 or dinasoleu@nationaltrust.org.uk

Dinefwr

Llandeilo, Carmarthenshire SA19 6RT

1990

A place of legends and folklore, Dinefwr's long history has featured power, glory, downfall and loss. There is even a direct link with the past through our iconic White Park cattle, which have been kept here for 1,000 years. Walks lead through ancient woods, with gnarled veteran trees, and you can seek the inhabitants of the Bogwood and Mill Pond and walk in the footsteps of medieval princes – viewing 'your kingdom' from the castle on the hill. After exploring the tranquil countryside, you can continue your adventure in atmospheric Newton House, discovering the many changes the years have wrought. **Note**: Dinefwr Castle is owned by the Wildlife Trust and is in the guardianship of Cadw.

The long history of Dinefwr, Carmarthenshire, above, features a heady mix of power, glory, downfall and loss. With legends and folklore thrown in for good measure

Eat, shop, stay: Billiard Tea-room (fully licensed). Castle Walk Café serving simple fare to parkland walkers (dogs welcome). Inner courtyard with a gift shop and plant sales. Pre-loved bookshop. Holiday cottages.

Things to see and do: **Indoors** Daily 'hidden house' tours. **Outdoors** Seasonal tours of parkland National Nature Reserve. Tractor trailer tours of estate and White Park cattle (Bank Holidays). School holiday and family activities. **Dogs**: welcome in outer park only. Please keep on leads (cattle/sheep grazing).

Access: **Castle** **Newton House** **Parkland**
Sat Nav: enter Dinefwr. **Parking**: 50 yards. Electric vehicle charging point at Home Farm on 'The Granary'.

Find out more: 01558 824512 or dinefwr@nationaltrust.org.uk

Dinefwr		M	T	W	T	F	S	S
1 Feb–30 Mar	11–3	M	T	W	T	F	S	S
31 Mar–3 Nov	10–5	M	T	W	T	F	S	S
4 Nov–31 Dec*	11–3	M	T	W	T	F	S	S

Newton House: closed 7 to 31 January for housekeeping and conservation (grounds remain open 10 to 3). Grounds: open all year 10 to 4 and 10 to 5 during the summer. *Everything closed 24 and 25 December.

Dolaucothi Estate Woodland

near Pumsaint, Llanwrda, Carmarthenshire 1944

Hours of woodland walks and multi-user trail with route information signage at the Gold Mines and Pumsaint village car parks. **Note**: for Sat Nav use SA19 8US.

Find out more: 01558 650809 or dolaucothi@nationaltrust.org.uk

Dolaucothi Gold Mines

Pumsaint, Llanwrda, Carmarthenshire SA19 8US

1941

Not your average National Trust visit, this hidden gem reveals the story of the quest for gold more than 2,000 years ago. Try your luck by panning for gold, and anything you find you keep. Or you can venture on an overground tour of the Roman archaeology, go underground to experience the harsh conditions of Victorian times and listen to what 1930s miners had to say in their very own words about their final efforts to search for gold. Why not join us for the ultimate adventure and discover centuries of stories in just one day? **Note**: steep slopes, stout footwear essential. Minimum height 1 metre, no carried children on underground tours.

Eat, shop, stay: enjoy a miner's lunch from our tea-room or treat yourself to a meal at the Dolaucothi Arms. Splash out on real Welsh gold jewellery from our gift shop. Sleep under dark skies, enjoy peace and tranquillity at our caravan site.

Things to see and do: guided tours throughout the day. Self-guided audio of the Roman workings. Gold panning. 1930s machinery display sheds. Network of footpaths across the 1,012-hectare (2,500-acre) estate. **Dogs**: welcome on leads, although not on guided tours.

Access: Tea-rooms **Machinery sheds** **Mine yard**
Parking: on site; overflow car park opposite main entrance.

Find out more: 01558 650809 (mines). 01558 650365 (caravan site) or dolaucothi@nationaltrust.org.uk

Dolaucothi Gold Mines		M	T	W	T	F	S	S
15 Mar–19 Jul	10:30–5	M	T	W	T	F	S	S
20 Jul–31 Aug	10–6	M	T	W	T	F	S	S
1 Sep–3 Nov	10:30–5	M	T	W	T	F	S	S

Shop: opens 10:30. Caravan site: open daily, dawn to dusk, 15 March to 3 November. Last tour leaves 90 minutes before closing.

Dolaucothi Gold Mines in Carmarthenshire: not your average National Trust visit

Dolmelynllyn Estate

Ganllwyd, Near Dolgellau, Gwynedd

1936

Ruins on the Dolmelynllyn Estate, Gwynedd

A 696-hectare (1,719-acre) estate, including woodland, two tenanted farms and Grade II-listed Dolmelynllyn Hall, with ornamental lake and parkland. There's a network of paths to explore with highlights which include the impressive Rhaeadr Ddu waterfall, ruins of Cefn Coch gold mines and wildlife-rich oak woodlands. **Note**: Dolmelynllyn Hall is a privately run hotel, not a pay-to-enter property.

Eat, shop, stay: four holiday cottages nearby. Two National Trust-owned but tenanted hotels on the estate offering refreshments and light meals. Picnic site.

Things to see and do: also in the area are the remote Cregennan Lakes (12 miles) and Dinas Oleu, at Barmouth, the first parcel of land donated to the National Trust (also 12 miles). **Dogs**: welcome on leads.

Sat Nav: use LL40 2TF. **Parking**: on site.

Find out more: 01341 440238 or dolmelynllyn@nationaltrust.org.uk

Dyffryn Gardens

St Nicholas, Vale of Glamorgan CF5 6SU

2013

A garden for all seasons, Dyffryn is celebrated for its botanical collection and is among the best in Wales. Meandering through the gardens, you will discover intimate garden rooms, formal lawns and an extensive arboretum. The reinstated glasshouse in the kitchen garden houses an impressive collection of rare cacti and orchids. Designed by the eminent landscape architect Thomas Mawson, the gardens are the early 20th-century vision of Reginald Cory. Standing at the heart of Dyffryn is a unique Victorian mansion.

The Grade II* listed Dyffryn House is an ongoing conservation project and has been partly furnished, but with a difference. The house is used as a canvas to interpret the gardens and Cory family history.

Eat, shop, stay: Gardens Café nestled by the Nant Bran stream at reception and The Gallery café within the gardens, connected to Dyffryn House. A large portion of produce comes directly from the kitchen gardens. Shop selling plants and gifts.

Things to see and do: network of garden rooms and champion trees in the arboretum to discover. Family events and wild play area inside arboretum and additional play area next to café. Second-hand bookshop inside the house. Tredegar House nearby. **Dogs**: welcome in gardens on short leads.

Exploring Dyffryn Gardens, Vale of Glamorgan

Access: **House**
Grounds
Parking: on site. Electric vehicle charging point in main car park beside play area.

Find out more: 02920 593328 or dyffryn@nationaltrust.org.uk

Dyffryn Gardens		M	T	W	T	F	S	S
Gardens, shop and café								
1 Jan–10 Feb	10–4	**M**	**T**	**W**	**T**	**F**	**S**	**S**
11 Feb–31 Mar	10–5	**M**	**T**	**W**	**T**	**F**	**S**	**S**
1 Apr–29 Sep	10–6	**M**	**T**	**W**	**T**	**F**	**S**	**S**
30 Sep–20 Oct	10–5	**M**	**T**	**W**	**T**	**F**	**S**	**S**
21 Oct–31 Dec*	10–4	**M**	**T**	**W**	**T**	**F**	**S**	**S**
House								
1 Jan–10 Feb	12–3:30	**M**	**T**	**W**	**T**	**F**	**S**	**S**
11 Feb–20 Oct	12–4	**M**	**T**	**W**	**T**	**F**	**S**	**S**
21 Oct–31 Dec*	12–3:30	**M**	**T**	**W**	**T**	**F**	**S**	**S**

Gardens: last entry one hour before closing. Gardens Café: opens 10 until 30 minutes before closing. Hot food orders 12 to 3:30. *Closed 25 and 26 December.

Erddig

Wrexham LL13 0YT

1973

A haven of natural beauty and modern sanctuary for well-being, Erddig's 485-hectare (1,200-acre) pleasure park, designed by William Emes, welcomes walkers (and their four-legged friends), beginner runners, Nordic walkers and those seeking a natural boost in the great outdoors. At its heart, above the River Clywedog, is Erddig Hall – an unexpected survivor, rescued from dereliction in the 1970s. Discover the story of a family's unique relationship with its servants – a large collection of servants' portraits and carefully preserved rooms capture their lives across the generations, where saw and spade are as treasured as silver and silk. Outdoors, relax in a restored 18th-century walled garden with tranquil water features, trained fruit trees and apple orchards growing over 180 varieties.

Eat, shop, stay: you can enjoy lunch in the Hayloft restaurant, light bites in the café and tea garden, or fresh coffee in Wolf's Den on busy days. Don't forget to visit our second-hand bookshop and gift shop before leaving.

Things to see and do: **Indoors** Discover how generations of the Yorke family took an almost curatorial attitude to their possessions, bequeathing one of the largest, most diverse and fragile collections in the National Trust.

Tulips on parade at Erddig, Wrexham, opposite, and children trying to catch falling leaves, below

Outdoors Year-long programme, including spring displays, atmospheric open-air theatre evenings, Christmas and Easter trails, garden tours and guided estate walks. Regular sporting activities on the estate include Nordic walking, beginner running groups and parkruns. Children can let off steam in the Wolf's Den natural play area and fly on the rope swing, climb the obstacles or enjoy building dens. **Dogs**: welcome in country park and tea garden, but not house, garden, stables and play area.

Access:
Building **Grounds**
Sat Nav: do not use, follow brown signs. **Parking**: on site, 200 yards from ticket office. Electric vehicle charging point available in the car park.

Find out more: 01978 355314 or erddig@nationaltrust.org.uk

Erddig		M	T	W	T	F	S	S
House								
9 Feb–22 Mar*	11:30–2:30	M	T	W	T	F	S	S
23 Mar–25 Oct	12:30–3:30	M	T	W	T	F	S	S
26 Oct–31 Dec*	11:30–2:30	M	T	W	T	F	S	S
Garden, restaurant and shop								
1 Jan–22 Mar**	11–4	M	T	W	T	F	S	S
23 Mar–25 Oct	10–5	M	T	W	T	F	S	S
26 Oct–31 Dec**	11–4	M	T	W	T	F	S	S

*Ground-floor servants' quarters only. Hourly tours weekdays, self-guided during school holidays and weekends. **Natural play area open as garden, but closed weekdays from 1 January to 16 February and closed completely from 4 November to 31 December. Closed 25 December. Timed tickets operate on Bank Holidays and during busy periods.

Freshwater West and Gupton Farm

Castlemartin, Pembrokeshire SA71 5HW

1976

Freshwater West is a wild stretch of coast that's great for water sports and sandy adventures. Beyond the beach, discover Gupton Farm, our campsite, farmhouse accommodation and visitor hub. A rustic escape for adventurous souls and nature lovers; go wildlife-watching, follow walking trails, make the most of the coast and sleep easy under the stars.

Both Freshwater West in Pembrokeshire, above, and Hafod y Llan in Gwynedd, right, offer space to enjoy the great outdoors, nature and adventure

Eat, shop, stay: farmhouse accommodation and campsite at Gupton Farm. Shop selling gifts, camping essentials and beach goods. Picnics welcome, seasonal catering also available at Freshwater West (concession).

Things to see and do: uncover the story of this special place at our visitor information hub. Follow walking trails, go wildlife-watching and try watersports with the on-site Surf and SUP school (concession).
Dogs: welcome under close control.

Access:
Sat Nav: for Gupton Farm use SA71 5HW.
Parking: on site.

Find out more: 01646 661640 or freshwater@nationaltrust.org.uk

Freshwater West and Gupton Farm	M	T	W	T	F	S	S
Campsite							
19 Apr–30 Sep	**M**	**T**	**W**	**T**	**F**	**S**	**S**

Interpretation room and farmhouse (National Trust holiday cottage) open every day all year.

Hafod y Llan

near Beddgelert, Gwynedd

1998

Hafod y Llan, in the beautiful Nantgwynant Valley, is the largest farm run by the National Trust, part of which is designated a National Nature Reserve and a Site of Special Scientific Interest. It extends from the valley floor to the summit of Snowdon and visitors are free to wander the many paths which cross this unique landscape. **Note**: as this is a working farm, access to the farmyard is on foot only.

Eat, shop, stay: holiday cottage, chalet and campsite on the farm. Refreshments available at nearby Caffi Gwynant (not National Trust).

Things to see and do: a network of paths cross Hafod y Llan, including a low-level adventure trail. At the farm entrance the Watkin Path leads to the summit of Snowdon.
Dogs: welcome on leads.

Sat Nav: use LL55 4NQ. **Parking**: on farm for campsite only. Car park near farm entrance for the Watkin Path (not National Trust). Electric vehicle charging point available when staying at the campsite.

Find out more: 01766 890473 or hafodyllan@nationaltrust.org.uk

The Kymin

Monmouth, Monmouthshire NP25 3SF

1902

Lord Nelson and Lady Hamilton were delighted with this Georgian banqueting house and Naval Temple (below) when they visited in 1802. The Kymin is still a great spot from which to enjoy panoramic views of the Brecon Beacons and Wye Valley. The woods and pleasure grounds are also perfect for picnics. **Note**: access via steep winding single lane with passing places.

Eat, shop, stay: cakes and refreshments available during special events. Picnics welcome.

Things to see and do: **Indoors** Our friendly guides offer a taste of a Georgian gentleman's picnic club. **Outdoors** Self-guided walks, featuring bluebells in spring. Children's nature quiz and special events throughout the year. **Dogs**: welcome in the Round House and grounds.

Access: **Round House** **Naval Temple** **Grounds**
Parking: limited on site, with Accessible parking bay adjacent to Round House.

Find out more: 01600 719241 or kymin@nationaltrust.org.uk

The Kymin		M	T	W	T	F	S	S
Round House*								
30 Mar–28 Oct	11–4	**M**	·	·	·	·	**S**	**S**
Grounds								
Open all year	7–9	**M**	**T**	**W**	**T**	**F**	**S**	**S**

*Open Good Friday. Car park: open daylight hours only.

Llanbedrog Beach

Llanbedrog, Gwynedd

2000

Best known for its colourful beach huts, this wonderful stretch of sand has been enjoyed by generations. Its sheltered waters, fantastic views over Cardigan Bay and adjacent wooded and craggy landscape make this a real gem of Llŷn. **Note**: toilet (not National Trust).

Eat, shop, stay: shops and cafés at Llanbedrog and at nearby Pwllheli and Abersoch (not National Trust).

Things to see and do: events during summer months. Children's adventure packs, maps and guides available at the visitor welcome cabin. Second-hand bookshop. Beach huts for hire (subject to availability). **Dogs**: welcome, but please be mindful of other beach users.

Access:
Sat Nav: use LL53 7TT.
Parking: on site. Electric vehicle charging point beside visitor welcome hut.

Find out more: 01758 740561 or llanbedrog@nationaltrust.org.uk

The wide sweep of golden sand and sheltered waters of Llanbedrog Beach, Gwynedd, have been loved by generations of families

Llanerchaeron in Ceredigion: this minor gentry estate boasts a working farm, where visitors are welcome to feed the hungry lambs

Llanerchaeron

Ciliau Aeron, near Aberaeron, Ceredigion SA48 8DG

1989

A self-sufficient 18th-century Welsh minor gentry estate. The villa, designed in the 1790s, is the most complete example of the early work of John Nash. It has its own service courtyard with dairy, laundry, brewery and salting house, giving a full 'upstairs, downstairs' experience. The walled kitchen gardens, pleasure grounds, ornamental lake and parkland offer peaceful walks, while the Home Farm complex has an impressive range of traditional, atmospheric outbuildings. The working farm has Welsh Black cattle, Llanwenog sheep and rare Welsh pigs as well as chickens, geese and turkeys. Woodland walks available.

Eat, shop, stay: café serving light meals and cakes (not National Trust). Picnic site. Fresh garden produce and plants, farm meat, gifts and books for sale. Second-hand bookshop. Two holiday cottages nearby.

Things to see and do: family activities during local school holidays, including craft activities, gardening, nature activities and self-led trails. Special events days. **Dogs**: welcome on the woodland walks and in the parkland on leads.

Access:
Visitor building **Villa**
Grounds
Parking: 50 yards. Electric vehicle charging point in front of visitor reception/café.

Find out more: 01545 570200 or llanerchaeron@nationaltrust.org.uk

Llanerchaeron		M	T	W	T	F	S	S
Whole property								
23 Feb–3 Mar	11:30–3:30	**M**	**T**	**W**	**T**	**F**	**S**	**S**
16 Mar–3 Nov*	10:30–5:30	**M**	**T**	**W**	**T**	**F**	**S**	**S**
Farm, shop and garden								
5 Jan–17 Feb	11:30–3:30	·	·	·	·	·	**S**	**S**
25 Feb–15 Mar	11:30–3:30	**M**	**T**	**W**	**T**	**F**	**S**	**S**
4 Nov–31 Dec**	11:30–3:30	**M**	**T**	**W**	**T**	**F**	**S**	**S**

Last admission one hour before closing. *Villa: opens 11:30, closes 4. **Closed 24 to 26 December. Geler Jones Rural Life Collection: open 12 to 4, Wednesday and Friday, 20 March to 1 November. Parkland and woodland walks: open daily.

Marloes Sands and Mere

Marloes, Pembrokeshire

1941

A hidden gem, this long sandy stretch of coast is perfect for making a splash, spotting marine life on the shore and gorgeous walks. Just inland you'll find Marloes Mere, a wetland bustling with birdlife. Bring along the binoculars and get closer to nature at our on-site bird hides. **Note**: nearest toilets by Runwayskiln farm, alongside track from the car park to Marloes Mere.

Eat, shop, stay: information point at Martin's Haven. Runwayskiln café and accommodation at Marloes Sands open throughout the season (concession).

Marloes Sands and Mere, Pembrokeshire, above and below

Things to see and do: for rock-pooling, birdwatching and getting closer to nature why not pick up a nature discovery Tracker Pack (available from the car park)? **Dogs**: welcome under close control.

Access:
Sat Nav: use SA62 3BH. **Parking**: on site.

Find out more: 01437 720385 or marloessands@nationaltrust.org.uk

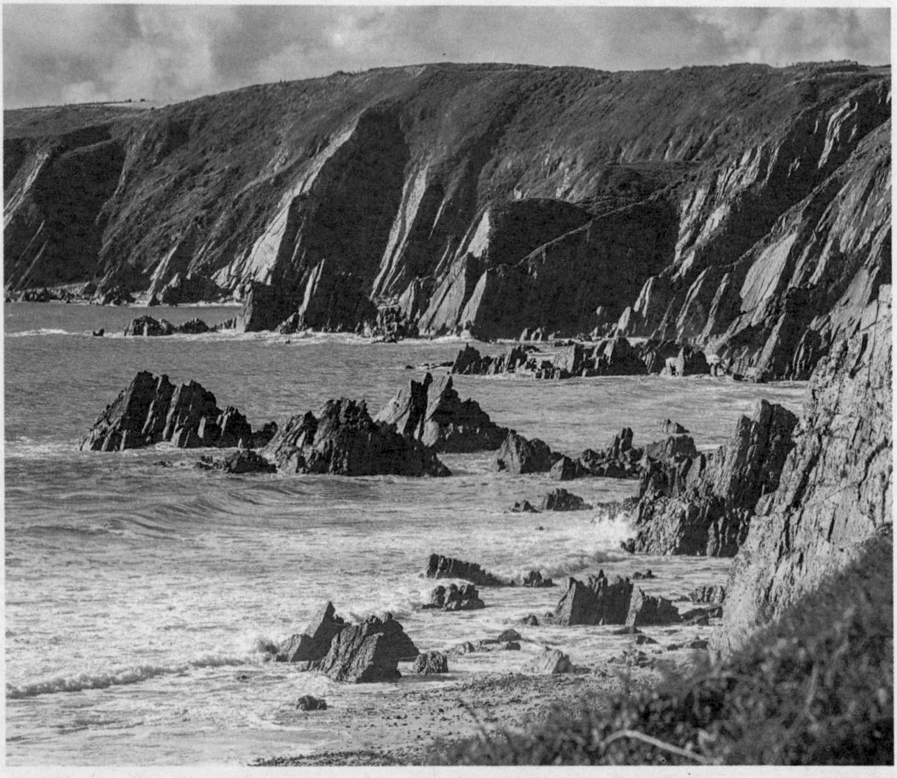

Ancient settlements, panoramic views and marine life – Martin's Haven in Pembrokeshire will fulfil every young adventurer's dream

Martin's Haven

near Marloes, Pembrokeshire

1981

The gateway to Skomer Island and a fabulously wild headland with fine panoramic views of St Bride's Bay. For a really varied and exciting day, why not combine spotting marine wildlife with discovering traces of ancient settlements? **Note**: nearest toilets by the slipway.

Eat, shop, stay: information point at Martin's Haven. Runwayskiln café and accommodation at Marloes Sands open throughout the season (concession).

Things to see and do: nature discovery Tracker Packs available from car park, for rock-pooling, birdwatching and getting closer to nature. **Dogs**: welcome under close control.

Access:
Sat Nav: use SA62 3BJ. **Parking**: on site.

Find out more: 01437 720385 or martinshaven@nationaltrust.org.uk

Mwnt

near Cardigan, Ceredigion 1963

Beautiful secluded bay with a sandy beach – perfect for spotting dolphins, seals and other amazing wildlife. **Note**: small café and shop (not National Trust). Steep steps to beach. For Sat Nav use SA43 1QH.

Find out more: 01545 570200 or mwnt@nationaltrust.org.uk

Ogwen Cottage

Nant Ffrancon, Bethesda, Gwynedd LL57 3LZ

2014

Ogwen Cottage is nestled between the dramatic Carneddau and Glyderau mountain ranges, at the starting point for numerous walking routes in the area. It includes a base for our local ranger team and an information point for walkers exploring nearby Cwm Idwal, Tryfan, Y Glyderau and Y Carneddau. This iconic building has long been associated with mountaineering and adventure, a tradition we're maintaining by providing outdoor learning experiences on site in partnership with The Outward Bound Trust.

Eat, shop, stay: food kiosk (not National Trust). Maps and guides available at the Ogwen ranger base. Two holiday cottages at Dyffryn Mymbyr (7 miles), and one at Tal y Braich (3 miles).

Things to see and do: **Indoors** Visit the ranger base for advice about the area. **Outdoors** Range of rock-climbing and mountain-walking routes available, as well as the National Cycle Network's Lon Las Ogwen. **Dogs**: on leads only.

Access: **Ranger base**
Sat Nav: use LL57 3LZ. **Parking**: at Ogwen Lake (not National Trust).

Find out more: 01248 605739 or ogwen@nationaltrust.org.uk

Ogwen Cottage
Ogwen Cottage Ranger Base: usually open during office hours, but opening times may vary (call for details).

Paxton's Tower

Llanarthne, near Dryslwyn, Carmarthenshire 1965

Known as 'Golwg y Byd' (Eye of the World), Paxton's Tower is said to offer views of seven counties. **Note**: sorry no toilet. Nearest National Trust facilities at Dinefwr in Llandeilo. For Sat Nav use SA32 8HX.

Find out more: 01558 823902 or paxtonstower@nationaltrust.org.uk

Penbryn

near Sarnau, Cardigan, Ceredigion 1967

One of Ceredigion's best-kept secrets, this beautifully secluded sandy cove lies down leafy lanes, edged with flower-covered banks. **Note**: café serving a selection of snacks and drinks (not National Trust). For Sat Nav use SA44 6QL. Electric vehicle charging point.

Find out more: 01545 570200 or penbryn@nationaltrust.org.uk

Ogwen Cottage in Gwynedd, left, and the spectacular cliffs at Pennard, Pwll Du and Bishopston Valley, Swansea, below

Pennard, Pwll Du and Bishopston Valley

near Southgate, Swansea

1954

Spectacular cliffs, caves where mammoth remains have been found, rare birds, an underground river, bat roosts, silver-lead mining, ancient woodland, smuggling and limestone quarrying are just a few of the wonders of this area. There are also numerous archaeological features and two important caves – Bacon Hole and Minchin Hole. **Note**: due to dangerous rip tides, swimming in Three Cliffs Bay is not advised.

Eat, shop, stay: coffee shop, village stores, tea-rooms and a pub in Pennard (none National Trust). Picnics welcome.

Things to see and do: Pennard provides a great starting point for a variety of walks, on which you can enjoy wild flowers and spot rare birds, such as choughs and Dartford warblers. **Dogs**: welcome, but please be aware livestock graze freely across Pennard Burrows.

Access:
Sat Nav: use SA3 2DH.
Parking: at Southgate car park.

Find out more: 01792 390636 or pennard@nationaltrust.org.uk

Penrhyn Castle and Garden

Bangor, Gwynedd LL57 4HT

1951

Penrhyn Castle is a vast neo-Norman castle with many different stories to tell. Extensive grounds and parkland include a Victorian walled garden, industrial Railway Museum and large Victorian kitchens. Set against the spectacular backdrop of Snowdonia and the North Wales coast, the castle's dominating stone façade hides more than just its internal red-brick construction. The unique architecture and opulent interiors mask a darker history of slavery and a bitter industrial dispute that changed Penrhyn's relationship with the local community for ever. Over the coming years Penrhyn will be exploring these difficult stories and presenting them in new and exciting ways.

The soaring castellated walls of Penrhyn Castle in Gwynedd, below, and visitors in the kitchen, above

Note: during this period of transformation, opening arrangements, room layout and tour availability may vary.

Eat, shop, stay: enjoy hot meals in the castle café or a lighter bite in the Stables. Browse through a range of National Trust and local products in our shop and find a bargain in our second-hand bookshop.

Things to see and do: **Indoors** Climb aboard an engine in the Railway Museum or see what life was like in the Victorian kitchens. **Outdoors** Find peace in Walter Speed's famous walled garden. **Dogs**: welcome on leads in grounds. Assistance dogs only in the castle.

Access:
Castle **Stable block** **Grounds**
Parking: 500 yards. Electric vehicle charging point in main car park, just below visitor reception.

Find out more: 01248 353084 or penrhyncastle@nationaltrust.org.uk

Penrhyn Castle and Garden		M	T	W	T	F	S	S
Castle*								
2 Mar–3 Nov	11-5	**M**	**T**	**W**	**T**	**F**	**S**	**S**
30 Nov–22 Dec	11-4	·	·	·	·	·	**S**	**S**
Garden, parkland and Railway Museum, café and shop								
5 Jan–10 Feb	11-3	·	·	·	·	·	**S**	**S**
16 Feb–3 Nov	10:30-5	**M**	**T**	**W**	**T**	**F**	**S**	**S**
9 Nov–29 Dec	11-4	·	·	·	·	·	**S**	**S**
Victorian kitchens								
2 Mar–3 Nov	11-5	**M**	**T**	**W**	**T**	**F**	**S**	**S**
9 Nov–22 Dec	11-4	·	·	·	·	·	**S**	**S**

*Last entry to castle one hour before closing.

Plas Newydd House and Garden

Llanfairpwll, Anglesey LL61 6DQ

1976

The ancestral home of the Marquess of Anglesey sits majestically on the shores of the Menai Strait, enjoying breathtaking views of Snowdonia. The surrounding gardens are great for exploring and include an Australasian arboretum, Italianate terrace garden and extensive woodland walks. There's plenty for little explorers too, including a hand-built tree house, nine-hole Frisbee™ golf course, and adventure playground – you might even meet one of the resident red squirrels! This family home houses a Waterloo-inspired military museum, works of art, regular exhibitions and, at its heart, Rex Whistler's famous 58-foot fantasy landscape painting. **Note**: due to reservicing works, some rooms may be closed, opening and tour arrangements may vary.

Eat, shop, stay: Plas café serving hot and cold lunches. Light bites and cakes available from the Old Dairy. The Old Dairy Shop, Siop Newydd and second-hand bookshop are the perfect place for gifts.

Things to see and do: **Indoors** Learn about family life at Plas Newydd and the secrets behind Rex Whistler's masterpiece. **Outdoors** Enjoy regular walks and talks with the gardeners and a full calendar of events. **Dogs**: welcome on short leads. Assistance dogs only in the house and terraced garden.

Access: **Building** **Grounds**
Parking: 400 yards from main entrance. Electric vehicle charging point in upper staff car park, beside the north wing.

Find out more: 01248 714795 or plasnewydd@nationaltrust.org.uk

Plas Newydd		M	T	W	T	F	S	S
Mansion								
16 Feb–3 Nov	11–4:30	M	T	W	T	F	S	S
Garden, shop and café								
5 Jan–10 Feb	11–3	·	·	·	·	·	S	S
16 Feb–10 Nov	10:30–5	M	T	W	T	F	S	S
16 Nov–29 Dec	11–3	·	·	·	·	·	S	S

Opening times may vary and some rooms may close occasionally due to major reservicing project.

The glorious position of Plas Newydd House and Garden, Anglesey, offers breathtaking views

Plas yn Rhiw

Rhiw, Pwllheli, Gwynedd LL53 8AB

1952

Nestled on a hillside overlooking Cardigan Bay, Plas yn Rhiw is a beautiful 16th-century manor house with Georgian additions. The house was rescued from neglect and lovingly restored by the three Keating sisters, who bought the property in 1938. The views from the grounds and gardens across the bay are among the most spectacular in Britain. The garden contains many beautiful flowering trees and shrubs, with beds framed by box hedges and grass paths – a real joy to explore and stunning whatever the season.

Eat, shop, stay: tea-room serving a selection of fresh sandwiches, soup, cakes, drinks and ice cream; picnics also available to take out. Shop selling gifts, plants, books and prints of Honora Keating's landscape watercolours. Three holiday cottages within walking distance.

Things to see and do: **Indoors** Virtual tour available on iPad and guided tours available by arrangement. **Outdoors** Woodland walks and a native-apple orchard. **Dogs**: on woodland walk below shop only (on leads).

Access:
Building **Grounds**
Parking: 100 yards (narrow lanes). Electric vehicle charging point in top car park beside tea-room.

Find out more: 01758 780219 or plasynrhiw@nationaltrust.org.uk

Plas yn Rhiw		M	T	W	T	F	S	S
House, garden, shop and tea-room								
21 Mar–30 Sep	11–5*	**M**	**T**	**W**	**T**	**F**	**S**	**S**
1 Oct–3 Nov	11–4*	**M**	**T**	**W**	**T**	**F**	**S**	**S**
Garden, shop and tea-room**								
9 Nov–15 Dec	11–3:30	·	·	·	·	·	**S**	**S**

*House opens at 12. **House closed.

Looking out over Cardigan Bay, the gardens at Plas yn Rhiw in Gwynedd, are a joy to explore

Porth Meudwy

near Aberdaron, Gwynedd

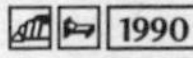 1990

Nowhere expresses the essence of the area better than this sheltered cove on the wild and rocky coastline west of Aberdaron. It was from here that the pilgrims set out to Ynys Enlli (Bardsey Island). Today fishermen still bring the daily catch into the cove. Don't miss the unique Aberdaron boats: small wooden beach boats designed to dance nimbly through the waves along the craggy coastline. **Note**: sorry no toilet.

Eat, shop, stay: shops, pubs and cafés in Aberdaron village (none National Trust). Four holiday apartments in Aberdaron.

Things to see and do: the Wales Coast Path – a birdwatchers' paradise – runs dramatically along the clifftop. **Dogs**: welcome, but please be mindful of other beach users.

Sat Nav: use LL53 8DA. **Parking**: ½ mile.

Find out more: 01758 760469 or porthmeudwy@nationaltrust.org.uk

Porth Meudwy, Gwynedd: the cove, above, offers shelter on this wild and rocky coastline, below

Porth y Swnt

Henfaes, Aberdaron, Pwllheli, Gwynedd LL53 8BE

This exciting interpretation centre, at the heart of the beautiful fishing village of Aberdaron, shines a light on Llŷn's unique culture, heritage and environment. You can experience the Bardsey Island lighthouse's retired optic up close, follow in the footsteps of pilgrims on a journey across the Sound in the video pod, catch up on what Llŷn's rangers are up to and form your reflective thoughts in the Sea of Words.

Eat, shop, stay: gift shop in visitor centre (not National Trust). Cafés, pubs and convenience stores in village (none National Trust). Henfaes holiday apartments (Meudwy, Enlli, Daron and Hywyn) are located at the centre of Aberdaron.

Things to see and do: **Indoors** Audio guide, children's scrapbooks, events during school holidays. **Outdoors** Walks and access to the Wales Coast Path. Adventure packs, beach fun days, guided walks and cycle rides. **Dogs**: beach access restricted during summer.

Access: Car park

Parking: on site. Electric vehicle charging point behind visitor centre.

Find out more: 01758 703810 or porthyswnt@nationaltrust.org.uk

Porth y Swnt		M	T	W	T	F	S	S
2 Jan–31 Mar*	10–4	M	T	W	T	F	S	S
1 Apr–30 Jun	10–5	M	T	W	T	F	S	S
1 Jul–31 Aug	10–6	M	T	W	T	F	S	S
1 Sep–30 Sep	10–5	M	T	W	T	F	S	S
1 Oct–31 Dec**	10–4	M	T	W	T	F	S	S

*Closed 23 to 29 January. **Closed 24 to 26 December.

Set at the heart of Aberdaron, a beautiful fishing village, the interpretation centre of Porth y Swnt, Gwynedd, offers thrills and unique experiences to excite and challenge visitors of all ages

Picturesque Porthdinllaen in Gwynedd

Porthdinllaen

Morfa Nefyn, Gwynedd

An old fishing village perched on the end of a thin ribbon of land stretching into the Irish Sea, with its clear sheltered waters lapping against stout stone houses, Porthdinllaen really is a jewel. You can watch fishermen bring in the daily catch, while relaxing with a drink at the Tŷ Coch Inn. In the summer you can view the ecologically rich seagrasses from a paddle board – and have fun trying to stand up. **Note**: nearest toilet in village, which can only be reached by foot. Steps down to beach.

Eat, shop, stay: two holiday cottages available in the heart of the village. Refreshments available at our tenanted pub, Tŷ Coch Inn.

Things to see and do: events during summer for all the family. Wonderful walking on the coastal path – maps and guides available at car park welcome cabin. **Dogs**: welcome, but please be mindful of other beach users.

Access:
Sat Nav: use LL53 6DA. **Parking**: on site for beach; 1 mile from village (no vehicular access to village). Electric vehicle charging point in Trust car park, beside visitor welcome hut.

Find out more: 01758 760469 or porthdinllaen@nationaltrust.org.uk

Porthor

Aberdaron, Gwynedd

1981

This wonderful beach is famous for its 'whistling sands' and glistening waters. The whistling happens because of the especially fine sand grains on the beach – perfect for building sandcastles. If the joys of sandcastles and sunbathing are not enough for you, then why not have a go at surfing? The sea here is perfect. In addition, the Wales Coast Path runs in both directions from the car park. **Note**: nearest toilet in car park. Please remember to scan your membership card.

Eat, shop, stay: National Trust tenanted beachside café and shop offering everything from lunch to sun cream. Four holiday apartments in Aberdaron.

Things to see and do: famous beach and glorious clifftop coast path to explore. Children's adventure pack available from car park. **Dogs**: seasonal restrictions on beach apply from 1 April to 30 September.

Access:
Sat Nav: use LL53 8LG. **Parking**: on site. Electric vehicle charging point.

Find out more: 01758 760469 or porthor@nationaltrust.org.uk

Porthor in Gwynedd, above and below: rock-pooling is irresistible, whatever your age

Powis Castle and Garden

Welshpool, Powys SY21 8RF

1952

Powis Castle and Garden in Powys

The Herbert family spent more than 400 years transforming a medieval fortress into the comfortable family home you see today. Furnished with sumptuous fabrics and exquisite works of art from around the world, including the unique Clive collection of Indian treasures, the interior reflects the Elizabethan period through to the 1940s when a girls' school was evacuated to the castle. With views across the Severn Valley, the world-renowned gardens are a mix of Italianate terraces filled with herbaceous borders, a formal garden with clipped yews and a woodland area which boasts a number of champion trees.

Eat, shop, stay: restaurant serving lunch, light bites, snacks and cakes (licensed) and garden coffee shop. Gift shop, garden shop, plant sales and second-hand books. Holiday cottage, The Bothy, is located in the heart of the garden.

Things to see and do: **Indoors** Themed castle tours, introductory talks (April to September). Family trails. New: Welsh Girls' School interactive installation. **Outdoors** Garden tours and talks. Family trails. Additional children's activities during school holidays.
Dogs: assistance dogs only.

Access:
Building **Grounds**
Sat Nav: postcode misdirects, enter Powis Castle. **Parking**: on site. Two electric vehicle charging points in car park.

Find out more: 01938 551920 or powiscastle@nationaltrust.org.uk

Powis Castle and Garden		M	T	W	T	F	S	S
Castle and shop								
1 Jan–31 Mar	11-4*	M	T	W	T	F	S	S
1 Apr–30 Sep†	11-5*	M	T	W	T	F	S	S
1 Oct–31 Dec	11-4*	M	T	W	T	F	S	S
Garden and café								
1 Jan–31 Mar††	10-4	M	T	W	T	F	S	S
1 Apr–30 Sep	10-5**	M	T	W	T	F	S	S
1 Oct–31 Dec	10-4	M	T	W	T	F	S	S

*Last entry to castle one hour before closing. **Garden: open to 6. †Garden coffee shop (opening times vary) and garden shop open. ††Reduced catering offer in January and February. Closed 25 December.

A herbaceous border at Powis Castle and Garden

Rhossili and South Gower Coast

on the Gower Peninsula, Swansea

1933

Rhossili lies at the far end of the beautiful Gower Peninsula. Blessed with 3 miles of golden, award-winning sands and spectacular coastal views, it's the perfect base from which to explore the stunning South Gower coastline – most of which is under the care of the National Trust. From the historically and environmentally important medieval strip farm system known as the The Vile, the instantly recognisable Worms Head tidal island, Iron Age earthworks, notable wildlife and geology, through to legends, shipwrecks and stories. Once visited, Rhossili will stay with you forever. **Note**: steep steps and a slope to the beach.

Eat, shop, stay: wide range of carefully selected gifts and limited refreshments (including Swansea's famous Joe's ice cream) available all year. Small outdoor catering offer from March to October (weather dependent). Three National Trust holiday cottages nearby.

Things to see and do: you can walk along the Coast Path and through The Vile, cross to Worms Head and explore the beach. Visitor information available all year. Regular free activities for all ages. **Dogs**: welcome (on leads near livestock please). Beach is dog-friendly all year.

Access: **Visitor centre**
Parking: large pay and display car park at end of village. Suitable for motorhomes.

Find out more: 01792 390707 or rhossili@nationaltrust.org.uk

Rhossili and Gower		M	T	W	T	F	S	S
Shop								
2 Jan–22 Feb	10–4	**M**	**T**	**W**	**T**	**F**	**S**	**S**
23 Feb–13 Apr*	10–4:30	**M**	**T**	**W**	**T**	**F**	**S**	**S**
14 Apr–19 Jul*	10–5	**M**	**T**	**W**	**T**	**F**	**S**	**S**
20 Jul–1 Sep*	10–6	**M**	**T**	**W**	**T**	**F**	**S**	**S**
2 Sep–6 Oct*	10–5	**M**	**T**	**W**	**T**	**F**	**S**	**S**
7 Oct–3 Nov*	10–4:30	**M**	**T**	**W**	**T**	**F**	**S**	**S**
4 Nov–23 Dec	10–4	**M**	**T**	**W**	**T**	**F**	**S**	**S**
27 Dec–30 Dec	11–4	**M**	·	·	·	**F**	**S**	**S**

*Outdoor food and beverages: open 1 March to 31 October (weather permitting). Car park open daily, dawn to dusk.

With its miles of golden sands and wonderful position on the beautiful Gower Peninsula, Rhossili and South Gower Coast, Swansea, is perfectly placed for exploration and adventure

St David's Visitor Centre and Shop

Captain's House, High Street, St David's, Pembrokeshire SA62 6SD

1974

Overlooking the Celtic Old Cross in the centre of St David's, Wales's smallest historic city, the visitor centre and well-stocked shop is open all year. For a complete guide to the National Trust in Pembrokeshire, visitors can take a tour of our special places, beaches and walks using interactive technology. **Note**: sorry no toilet.

St David's, Pembrokeshire: pony grazing on the peninsula, below, and the view from St David's peninsula, above

Eat, shop, stay: books, cards, maps, wide range of gifts and local produce. Walks leaflets available. Holiday cottages nearby.

Things to see and do: visitor information and advice about Pembrokeshire's special places; speak to the team about access, facilities and walks. St David's Head, Porth Clais, Solva and Abereiddi nearby.

Access: Building

Parking: none on site.

Find out more: 01437 720385 or stdavidsshop@nationaltrust.org.uk

St David's Visitor Centre		M	T	W	T	F	S	S
2 Jan–23 Mar	9–4	M	T	W	T	F	S	·
24 Mar–31 Dec	9–5*	M	T	W	T	F	S	S

*Open 10 to 4 on Sundays. Closed 1 January and 25 and 26 December.

Segontium

Caernarfon, Gwynedd 1937

Fort built to defend the Roman Empire against rebellious tribes. **Note**: in the guardianship of Cadw – Welsh Government's historic environment service. Museum not National Trust. For Sat Nav use LL55 2LN. Please call for opening arrangements.

Find out more: 01443 336000 or segontium@nationaltrust.org.uk

Skenfrith Castle

Skenfrith, near Abergavenny, Monmouthshire NP7 8UH 1936

Remains of early 13th-century castle, built beside the River Monnow to command one of the main routes from England. **Note**: in the guardianship of Cadw – Welsh Government's historic environment service. Open every day all year.

Find out more: 01874 625515 or skenfrithcastle@nationaltrust.org.uk

Southwood Estate

Newgale, Roch, Pembrokeshire

2003

A timeless landscape of wooded valleys, floral fields and craggy cliffs, the Southwood Estate is full of scenic surprises. Follow the waymarked walking trails and explore the best of coast and countryside; spot flora and fauna and see how we're working hard to safeguard this special place.

Timeless Southwood Estate in Pembrokeshire

Eat, shop, stay: shop, café and pub in nearby Newgale and Roch (not National Trust). St David's Visitor Centre and Shop nearby. Bed and breakfast at Southwood Farm (concession).

Things to see and do: walking trails and seasonal programme, including guided walks, talks, craft fair and children's holiday activities. Information points at Southwood Farm and Maidenhall car parks. Shearing shed interpretation telling Southwood's story. **Dogs**: welcome under close control.

Access:
Sat Nav: for Maidenhall car park use SA62 6BD; Southwood Farm car park use SA62 6AR. **Parking**: on site.

Find out more: 01437 720385 or southwoodestate@nationaltrust.org.uk

Stackpole

near Pembroke, Pembrokeshire

1976

A former grand estate stretching down to some of the most beautiful coastline in the world, including Broad Haven South, Barafundle Bay and Stackpole Quay. Today, Stackpole is a National Nature Reserve, recognised for its abundant flora and fauna; Bosherston Lakes are famous for their superb display of lilies and resident otters; and the dramatic cliffs of Stackpole Head are great for wildlife watching. You can uncover the history and heritage of this special place too; the former Stackpole Court site and nearby Lodge Park Woods reveal the story behind the magnificent designed landscape.

Eat, shop, stay: Boathouse tea-room offering drinks, light lunches, sandwiches and a selection of cakes and cream teas. Wide range of gifts and local goods available at shop. Stay longer at Stackpole's holiday cottages, Outdoor Learning Centre or Gupton campsite and farmhouse.

Things to see and do: guided kayaking and coasteering (concession). Wildlife walks and talks. Coarse fishing (close season 15 March to 15 June). Family events, including fun runs, beach activity days and bushcraft with rangers. **Dogs**: under close control on the estate.

Access: **Building** **Grounds**
Sat Nav: for Stackpole Quay use SA71 5LS; Broad Haven South SA71 5DR; Bosherston Lakes SA71 5DR; Stackpole Court SA71 5DE.
Parking: car parks at Stackpole Quay, Broad Haven South, Bosherston Lakes and Stackpole Court. Electric vehicle charging point at Stackpole Outdoor Learning Centre (SA71 5DQ).

Find out more: 01646 623110 or stackpole@nationaltrust.org.uk

Stackpole		M	T	W	T	F	S	S
Estate								
Open all year	Dawn–dusk	**M**	**T**	**W**	**T**	**F**	**S**	**S**
Boathouse tea-room								
9 Feb–5 Apr*	11–4	**M**	**T**	**W**	**T**	**F**	**S**	**S**
6 Apr–29 Sep	10–5	**M**	**T**	**W**	**T**	**F**	**S**	**S**
30 Sep–3 Nov*	11–4	**M**	**T**	**W**	**T**	**F**	**S**	**S**
9 Nov–29 Dec*	11–4	·	·	·	·	·	**S**	**S**

*Reduced catering offer.

Stackpole in Pembrokeshire boasts some of the most beautiful coastline in the world

Stackpole Outdoor Learning Centre

Old Home Farm Yard, Stackpole, near Pembroke, Pembrokeshire SA71 5DQ

1976

Stackpole Outdoor Learning Centre in Pembrokeshire: activities and adventure

Located in the heart of the Stackpole Estate, our eco-award-winning centre provides residents with easy access to Bosherston Lakes, Stackpole Quay and award-winning beaches – including Barafundle and Broad Haven South – as well as the historic site of Stackpole Court. The recently refurbished centre can house up to 147 guests and offers flexible accommodation with modern facilities, including a theatre, meeting and classroom space. It is ideal for groups, corporate clients, celebrations and family holidays. **Note**: contact the centre for activity programmes, prices and availability.

Eat, shop, stay: self-catering or chef-catered options. Meals provided by in-house catering team. Full entertainment licence for events with bar. Wide range of gifts and local goods available at on-site shop. Single and double rooms, farmhouse accommodation and campsite at nearby Gupton Farm.

Things to see and do: events, including rock-pool rambles, bushcraft, guided walks and talks. Explore the area from an alternative angle with kayaking and coasteering guided tours (concession). **Dogs**: assistance dogs only.

Access: [access symbols]
Parking: free for guests. Electric vehicle charging point.

Find out more: 01646 623110 or stackpoleoutdoorlearning@nationaltrust.org.uk

Stackpole Outdoor Centre
Please contact the centre for information on residential group bookings, courses and activities.

Exploring and hiking at Stackpole Outdoor Learning Centre

Sugar Loaf and Usk Valley

Abergavenny, Monmouthshire NP7 7LA

[symbols] 1936

Sugar Loaf and Usk Valley in Monmouthshire

Discover glorious views across Monmouthshire and the borders from the peaks of Sugar Loaf and The Skirrid. Alternatively explore seasonal changes through the ancient woodland that straddles their slopes. By contrast, meander through parkland at Clytha and the Usk Valley, perfect for picnics or short walks. **Note**: sorry no toilets. Some car parks not National Trust.

Eat, shop, stay: many shops and restaurants at nearby Abergavenny (none National Trust).

Things to see and do: **Indoors** Visit the nearby Georgian Round House at The Kymin. **Outdoors** Family activities during school holidays, including Wild Wednesdays at Sugar Loaf or The Skirrid. Visit nearby Skenfrith Castle. **Dogs**: welcome on leads.

Sat Nav: for Llanwenarth car park, follow signs for Sugar Loaf vineyard and continue uphill. **Parking**: at Llanwenarth car park for Sugar Loaf; numerous on-site car parks for Usk Valley.

Find out more: 01874 625515 or sugarloaf@nationaltrust.org.uk

Tredegar House

Newport NP10 8YW

2012

Tredegar House and the Morgan family have been an important part of the Newport community for more than 500 years. Captivating tales of war heroism, inheritance disputes, Russian princesses and sprawling influence bring alive a home designed to impress and entertain, while the small but elegant contrasting formal gardens pay homage to life at Tredegar House. Those who keep the mansion, gardens and parkland running today are working in partnership with local organisations to combine colourful histories and modern programmes with an ambition to bring genuine benefit to the community and all who visit. **Note**: tea-room renovations taking place this year.

Eat, shop, stay: tea-room serving light lunches, homemade cakes and hot drinks. Gift shop selling souvenirs, books, gifts and plants.

Things to see and do: **Indoors** Beautiful architectural decoration and intriguing stories. **Outdoors** Lakeside walks, formal gardens and programmed activities. **Dogs**: welcome in the parkland, formal gardens and tea-room.

Access:
House **Reception** **Grounds**
Parking: on site.

Find out more: 01633 815880 or tredegar@nationaltrust.org.uk

Tredegar House		M	T	W	T	F	S	S
House and gardens*								
16 Feb–5 Apr	11-4	M	T	W	T	F	S	S
6 Apr–29 Sep	11-5	M	T	W	T	F	S	S
30 Sep–3 Nov	11-4	M	T	W	T	F	S	S
30 Nov–22 Dec	11-4**	·	·	W	T	F	S	S
Tea-room and shop								
5 Jan–10 Feb	10-3:30	·	·	·	·	·	S	S
16 Feb–5 Apr	10-4	M	T	W	T	F	S	S
6 Apr–28 Jul	10-5	M	T	W	T	F	S	S
29 Jul–1 Sep	10-6	M	T	W	T	F	S	S
2 Sep–29 Sep	10-5	M	T	W	T	F	S	S
30 Sep–3 Nov	10-4	M	T	W	T	F	S	S
6 Nov–20 Dec	10-4	·	·	W	T	F	·	·
9 Nov–22 Dec	10-5	·	·	·	·	·	S	S
Park								
Open all year	Dawn–dusk	M	T	W	T	F	S	·

*Gardens: open from 10:30. **Wednesday to Friday entry by tour only. Last entry one hour before closing.

Tredegar House, Newport, the formal garden is accessible to everyone, even if walking is difficult

Tudor Merchant's House

Quay Hill, Tenby, Pembrokeshire SA70 7BX

1937

Over 500 years ago when Tenby was a busy trading port, a merchant built this three-storey house (above) to live in and trade from. Today, the house and shop have been furnished with exquisitely carved replicas and brightly coloured wall-hangings which recreate the atmosphere of life in Tudor Tenby. **Note**: sorry no toilet.

Eat, shop, stay: shop range includes specially made Tudor-style pottery (design based on finds at the house), pewterware, horn cups, glass, beeswax candles and books about the Tudors.

Things to see and do: you can lay the high table, see the wall-paintings, try on traditional costumes and play with replica games and toys. Tudor-themed family activities year-round. **Dogs**: assistance dogs only.

Access: Building
Parking: very limited on-street parking. Several pay-and-display car parks, not National Trust (charge including members).

Find out more: 01834 842279 or tudormerchantshouse@nationaltrust.org.uk

Tudor Merchant's House		M	T	W	T	F	S	S
16 Feb–3 Mar	11-3	M	T	W	T	F	S	S
9 Mar–7 Apr	11-3	·	·	·	·	·	S	S
8 Apr–3 Nov	11-5	M	T	W	T	F	S	S

Tŷ Isaf

Beddgelert, Gwynedd LL55 4YA

1985

Brimming with character, Tŷ Isaf lies in the very heart of Beddgelert. Dating back to the late 17th century, this Grade II listed building is the oldest property in the village and has fulfilled many roles over the centuries – from tavern to farmhouse and, now, shop.

Eat, shop, stay: fantastic range of local produce and crafts, alongside National Trust products, for sale. Second-hand books and gallery upstairs.

Things to see and do: free family adventure packs. Go for a ramble beside the river and see how many activities you can complete.

Access:
Parking: car parks in village, not National Trust (charge including members).

Find out more: tyisaf@nationaltrust.org.uk

Tŷ Isaf		M	T	W	T	F	S	S
6 Apr–3 Nov	11-5*	M	T	W	T	F	S	S
9 Nov–22 Dec	11-4	·	·	·	·	·	S	S

*Open to 4 on Sundays.

Tŷ Isaf, Gwynedd: dates back to the late 17th century

 For information about getting to National Trust places, please see page 3

Tŷ Mawr Wybrnant

Penmachno, Betws-y-Coed, Conwy LL25 0HJ

1951

Modest 16th-century farmhouse with huge cultural significance. Birthplace to Bishop William Morgan, whose 10-year endeavour to translate the Bible into Welsh helped ensure the survival of the language. You can view an original copy of the 1588 Welsh Bible at the house, which is situated on the old drovers' road. **Note**: access via narrow road from Penmachno. Once you reach forestry, follow signs.

Eat, shop, stay: picnics welcome. Four holiday cottages available near Betws-y-Coed and Hendre Isaf bunkhouse at Pentrefoelas (9 miles).

Tŷ Mawr Wybrnant in Conwy: the modest farmhouse, left, and fun in the grounds, above

Things to see and do: **Indoors** Enjoy an introductory talk, visit the exhibition room and browse the extensive Bible collection. Virtual tour also available. **Outdoors** Tudor kitchen garden, woodland walk and animal puzzle trail. **Dogs**: under close control.

Access: **Building** **Grounds**
Sat Nav: do not use. No access from A470.
Parking: 500 yards.

Find out more: 01690 760213 or tymawrwybrnant@nationaltrust.org.uk

Tŷ Mawr Wybrnant		M	T	W	T	F	S	S
4 Apr–29 Sep	12–5	·	·	·	T	F	S	S
3 Oct–3 Nov	12–4	·	·	·	T	F	S	S

Open Bank Holiday Mondays.

Additional coastal and countryside car parks in Wales

Ceredigion

Mwnt	SA43 1QF
Penbryn	SA44 6QL
Llŷn Peninsula	
Uwchmynydd	LL53 8DD
Pembrokeshire	
Broad Haven South	SA71 5DR
Bosherston Lakes	SA71 5DR
Porth Clais	SA62 6RR
Snowdonia	
Cregennan	LL39 1LX
Nantmor	LL55 4YG
Swansea (Gower)	
Rhossili	SA3 1PR

Northern Ireland

Jumping the waves at Murlough National Nature Reserve, County Down Competition entry from Paul McCartan

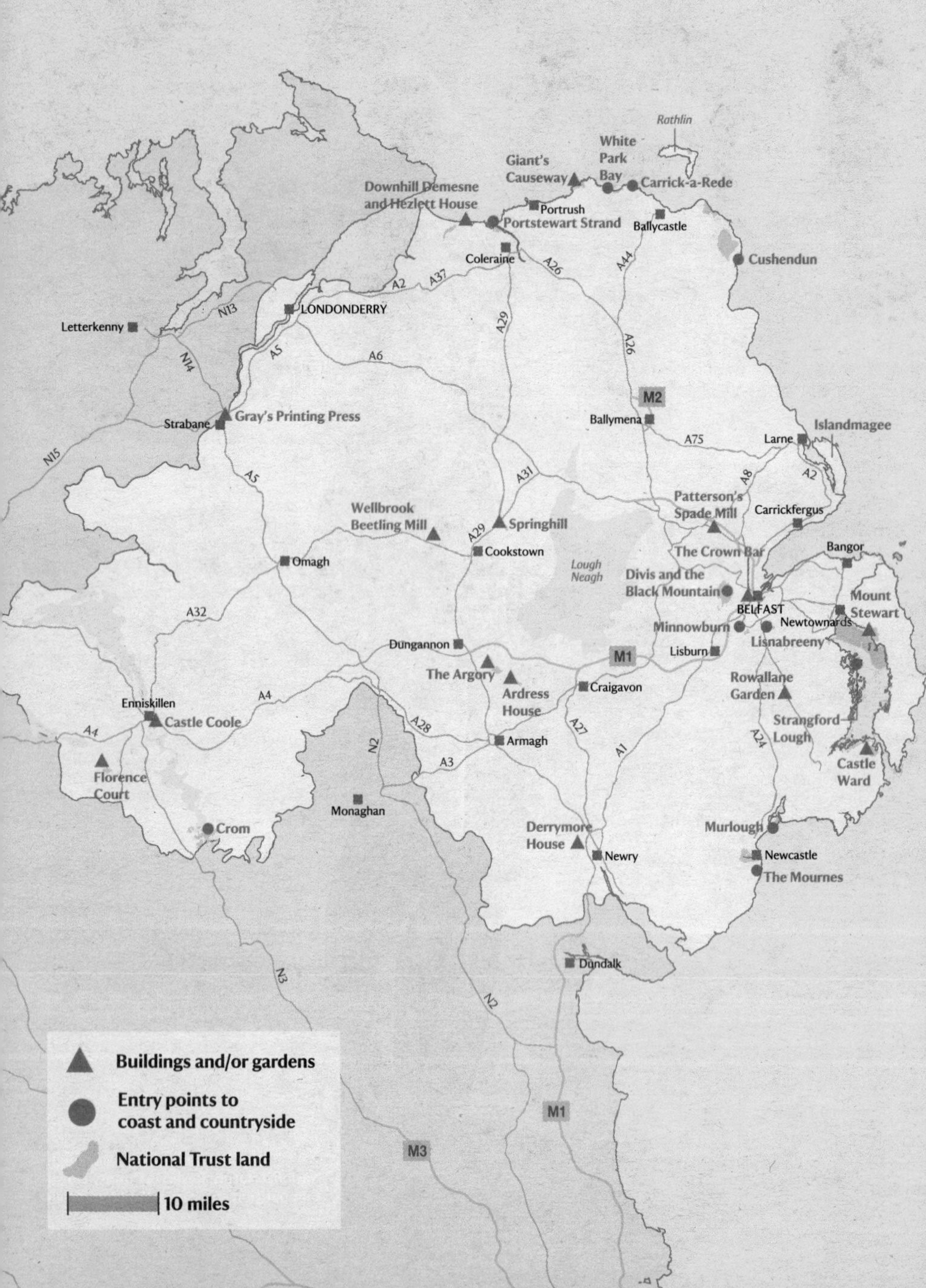

Rathlin
White Park Bay
Giant's Causeway
Carrick-a-Rede
Downhill Demesne and Hezlett House
Portrush
Portstewart Strand
Ballycastle
Cushendun
Coleraine
LONDONDERRY
Letterkenny
Gray's Printing Press
Strabane
Ballymena
Islandmagee
Larne
Patterson's Spade Mill
Carrickfergus
Wellbrook Beetling Mill
Springhill
Cookstown
The Crown Bar
Bangor
Omagh
Lough Neagh
Divis and the Black Mountain
BELFAST
Mount Stewart
Newtownards
Minnowburn
Lisnabreeny
Dungannon
Lisburn
The Argory
Ardress House
Craigavon
Rowallane Garden
Enniskillen
Castle Coole
Strangford Lough
Armagh
Florence Court
Castle Ward
Monaghan
Crom
Derrymore House
Murlough
Newry
Newcastle
The Mournes
Dundalk
A2
A37
A26
A44
A29
N13
N14
A5
A6
M2
A75
N15
A8
A31
A29
A32
M1
A4
A28
N2
A27
A1
A24
A3
N3
M3
Buildings and/or gardens
Entry points to coast and countryside
National Trust land
10 miles

Ardress House

64 Ardress Road, Annaghmore, Portadown, County Armagh BT62 1SQ

Nestled in 40 hectares (100 acres) of rolling countryside, this 17th-century farmhouse, with detailed plasterwork and fine Georgian interiors, offers afternoons of fun and relaxation for everyone. The cobbled farmyard is the perfect spot for children to feed the resident chickens, and the nearby apple orchards are great for exploring.

Eat, shop, stay: takeaway hot and cold drinks and ice cream available. Picnics welcome in the garden or woodlands.

Things to see and do: original cobbled farmyard, including dairy, smithy and threshing barn, miniature Shetland ponies, donkeys, nanny goats and chickens. Lady's Mile walking trail. Children's outdoor and indoor play.
Dogs: on leads in garden only.

Access: **Building** **Grounds**
Parking: 10 yards.

Find out more: 028 8778 4753 or ardress@nationaltrust.org.uk

Ardress House		M	T	W	T	F	S	S
House and farmyard								
9 Mar–14 Apr	11–5	·	·	·	·	·	**S**	**S**
19 Apr–28 Apr	11–5	**M**	**T**	**W**	**T**	**F**	**S**	**S**
4 May–30 Jun	11–5	·	·	·	·	·	**S**	**S**
1 Jul–31 Aug	11–5	**M**	·	·	**T**	**F**	**S**	**S**
1 Sep–29 Sep	11–5	·	·	·	·	·	**S**	**S**
6 Oct–27 Oct	11–5	·	·	·	·	·	·	**S**
Lady's Mile Walk								
Open all year	Dawn–dusk	**M**	**T**	**W**	**T**	**F**	**S**	**S**

House: admission by guided tour (last tour one hour before closing). Open Bank Holiday Mondays and all other public holidays in Northern Ireland. Closed 25, 26 December and 1 January 2020.

Ardress House, County Armagh: enjoying the art, above, and feeding chickens in the farmyard

The Argory

144 Derrycaw Road, Moy, Dungannon, County Armagh BT71 6NA

1979

This Irish gentry house can trace more than 190 years of history. Built in the 1820s for the MacGeough Bond family, the house and surrounding riverside estate came into existence due to a quirky stipulation in a will. The interior of this understated and intimate house still evokes the eclectic tastes and interests of the family. The small rose garden with its unusual sundial, pleasure gardens and wooded walks along the River Blackwater are ideal for exploring.

Eat, shop, stay: Courtyard Café serving home-baked scones, sandwiches, paninis and cakes. Gift shop offering a wide range of products. Second-hand bookshop (volunteer-run). Picnics welcome.

The Argory, County Armagh: eclectic interests

Letting off steam in The Argory's play area

Things to see and do: **Indoors** Guided house tours and children's indoor Pest Quest. **Outdoors** Variety of walks and trails. Children's play area with zip line. Events throughout the year, including Vintage Rally. **Dogs**: on leads in grounds and garden.

Access: Grounds
Parking: 100 yards.

Find out more: 028 8778 4753 or argory@nationaltrust.org.uk

The Argory		M	T	W	T	F	S	S
House, café and shop								
2 Feb–24 Feb*	11–5	·	·	·	·	·	**S**	**S**
9 Mar–14 Apr	11–5	·	·	·	**T**	**F**	**S**	**S**
15 Apr–28 Apr	11–5	**M**	**T**	**W**	**T**	**F**	**S**	**S**
2 May–31 May	11–5	·	·	·	**T**	**F**	**S**	**S**
1 Jun–30 Jun	11–5	·	·	**W**	**T**	**F**	**S**	**S**
1 Jul–31 Aug	11–5	**M**	**T**	**W**	**T**	**F**	**S**	**S**
1 Sep–29 Sep	11–5	·	·	·	**T**	**F**	**S**	**S**
5 Oct–27 Oct	11–4	·	·	·	·	·	**S**	**S**
28 Oct–3 Nov	11–4	**M**	**T**	**W**	**T**	**F**	**S**	**S**
Grounds								
Open all year	10–5	**M**	**T**	**W**	**T**	**F**	**S**	**S**

*Also open 18 and 19 February for local half term. House: admission by guided tour (last tour one hour before closing). Open Bank Holiday Mondays and all public holidays in Northern Ireland. Grounds closed 25, 26 December and 1 January 2020.

Carrick-a-Rede

Ballintoy, County Antrim BT54 6LS

Connected to the cliffs by a rope bridge across the Atlantic Ocean, this rocky island is the ultimate clifftop experience. Jutting out from the Causeway Coastal Route, the 30-metre-deep and 20-metre-wide chasm separating Carrick-a-Rede from the mainland is traversed by an amazing rope bridge that was traditionally erected by salmon fishermen. Wildlife-rich and with views across the seas to Rathlin Island, this is also home to Larrybane old quarry, recently featured in the television series *Game of Thrones*. **Note**: timed-ticketing system in operation (online booking). Bridge access dependent on weather.

Eat, shop, stay: Weighbridge tea-room offering great coffee, delicious scones and sweet treats, hot snacks and light lunches. Gift shop area showcasing local crafts and unique range of Carrick-a-Rede souvenirs.

Things to see and do: coastal path – part of the Causeway Coast Way walking route from Portstewart to Ballycastle. Birdwatching and coastal scenery. Unique flora and fauna. Guided tours (by arrangement).
Dogs: on leads (not permitted to cross bridge).

Access: Grounds
Parking: on site.

Find out more: 028 2076 9839 or carrickarede@nationaltrust.org.uk

Carrick-a-Rede		M	T	W	T	F	S	S
Rope bridge								
1 Jan–31 Jan	9:30–3:30	**M**	**T**	**W**	**T**	**F**	**S**	**S**
1 Feb–28 Feb	9:30–5	**M**	**T**	**W**	**T**	**F**	**S**	**S**
1 Mar–30 Jun	9:30–6	**M**	**T**	**W**	**T**	**F**	**S**	**S**
1 Jul–31 Aug	9:30–8	**M**	**T**	**W**	**T**	**F**	**S**	**S**
1 Sep–31 Oct	9:30–6	**M**	**T**	**W**	**T**	**F**	**S**	**S**
1 Nov–31 Dec	9:30–3:30	**M**	**T**	**W**	**T**	**F**	**S**	**S**

Bridge: open weather permitting; last entry 45 minutes before closing. Car park and North Antrim coastal path open all year. Closed 24 to 26 December.

Have you got what it takes to cross the rope bridge at Carrick-a-Rede in County Antrim?

Castle Coole

Enniskillen, County Fermanagh BT74 6HN

1951

Surrounded by a stunning landscape park, the majestic 18th-century home of the Earls of Belmore was created to impress. One of the finest examples of Neo-classical architecture in Ireland, the rooms at Castle Coole are brimming with opulence, luxury and colour. There are interesting pieces of history to explore, such as the servants' tunnel and ice house. The parkland, interspersed with mature oaks, woodlands and paths, is perfect for refreshing walks, while the outdoor play area is great for families.

Eat, shop, stay: Tallow House tea-room serving snacks, lunches and afternoon teas. Gift shop selling souvenirs and local crafts. Second-hand bookshop (volunteer-run).

Things to see and do: **Indoors** Events throughout the year. 'Upstairs downstairs' guided tours of the mansion. Enjoy the cosy Tallow House tea-room. **Outdoors** Events throughout the year, including summer music sessions. Trails and walks. **Dogs**: under control.

Access:
Building **Grounds**
Parking: 150 yards.

Find out more: 028 6632 2690 or castlecoole@nationaltrust.org.uk

Castle Coole		M	T	W	T	F	S	S
Grounds								
1 Jan–28 Feb	10-4	**M**	**T**	**W**	**T**	**F**	**S**	**S**
1 Mar–31 Oct	10-7	**M**	**T**	**W**	**T**	**F**	**S**	**S**
1 Nov–31 Dec	10-4	**M**	**T**	**W**	**T**	**F**	**S**	**S**
House, tea-room and shop								
9 Mar–14 Apr	11-5	·	·	·	·	·	**S**	**S**
19 Apr–28 Apr	11-5	**M**	**T**	**W**	**T**	**F**	**S**	**S**
29 Apr–31 May	11-5	**M**	·	**W**	**T**	**F**	**S**	**S**
1 Jun–1 Sep	11-5	**M**	**T**	**W**	**T**	**F**	**S**	**S**
2 Sep–30 Sep	11-5	**M**	·	**W**	**T**	**F**	**S**	**S**

House: admission by guided tour (last tour one hour before closing). Open Monday 18 March, Bank Holiday Mondays and all other public holidays in Northern Ireland.

Castle Coole in County Fermanagh, above and below, was created to impress

For information about getting to National Trust places, please see page 3

Castle Ward

Strangford, Downpatrick,
County Down BT30 7LS

1953

High on a hillside, with views across the tranquil waters of Strangford Lough, the Gothic and classical collide at Castle Ward. This eccentric 18th-century mansion within a 332-hectare (820-acre) walled demesne, is one of the most peculiar architectural compromises between two people. The story behind the different façades of the former home of the Viscounts Bangor is revealed by guided tours. In the farmyard, visit the water-powered corn mill, or stroll among flowers and subtropical plants in the newly restored Sunken Garden. The laundry, tack room and dairy give an insight into life 'below stairs'. Discover more on the 21 miles of family-friendly multi-use trails, while the woodland and adventure playground are great for children.
Note: 1 March to 30 November visitor access to livestock grazing areas may be restricted.

Eat, shop, stay: Stableyard tea-room. Gift shop selling local produce and souvenirs. Second-hand bookshop. Holiday cottage, bunkhouse, caravan and campsite with glamping pods.

Things to see and do: **Indoors** Guided house tours. Victorian laundry, dairy and corn mill. You can visit the 16th-century Tower House. **Outdoors** Network of multi-use trails. Bicycles for hire (not National Trust). Farmyard with animals. Woodland and Adventure playground. Tracker Packs and children's activities.
A series of family events throughout the year including Easter, Pumpkinfest and Winterfell Festival. Why not visit some of the iconic filming locations – Winterfell in HBO's *Game of Thrones*? **Dogs**: welcome on leads (livestock grazing areas out of bounds).

Castle Ward in County Down: this split-personality house sits high on a hill offering views for miles

Castle Ward's classical façade, above, and one of its endearingly eccentric Gothic interiors, left

Access:
Building **Grounds**
Parking: on site.

Find out more: 028 4488 1204 or castleward@nationaltrust.org.uk

Castle Ward		M	T	W	T	F	S	S
Parkland, trails and garden								
1 Jan–15 Mar	10–4	**M**	**T**	**W**	**T**	**F**	**S**	**S**
16 Mar–3 Nov	10–6	**M**	**T**	**W**	**T**	**F**	**S**	**S**
4 Nov–31 Dec	10–4	**M**	**T**	**W**	**T**	**F**	**S**	**S**
House, stableyard and farmyard*								
16 Mar–3 Nov	12–5	**M**	**T**	**W**	**T**	**F**	**S**	**S**
Tea-room, gift shop and second-hand bookshop								
1 Jan–15 Mar	10–4	**M**	**T**	**W**	**T**	**F**	**S**	**S**
16 Mar–3 Nov	10–5	**M**	**T**	**W**	**T**	**F**	**S**	**S**
4 Nov–31 Dec	10–4	**M**	**T**	**W**	**T**	**F**	**S**	**S**

*Stableyard and farmyard: open at 10. House: admission by guided tour (last tour one hour before closing). Corn mill demonstration: 7 April to 22 September, Sundays, 2 to 5. Gates and parkland close same time. Everything closed 25 and 26 December.

Crom

Upper Lough Erne, Newtownbutler,
County Fermanagh BT92 8AJ

1987

Home to islands, ancient woodland and historical ruins, this 810-hectare (2,000-acre) demesne sits in a tranquil landscape on the peaceful southern shores of Upper Lough Erne. One of Ireland's most important conservation areas, it has many rare species and is great for relaxing walks, cycling and boat trips.
Note: 19th-century castle not open to public.

Eat, shop, stay: lunch, snacks and afternoon tea, gifts and souvenirs available in visitor centre. Convenience goods and outdoor clothing also for sale. Holiday cottages, campsite (tents only) and glamping pods.

Things to see and do: historic castle ruins. Cot trips (Bank Holiday Mondays). Boat and canoe hire. Children's Tracker Packs and GPS devices available. Events, including Outdoor Adventures, Easter hunts and Music by the Lake. **Dogs**: under control.

Tranquil Crom in County Fermanagh, above and below, is home to many rare species

Access:
Building **Grounds**
Parking: 100 yards.

Find out more: 028 6773 8118 or crom@nationaltrust.org.uk

Crom		M	T	W	T	F	S	S
Grounds								
1 Jan–28 Feb	10–4	M	T	W	T	F	S	S
1 Mar–31 Oct	10–7	M	T	W	T	F	S	S
1 Nov–31 Dec	10–4	M	T	W	T	F	S	S
Visitor centre and tea-room								
9 Mar–30 Sep	11–5	M	T	W	T	F	S	S
5 Oct–27 Oct*	11–5	·	·	·	·	·	S	S

Open Bank Holiday Mondays and all other public holidays in Northern Ireland. Last admission one hour before closing.
*Tea-room closed October.

The Crown Bar

46 Great Victoria Street, Belfast, County Antrim BT2 7BA 1978

Belfast's most famous pub remains one of the finest examples of a high-Victorian gin palace complete with period features. **Note**: run by Mitchells & Butlers.

Find out more: 028 9024 3187 or info@crownbar.com

Cushendun

County Antrim

 1954

Charming, historic Cushendun, County Antrim

Nestled at the mouth of the River Dun (Brown River) at the foot of Glendun, Cushendun is a very charming historic village steeped in character and folklore. The surrounding hills are a patchwork of farms, small fields, hedgerows and traditional stone walls. Sheltered harbour and beautiful beach. Views of Scotland.

Eat, shop, stay: pub and restaurant facilities available in the village (none National Trust).

Cushendun sits at the mouth of the River Dun

Things to see and do: attractive white Cornish-style houses designed by Clough Williams-Ellis. Explore the grounds of historic Glenmona House. Circular walking trail. River fishing, sea angling, boating, horse-riding and golf course nearby.

Sat Nav: use BT44 0PH. **Parking**: car park adjacent to Corner House tea-room and at Glenmona House.

Find out more: 028 2073 3419 or cushendun@nationaltrust.org.uk

Derrymore House

Bessbrook, Newry, County Armagh BT35 7EF 1953

Resting peacefully in a landscape demesne, this 18th-century thatched cottage is rich in history and a great place for walks. **Note**: sorry no toilet. Grounds open dawn to dusk. Drawing room open 6 and 27 May, 12 July, 26 August and 7 September, 2 to 5. Last admission 45 minutes before closing.

Find out more: 028 8778 4753 or derrymore@nationaltrust.org.uk

Divis and the Black Mountain

Hannahstown, near Belfast, County Antrim

2004

Sitting in the heart of the Belfast Hills, this 809-hectare (2,000-acre) mosaic of upland heath and blanket bog is a great place for a wild countryside experience. There are four walking trails to explore, affording panoramic views across Belfast and a wealth of flora, fauna and archaeological remains to discover. **Note**: cattle roam freely during summer months. Mountain environment and weather conditions can change rapidly.

Eat, shop, stay: tea, coffee and light refreshments available in The Barn.

Things to see and do: guided walks on biodiversity and archaeology. **Dogs**: welcome, but please note cattle roam freely during summer.

Access: **Visitor centre**
Sat Nav: use BT17 0NG.
Parking: beside The Barn or on Divis Road, opposite entrance gates.

Find out more: 028 9082 5434 or divis@nationaltrust.org.uk

Divis and the Black Mountain
Café and Information Barn: seasonal opening (contact property for details).

Storm clouds mass over Divis and the Black Mountain in County Antrim

Downhill Demesne and Hezlett House

Mussenden Road, Castlerock, County Londonderry BT51 4RP

1949

The sheltered gardens, cliff-edge landmark and striking ruins of a grand headland mansion bear testament to the eccentricity of the Earl Bishop who once made this 18th-century demesne his home. Mussenden Temple, perched atop sheer cliffs, offers panoramic views of the famous north coast and is a great place for walking and kite-flying. Nearby at Hezlett House, life in a rural 17th-century cottage is told through the people who once lived there. One of the oldest thatched cottages left standing in Northern Ireland, it boasts a rare cruck frame and houses the Downhill Marble Collection.

Eat, shop, stay: tea and coffee facilities at Hezlett House and Bishop's Gate. Picnics welcome in gardens.

Things to see and do: **Indoors** Hezlett House guided tours on request (booking essential).

Outdoors Numerous events throughout year, including Easter hunts and Kite Festival. Bishop's Play Trail and new Bishop's Tree Trail. **Dogs**: on leads only.

Access: **Building** **Grounds**
Sat Nav: use BT51 4TW for Hezlett House.
Parking: at Lion's Gate.

Find out more: 028 7084 8728 or downhilldemesne@nationaltrust.org.uk Hezlett House, 107 Sea Road, Castlerock, County Londonderry BT51 4TW

Downhill and Hezlett		M	T	W	T	F	S	S
Downhill Demesne grounds								
Open all year	Dawn-dusk	**M**	**T**	**W**	**T**	**F**	**S**	**S**
Downhill Demesne facilities								
9 Mar-15 Sep	10-5	**M**	**T**	**W**	**T**	**F**	**S**	**S**
21 Sep-27 Oct	10-5	·	·	·	·	·	**S**	**S**
Hezlett House								
16 Mar-7 Apr	11-5	·	·	·	·	·	**S**	**S**
13 Apr-28 Apr	11-5	**M**	**T**	**W**	**T**	**F**	**S**	**S**
4 May-16 Jun	11-5	·	·	·	·	·	**S**	**S**
17 Jun-8 Sep	11-5	**M**	**T**	**W**	**T**	**F**	**S**	**S**

Open Bank Holiday Mondays and all other public holidays in Northern Ireland.

Clockwise from top left: Mussenden Temple, Hezlett House and the striking ruins of Downhill Demesne, County Londonderry

Florence Court

Enniskillen, County Fermanagh BT92 1DB

1954

Florence Court enjoys a majestic countryside setting in West Fermanagh, surrounded by lush parkland with Benaughlin mountain rising in the background. There is something for everyone to enjoy at this extensive and welcoming place. On a guided tour of the Georgian mansion you can hear stories about the Earls of Enniskillen and their staff, who lived here for more than 250 years. Outdoors take a gentle walk or long cycle along 10 miles of trails in the adjoining forest park and see fascinating industrial heritage features, including the water-powered sawmill and blacksmith's forge. The gardens are home to the mother of all Irish yew trees, as well as the kitchen garden which is being restored to its 1930s character.

Eat, shop, stay: Stables tea-room serving snacks, lunches and afternoon tea. Coach House gift shop. Second-hand bookshop (volunteer-run). Visitor centre providing information, house tour tickets, retail and drinks to go. You can stay for longer and enjoy a holiday in the Butler's Apartment.

Things to see and do: Indoors Guided house tours. Laundry yard with washroom, dairy, ironing and drying room. Explore our forge, sawmill and carpenters shop. **Outdoors:** Events and ranger walks throughout year. Children's Tracker Packs. Network of 10 miles of multi-use trails. Bike hire available from the visitor centre. Kitchen garden restoration project. **Dogs**: under control, on leads in walled garden.

Access:
Building **Grounds**
Parking: 100 yards to visitor centre.

Find out more: 028 6634 8249 or florencecourt@nationaltrust.org.uk

Florence Court in County Fermanagh, this page and opposite, has something to offer every visitor

Florence Court		M	T	W	T	F	S	S
Gardens and park								
1 Jan–28 Feb	10–4	**M**	**T**	**W**	**T**	**F**	**S**	**S**
1 Mar–31 Oct	10–7	**M**	**T**	**W**	**T**	**F**	**S**	**S**
1 Nov–31 Dec	10–4	**M**	**T**	**W**	**T**	**F**	**S**	**S**
House, tea-room, visitor centre and shop								
9 Mar–14 Apr	11–5	·	·	·	·	·	**S**	**S**
19 Apr–28 Apr	11–5	**M**	**T**	**W**	**T**	**F**	**S**	**S**
29 Apr–2 Jun	11–5	**M**	**T**	**W**	**T**	·	**S**	**S**
3 Jun–31 Aug	11–5	**M**	**T**	**W**	**T**	**F**	**S**	**S**
1 Sep–30 Sep	11–5	**M**	**T**	**W**	**T**	·	**S**	**S**
5 Oct–27 Oct	11–5	·	·	·	·	·	**S**	**S**

House: admission by guided tour (last tour one hour before closing). Open 18 March, Bank Holiday Mondays and all other public holidays in Northern Ireland. Open Republic of Ireland Bank Holiday, 28 October. Grounds closed 25 December. Visitor centre: open daily October and weekends in November and December.

Giant's Causeway

44 Causeway Road, Bushmills,
County Antrim BT57 8SU

Follow in the legendary footsteps of giants at Northern Ireland's iconic UNESCO World Heritage Site. The famous basalt columns of the Causeway landscape, left by volcanic eruptions 60 million years ago, are home to more than Finn McCool. Its nooks and crannies are dotted with dainty sea campion, and defensive fulmars protect their cliff nests. Windswept walking trails wind through this Area of Outstanding Natural Beauty, with an all-accessible walk at Runkerry Head and more challenging terrain along the Causeway Coast Way. The interactive exhibition and innovative audio-guides unlock secrets of the landscape and regale visitors with legends of giants.

Eat, shop, stay: light lunches and tasty snacks available in Visitor Centre café. Causeway Hotel bar and restaurant offer delicious lunch and evening meal menus based around fresh local produce. The award-winning gift shop showcases locally handcrafted gifts and exclusive Giant's Causeway souvenirs.

Things to see and do: **Indoors** Interactive exhibition brings the stories of the Causeway to life. **Outdoors** Audio-guides (11 languages) reveal the landscape's secrets. Walking trails for all abilities. Entertaining guided tours. Family fun events. **Dogs**: on leads only.

Access: **Grounds** **Visitor Centre** **Causeway Hotel**
Parking: on site and park and ride in Bushmills Village. Electric vehicle charging point in car park two.

Find out more: 028 2073 1855 or giantscauseway@nationaltrust.org.uk

Giant's Causeway		M	T	W	T	F	S	S
Stones and coastal path								
Open all year	Dawn–dusk	**M**	**T**	**W**	**T**	**F**	**S**	**S**
Visitor Centre								
1 Jan–28 Feb	9–5	**M**	**T**	**W**	**T**	**F**	**S**	**S**
1 Mar–31 May	9–6	**M**	**T**	**W**	**T**	**F**	**S**	**S**
1 Jun–30 Sep	9–7	**M**	**T**	**W**	**T**	**F**	**S**	**S**
1 Oct–31 Oct	9–6	**M**	**T**	**W**	**T**	**F**	**S**	**S**
1 Nov–31 Dec	9–5	**M**	**T**	**W**	**T**	**F**	**S**	**S**

Last admission to Visitor Centre one hour before closing.
Closed 24 to 26 December.

Gray's Printing Press

49 Main Street, Strabane,
County Tyrone BT82 8AU 1966

The indelible story of printing is told behind this Georgian shop front in Strabane, once reputed as Ireland's printing capital. **Note**: Open 6 and 27 May, 4 July, 26 August and 7 September, 12 to 4 (times subject to change). Last admission 45 minutes before closing.

Find out more: 028 8674 8210 or grays@nationaltrust.org.uk

Islandmagee

near Larne, County Antrim 1996

An Area of Special Scientific Interest, the peninsula at Islandmagee has some of Northern Ireland's largest colonies of cliff-nesting seabirds. **Note**: paths uneven and steep in places.

Find out more: 028 9064 7787 or islandmagee@nationaltrust.org.uk

Lisnabreeny

near Belfast, County Down 1938

On the edge of Belfast, paths through a wooded glen cross farmland, emerging at a rath on the Castlereagh Hills. **Note**: uneven paths and steps.

Find out more: 028 9064 7787 or lisnabreeny@nationaltrust.org.uk

The dramatic basalt stone columns of the Giant's Causeway in County Antrim, left, and the broad, meandering River Lagan at Minnowburn, County Down, above right

Minnowburn

near Belfast, County Down

1952

Nestled in the heart of Lagan Valley Regional Park, where meadows and woodlands roll down to the River Lagan. Perfect for a short stoll or longer walk. Climb Terrace Hill to discover the garden built by linen merchant Ned Robinson, and stop for a picnic and to admire the views. **Note**: trails are uneven and steep in places.

Eat, shop, stay: coffee van (not National Trust) serves food, tea and coffee in car park six days a week. Lock Keeper's Inn (not National Trust) serving food, tea and coffee, ¾ mile along riverside path. Picnic tables in Terrace Hill garden.

Things to see and do: guided walks, including heritage, history and woodlands. Natural play area and walking trails to discover, including the Giant's Ring and Terrace Hill trails. **Dogs**: on leads only.

Sat Nav: use BT8 8LD. **Parking**: on site.

Find out more: 028 9064 7787 or minnowburn@nationaltrust.org.uk

Mount Stewart

Portaferry Road, Newtownards, County Down BT22 2AD

1976

Voted one of the world's top 10 gardens, Mount Stewart reflects a rich tapestry of design and planting artistry bearing the hallmark of its creator. Edith, Lady Londonderry's passion for bold planting schemes, coupled with the mild climate of Strangford Lough, means rare and tender plants from across the globe thrive in this celebrated garden, with the formal gardens exuding a distinct character and appeal. Explore the exquisite house, recently restored to glory. Hear fascinating stories about the Londonderry family, and enjoy a world-class collection of paintings and many other internationally significant items. For a different view of Mount Stewart, stroll around miles of new walking trails and discover a landscape lost in time.

Eat, shop, stay: gift shop selling local gifts. Garden shop offering a range of plants specially propagated from our world-class garden. Second-hand bookshop. Tea-room serving a range of homemade seasonal hot and cold food. Coffee and ice-cream kiosk in the courtyard.

Things to see and do: **Indoors** Explore the recently restored house and discover the impressive collection of artwork and objects. Guided tours on selected days. **Outdoors** World-class gardens, walking trails, new red squirrel hide, natural play area and garden tours. The natural play area and walking trails will take you through a magical landscape of woodland and farmland, set within the iconic drumlin landscape of Strangford Lough. Events throughout the year: Jazz in the Gardens (April to September), Teddy Bears' Picnic (July), Mount Stewart Conversations Festival and Red Squirrel Day (both in September). **Dogs**: welcome on short leads in grounds, trails and gardens. Elsewhere, assistance dogs only.

The lavish house interiors at Mount Stewart in County Down, right, complement the bold design, colour and sheer exuberance of the world-famous gardens, below

Discovering Strangford Lough at Mount Stewart

Access:
Reception, shop and tea-room
House **Grounds**
Sat Nav: use BT22 2AD. Access via second gate into Mount Stewart identified by brown sign.
Parking: 200 yards from main car park. Overflow car park approximately 465 yards. Two electric vehicle charging points in rear car park. Accessible and family parking spaces in main car park.

Find out more: 028 4278 8387 or mountstewart@nationaltrust.org.uk

Mount Stewart		M	T	W	T	F	S	S
Formal and lakeside gardens, trails, tea-room and shop								
1 Jan–3 Mar	10–4*	M	T	W	T	F	S	S
4 Mar–3 Nov	10–5	M	T	W	T	F	S	S
4 Nov–31 Dec	10–4*	M	T	W	T	F	S	S
House								
3 Jan–3 Feb**	11–3	·	·	·	T	F	S	S
9 Feb–17 Mar†	11–3	·	·	·	·	·	S	S
18 Mar–31 Oct	11–5	M	T	W	T	F	S	S
1 Nov–29 Dec†	11–3	·	·	·	T	F	S	S

*Tea-room and shop: close 5 at weekends, Bank Holidays and public holidays. Open Bank Holiday Mondays and all other public holidays in Northern Ireland. Closed 25 and 26 December. Temple of the Winds open once a month. **Freeflow only. †Guided tours only.

The Mournes

near Newcastle, County Down

1992

These famous wildlife-rich mountains are criss-crossed by well-marked coastal and mountain paths. Great for exploring, the National Trust-maintained paths stretch from the shore into the heart of the Mournes, offering views over Dundrum Bay to the Isle of Man on a clear day.

Eat, shop, stay: picnics welcome. Shops, restaurants and cafés in nearby Newcastle (none National Trust).

Things to see and do: outstanding views from Bloody Bridge or the coastal path to St Mary's Chapel ruins. Birdwatching.
Dogs: welcome under control and on leads.

Sat Nav: use BT33 0EU for Slieve Donard and BT33 0LA for Bloody Bridge.
Parking: for Slieve Donard, park in Newcastle; for Bloody Bridge, park on A2.

Find out more: 028 4375 1467 or mournes@nationaltrust.org.uk

The Mournes, County Down: haunting mountains

Murlough National Nature Reserve

near Dundrum, County Down

1967

Home to seals, Neolithic sites and Ireland's first nature reserve, Murlough is one of the most extensive examples of dune landscape in Ireland and an important wildlife conservation site. A network of paths and boardwalks through ancient dunes, woodland and heath make it ideal for relaxed walks and wildlife spotting. **Note**: limited toilet facilities.

Eat, shop, stay: beach café (seasonal opening, not National Trust). Picnics welcome on beach or in car park.

Things to see and do: explore the dune network and discover the wildlife that live here on one of the ranger-led guided walks. Family activities throughout the year and new natural play area. **Dogs**: on leads are welcome, restrictions apply when ground-nesting birds are breeding or cattle grazing.

Two very different views of Murlough National Nature Reserve in County Down

Access:
Sat Nav: use BT33 0NQ. **Parking**: on site.

Find out more: 028 4375 1467 or murlough@nationaltrust.org.uk

Murlough		M	T	W	T	F	S	S
Nature reserve								
Open all year	9:30–7	**M**	**T**	**W**	**T**	**F**	**S**	**S**
Facilities								
9 Mar–14 Apr	10–6	·	·	·	·	·	**S**	**S**
19 Apr–28 Apr	10–6	**M**	**T**	**W**	**T**	**F**	**S**	**S**
4 May–26 May	10–6	·	·	·	·	·	**S**	**S**
1 Jun–1 Sep	10–6	**M**	**T**	**W**	**T**	**F**	**S**	**S**
7 Sep–29 Sep	10–6	·	·	·	·	·	**S**	**S**

Open Bank Holiday Mondays and all other public holidays in Northern Ireland. Car park gates: open at 8 and close at 7.

Patterson's Spade Mill

751 Antrim Road, Templepatrick, County Antrim BT39 0AP

1991

Patterson's Spade Mill in County Antrim

Travel back in time and witness history literally forged in steel at the last working water-driven spade mill in daily use in the British Isles. Dig up the history and culture of the humble spade and visit bygone life fashioning steel into spades during the industrial era.

Eat, shop, stay: handcrafted spades on sale and made to specification.

Things to see and do: guided tours and demonstrations for all the family. **Dogs**: on leads only.

Access: Building Grounds
Parking: 50 yards.

Find out more: 028 9443 3619 or pattersons@nationaltrust.org.uk

Patterson's Spade Mill		M	T	W	T	F	S	S
19 Apr–28 Apr	12–4	**M**	**T**	**W**	**T**	**F**	**S**	**S**
4 May–26 May	12–4	·	·	·	·	·	**S**	**S**
27 May–25 Aug	12–4	**M**	**T**	**W**	·	·	**S**	**S**
31 Aug–29 Sep	12–4	·	·	·	·	·	**S**	**S**

Admission by guided tour, last admission one hour before closing. Open Bank Holiday Mondays and all other public holidays in Northern Ireland, 19 April to 29 September.

Portstewart Strand

Portstewart, County Londonderry

1981

Sweeping along the edge of the north coast, this 2-mile stretch of golden sand is one of Northern Ireland's finest beaches and affords uninterrupted views of the coastline. It's an ideal place for lazy picnics, surfing and long walks into the wildlife-rich sand dunes.

Eat, shop, stay: award-winning Harry's Shack with great new catering offer (not National Trust). Mobile beach information service.

Things to see and do: waymarked nature trail. Barmouth Estuary bird hide. Events during peak season. **Dogs**: on leads only.

Access: Café Beach
Sat Nav: use BT55 7PG. **Parking**: on beach.

Find out more: 028 7083 6396 or portstewart@nationaltrust.org.uk

Portstewart Strand		M	T	W	T	F	S	S
Beach								
Open all year*	Dawn–dusk	**M**	**T**	**W**	**T**	**F**	**S**	**S**
Facilities								
9 Mar–12 Apr	10–5	**M**	**T**	**W**	**T**	**F**	**S**	**S**
13 Apr–28 Apr	10–6	**M**	**T**	**W**	**T**	**F**	**S**	**S**
29 Apr–1 Sep	10–7	**M**	**T**	**W**	**T**	**F**	**S**	**S**
2 Sep–6 Oct	10–5	**M**	**T**	**W**	**T**	**F**	**S**	**S**
12 Oct–29 Dec	10–3	·	·	·	·	·	**S**	**S**

*Open to pedestrians. Beach closed to vehicles one hour after last admission. Opening times vary depending on weather and tides.

Golden Portstewart Strand, County Londonderry

For information about getting to National Trust places, please see page 3

Rowallane Garden

Saintfield, County Down BT24 7LH

1956

Carved into the County Down drumlin landscape since the mid-1860s, this inspirational 21-hectare (52-acre) garden is 'a world apart'. The passion and shared vision of the Reverend John Moore, and later his nephew Hugh Armytage Moore, created a garden where you can leave the outside world behind and immerse yourself in nature's beauty. The formal and informal garden spaces are home to magical features mingled with native and exotic plants, such as drifts of rare rhododendrons. It is a great place for a leisurely walk or just to relax on a seat and soak up the atmosphere.

Eat, shop, stay: garden café with views across the gardens. Café gift shop. Second-hand bookshop. Pottery providing unique Rowallane Garden items and garden pots.

Things to see and do: exciting activities and events for all ages throughout the year.
Dogs: on leads in garden.

Access: Grounds
Parking: on site.

Find out more: 028 9751 0131 or rowallane@nationaltrust.org.uk

Rowallane Garden		M	T	W	T	F	S	S
Garden								
1 Jan–28 Feb	10–4	M	T	W	T	F	S	S
1 Mar–30 Apr	10–6	M	T	W	T	F	S	S
1 May–31 Aug	10–8	M	T	W	T	F	S	S
1 Sep–31 Oct	10–6	M	T	W	T	F	S	S
1 Nov–31 Dec	10–4	M	T	W	T	F	S	S
Café								
1 Jan–30 Apr	11–4	M	T	W	T	F	S	S
1 May–31 Aug	11–5	M	T	W	T	F	S	S
1 Sep–31 Dec	11–4	M	T	W	T	F	S	S

Open Bank Holiday Mondays and all other public holidays in Northern Ireland. Closed 25 and 26 December.

Immerse yourself in nature's beauty at Rowallane Garden in County Down, above and below

Springhill

20 Springhill Road, Moneymore, Magherafelt, County Londonderry BT45 7NQ

1957

Hundreds of years ago the Lenox-Conyngham family chose this idyllic spot to build their home and, after 10 generations, this 17th-century plantation house is still regarded as 'one of the prettiest houses in Ulster'. The welcoming family home they created is brought to life on guided tours of its portraits, furniture and decorative arts. The old laundry houses Springhill's celebrated costume collection of 18th- to 20th-century pieces that capture its enthralling past. There is a visitor centre, a natural play area and short trails that are perfect for a leisurely stroll.

Eat, shop, stay: soup, scones, hot and cold drinks, snacks and ice cream available from the Barn Café. Retail area with a range of items for the home and garden. Second-hand bookshop.

Things to see and do: **Indoors** Guided house tours and children's indoor Pest Quest. Costume exhibition and children's dressing-up area. **Outdoors** Woodland walks and children's natural play trail. **Dogs**: on leads in grounds only.

Access: Building
Parking: 50 yards.

Find out more: 028 8674 8210 or springhill@nationaltrust.org.uk

Springhill		M	T	W	T	F	S	S
House, visitor centre, café and costume museum								
2 Feb–14 Apr*	11-5	·	·	·	·	·	S	S
15 Apr–28 Apr	11-5	M	T	W	T	F	S	S
3 May–31 May	11-5	·	·	·	·	F	S	S
1 Jun–30 Jun	11-5	·	·	·	T	F	S	S
1 Jul–31 Aug	11-5	M	T	W	T	F	S	S
1 Sep–29 Sep	11-5	·	·	·	·	·	S	S
6 Oct–27 Oct	11-4	·	·	·	·	·	·	S
28 Oct–3 Nov	11-4	M	T	W	T	F	S	S
Grounds								
Open all year	10-5	M	T	W	T	F	S	S

*Also open 18 and 19 February for local half term. House: admission by guided tour (last tour one hour before closing). Open Bank Holiday Mondays and all other public holidays in Northern Ireland. Closed 25, 26 December and 1 January 2020.

Idyllic Springhill in County Londonderry, left and below, is a welcoming family home

Strangford Lough

County Down 1969

The tidal treasures of Britain's largest sea lough and one of Europe's key wildlife habitats await discovery.

Find out more: 028 4278 7769 or strangford@nationaltrust.org.uk

Wellbrook Beetling Mill

20 Wellbrook Road, Corkhill, Cookstown, County Tyrone BT80 9RY 1968

Discover how yarn was spun at Northern Ireland's last working water-powered linen beetling mill and enjoy a woodland river walk. **Note**: open weekends, 9 March and 29 September, 1 to 5. Admission by guided tour, last tour one hour before closing. Open Bank Holiday Mondays and all other public holidays in Northern Ireland. Closed 25, 26 December and 1 January 2020.

Find out more: 028 8674 8210 or wellbrook@nationaltrust.org.uk

White Park Bay

near Ballintoy, County Antrim

1939

Embraced by ancient dunes and once home to Neolithic settlements, this arc of white sand nestles between two headlands on the North Antrim coast. Containing a range of rich habitats for a myriad of wildlife, its seclusion makes it ideal for relaxation and quiet walks.

Eat, shop, stay: shops, restaurants and cafés in nearby towns (none National Trust). Picnics welcome.

White Park Bay in County Antrim: this arc of white sand nestles between two headlands

Things to see and do: discover one of the first Neolithic settlements in Ireland, including Druid's Altar (not on National Trust land). Part of the Causeway Coast Way, a section of the Ulster Way. **Dogs**: welcome on leads.

Access:
Sat Nav: use BT54 6NH. **Parking**: on site.

Find out more: 028 2073 3320 or whiteparkbay@nationaltrust.org.uk

Additional coastal and countryside car parks in Northern Ireland

Belfast	
Glenoe	BT40 3LG
East Down	
Kearney	BT22 1QF
Strangford Lough	BT22 2RU
Mid Ulster	
Ballymoyer	BT60 2LA
North Coast	
Cushendun	BT44 0PH
Dunseverick	BT57 8SY
Fair Head and Murlough Bay	BT54 6RG
South Down	
Dundrum Coastal Path	BT33 0NG

Themed index

General interest

1 Adventure playgrounds/play areas
2 Boat hire
3 Bicycle hire
4 Camping and caravanning
5 Gardens
6 Ghosts
7 Industrial heritage

General interest continued

1 Adventure playgrounds/play areas
2 Boat hire
3 Bicycle hire
4 Camping and caravanning
5 Gardens
6 Ghosts
7 Industrial heritage

Berkshire, Hampshire and the Isle of Wight

Bembridge Windmill, Isle of Wight

Kent, Surrey and Sussex

Polesden Lacey, Surrey

London

Ham House and Garden, London

East of England

Hatfield Forest, Essex

East Midlands

Clumber Park, Nottinghamshire

West Midlands

Birmingham Back to Backs, West Midlands

North West

Quarry Bank, Cheshire

The Lakes

Great Langdale Campsite, Cumbria

Yorkshire

Yorkshire Coast, North Yorkshire

General interest continued

1 Adventure playgrounds/play areas
2 Boat hire
3 Bicycle hire
4 Camping and caravanning
5 Gardens
6 Ghosts
7 Industrial heritage

North East

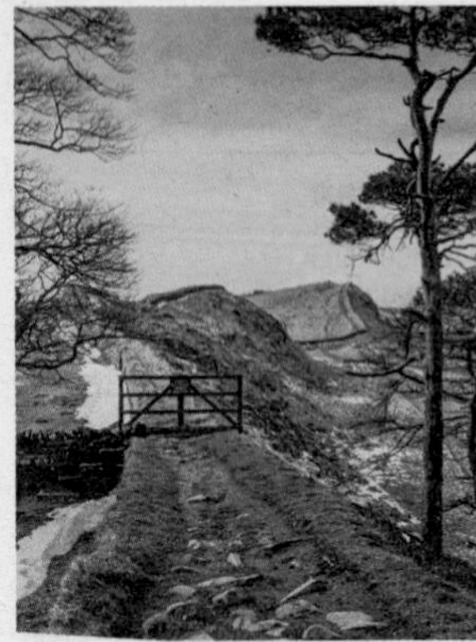

Hadrian's Wall and Housesteads Fort, Northumberland

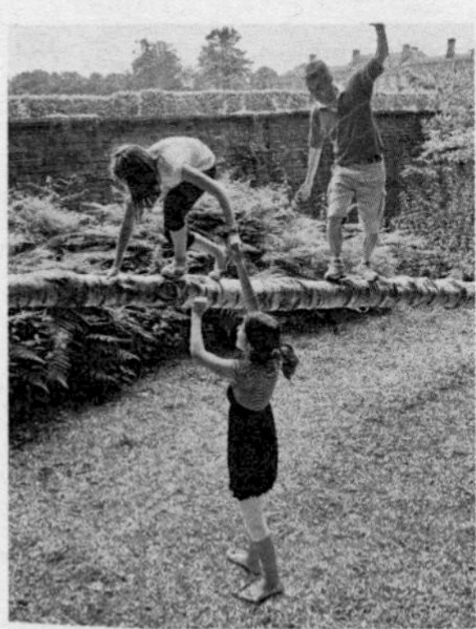

Wales

Erddig, Wales

Northern Ireland

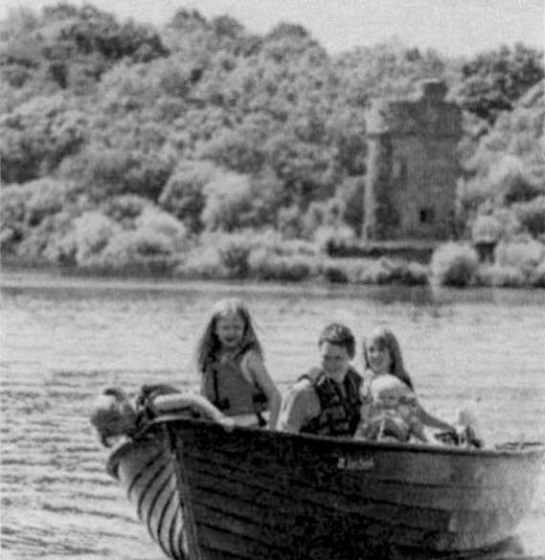

Crom, Northern Ireland

Additional coastal and countryside car parks

Quick stops

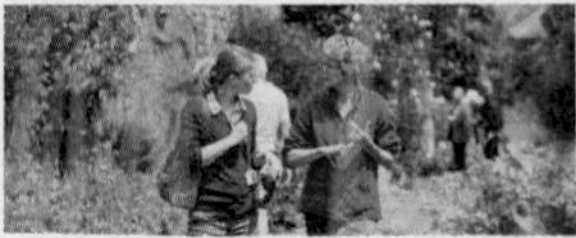

Dyffryn Gardens, Wales

Collections

1 Armour
2 Carriages
3 Ceramics
4 Costume and fashion
5 Dolls, doll's houses and miniature rooms
6 Furniture
7 Glass and silverware
8 Musical instruments
9 Paintings
10 Taxidermy
11 Wall-hangings, embroideries and needlework

Lanhydrock, Cornwall

Montacute House, Somerset

Snowshill Manor and Garden, Gloucestershire

Petworth, West Sussex

Collections continued

1 Armour
2 Carriages
3 Ceramics
4 Costume and fashion
5 Dolls, doll's houses and miniature rooms
6 Furniture
7 Glass and silverware
8 Musical instruments
9 Paintings
10 Taxidermy
11 Wall-hangings, embroideries and needlework

East Midlands

West Midlands

North West

Gawthorpe Hall, Lancashire

The Lakes

Yorkshire

North East

Wallington, Northumberland

Wales

Northern Ireland

Notable people

People with connections to places listed in this *Handbook*.

Lancelot 'Capability' Brown

Winston Churchill

Emma Hart (Lady Hamilton)

Octavia Hill

Florence Nightingale

Otto Overbeck

George Bernard Shaw

Rex Whistler

Film and television

This is a small selection of the largest and most popular films and television dramas filmed at National Trust places.

Ashridge Estate, Hertfordshire

Downhill Demesne, Northern Ireland

Lavenham Guildhall, Suffolk

Levant Mine and Beam Engine, Cornwall

Osterley Park and House, London

Chastleton House, Oxfordshire

Alphabetical index

Photography credits

National Trust Images' photographers and copyright holders:

Solent News and Photography Agency
James Aitken
Matthew Antrobus
Steven Barber
Paul Barker
Sam Bayley
John Bethell
Rebecca Bevan
Dawn Biggs
Jon Bish
Tracey Blackwell
Sue Brackenbury
April Braund
Heather Broughton
Matthew Bruce
Andrew Butler
Mike Calnan
Tom Carr
Alan Clamp
Tony Cobley
Rob Coleman
Peter Cook
Joe Cornish
Stuart Cox
Derek Croucher
Hilary Daniel
Andy Davies
Malcolm Davies
Tiree Dawson
Paul Delaney
David Dixon
James Dobson
Carole Drake
Andreas von Einsiedel
Jim Elliott
Claire Evans
Jemma Finch
Simon Fraser
Geoffrey Frosh
Abby George
Dennis Gilbert
Peter Greenway
Martin Hailey
Michael Hall
Peter Hall
John Hammond
Paul Harris
Trevor Ray Hart
Christopher Heaney
Rob Hewer
Elaine Hill
Jim Holden
Fisheye Images
Neil Jakeman
Sue James
Gareth Jenkins
Jill Jennings
David Johnson
Barry Keen
Anna Kilcooley
Allan King
Chris Lacey
Chee Wai Lee
David Levenson
Paul Lewis
Gary Lomas
Nadia Mackenzie
Esme Mai
Marianne Majerus
John Malley
Paul McCartan
Eric McDonald
Nick Meers
David Midgelow
John Millar
John Miller
Sam Milling
Justin Minns
Robert Morris
Hugh Mothersole
Clive Nichols
David Noton
Matthew Oates
Wynn Owen
John Parker
Gwenno Parry
Robin Pattinson
Mel Peters
Chris Hill
Alex Prain
Oskar Proctor
Stephen Robson
Emily Roe
Marina Rule
Emma Ryan
Mark Saunders
Sophia Schorr-Kon
Richard Scott
David Sellman
Ben Selway
Arnhel de Serra
Ian Shaw
Claire Shuter
Ed Silvester
Mike Simmonds
Stewart Smith
Tom Soper
Rob Stothard
Pete Tasker
Megan Taylor
Tony Temple
Robert Thrift
Rupert Truman
Nick Upton
Joe Wainwright
Paul Wakefield
Emma Wakeham
Ian Ward
Frances Warnell
David Watson
Penny Webb
Emma Weston
Mark Wigmore
Derrick E. Witty
Alana Wright
Andrew Wright
McCoy Wynne

Accessibility: notes and information

- You can find information on access and facilities for every place listed in this *Handbook* in their entry. For the key to the symbols, please see the bookmark at the front of this book.
- If you have specific requirements, please ring before you visit in case something needs to be booked in advance.
- Disabled people can bring up to two essential companions free of charge. Get in touch with our Supporter Services team on **0344 800 1895** or **enquiries@nationaltrust.org.uk** for a companion card, so you can bring the person or people you need. Alternatively, on arrival just let our reception team know that you need someone to accompany you.
- Blue Badge holders park free.
- Assistance dogs are welcome at virtually all of our places.
- All the places we care for are writing their own access statements with more detailed accessibility information. These can be found on our website.

Accessible paths allow visitors with mobility problems to explore glorious gardens and enjoy the many delights they have to offer

Improving access

We're constantly working to improve accessibility at the places we look after, for example:

- We have around 100 powered mobility vehicles which visitors can use free of charge at about 67 places. We are increasing this number, together with organisations such as Countryside Mobility South West.
- Seven locations have Changing Places toilets, which include hoists and changing tables for people who can't use standard accessible toilets. We have plans for many more too.

About your membership

Important information to help you make the most of your membership this year.

With access and parking free for members to most of the places we look after, visiting opportunities are endless – whether you fancy exploring an archetypal English formal garden or a centuries-old castle

Experience unlimited access

Your member card gives you free access to most of the places we look after, during normal opening hours. (Just remember to bring it along with you every time you visit.)

Get free parking

Your membership also gives you free parking at most of the places we care for*, even when there's a sign saying 'pay and display'. Just scan your member card at the pay and display machine for your free ticket.

Every time you scan your card for free parking, you're helping to care for the places you love. To find out how, or if you have a question about parking, visit **nationaltrust.org.uk/features/car-parking-faqs**, or feel free to ask a member of staff at the property. Please keep your card handy in case you need to show it.

*You can use your card at the places we look after across England, Wales and Northern Ireland, as well as National Trust for Scotland heritage sites too. The main exceptions are Tatton Park and Wakehurst, which are managed and financed by Cheshire East Council and Royal Botanic Gardens, Kew, respectively.

Find dog-friendly places

We welcome dogs wherever we can. Just check the 'Dogs' information at the end of the 'Things to see and do' section of the place you're visiting before you set out.

Visit special places overseas

We have special visiting arrangements with heritage organisations in a number of other countries, giving you free or discounted entry on showing your member card. To see where your membership could take you, visit **nationaltrust.org.uk/features/overseas-organisations**

There are hundreds of places across England, Wales and Northern Ireland to discover as a National Trust member

Know before you go

Check facilities and plan ahead

Our places offer different types of access and a range of facilities, as indicated by the symbols in this *Handbook*. Please check before you visit, and do ring ahead in case anything needs to be booked.

Carers go free

Carers can accompany you free of charge. To make things easier, you can order an annual Essential Companion Card – just call **0344 800 1895** or email **enquiries@nationaltrust.org.uk**

Be photo sensitive

For the safety and comfort of other visitors, please don't use a flash or tripod when you take pictures indoors. Also, pay attention to any notices about photography, as loan items on display may require permission to be photographed from the owner.
For commercial filming and photography, please call us on **020 7824 7128**.

Flash and tripods disturb other visitors, so please do not use them, right. Also keep an eye open for notices about photography. As facilities vary from place to place, please check this book and ring ahead if anything needs to be booked

More ways to support the places you love

As a member, you're already helping us look after special places for future generations. If you'd like to do even more, here are some other great ways to get involved.

Cosy up in a café

After a day of seeing the sights, reward yourself with something sweet and sticky at one of our cafés. With baked treats, seasonal dishes and refreshing cuppas, they're perfect for a natter with friends. Whet your appetite at **nationaltrust.org.uk/food**

Pop to the shop

Pick up a treat for yourself or a gift for a loved one at one of our shops. Handcrafted homeware, beautiful accessories, tasty delights and much more – all inspired by the places you love. Shop online at **nationaltrust.org.uk/shop**

Have a holiday

From grand manor houses and cosy cottages, to rustic bunkhouses and camping in the great outdoors, we've got hundreds of different breaks to choose from. Get some inspiration at **nationaltrust.org.uk/holidays**

Add an event to your diary

Whether it's enjoying live music or open-air theatre, or taking part in organised sports or a conservation walk, there's a busy calendar of events to choose from. Find out what's happening near you at **nationaltrust.org.uk/visit/whats-on**

Volunteer for somewhere special

Learn some new skills, share your knowledge and help protect your favourite places for years to come. Get involved at **nationaltrust.org.uk/volunteer**

Help out when you visit

Keep an eye out for our conservation events, such as cleaning up a beach, planting native trees or helping out with a wildlife survey.

Be part of a supporter group

Meet like-minded people, support a cause you love and have some fun together with group walks, talks and conservation activities. Learn more at **nationaltrust.org.uk/supporter-groups**

Donate or leave a gift in your will

From supporting an appeal for a special place to leaving a gift in your will, every donation helps look after stunning beaches, rolling countryside and historic properties: **nationaltrust.org.uk/donate**

Share the joy of membership

With a gift membership you could give someone special a whole year's worth of new discoveries. You could also buy junior, family, joint or life memberships, to suit your situation. More at **nationaltrust.org.uk/membership**